THIRD EDITION

Teaching Elementary Social Studies

Principles and Applications

JAMES J. ZARRILLO
California State University, East Bay

PEARSON
_____
Merrill
Prentice Hall

Upper Saddle River, New Jersey
Columbus, Ohio

Library of Congress Cataloging-in-Publication Data

Zarrillo, James.
  Teaching elementary social studies: principles and applications / James J. Zarrillo.—3rd ed.
    p. cm.
  Includes bibliographical references and index.
  ISBN-13: 978-0-13-613391-9 (pbk)
  ISBN-10: 0-13-613391-6 (pbk.)
  1. Social sciences—Study and teaching (Elementary)—United States.   2. Multicultural education—United States.
  I. Title.
  LB1584.Z27 2008
  372.8'004—dc22

                                                                                    2007004020

Vice President and Executive Publisher: Jeffery W. Johnston
Acquisitions Editor: Meredith D. Fossel
Senior Editorial Assistant: Kathleen S. Burk
Production Editor: Alexandrina Benedicto Wolf
Production Coordination: Thistle Hill Publishing Services, LLC
Design Coordinator: Diane Lorenzo
Photo Coordinator: Valerie Schultz
Cover Designer: Jeff Vanik
Cover Image: SuperStock
Production Manager: Pamela D. Bennett
Director of Marketing: David Gesell
Marketing Coordinator: Brian Mounts

This book was set in ITC Garamond by Integra Software Services. It was printed and bound by Edwards Brothers. The cover was printed by Phoenix Color Corp.

Photo credits: Scott Cunningham/Merrill, pp. 1, 25; Anne Vega/Merrill, pp. 54, 287; Barbara Schwartz/Merrill, p. 80; Tom Watson/Merrill, p. 123; Tom Stewart/Corbis/Bettmann, p. 140; Krista Greco/Merrill, p. 171; David Mager/Pearson Learning Photo Studio, pp. 196, 323; Anthony Magnacca/Merrill, p. 222; Bill Bachmann/Photo Researchers, Inc., p. 258.

Pearson Education Ltd.
Pearson Education Singapore Pte. Ltd.
Pearson Education Canada, Ltd.
Pearson Education—Japan

Pearson Education Australia Pty. Limited
Pearson Education North Asia Ltd.
Pearson Educación de Mexico, S.A. de C.V.
Pearson Education Malaysia Pte. Ltd.

10 9 8 7 6 5 4 3 2 1
ISBN-13: 978-0-13-613391-9
ISBN-10:   0-13-613391-6

Preface

The third edition of *Teaching Elementary Social Studies: Principles and Applications* reflects a national trend toward standards-based curricula and the need to differentiate instruction to meet the needs of a highly diverse student population. Specifically, the most significant *new features* are the following:

- A new section in Chapter 2 on teaching gifted students and students with mild learning disabilities.
- Throughout the book, the sample lessons and units include suggestions for meeting the needs of students with learning disabilities and gifted students, along with the suggestions for English learners.
- A new section, which includes 10 specific suggestions to help children who can't read their grade-level social studies textbook, has been added to Chapter 9.
- A new section, "Teaching the Electoral Process," has been added to Chapter 10.
- The third edition is shorter than the previous edition—chapters on units of instruction and lesson planning have been combined into Chapter 4.
- To make the text easier to read, the sample lesson plans and units have been moved to the end of each chapter.
- The references, websites, and children's books have been significantly updated. There are over 100 new professional references, and over 100 older references were deleted.

The conceptual framework for the book is unchanged. The field of social studies has a rich history. Driven by the dynamic nature of human society, social studies has evolved into a lively and challenging pursuit, drawing concepts and ideas from history, geography, political science, economics, sociology, and anthropology. Thus, the possibilities to create meaningful, engaging, and stimulating experiences in social studies are endless. The dilemma for many educators, however, has been how to teach such a vast and expanding bed of knowledge.

Fortunately, researchers in education, psychology, and linguistics provide some answers. How we teach should be dictated by how children learn, and research tells us that children learn best when teachers do the following:

- Allow children to construct knowledge as they become active participants in a wide range of learning experiences
- Give all children a variety of materials to manipulate, question, and puzzle over
- Encourage children to think critically about the content they learn
- Plan opportunities for children to interact with one another on a regular basis
- Recognize the cultural and linguistic diversity in their classroom and build enriched learning experiences around that diversity

It is from these perspectives that I have made the revisions to this edition. Part I (Chapters 1 to 3) defines social studies and differentiated instruction, and explains culturally responsive teaching. Chapter 2 describes the students you will teach, with special emphasis on language, culture, and exceptionality. Chapter 3 explains how teachers can transform the social studies curriculum to reflect a multicultural perspective. Part II (Chapters 4 to 9) presents the fundamentals of social studies teaching. Its focus is on how to plan lessons and units that include many opportunities for students to work cooperatively, engage in inquiry, and think critically. Chapter 4 now includes both lesson and unit planning. Chapter 7 examines teaching with computer-based resources. Chapter 8 addresses how to assess each child's performance in social studies in a standards-based curriculum, and Chapter 9 discusses how teachers can integrate the social studies curriculum. Part III (Chapters 10 to 12) highlights the sources of content for the social studies curriculum, especially citizenship education, history, and geography. Within this organizational framework is an underlying theme—diversity.

◆ Diversity: The Unifying Theme for This Text

Diversity continues to be the unifying theme for this text. It is impossible to discuss current social studies teaching and learning without acknowledging the crucial importance of understanding diversity. Teachers in the United States now face two extraordinary challenges. They must teach about those values that unite us, while at the same time help students accept disparate perspectives. Teachers must help their students better understand different cultures and also avoid stereotypical and biased views of other people. These challenges, it seems, reinforce the power of a text based on understanding diversity.

Diversity has several dimensions. First, our student population continues to be increasingly pluralistic. Data gathered by the U.S. Census Bureau confirms a trend that has been constant for the past four decades. The percentage of Americans who identify themselves as "white" is steadily decreasing, while the percentage who are either African

American, Asian American, or Hispanic American is steadily on the rise. In 2000, the non-Hispanic, white population was 69 percent of the total; projections are that this percentage will shrink to 52 percent by 2050. African American, Asian American, and Hispanic American students currently represent over one-third of the K–12 population. They already are the majority in the nation's 25 largest school districts.

Second, our teaching should use a variety of instructional strategies and resources to meet the needs of students from various cultural backgrounds and experiences. Third, we need to adapt how we teach to provide meaningful instruction to students with special needs (this book focuses on children with mild learning disabilities and gifted children). Fourth, the content of the social studies curriculum should be diverse because social studies is the study of people, and the curriculum should introduce our students to a wide array of individuals and groups. Finally, teachers need to prepare students to live in a democracy where citizens celebrate divergent beliefs and perspectives, no matter how great the pressure is to adhere to a single point of view. Diversity is a theme that unifies social studies teaching and learning: we must acknowledge it in our students, present it as our curriculum, and build on it as a civic value.

To accomplish these goals, we need to infuse our lessons with pluralistic, multidimensional resources. For example, children's literature provides authentic accounts of the experiences of people from many cultural heritages. Of particular note are books that share diaries, journals, and oral histories of people who are "distant," either by time or place, from our students. The authentic nature of this literature helps children better understand the difficult decisions other people have made. In this book, many lessons model how to incorporate children's literature in the social studies curriculum. At the end of each of these lessons—and the projects and activities provided—are ideas for providing additional multicultural experiences. In addition, a reference list of children's literature that can be used to develop elementary social studies lessons is provided at the end of this text.

Visual media and computer resources are essential resources for a classroom with a diverse student population. This text illustrates the use of videos, CD-ROMs, and Internet websites. The Internet has changed the nature of social studies teaching and has immense potential, especially as a resource for students as they engage in the process of inquiry. Finally, the visual and performing arts should play prominent roles in elementary social studies. Applying a variety of instructional strategies and resources will increase the chances that every child in your classroom will be successful and be better prepared for a productive life in the 21st century.

◆ Supplements

The text has the following ancillary materials available to instructors using the text:

Online Instructor's Manual with Text Bank, ISBN 0-13-613393-2
Online PowerPoint Slides, ISBN 0-13-613392-4

Contact your Merrill/Prentice Hall sales representative, call Faculty Services at 1-800-526-0458, or e-mail us at Merrill.marketing@pearsoned.com

◆ Acknowledgments

I wish to thank the elementary school teachers from whom I borrowed ideas for this book: my colleagues in Burbank, California; the teachers I observed during research projects from school districts in Los Angeles County; the cooperating teachers in the ABC, Castro Valley, Dublin, Hayward, and Long Beach Unified School Districts who guided my student teachers; and my students at California State University, East Bay. Many thanks also to Meredith Fossel, my editor at Merrill/Prentice Hall, and Thistle Hill Publishing Services for production coordination and copyediting for this book—all contributed to the book and I truly appreciate it.

I also wish to thank my reviewers: Ernest Barnett, Northern Kentucky University; Melinda Cowart, University of North Texas; and Laurie Katz, The Ohio State University.

In the first edition of this book, I mentioned my mother, Lois Zarrillo, who taught junior high and senior high school social studies from 1937 to 1981 and based her teaching on the belief that every student could succeed. In the second edition, I wrote about my father, Joseph Zarrillo, who had an unquenchable thirst for knowledge about people from every corner of the globe. Sadly, both my parents are gone now, but on a happier note, my first grandchild, Hannah, was born while I was working on this edition. I hope that this book will be of some help to the teachers who teach Hannah and the other children who are a part of her generation.

James J. Zarrillo

Brief Contents

Part I   **The Foundations of Social Studies Teaching**   1

Chapter 1   An Introduction to the Social Studies: Linking the Past and the Present   2

Chapter 2   Children, Diversity, and Learning: Implementing Differentiated Instruction   25

Chapter 3   The Transformed Curriculum: Infusing Multicultural Perspectives   54

Part II   **The Fundamentals of Social Studies Teaching**   79

Chapter 4   Lesson and Unit Plans: Organizing Instruction   80

Chapter 5   Cooperative Learning: Enhancing Skills and Knowledge Through Group Activities   123

Chapter 6   Inquiry and Critical Thinking: Challenging Students with the Complex and the Controversial   140

Chapter 7   Technology: Teaching with Computer-Based Resources   171

Chapter 8   Assessment: Acquiring and Analyzing Data on Student Achievement   196

Chapter 9   The Integrated Curriculum: Incorporating
the Language Arts, the Performing Arts,
and the Visual Arts   222

Part III   Sources of Content for Social
Studies Teaching   257

Chapter 10   Democratic Citizenship: Participating in Civic Life   258

Chapter 11   History and Geography: Understanding
People of Different Times and Places   287

Chapter 12   The Other Social Sciences and Topics
of Special Interest: Completing the Social
Studies Curriculum   323

Children's Literature to Support
Social Studies Instruction   356

References   361

Author Index   388

Subject Index   394

Contents

Part I **The Foundations of Social Studies Teaching** **1**

Chapter 1 **An Introduction to the Social Studies: Linking the Past and the Present** **2**

Definitions of Social Studies 4

A Brief History of Social Studies Teaching 6

The Influence of Progressive Education and the New Social Studies 7

The Role of History, Standards, Technology, and Diversity 9

Social Studies: The Curriculum 14

Content 14

Processes 18

Values 18

Summary of Key Points 19

For Further Reading 19

Chapter 2 **Children, Diversity, and Learning: Implementing Differentiated Instruction** **25**

Linguistic Diversity 29

English Learners 29

Second-Language Acquisition and Learning in Social Studies 29

Cultural Diversity 35

Definitions of Key Words and Descriptors 35

How Culture Shapes Learning 37

Exceptionality 40

Differentiating Instruction for Children with Learning Disabilities 40

Gifted Children 45

Summary of Key Points	47
For Further Reading	47

Chapter 3   **The Transformed Curriculum: Infusing Multicultural Perspectives** — **54**

The Dimensions of Multicultural Education	56
Levels of Curricular Integration	56
The Transformation Process	57
In Their Own Words: Children's Books	59
In Their Own Words: Oral History	61
The Benefits of Oral History	61
Guidelines for Oral History Projects	62
Incorporating the Personal Experiences of Your Students	66
Adapting a Traditional Unit of Study	69
Summary of Key Points	72
For Further Reading	73

Part II   **The Fundamentals of Social Studies Teaching   79**

Chapter 4   **Lesson and Unit Plans: Organizing Instruction** — **80**

General Guidelines for Planning Social Studies Lessons	82
Lesson Plan Formats	83
The Comprehensive Lesson Plan	84
The Abbreviated Lesson Plan	84
Writing Lesson Objectives	87
Making Objectives More Meaningful	87
Raising the Levels of Performance: Objectives in the Cognitive Domain	87
Perspectives on the Teaching Sequence	89
Hunter's Seven-Step Model: Direct Instruction	89
The Concept Attainment Model	90
Principles for Planning Instructional Units	93
Units Should Be Integrated	93
The Scope of Each Unit Should Be Clearly Defined	93
Activities in a Unit Should Follow a Logical Sequence	94
Units Should Feature a Variety of Instructional Resources	96
Units Should Include Whole-Group, Small-Group, and Individual Activities	97
Summary of Key Points	98
For Further Reading	99

Chapter 5   **Cooperative Learning: Enhancing Skills
and Knowledge Through Group Activities**   **123**
    Introduction to Cooperative Learning   125
    A Research-Based Rationale for Cooperative Learning   126
        Group Projects   127
        Student Teams–Achievement Divisions (STAD)   129
        Jigsaw   130
        Think–Pair–Share   130
        Three-Step Interview   131
    Making Cooperative Learning Work   132
        Group Goals   132
        Individual Accountability   132
        Social Skills   132
        Effective Planning   133
    Other Issues in Grouping   134
        *What Is the Proper Place of Cooperative Learning
            in Social Studies?*   134
        *What Criteria Should Be Used to Place Students
            in Groups?*   134
        How Long Should Students Stay in a Group?   135
    Summary of Key Points   135
    For Further Reading   136

Chapter 6   **Inquiry and Critical Thinking: Challenging
Students with the Complex and the
Controversial**   **140**
    Inquiry: An Overview   142
    A Teaching Sequence for an Inquiry   143
    Inquiry as Cooperative Learning: Group Investigation   147
        Suchman's Inquiry Model   148
    Critical Thinking: An Overview   149
        What Are Critical Thinking Skills?   150
        Developing Critical Thinking Skills   152
        *Newmann's Research on Critical Thinking
            in Social Studies*   152
        Taba's Strategies for Concept Formation   153
        *An Integrative Model for Teaching Reasoning
            with Content*   154
        *Using Reference Books and Multimedia to Develop
            Inquiry and Critical Thinking*   156
        Audio and Visual Resources   158
        Inquiry and Critical Thinking for All Students   160
    Summary of Key Points   161
    For Further Reading   161

Chapter 7   **Technology: Teaching with Computer-Based Resources**   **171**

Gathering Information   174
The Internet and Elementary School Students   174
Cybersafety: Keeping Children Safe When They Use the Web   174
Accuracy of Information on Websites   175
Website Literacy   177
Virtual Field Trips and Online Expeditions   179
CD-ROM Resources   180
Recording and Sharing   181
Word Processing   182
Databases and Spreadsheets   182
Linear Presentation Software   182
Hypermedia   184
Concept Mapping   184
E-Mail   185
Gather Information   187
E-Pals (Electronic Pen Pals)   188
Civic Communication   188
Summary of Key Points   188
For Further Reading   189

Chapter 8   **Assessment: Acquiring and Analyzing Data on Student Achievement**   **196**

Purposes and Goals of Assessment   197
Authentic Assessment   199
Characteristics of Authentic Assessment   199
Student Portfolios in a Standards-Based System   199
Tests and Authentic Assessment   201
Gathering Data   201
Contents of Student Portfolios   209
Records Teachers Should Keep   210
Analyzing and Sharing Assessment Data   212
Verifying Acquisition of Content   212
Measuring the Understanding of Processes   212
Evaluating Development of Values   214
Evaluating Achievement of Standards   216
Sharing What Has Been Learned   218
Assessment and Diversity: Final Thoughts   220
Summary of Key Points   220
For Further Reading   221

Chapter 9   **The Integrated Curriculum: Incorporating the Language Arts, the Performing Arts, and the Visual Arts**   **222**

     The Integrated Curriculum   224
     The Language Arts   224
       Social Studies Textbooks   224
       Instructional Strategies: Reading the Textbook   225
       Children's Literature: Information Books and Biography   236
       Children's Literature: Fiction   239
       Writing in the Social Studies Program   241
       Forms of Writing Well Suited to the Social Studies   241
       Speaking and Listening in the Social Studies Program   244
     The Performing Arts and the Visual Arts   247
       The Performing Arts   248
       The Visual Arts   250
     Summary of Key Points   251
     For Further Reading   251

Part III   **Sources of Content for Social Studies Teaching**   **257**

Chapter 10   **Democratic Citizenship: Participating in Civic Life**   **258**

     Democratic Citizenship: The First Goal of Social Studies   260
       Citizenship Education and Diversity   261
       Research on Citizenship Education   262
     Competing Perspectives on Citizenship Education   263
       National Projects on Citizenship Education   265
     Citizenship Education: Content   265
       Teaching the Electoral Process   267
     Citizenship Education: Values   268
       Teaching Democratic Values   269
     Citizenship Education: Processes   271
       Participatory Writing   274
       Service Learning   274
       Citizenship and Classroom Management   276
     Summary of Key Points   277
     For Further Reading   278

Chapter 11   **History and Geography: Understanding**
                 People of Different Times and Places   **287**

History in the Elementary School: Overview
  and Research   289
History in the Elementary School: Content   291
History in the Elementary School: Processes   294
Teaching History in the Elementary School   295
  Primary Sources   296
  Children's Fiction: History as a Story
    Well Told   298
  Time Lines   300
Geography in the Elementary School: Overview
  and Research on Children's Understanding of
  Geography   301
  Research on Geographic Learning and
    Teaching   302
Geography in the Elementary School: Content   304
Geography in the Elementary School:
  Processes   305
Teaching Geography in the Elementary School   306
  Symbols, Scale, Grid, and Direction   307
  Reporting Geographic Data: Student-Made Maps   311
Summary of Key Points   312
For Further Reading   313

Chapter 12   **The Other Social Sciences and Topics**
                 of Special Interest: Completing the Social
                 Studies Curriculum   **323**

Completing the Social Studies Curriculum   324
Anthropology   325
  Single Group Studies   326
  Doing Anthropology: A Dig   327
Economics   329
  Economics: The Curriculum   331
  Teaching Ideas for Economics   332
Psychology and Sociology   335
  Reducing Stereotyping and Prejudice   337
  Families and Friendship   338
Global Education, Environmental Education,
  and Current Events   340
  Global Education   340
  Teaching Global Education   341
  Environmental Education   344
  Current Events   345

Summary of Key Points 347
For Further Reading 347

**Children's Literature to Support Social
Studies Instruction** **356**

References **361**

Author Index **388**

Subject Index **394**

Note: Every effort has been made to provide accurate and current Internet information in this book. However, the Internet and information posted on it are constantly changing, and it is inevitable that some of the Internet addresses listed in this textbook will change.

Lesson Plans and Instructional Activities

More than 150 instructional activities appear in this book in a variety of formats. Many are described briefly, usually as examples of instructional strategies discussed in the text. Following is a list of the lessons, projects, units, and other activities presented in detail:

Chapter 1

Classroom Vignette
Grade Six

Multiple Activities During a Unit on Ancient Greece   21

Lesson Plan
Kindergarten

Cooperation and *A Chair for My Mother*   22

Chapter 2

Opening Vignette
Grade Two

Description of Activities from a Unit—Families and Friends   26

Mini-Unit
Grade Four

Chinese Writing   49

Chapter 3

Opening Vignette
Grade Five

Description of a Writing Activity from a Unit—The American Revolution   55

Lesson Plan
Grade Five

From *To Be a Slave*   74

Group Project
Grade Three

Oral History Project—The History of Our School   76

Chapter 4

Opening Vignette   Description of a Lesson from a Unit—
Grade Five   19th-Century Native Americans   81

Lesson Plan   Comprehensive Format: *Buffalo Chase,*
Grade Five   *Upper Missouri*   101

Lesson Plan   The Hunter Format: *Buffalo Chase,*
Grade Five   *Upper Missouri*   105

Lesson Plan   The Concept Attainment Model: The Sioux
Grade Five   of the Plains   106

Unit   Boats   107
Grade Three

Chapter 5

Opening Vignette   Description of an Activity from a Unit—
Grade Three   Boats   124

Group Project   Chronological Mural   137
Grade Three

Chapter 6

Opening Vignette   Description of an Inquiry Activity from
Grade Four   a Unit—The California Missions   141

Lesson   A Suchman Inquiry—Samoset Greets
Grade Five   the Pilgrims   162

Lesson Plan   Using an Integrative Model—Summer
Grade One   and Winter   165

Lesson Plan   A Roman Coin   168
Grade Six

Chapter 7

Opening Vignette   Descriptions of Students Using
Grade Four   Computers   172

Project   Description of a Web-Based Project—
Grade Six   A WebQuest on Ancient Egypt   190

Lesson Plan   A Virtual Field Trip to Monticello   191
Grade Five

Lesson   Description of a Student Using a CD-ROM
Grade Two   Encyclopedia—Tamika Sees and Hears
                         Dr. Martin Luther King Jr.   194

Chapter 8
Opening Vignette   Evaluation of Students Participating
   Grade Three   in a Project   197

Chapter 9
Lesson Plan   *Grandfather's Journey*   253
   Grade Three

Project   A Picture History of *Lone Bull's Horse*
   Grade Five   *Raid*   255

Chapter 10
Opening Vignette   Description of a Project—Welcome to Cesar
   Grade Three   Chavez School   259
Lesson Plan   Walking Field Trip—Rules on Signs   280
   Grade Two
Mini-Unit   Fair Trials   282
   Grade Five

Chapter 11
Opening Vignette   Description of an Activity from a Unit—All
   Grade Three   About Us   288
Mini-Unit   The Historian as Detective   314
   Grade Six
Lesson Plan   *Ox-Cart Man*   317
   Kindergarten
Lesson Plan   Using a Scale of Miles to Calculate Distance:
   Grade Four   A First Lesson   318
Mini-Unit   Using Grid Systems to Find Places
   Grade Three   on Maps   320

Chapter 12
Opening Vignette   Description of a Project—Anger
   Grade Five   Management   324
Lesson Plan   Jobs Offered: The Classified Ads   348
   Grade Six
Group Project   A Mini-Book on My Family   350
   Grade Two

Part I

The Foundations of Social Studies Teaching

Chapter 1 An Introduction to the Social Studies: Linking the Past and the Present

Chapter 2 Children, Diversity, and Learning: Implementing Differentiated Instruction

Chapter 3 The Transformed Curriculum: Infusing Multicultural Perspectives

Chapter 1

An Introduction
to the Social Studies:
Linking the Past
and the Present

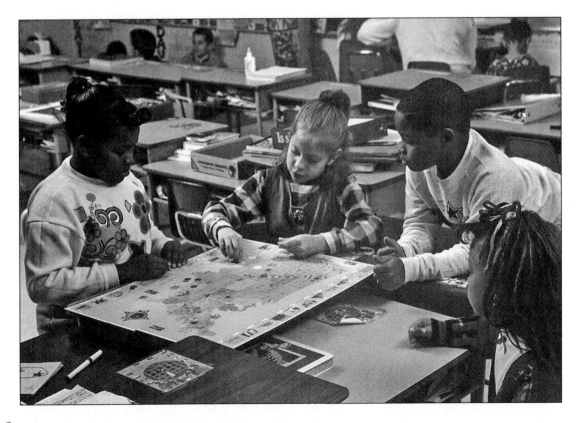

n a kindergarten classroom, the teacher reads aloud the picture book *A Chair for My Mother*. Afterward, the children discuss how characters in the story cooperated to solve a problem. Then the children help their teacher make a list of ways they can work together to make their classroom a happier, more productive place.

A first-grade teacher wants his students to engage in a simple form of critical thinking, comparing and contrasting, so he has gathered one set of photographs of people doing things in the winter and another set showing people doing things in the summer. His first graders will work in small groups to identify how weather affects the way people live.

Twenty-three second graders follow their teacher on a "walking" field trip around the playground of their school and the adjoining streets. They look at signs that state rules people must follow. Afterward, the children will be asked to provide a rationale for each rule they observed. Then a group of five students will devise a set of new signs that will make their school safer. They will present their suggestions to the school principal and the PTA.

As part of their yearlong study of their community, six third graders undertake a bold project: to compile an oral history of their school. During this project, they will interview former students, teachers, and community leaders.

In a fourth-grade classroom, one Chinese American girl is working with her mother to learn to write in Chinese. She shares some examples of her writing and her classmates want to learn more. Her teacher prepares a four-day "mini-unit" that will allow all the students in the room to learn about the logographic Chinese system and write a few Chinese characters.

Working in small groups, fifth graders read the first-person narratives of former enslaved people found in the book *To Be a Slave*. Later each group will share what they have learned about American slavery with their classmates.

A sixth-grade classroom is alive with many activities as the children learn about ancient Greece. Some students rehearse a play on the myth of Daedulus, others paint a mural of the Acropolis, a third group works on a CD-ROM presentation on the Greeks, while three students explore an Internet Website with photographs of the Parthenon.

• • •

All this and much more is social studies in the elementary school. During social studies, children learn about people—people who lived long ago and people who live today. It is when they become more proficient as thinkers, researchers, readers, writers, speakers, listeners, artists, and technologists, and it is the time when students use what they have learned to become good citizens in our democratic society.

In this chapter, you will read about

- Perspectives that currently define social studies
- Two historical, influential movements that still characterize the discipline of social studies—Progressive Education and the New Social Studies
- Three components that frame a responsible social studies curriculum: content, processes, and values

◆ Definitions of Social Studies

In 1992, the National Council for the Social Studies (NCSS) adopted the following definition of "social studies":

> Social studies is the integrated study of the social sciences and humanities to promote civic competence. Within the school program, social studies provides coordinated, systematic study drawing upon such disciplines as anthropology, archaeology, economics, geography, history, law, philosophy, political science, psychology, religion, and sociology, as well as appropriate content from the humanities, mathematics, and natural sciences. The primary purpose of social studies is to help young people develop the ability to make informed and reasoned decisions for the public good as citizens of a culturally diverse, democratic society in an interdependent world. (NCSS Task Force on Standards for Teaching and Learning in the Social Studies, 1993, p. 213)

The NCSS, the professional organization of social studies educators, has played an essential role since 1921 (www.ncss.org). The NCSS definition seems to be a good place to start our discussion of how to teach social studies in an elementary school classroom. The existence of an "official" definition is somewhat misleading because authorities in the field have long debated the dimensions of an appropriate definition of social studies (Barr, Barth, & Shermis, 1977; Barth & Shermis, 1970; Dougan, 1988; Evans, 2004; Griffith, 1991). The NCSS definition states the topics covered in social studies and clarifies the purposes of social studies teaching and learning. Barth (1993) provides a simpler definition of social studies:

> Social studies is the interdisciplinary integration of social science and humanities concepts for the purpose of practicing problem solving and decision making for developing citizenship skills on critical social issues. (p. 57)

I think this is a useful definition. It emphasizes the ultimate goal of social studies teaching—to help students think critically *and to use what they know to be active citizens.* I have a definition, too:

> Social studies is the study of people. Social studies should help students acquire knowledge, master the processes of learning, and become active citizens.

A closer look at my definition and a discussion of those provided by the NCSS and Professor Barth should bring social studies into sharper focus.

Social Studies Is the Study of People.   People are the domain of social studies. This includes people as nearby as family and as far away as those who live in the most distant nations. It includes people living now, those who lived long ago, and those who will live in the future. Social studies has the potential to be the best part of the school day because it is when children connect with other people. As children learn about others, they will be fascinated by differences among cultural groups, while at the same time they will find the commonalities that create a shared sense of humanity. It is a complex task to teach about people, and information must come from many fields of study. The NCSS definition points out that it is the various disciplines of the social sciences and humanities that provide the content for what is taught during social studies. While history and geography should serve as the core of social studies, it is imperative that the other social sciences are not neglected; rather, they should be a significant part of every social studies program. The other social sciences are anthropology, economics, philosophy, political science, psychology, religion, and sociology.

The humanities (literature, the performing arts, and the visual arts) are an important part of social studies, too (Eisner, 1991). The arts serve two functions. First, they help children better understand the people, places, and ideas they study. Stories, songs, dances, plays, paintings, statues, and other works of art allow students to become acquainted with the people who created them. Second, children can show us what they know by expressing themselves through the arts. As Barth (1993) points out, social studies involves *integration* of the social sciences and the humanities. A good social studies unit of study should pull information and ideas from several different fields.

Social Studies Should Help Students Acquire Knowledge, Master the Processes of Learning, and Become Active Citizens.   The knowledge children acquire as a part of social studies tends to be the highest priority for teachers, parents, and the children. The common perception is that this is what social studies is all about—knowing things like the location of the Rocky Mountains, the conditions aboard a slave ship, and the purpose of a mailbox. This is too limited a view because social studies must be a vehicle for children to become better communicators, thinkers, researchers, computer users, and artists. Finally, all three definitions state that the ultimate goal of social studies is active citizenship in our society, as our students *use* the knowledge they have acquired and the processes they have mastered to make communities, the nation, and the world better places. This is the position of the NCSS, that the "core mission of social studies education is to help students develop the knowledge, skills, and values that will enable them to become effective citizens" (NCSS Task Force on Revitalizing Citizenship Education, 2001, p. 319).

In the end, there probably will never be one universally accepted definition of social studies. This lack of consensus reflects fundamental disagreements on the primary purpose of social studies. Consider the following points of view on social studies teaching and learning, expressed throughout the last 100 years:

- Social studies should promote the acceptance of cultural diversity (national survey of elementary and middle school teachers reported by Leming, Ellington, & Schug, 2006).
- Social studies should focus on the major events and important individuals in American history and seek to transmit to young people the American concepts of liberty and equality (Leming, Ellington, & Porter-Magee, 2003).
- Social studies should be issues centered, as students search for answers to problems and dilemmas confronted by people today and in the past (Evans, 1992).

Barbara Schwartz/Merrill

Children are interested in how other people live. This class obviously enjoyed their study of Greece.

- Social studies should develop democratic citizens who are more than loyal and patriotic; good citizens are also critics of, and participants in, their government (Engle & Ochoa, 1988).
- Social studies should focus on the big ideas of the social science disciplines, and the essential activity for children is problem solving (Fenton, 1967).
- Social studies should be child centered and permit students to pursue topics of personal interest (Kilpatrick, 1918).

Perhaps a good way to conclude our discussion of the definition of social studies is through example. At the end of this chapter, you will find the field notes I took while visiting Mrs. Denise Winslow's sixth-grade classroom one Tuesday afternoon. Her class was studying ancient Greece.

◆ A Brief History of Social Studies Teaching

Now that we have some sense of what social studies is, let's turn to another topic that will help establish a foundation for our teaching. Over the past 150 years, some of the greatest educational thinkers have turned their attention to social studies. Indeed, the history of social studies, in regard to both *what* should be taught and *how* to teach it, makes fascinating reading for anyone interested in teaching and learning. This is too large a topic for a thorough discussion in a methods text, however, so I suggest you read other sources for a more comprehensive treatment: Atwood (1991), Cremin (1961), Douglass (1967, 1998), Evans (2004, 2006), Hertzberg (1981), Jenness (1990), Lybarger (1991), and Saxe (1991, 1992). I first focus briefly on two "educational movements" that we can learn a great deal from: Progressive Education and the New Social Studies. Our discussion of the history of social studies concludes with a look at contemporary issues in the field.

The Influence of Progressive Education and the New Social Studies

Progressive Education.   From colonial times to the end of the 19th century, social studies was a dreary, unimaginative business. The phrase *social studies* was not used in regard to what was taught in elementary schools until 1897. In the place of the integrated social studies, time was devoted to the separate topics of history, geography, and civics (the study of how federal, state, and local governments work). Until the 20th century, students were expected to memorize information in their textbooks and then recite it in front of their classmates. The textbooks were organized around questions, and teachers called on a student who stood and recited the answer (Douglass, 1967).

Fortunately, the late 19th century brought great changes to social studies curriculum and instruction. This was the period of Progressivism, the social and political movement that reformed American life between 1880 and 1920. Profoundly influenced by the educational philosophy of John Dewey (1900, 1902) and the innovations of Francis W. Parker (1883, 1894), social studies was born during this period. Parker boldly asserted that "we learn to do by doing, to hear by hearing, and to think by thinking" (1883, p. 115). He introduced teacher-made materials, field trips, and what we would call today "hands-on experiences." Study in geography began with trips to the surrounding countryside. Children observed and described what they saw. Following this firsthand experience, children made maps by molding sand. Later they would draw their own maps. When studying history, Parker believed that students should learn different points of view and not rely on the textbook as the sole source of information. Parker sought to develop each child's "power of organized inference" (1894, p. 269). Children should compare and contrast, speculate, and find generalizations. Teachers should lead this process by planning activities, asking questions, and suggesting places where answers could be found. Francis Parker's reforms were among the most significant in the history of American education. It was John Dewey, however, who gave Progressive Education a unifying, underlying philosophy. One of the key elements of Dewey's philosophy was the importance of "child-centered" education. Children, he argued, will receive the best education if they are given choices over what they learn and when they learn it. Dewey also stressed the importance of "activity-based" learning, calling for a challenging curriculum that provided children with many opportunities to build things, manipulate things, and create things. During the first 20 years of the 20th century, the influence of Progressive Education was considerable. There were, however, problems with some Progressive ideas. Some Progressive schools were too permissive—any activity children decided to pursue was viewed as worthwhile. Between 1920 and 1960, the influence of the Progressives steadily weakened. Today's teachers should remember four ideas from Progressive Education:

1. Social studies is more than the memorization of facts. It is where students learn to think, to make hypotheses, and to find answers.
2. Social studies should be activity based. Learning requires firsthand experiences. Children need to act, sing, build, dance, take field trips, and have hands-on activities.
3. Social studies requires the use of many instructional materials. Textbooks can play an important role in social studies teaching, but many other learning resources must be used.
4. Social studies instruction should build on the interests of children. To put this in practical terms, every instructional unit should be structured so children select some of their learning activities.

Bruner and the New Social Studies.   In the 1960s, social studies was reexamined. In 1959, the National Academy of Sciences sponsored a summer study group of scientists, scholars from other fields, and educators. Their purpose was to discuss how science education could be improved in elementary and secondary education. The results of this meeting, however, would play an influential role not just in science education but in social studies as well. Jerome Bruner, a psychologist from Harvard, wrote *The Process of Education* (1960), a little book reporting on the conference that sounded the keynote for a period of considerable reform in elementary education. *The Process of Education* provided the theory for instructional programs that became known as the "New Social Studies" (and the "New Math"). The federal government provided millions of dollars for reform-oriented social studies projects during the 1960s (Hertzberg, 1981). Bruner himself played a key role in the development of a highly innovative and controversial curriculum called "Man: A Course of Study" (MACOS; Dow, 1991; Schaffarzick, 1979). Bruner's ideas were at the heart of MACOS and many other New Social Studies programs. Bruner (1960) believed that the subject matter for social studies should be organized around two concepts: the "structure of the disciplines" and "the spiral curriculum." He thought that what students learn about any subject "should be determined by the most fundamental understanding that can be achieved of the underlying principles that give structure to that subject" (p. 31). Thus, if we wanted elementary students to learn from the field of economics, we would first define the most important principles of economics and then develop materials and activities to teach them. Bruner also asserted that the curriculum should "spiral." That is, these important concepts or principles would be taught at several grade levels; as the children grow older, the principles would be covered with greater sophistication. And Bruner believed that *any* concept could be simplified and taught to a child at *any* age. The task for authors of social studies textbooks and curriculum guides and for the teachers who used them was to take big ideas and present them so that small children would understand them.

The instructional programs developed as part of the New Social Studies attempted to teach children the fundamental principles from many social science disciplines, especially anthropology and sociology. Bruner had strong ideas about what learning activities should dominate social studies. He felt that social studies should be based on inquiry learning (*inquiry* is a process of solving problems and answering questions). He wrote that one of the purposes of social studies was "the development of an attitude toward learning and inquiry, toward guessing and hunches, toward the possibility of solving problems on one's own" (Bruner, 1960, p. 96). He believed that the best way for students to learn how to solve problems was for them to do the same type of activities as grown-up practitioners. If children were studying history, they should go about answering questions the same way real historians do. The programs created as part of the New Social Studies were popular during the 1960s and 1970s. For several reasons, however, they were abandoned in favor of traditional, textbook-oriented approaches (Engle, 1986; Evans, 1989b; Fenton, 1991). Nonetheless, today's teachers should remember three ideas from Jerome Bruner and the New Social Studies:

1. Social studies should introduce students to the important principles of several social science disciplines (especially anthropology, economics, and sociology). Teaching these principles requires children to learn more than bits of information. For example, second graders who are learning about how food moves from farms to markets should be introduced to the concept of *economic interdependence*—how people rely on others for their basic needs.
2. Social studies should include the *doing* of social science; that is, children should do the same things that historians, geographers, anthropologists, and political scientists do. For example, children can examine primary sources, such as diary entries and old newspapers, just like historians.
3. Social studies should involve many opportunities for children to solve problems and answer complex questions. This is one factor that distinguishes effective teachers: They challenge their students to use the facts they have learned to complete tasks that require critical thinking. For example, a group of second graders could use what they have learned about their community to propose a location for a new park.

The Role of History, Standards, Technology, and Diversity

Controversy Over History.   During the past 30 years, there has been considerable debate regarding the role of the history in elementary social studies. Should it be the dominating center of the curriculum, or should the fields of anthropology, economics, geography, political science, sociology, the arts, and the humanities play significant roles (Brophy & Van Sledright, 1997; Cardis & Risinger, 1994; Evans, 2004,

2006; Phipps & Adler, 2003)? Currently, most state social studies curricula emphasize historical content at the expense of the other disciplines. On the other hand, the NCSS standards for social studies have been sharply criticized because of an alleged lack of historical content (Phipps & Adler, 2003). In addition to arguments over the relevant importance of historical study, the historical content students will be expected to learn has also been controversial. Once the decision is made to focus on history, conflicting viewpoints immediately emerge. Whose history will be examined? Which view of the past will be presented? It is impossible to please everyone across the political spectrum, and it seems any historical scope and sequence becomes a political document, subject to criticism from either the Left or the Right, or both (Grant, 1997; Leming, Ellington, & Porter-Magee; 2003; Nash & Dunn, 1995; Saxe, 1996; Spies et al., 2004; Symcox, 2002).

Standards and the "Squeezing Out" of Social Studies.   Another trend of great importance is the movement to standards-based instructional programs. Standards define what students should know and be able to do, and define at what age those goals should be accomplished. Standards have been created by school districts, by state departments of education, and by national organizations. For you, the standards adopted by your state department of education will determine the social studies curriculum you teach. The George W. Bush administration's "No Child Left Behind" legislation of January 2002 provided funds for each state to create standards, but only in the areas of reading, math, and science, not in social studies (see the U.S. Department of Education Website, www.ed.gov). Nonetheless, almost all states have adopted standards for elementary social studies. Sometimes the process has been controversial, as it was in Minnesota (Spies et al., 2004). For examples of state social studies standards, take a look at the Texas Essential Knowledge and Skills—Social Studies (www.tea.state.tx.us/teks/); California's History/Social Science Content Standards (www.cde.ca.gov); or Florida's Sunshine State Standards (www.fldoe.org).

The emphasis on having every child achieve state standards in reading and math has led to less time for social studies teaching and learning in many elementary classrooms. While almost all states have social studies standards, not all states have mandatory *assessments* of those standards. The No Child Left Behind legislation requires tests only of math and reading and, as a result, many states have mandated that children be assessed only in reading, writing, and mathematics. Thus, the time devoted to teaching social studies in some elementary schools has shrunk considerably over the last 5 years (Hinde & Ekiss, 2005; Howard, 2003; Neill & Guisbond, 2005). One writer considers this to be a crisis that has created a situation in which "youngsters are growing up with little or no knowledge of their own and their neighbors' histories, ironically when the nation is debating many foreign policy issues" (Pascopella, 2005, p. 30). Further, fewer and fewer teachers teach social studies during a separate, dedicated part of the day. In a recent national survey, about half of second- and fifth-grade teachers stated that what little social studies they taught, contained in fewer than four hours a week, was taught in an integrated fashion with language arts or science (Leming, Ellington, & Schug, 2006).

Standards in social studies written for national audiences influenced state-adopted standards and are also important because they reflect the perspectives of experts in many different subject areas. The development of national standards started in 1994 when President Clinton signed into law the Goals 2000: Educate America Act, which enabled the federal Department of Education to fund the development of curriculum standards in the several areas, including the specific social studies disciplines of civics and government, economics, geography, and history. The NCSS created a task force to write national standards for social studies.

All the national standards projects, those funded by Goals 2000 and the independent initiative of the NCSS, have now been in place for over 10 years:

> Standards for social studies in general: *Expectations of Excellence: Curriculum Standards for the Social Studies* (www.ncss.org, NCSS, 1994)
>
> Standards for civics and government: *National Standards for Civics and Government* (www.civiced.org, Center for Civic Education, 1994)
>
> Standards for economics: *National Content Standards in Economics* (www.ncee.net, National Council on Economic Education, 1997)
>
> Standards for geography: *Geography for Life* (www.ncge.org, Geography Education Standards Project, 1994)
>
> Standards for history: *National Standards for History* (www.sscnet.ucla.edu/nchs, National Center for History in the Schools, 1996)

Again, in your teaching assignment, standards adopted by your state department of education will be the ones you are expected to follow. Since this book is written for a national audience, I will use examples from each of these national sets of standards as the basis for sample lessons and units.

A brief look at *Expectations of Excellence: Curriculum Standards for the Social Studies* would seem to be in order since these standards represent the vision of the NCSS (Alter, 1995a; Handley & Adler, 1994). Remember, standards are statements of what students should know and when they should know it. Rather than proposing topics for each grade level, K–12, the NCSS standards are organized under 10 themes. For each theme, there are "performance standards" for the early grades, the middle grades, and high school. The national social studies standards also include examples of exemplary instructional activities. The 10 themes are shown in Table 1.1.

For example, for the theme of "culture," there are five performance standards for the early grades. The first two are the following:

> Social studies programs should include experiences that provide for the study of culture and cultural diversity, so that the learner can:
>
> a. explore and describe commonalities and differences in the ways groups, societies, and cultures address similar human needs and concerns;
> b. give examples of how experiences may be interpreted differently by people from diverse cultural perspectives and frames of reference (NCSS, 1994, p. 33)

Table 1.1   Ten Organizational Themes for Social Studies

Themes	Theme Descriptions
1. *Culture*	Students will learn the common characteristics and significant differences among the world's cultural groups. The content related to this theme comes primarily from the social science field of anthropology.
2. *Time, Continuity, and Change*	Students will learn how to reconstruct the past and develop a historical perspective to interpret the present. The content related to this theme comes primarily from the social science field of history.
3. *People, Places, and Environments*	Students will learn to understand the significance of place and develop a geographic perspective to interpret current social conditions. The content related to this theme comes primarily from the social science field of geography.
4. *Individual Development and Identity*	Students will learn how culture, social groups, and institutions shape personal identity. The content related to this theme comes primarily from the social science field of psychology.
5. *Individuals, Groups, and Institutions*	Students will learn how institutions such as schools, churches, families, and government influence people's lives. The content related to this theme comes primarily from the social science field of sociology.
6. *Power, Authority, and Governance*	Students will learn how forms of government distribute power and authority. The content related to this theme comes primarily from the social science field of political science.
7. *Production, Distribution, and Consumption*	Students will learn that resources are limited and that people must make decisions on what things will be produced, how those things will be distributed, and the rate at which they will be consumed. The content related to this theme comes primarily from the social science field of economics.
8. *Science, Technology, and Society*	Students will learn that new technology changes the way people live. The content related to this theme comes from several social sciences fields.
9. *Global Connections*	Students will learn about the global connections among the world's societies. The content related to this theme comes from social science fields.
10. *Civic Ideals and Practices*	Students will learn the importance of civic participation in a democratic society. The content related to this theme comes primarily from political science.

Diversity.   In the 21st century, teachers will work with students who are highly diverse, especially in regard to language, culture, and exceptionality (Banks et al., 2005). The results of the 2000 census confirmed a trend that has been constant for the last four decades (www.census.gov). The percentage of Americans who identify themselves as "white" is steadily decreasing, as the percentage who are either African American, Asian American, or Hispanic American is steadily on the rise. In 2000, the non-Hispanic, white population was 69% of the total; projections are that this percentage will shrink to 63% in 2020 and to 52% in 2050. In California, by far the most populous state, the 2000 census revealed that "minorities" are now the majority! There, the non-Hispanic, white population is just 46.7%. There are two paramount issues regarding diversity. First, more and more of our students are acquiring English as a second language and in this book will be called "English learners," or "ELs." These children face the challenge of learning social studies content at the same time they are learning English. Effective teachers must know how to "shelter" instruction so that English learners acquire the same content as their English-only peers (Echevarria & Graves, 2006; Echevarria, Vogt, & Short, 2003; Kurtz-Costes & Pungello, 2000). Second, teachers face the challenge of educating their students about different cultural groups, including, of course, those who make up an increasingly large percentage of the U.S. population. The need for American children to better understand disparate cultural groups outside the United States has taken on a special urgency. All this requires considerable skill as we seek to provide information that is at the same time comprehensible and free of bias (Alvi, 2001; Foster & Hoge, 2000; Seikaly, 2001; Wilhelm, 1999). Finally, almost every classroom will include students with special needs, and good teachers will successfully "differentiate," or modify how they teach to meet the needs of students with learning disabilities and gifted students (Tomlinson, 2001; 2003).

The Information Age.   Technology has transformed all aspects of contemporary life, and the classroom is no exception. The explosion of information that is easily available to those who are interested has resulted in new challenges for both students and teachers. Fitzpatrick (2000) noted that the irony is that students born and raised in the era of the computer and the Internet are better prepared to work in information-age classrooms than their teachers, most of whom are more comfortable with television, newspapers, and encyclopedias. He concluded that "the greatest challenge of the new millennium is therefore not the one facing *students,* but the one facing *teachers* as they work to help fresh, young minds grow toward their fullest potential" (p. 33, emphasis added). Computer-based resources are replacing more traditional, hard-copy sources, like pull-down classroom maps, multivolume encyclopedias, and films. The NCSS journals *Social Education* and *Social Studies and the Young Learner* regularly publish articles about the advantages and potential problems with Internet resources. Also, the computer allows students to reveal what they have learned in exciting new ways as children create multimedia products that are "recorded" on CD-ROM and school Websites. In many classrooms, the hand-painted mural and painstakingly printed caption have given way to presentations using sophisticated word processing and graphics programs (Simpson, 2005; 2006; VanFossen, 2004a).

◆ Social Studies: The Curriculum

Whatever set of standards you follow as a teacher, the structure of the social studies curriculum will have three organizational components: content, processes, and values.

Content

Scope and Sequence.   Given the domain of social studies—the study of people—there is far more content than can be presented in the seven elementary grades. Therefore, anyone planning a social studies curriculum must design a *scope and sequence*. A scope and sequence is an outline of the content studied at each grade level. *Scope* refers to the topics covered, *sequence* to the order of their presentation. The scope and sequence of any curriculum is organized around grade levels. The topics chosen and the concepts related to those topics should be dependent on the developmental level of students. Thus, simpler concepts are usually chosen for earlier grade levels. For the purposes of this textbook, I provide lesson examples for grades K–6.

One scope and sequence has dominated elementary social studies, namely, the *expanding environments* approach (also called *expanding communities* or *expanding horizons*). Some authorities question when this framework was first implemented; social studies programs from as far back as 1900 in some ways resemble it (LeRiche, 1987). Paul Hanna (1963, 1987a, 1987b) first advocated it as a distinct theory in 1956. The essence of expanding environments is that children should learn about what is nearest to them first and then, as they grow older, about people and places that are progressively more remote. A scope and sequence following the expanding environments model would be as follows:

> Kindergarten: Self, Family, School
> First Grade: Family and School
> Second Grade: Neighborhood and Community
> Third Grade: Our Community and Other Communities
> Fourth Grade: Our State
> Fifth Grade: United States History
> Sixth Grade: World Studies

The expanding environments scope and sequence has been criticized for its lack of substance in the primary grades and for its too narrow scope (Akenson, 1989; Larkins & Hawkins, 1990). Young children need to learn about the many cultural groups in the United States and around the world. Devoting four grades to family, school, and community provides children with too limited a view. Certainly, in a time of increased cultural diversity in the United States and of interdependence internationally, the expanding environments concept needs to include cross-cultural and global perspectives whenever possible. The elementary social studies curriculum of the Gwinnett County, Georgia, Public Schools is an example of a curriculum that is more international in its scope and sequence. This curriculum is based on a set of standards called "Academic Knowledge and Skills" (AKS) and features the study of

Canada, Mexico, or Brazil in first grade and Japan and Australia in second grade (www.gwinnett.k12.ga.us). An outline of this curriculum is included in Table 1.2.

The expanded environments concept, however, remains a strong influence on curriculum planners. Alternative outlines, while emphasizing other themes and presenting new topics, generally reflect the self–family–school–neighborhood––community–state–nation–world sequence of expanding environments. For example, California's content standards for history and social science introduced new topics

Table 1.2   Social Studies Scope and Sequence: Three Perspectives

	Expanded Environments	California, 1998	Gwinnett County, 2006
Kindergarten	Self, family, and school	Learning and working, now and long ago	Myself; families and communities in Georgia, now and long ago
Grade 1	Family and school	A child's place in time and space (social skills, geography of neighborhood, folktales)	Geography and national symbols and celebrations of United States, Canada, and Mexico or Brazil
Grade 2	Neighborhood and community	People who make a difference (suppliers of food, family history, biographies)	Basic economics; Native Americans; geographic and cultural comparison of United States, Japan, and Australia
Grade 3	Our community	Continuity and change (local history, U.S. history through biography and folklore)	History, civics, and economics of the United States; Native Americans in Georgia and early settlers
Grade 4	Our state or region of the United States	California history and geography	U.S. geography and history to 1875
Grade 5	U.S. geography and history	U.S. history (to about 1850)	U.S. history from 1875 to present
Grade 6	World geography and history; usually Canada and Latin America	World history: ancient civilizations (to about A.D. 500)	Geographic and cultural comparison of Canada, Mexico, Brazil, Germany, Russia, Australia, or New Zealand

in the primary grades. Otherwise, planners followed the expanded environments scope and sequence, especially in the upper grades with study of the local community in grade 3, state history in grade 4, U.S. history in grade 5, and world history in grade 6 (California Department of Education, 1998; www.cde.ca.gov).

As teachers, we are expected to follow the curriculum scope and sequence that is used as the basis for the set of social studies standards our school district follows. You may have a personal interest in the American Civil War, for example, but that does not mean you are free to make it a part of your social studies curriculum unless, of course, the standards you are following make it a topic you are supposed to teach. At the same time, we and our students should have the freedom to pursue topics of interest within our grade-level curriculum. For example, suppose a third-grade class is studying community workers. If a child shows a keen interest in firefighters, then she should be encouraged to complete unique activities relating to fighting fires while other students do other things.

One other point related to scope and sequence: The elementary school is the ideal place for teachers to plan cross-curricular units of instruction. These units combine one or more of the following: social studies, science, math, literature, language arts, the performing arts, and the visual arts. One factor that has stimulated the development of cross-curricular units of study has been the reorganization of junior high schools into middle schools, where sixth and seventh graders frequently are taught in "humanities blocks," or two-hour periods with an integrated curriculum of social studies and language arts (Field et al., 2001; Kellough, 1995; Young, 1994).

Concepts, Generalizations, and Facts.   A scope and sequence will define what is to be covered, though there still remains the large question of what specific content children will be expected to acquire. If fourth graders study their state, what about their state should they learn? Again, the relevant set of standards your school district has adopted will determine the content your children are expected to master. The content students learn should consist of concepts, generalizations, and facts. This three-level categorization of the content component of social studies is based on the work of Hilda Taba (Bernard-Powers, 2002; Fraenkel, 1992; Taba, 1967). Note that other authorities in the social studies offer different definitions for generalizations and concepts. Here, though, we will use Taba's system:

- *Concepts* are ideas. They may be stated in a variety of ways. They tend to be broad and somewhat fuzzy. Conflict, justice, and family are all concepts. Perhaps the easiest way to think of concepts is as the big ideas that we want students to understand.
- *Generalizations* are content-specific statements. They are more specific than concepts and are based on the factual content of the social studies curriculum.
- *Facts* support concepts and generalizations.

It is essential that we understand the relationship among concepts, generalizations, and facts. Children learn facts so that they can make generalizations. Several

Barbara Schwartz/Merrill

Some social studies concepts are relatively easy to understand while others are more difficult. Effective teachers provide assistance to those students who need it.

generalizations, when understood in concert, explain a concept. Generalizations and concepts enable children to make sense of what they study because facts, if unconnected to larger ideas, are of little value. Taba (1967) points out that the purpose of teaching facts "is to explain, illustrate, and develop main ideas" (p. 19). Figure 1.1 shows the hierarchical relationship among concepts, generalizations, and facts for one part of a third-grade social studies curriculum.

Figure 1.1   Concepts, Generalizations, and Facts for "Coming to Our City" in a Third-Grade Curriculum

---

Concept: Movement (A geographic concept—that people, products, and ideas move across political and natural borders.)

Generalization: People have come to our city throughout its history.

Facts:

- In about A.D 1000, Native Americans first settled in what was to become our city.
- In 1792, the Franciscan missionaries built a mission near our city.
- During the 10 years after World War II (1945–1955), the population of our city doubled, from 40,000 to 80,000 people.
- From 1975 to 1990, 9,500 immigrants from Southeast Asia moved to our city.

Processes

In addition to teaching children concepts, generalizations, and facts, social studies programs also should improve students' ability in several processes. A *process* involves doing—it usually can be stated in a single word ending with *-ing*. Sets of social studies standards, whether produced at the national, state, or local level, will have a list of the processes students should master as they learn the content of the curriculum. The processes related to social studies can be categorized as follows:

- *Inquiry processes,* in which children formulate questions, gather data, analyze what they have found, and share what they learned
- *Thinking processes,* in which children develop the ability to apply, analyze, synthesize, and evaluate information
- *Language arts processes,* especially as they relate to the social science disciplines, as students read, write, speak, and listen
- *Visual and performing arts processes,* which are of two kinds, as students learn to *appreciate* the arts and learn to *use* the arts for expression
- *Technology processes,* in which children manipulate computer-based resources
- *Participation processes,* as children express personal views, work cooperatively with others toward common goals, and become active citizens

Values

Content is the *what* of social studies, and processes are the *how to*. That is not all there is to social studies. Recall from the definitions of the first part of this chapter that an important part of social studies is teaching values. The NCSS provided this definition of *values:*

> Values constitute the standards or criteria against which individual behavior and group behavior are judged. Beliefs represent commitments to those values. (NCSS Task Force on Scope and Sequence, 1989, p. 378)

Honesty, for example, is a value. If we are honest, then we will adopt a certain way of living and expect others to behave in a way that reflects that value. The set of values social studies emphasizes are *civic values,* beliefs that lead to active citizenship. It is not enough that students acquire content and become skillful in a variety of processes. Children should *use* what they know to make their family, school, community, state, nation, and world a better place. This part of the elementary curriculum has existed since colonial times and is fundamental to public schooling in a democratic society. Democracies must have citizens who are knowledgeable and active. Other than civic values, social studies should teach children to value themselves by nurturing positive self-concepts. Along with the rest of the elementary curriculum, social studies programs should help children adopt healthy values toward school and learning (NCSS Task Force on Early Childhood/Elementary Social Studies, 1989).

It should be stressed from the beginning, however, that values education should not be a process of indoctrination. Rather, children should adopt civic values because they understand the importance of them in a free society. As children learn to treasure our democratic system, they must concurrently learn of the differences in all aspects of life in a democratic society. In other words, diversity is inevitable in a democracy. The values component of the social studies curriculum can be difficult to teach, but we should not shy away from it. Engle and Ochoa (1988) stated it nicely:

> It is much easier and more straightforward to ask what are the facts than to ask what value or values should we subscribe to in a given instance. Despite the difficulty, a social studies program that neglects to deal with value problems stops far short of teaching students how to think intelligently about the real world. (p. 120)

At the end of this chapter, there is a lesson plan for a kindergarten classroom that is standards based and has objectives from each component of the social studies curriculum: content, processes, and values.

No one can tell what the future will bring for social studies. It seems safe to say that debates about both curricular and instructional issues will be ongoing. As elementary schoolteachers, we will become a part of the history of social studies as we guide our students to become active citizens.

◆ Summary of Key Points

- Social studies is integrated and interdisciplinary in that ideas and information come from many fields of study.
- Social studies goes beyond the textbook and rote memorization of facts.
- Social studies adopts the best ideas from the period of Progressive Education, including hands-on experiences, student selection of activities, thematic units, and the integration of social studies with the arts.
- Social studies continues the innovations of the New Social Studies, such as teaching children the fundamental concepts of the social sciences through inquiry learning.
- Social studies teaching and learning has become standards based.
- Social studies content includes concepts, generalizations, and facts.
- Social studies processes fall under the following categories: inquiry, thinking, language arts, visual arts, performing arts, technology, and participatory.
- Social studies emphasizes acquisition of civic values, the set of beliefs that lead to active citizenship.

FOR FURTHER READING

General Sources of Information on Social Studies

- The Website of the NCSS is www.ncss.org. There are many journals that focus on social studies. Most of my references are from three journals: *Social Education, Social Studies and the Young Learner,* and *The Social Studies.* If you want to get acquainted with research on social studies, start with the 660-page *Handbook of Research on Social Studies Teaching and Learning* (Shaver, 1991).

Definitions of Social Studies

- Check out the national survey of elementary and middle school teachers reported by Leming, Ellington, and Schug, 2006. Their report provides a portrait of how social studies is being taught. Unfortunately, they found "teachers in two of the three grades surveyed (second and fifth), spend little classroom time on social studies" (p. 325).
- Interested in reading more definitions of social studies? A good book written some time ago is *Defining the Social Studies* (Barr et al., 1977). Engle and Ochoa (1988) provided an excellent critique of the confusion over social studies definitions in Chapter 7 of their book. The January/February 2000 issue of *Social Education* had several good articles on speculating on how social studies teaching and learning would change in the 21st century (Hartoonian & Van Scotter, 2000). It would be interesting for our students to see if their predictions are coming true.

Social Studies: A History

- We can all learn a great deal by exploring classrooms of the past. Lawrence Cremin's *The Transformation of the School* is about Progressive Education and is fascinating reading. *How Teachers Taught* (Cuban, 1984) is another excellent book with a general focus. For a closer look at social studies in Dewey's Laboratory School, see Dewey (1976) and Mayhew and Edwards (1936). For criticisms of Progressive Education, see Bestor (1953, 1955). A great deal was written about MACOS. Inkpen (1974) compiled a bibliography. See also Cort and Peskowitz (1977), Dow (1976), and Herlihy (1974). On the contributions of women from 1784 to 1984, see Crocco and Davis (2002). On the challenge of teaching tolerant attitudes toward Muslim Americans and Arab Americans after September 11, see Alvi (2001) and Seikaly (2001). For a debate over the NCSS standards, see Adler (2001), Ochoa-Becker (2001); and Phipps & Adler (2003).
- A harsh critique of the way social studies is taught in the United States is *Where Did Social Studies Go Wrong?* (Leming, Ellington, & Porter-Magee, 2003). Authors in that book claim that the social studies curriculum is too left-leaning and politically correct, void of traditional American history, filled with too much content from the other social sciences and multiculturalism, and is taught by teachers who favor student-centered activities over direct instruction. To say the least, many social studies educators disagreed. The July/August (volume 96, number 4) and the September/October (volume 96, number 5) issues of the journal *The Social Studies* were devoted to rebuttals to *Where Did Social Studies Go Wrong?*

Instructional Activities

- For more picture books with the theme of working together with family and friends, take a look at Chapter 5 of *Multicultural Literature, Multicultural Teaching* (Zarrillo, 1994).

LESSON PLANS AND INSTRUCTIONAL ACTIVITIES

At the end of each chapter you will find sample instructional plans in several formats. Most will be *lesson plans,* a teacher's written plan for a social studies lesson of 20 to 40 minutes. Others will be *mini-units,* a series of three or four lessons on a single topic. Some of will be *projects,* an activity that takes more than one day to complete. Finally, at the end of Chapter 4, you will find a fully developed *unit of study,* a set of lesson plans and instructional activities, all related to a single topic, spanning several days. Each chapter will begin with a *vignette,* a description of a social studies activity in an elementary classroom. At the end of this chapter you will find: (a) A classroom vignette describing a sixth-grade class immersed in a unit on ancient Greece; and (b) A lesson plan for a kindergarten activity on cooperation.

Classroom Vignette/Grade Six

Multiple Activities During a Unit on Ancient Greece

There is a lot going on here! Some students rehearse a play they have written on the myth of Daedalus. Another group is busy painting the Acropolis for a large mural on the ancient Greeks. Some kids are in their seats reading books. Mrs. Winslow has brought several books to class from the local library. Matt reads Margaret Hodges's *The Arrow and the Lamp,* a retelling of the myth of Eros and Psyche. Julie examines an information book, *The Parthenon,* written by Susan Woodford. Ricardo and Thuy, working on a computer, are looking at photographs of the Parthenon through an Internet Website (History/Social Science for K–12 Teachers; http://k-12historysocialstudies.com). Mrs. Winslow works with a group of students who are producing a CD-ROM on ancient Greece. This electronic encyclopedia will have photographs, maps, charts, and written text. (Ouch! The students know much more about this technology than I do!)

I also copied a page from Mrs. Winslow's plan book. This is what she wrote for the day I observed:

1:05–2:00 Social Studies
Ancient Greek unit, Day 10, Multiple Activities:

1. "Daedalus" play group—read through second part of script—first walkthrough tomorrow
2. Mural group—paint Acropolis
3. CD-ROM encyclopedia group—I will spend most of my time with this group—edit rough drafts of text, answer questions
4. Computer/Internet—view photographs of the Parthenon available through History/Social Science Website for Teachers
5. Other students—read independently

Let's consider these activities in the context of the definitions presented earlier. Both the NCSS definition and Barth's definition stress that social studies must integrate the social sciences and humanities. The focus of the unit was historical, but Mrs. Winslow did a good job of integrating the arts with the historical content of the unit. The play on Daedulus and books like *The Arrow and the Lamp* were just a few of the ways she introduced her students to the Greek myths. Development of the mural helped students understand Greek architecture and would be followed with lessons showing Greek influence on American architecture. The arts were also a means for student expression. Rather than limit her students to written assignments, Mrs. Winslow provided opportunities for expression through the visual arts and performing arts. My definition stresses that social studies should help students master several processes; and in this one day, I saw students reading, writing, acting, talking, cooperating, drawing, painting, and "computing" (using the computer to gather and present information). Remember, too, that each definition stated that the ultimate purpose of social studies is good citizenship. Mrs. Winslow's unit on the ancient Greeks provided her students with knowledge of the link between ancient Greece and contemporary America and the influence of their democratic governments on society.

 Effective Teaching in Today's Diverse Classroom: It is important to note that the multiple-activity approach used by Mrs. Winslow is essential in a classroom with diverse students. While engaging in different types of experiences, each student in her room was learning more about the ancient Greeks. Some students will learn more through the visual arts, others through reading and writing, and others through the performing arts. Howard Gardner (1983) describes the "multiple intelligences" that people possess, and our teaching should allow children to learn social studies content in a variety of ways. This is especially important for children with learning disabilities. Also, the multiple activities Mrs. Winslow planned provided for both group and individual work. Even though all students need to work with their classmates in small-group formats, it was good to see that she provided an opportunity for students to choose to work individually or with their peers.

 LESSON PLAN

Kindergarten: Cooperation and *A Chair for My Mother*

Overview: This is a lesson for kindergarten. It is part of a unit titled "Happy Together—Family and Friends." It is planned for 25 students.

Resources and Materials: (a) One copy of *A Chair for My Mother* by Vera B. Williams, (b) paint and paper for bulletin board illustrations, (c) 25 sheets of primary-level drawing/writing paper.

Standard: One of the themes in the national social studies standards is "Individuals, Groups, and Institutions." One performance expectation for the early grades is that children can "show how groups and institutions work to meet individual needs and promote the common good, and identify examples of where they fail to do so" (NCSS, 1994, p. 38).

Content Objectives: This lesson will help children see how members of a family and their friends help each other in a time of need. They will consider how they can cooperate in our classroom. It will help children build their understanding of the concepts of cooperation and family.

Process Objectives: The students will (a) *listen* to the book read aloud, (b) *respond* orally to the teacher's questions, (c) *identify* how several characters help Rosa and her family, and (d) complete one of three postreading optional activities.

Value Objectives: This activity should help students acquire the value of "Consideration for Others"—that we should help people who have suffered from an unforeseen circumstance.

Teaching Sequence:

1. Before the lesson begins, be sure all materials and resources are ready; on the blackboard, write the names of the following characters: Rosa, Grandmother, Aunt Ida and Uncle Sandy, neighbors.
2. On a sheet of chart paper, write the following postreading options: (a) Go with Ms. Sanchez (the instructional aide). Draw pictures for *A Chair for My Mother* section of "Our Favorite Books" bulletin board. (b) Go to your seat. Draw and write anything you want about *A Chair for My Mother.* (c) Stay with Mr. Wong (the teacher). Talk about what makes working together difficult and what makes it easy.
3. Ask children to sit on the carpet and read aloud *A Chair for My Mother.*
4. Ask the children if there is anything they would like to say about the book (use what the children say as a basis for further discussion).
5. Discuss with the children how Rosa, Grandmother, Aunt Ida and Uncle Sandy, and the neighbors helped. Refer back to illustrations in the book.
6. Lead discussion on how class members can work together and help each other. Begin by making a list of all the classroom chores that are easier to complete if members of the class work together. Other than classroom tasks, ask what other things members of the class can do for each other (many things should come to mind, like sharing supplies or cheering up classmates who are sad). Use a piece of chart paper to record the ideas of the students.
7. Explain options to children (see item 2).
8. Be sure all children are either working with Ms. Sanchez, in their seats, or still on the carpet.
9. Later, bring the group together. Have children share their pictures, dictated narratives, and the results of the discussion.

Evaluation: At the kindergarten level, evaluation is often informal. The pictures the children draw and the texts they write or dictate can be saved in student portfolios.

Effective Teaching in Today's Diverse Classroom: Mr. Wong's class included several Spanish-speaking English learners. These children spoke some English. The excellent illustrations in the book allowed the English learners to understand the story, even though they did not know the meaning of every word in the story's text. Like most kindergarten teachers, Mr. Wong modified his speech when talking to his 5-year-old students. He slowed down, repeated things, and avoided large words. This, too, helped the English learners understand what he was saying. If the class had included English learners who spoke almost no English, then the activity would need the assistance of a bilingual person (the teacher, an instructional aide, a parent volunteer, or an older student). Each of the following adjustments could be added: (a) Someone should explain the plot of the story in the native language of the English learners (in this case, Spanish), and (b) the postreading discussion could be conducted in the English learners' native language. We want children to understand the concepts of cooperation and to see their importance in the story and in the classroom. To achieve this objective, it might be necessary to conduct all or part of the lesson in a language other than English.

Chapter 2

Children, Diversity, and Learning: Implementing Differentiated Instruction

Matt Marcella's second-grade classroom reflected the diversity of his community. Twelve children were Hispanic, five were Vietnamese American, four were African American, and nine were European American. Eight children were immigrants to the United States. Mr. Marcella wanted to start the year with a social studies unit that incorporated the diversity of his students and, at the same time, introduced his students to each other. He planned a unit called "Families and Friends." During the unit, his students listened while he read picture books about friendship and families. The children's favorites were *Abuela,* Arthur Dorris's charming fantasy about a Latina girl and her grandmother who fly above New York; *Peter's Chair,* Ezra Jack Keats's story about an African American boy who runs away from home because of the arrival of his new sister; and *The Lost Lake,* Allen Say's beautifully illustrated tale about a Japanese American father and son who go backpacking.

Mr. Marcella's class sang songs about families and friendship. His favorite was "Five People in My Family," a song he had learned when he was a boy (from the *Sesame Street Song Book* [Raposo & Moss, 1971]). His students liked "I Live in the City" by Malvina Reynolds, a song about how people of many colors build a city. Throughout the unit, the children worked in small groups to define friendship, focusing on a list of things that friends do for their friends. During the unit, Mr. Marcella gave the children many opportunities to write about their families, their feelings, and their friends. Then, because Mr. Marcella knew that autobiographies would help the children appreciate the diverse backgrounds of their classmates, he made the creating of autobiographies a culminating activity. Some children were able to bring photographs from home to illustrate their books, while others drew pictures. Mr. Marcella helped each student organize his or her book around topics such as celebrating holidays, starting school, moving to a new apartment, and enjoying summer vacations. First, the children drew pictures or used their photographs to help recall details. Then they wrote descriptive sentences that related what was happening in their illustrations. Although most children were able to write a few sentences about each illustrated event, some needed to dictate their text, and three wrote in Spanish. When completed, the autobiographies were shared with the whole group as either the child or the child with Mr. Marcella's help read his or her book aloud.

As a culminating activity, Mr. Marcella and his students created a classroom quilt. Each child was represented on the quilt with either a self-portrait or an illustration showing something that the child considered special.

•   •   •

In this chapter, you will read about

- The ideas of Stephen Krashen and James Cummins on linguistic diversity and language acquisition, important to lesson planning for students acquiring English as a second language.
- The advantages of planning social studies programs that meet the needs of culturally diverse classrooms.
- Instructional strategies that will help children with learning disabilities and children who are gifted.

Like Mr. Marcella, we teach social studies in the context of an increasingly diverse society. We need to adapt our teaching to fit the backgrounds, abilities, interests, and needs of our students. In fact, our success as teachers depends on our ability to plan an instructional program that accounts for the diversity of our students. This is a tall order, so let's take a look at how students in our classrooms might differ.

Dictionary definitions of *diversity* use words like "different," "varied," or "diversified," and these are good descriptors of the children we teach. Capitalizing on the diversity of our students will enhance our joy of teaching. As a group of scholars aptly put it, "Diversity in the nation's schools is both an opportunity and a challenge. The nation is enriched by the ethnic, cultural, and language diversity among its citizens and within its schools" (Banks et al., 2005, p. 39). Every year, we will work with a group of different individuals, each with unique challenges and gifts, so each class we teach will be delightfully different.

How will our students differ? Students in all elementary school classrooms vary in a number of ways. Both girls and boys will be assigned to our rooms, and some will be older (or younger) than most of their classmates. Although students usually are assigned to classes by age, a variety of factors can result in a group with significant age differences, and the "higher" the grade we teach (e.g., fourth, fifth, or sixth), the greater the span between our oldest and youngest students. Some of our students will be well adjusted, confident, and happy. Others, however, will struggle with personal issues and the effects of difficult past experiences. Most public elementary schools reflect the concept of the neighborhood school, and the level of homogeneity in family income status among the students will be high. There is a good chance, however, that some of our students will be significantly more affluent (or impoverished) than their classmates.

Students will differ widely in their native talents and abilities, with variation in all areas of mental and physical performance. If we are good teachers, we will be able to develop an instructional program that allows each child to develop the full limit of his or her ability. Public Law 94–102, the Education for All Handicapped Children Act of 1975 (now called the Individuals with Disabilities Education Act [IDEA]), established the requirements for children with special needs in public schools. Congress reauthorized IDEA in 2004. Among these requirements is that each child is placed in his or her "least restrictive environment." This requires schools to educate students with disabilities with nondisabled students to the maximum extent appropriate for the student with disabilities (Lewis & Doorlag, 2006; Turnbull, Turnbull, & Wehmeyer, 2007). Thus, we might teach children with exceptionalities for part or all of the school day. By the time they reach our classrooms, our students will have clearly defined tastes, interests, and preferences. Without any special effort on our part, many of our students will be interested in the topics presented in social studies. Others, though, will become engaged only if the activities we plan and the resources we select are exciting and challenging.

An ever increasing percentage of students first acquire a language other than English. These children will face the challenge of learning social studies content, mastering social studies processes, and adopting social studies values *at the same time* they are learning to read, write, speak, and listen in English (Rodriguez, Salinas, & Guberman, 2005). The United States is a pluralistic society. Our cultural identity plays a primary role in shaping our values and behaviors. Research shows that there are important differences in the way children of different cultural groups communicate, interact, and learn.

The only way to meet the needs of our diverse student populations is to "differentiate" instruction (Tomlinson, 2001; 2003). Differentiated instruction abandons a "one size fits all" mentality in favor of modifying how we teach to meet the needs of our students. We can make three categories of modifications. First, we can change *content* we teach, perhaps by breaking an area of study into smaller units or, for our gifted students, by introducing more challenging topics. Second, we can change the *instructional process* through a number of interventions, such as simplifying the way we talk to make our presentations comprehensible to our English learners. Finally, we can change the work *products* we expect students to complete; one possibility would be to let students who have difficulty with written tasks present a report orally. This chapter focuses on these three aspects of diversity—language, culture, and exceptionality (children with learning disabilities and gifted children).

Scott Cunningham/Merrill

In the 21st century, the student population in our classrooms will be increasingly diverse. Small-group work gives children from different cultural groups the opportunity to develop positive attitudes towards each other.

◆ Linguistic Diversity

First, let us look at the challenge children face when they are learning social studies at the same time they are learning English as a second language.

English Learners

Children with native languages other than English may be called "language minority students." Those language minority students who have not achieved a level of English language proficiency (reading, writing, and speaking) comparable to a monolingual child of the same age have been classified as "limited English proficient" (LEP) or English learners (EL). Remember, not all language minority students have EL status; some will come to your classroom fully bilingual. They astound us with their ability to use their native language and English. There will be a wide range of English competency among our EL students: Some will have virtually no English, whereas others will be on the threshold of becoming fluent in English. The level of each child's English proficiency will be a key factor in designing appropriate social studies instruction.

I find the label *limited* English proficient unfortunate and misleading because all of us grow as language users over a lifetime. The extent of our language proficiency is without limits, so all of us are to some degree "limited." The use of *limited,* with its negative connotation, is unfair to the children who are classified as LEP. In this book, I will use the descriptor "English learner" (EL).

The number of English learners in our schools has increased dramatically in the past 40 years. In 1993, there were over 2 million English learners in public schools in the United States. Data from the National Center for Education Statistics revealed that by 2004 the number of English learners had increased to 3.8 million (about 11% of the total). The U.S. Census Bureau's 2005 American Community Survey showed that 19% of all Americans speak a language other than English in their homes. Since 1960, the pattern of immigration has shifted from Europeans to immigrants from Asia and the Spanish-speaking Americas. Recently, there have been significant increases of immigrants from India and Pakistan, the former Soviet Union, and the Middle East. Thus, many schools now have significant populations of Mandarin, Vietnamese, Arabic, Hindi, Farsi, and Russian-speaking English learners. The 2005 American Community Survey showed that immigrants are settling all over the United States. From 2000 to 2005, for example, South Carolina saw the largest increase in foreign-born residents and Arkansas experienced the largest increase in Latino residents (for more sources of data, see the Websites of the U.S. Census Bureau, www.census.gov; and the National Center for Education Statistics, www.nces.ed.gov).

Second-Language Acquisition and Learning in Social Studies

The ideas of Stephen Krashen and James Cummins provide a theoretical framework for effective social studies teaching with English language learners.

Krashen: Second-Language Acquisition.   Stephen Krashen is a linguist who has developed a model of second-language acquisition that has been adopted widely in the United States by second-language teachers (1982; 1986; 2003; Krashen & Terrell, 1995). Although his ideas are controversial among linguists, Krashen's perspectives have helped teachers be more effective in teaching their English learners (McLaughlin, 1987). There is no need in a book about social studies teaching and learning to explore all of Krashen's theory of second-language acquisition, but two of his ideas are essential: (a) the concept of *comprehensible input* and (b) the impact of the *affective filter.*

Krashen believes that second languages are acquired when a person is exposed to *comprehensible input in a low anxiety environment.* We acquire a second language by listening to spoken language and reading written language that is slightly more advanced than what we know. The goal of English-speaking teachers is to make the English understandable, and this requires teachers to modify what they say and how they say it. Also, English learners should read materials with English words, phrases, and ideas that are just slightly beyond what they know. If we want English learners to understand what we are saying and at the same time acquire English, then our goal must be to provide comprehensible input.

For example, a teacher working with English learners during a social studies lesson will repeat certain key words and phrases, slow his or her speech, and refrain from using difficult vocabulary that is not essential in the lesson. Although the teacher's speech will be simplified, it will not change to the point where it seems artificial. The key, of course, is for the teacher to communicate with the students. The social studies textbook is often not comprehensible input for English learners. So we as teachers may read the text aloud to students or present the material through charts and graphs, illustrations, or films. Some of us rewrite important sections of the textbook in simplified English so that English learners have a version to read that they can understand.

Krashen argues that an *affective filter* can make it difficult for students to acquire a second language. The affective filter is an attitude or feeling that works as a mental block. Anxiety, fear, and a lack of motivation can operate as affective filters. To put it simply, if we want to make it difficult for students to understand something, we should scare them or bore them! Even if we or other students are providing comprehensible input, the input might not get through if the student is worried, upset, frightened, or disinterested. Worry, anxiety, fear, and boredom work as filters, and the input we so carefully offered is wasted. Consider the following examples: In one classroom, most of the social studies "talk" is among children working in small groups. These conversations are among peers, and there are no affective filters; all the comprehensible input an English learner hears will "get through." In another classroom, in contrast, the teacher asks questions from the textbook and randomly calls on children to answer. The affective filter will be "thick," as the fear of being called on blocks the available comprehensible input. The implication for social studies teaching with English learners is quite clear. Our teaching must provide comprehensible input in a situation where the students' affective filters have "dropped," and are low enough to allow the input in.

Cummins: Dimensions of Language Proficiency. Canadian linguist James Cummins has had an immense influence on educators in the United States (1979, 1986a, 1986b, 1989, 1992; see also Chapter 1 in Cruz, Nutta, O'Brien, Feyten, and Govoni, 2003). As with Krashen, our discussion of Cummins's ideas must be selective. Most significant to the teaching of social studies is his description of the *dimensions of language proficiency.* His discussion of *cognitive demand* and *contextual support* provides us with a useful framework for planning effective lessons for all students, particularly for students whose first language is not English.

Cognitive demand is the level of thinking a student must do to complete a task. Cognitively *undemanding* tasks include writing a description of a new pair of shoes, asking to borrow a pair of scissors, or reading the television program listings in the entertainment section of a newspaper. At the other end of the continuum are cognitively *demanding* tasks, which require complex thinking, such as discussing the relative merits of capitalism and socialism, reading and understanding information about the Russian monetary system, or writing an essay on comprehensive health care. In social studies, students should be asked to complete tasks at all points along the cognitive demand continuum, from the facile to the most difficult.

Contextual support is the level of help a person has to complete a task. Many language tasks have a great deal of contextual support. The person performing the task can ask questions, seek help from other people, and refer to illustrations or real objects. At the other end of the continuum are tasks for which the person who is to perform them has little, if any, support. Any task, regardless of its cognitive demand, can have either a great deal of contextual support or very little, depending on how teachers structure the situation. For example, a group of students are asked to compare and contrast a Mohawk longhouse and a Sioux tipi. If the students can work together to write their answer, if they can ask the teacher for help, if they have accurate illustrations to examine, then the task has a high level of contextual support. In contrast, if students must work individually, are given 15 minutes to write their answers, and are not permitted to ask anyone for help, then there is no contextual support to complete the task.

Cummins developed a diagram to help educators understand the roles of cognitive demand and contextual support in school-related tasks (1986b, 1992). The diagram, consisting of four quadrants, classifies the way language is used. My students have found it easier to understand and apply these concepts if they are presented in a four-level chart. Figure 2.1 places social studies activities in four categories, explains the level of cognitive demand and contextual support in each of the categories, and provides an example in each category of an activity from a third-grade unit on boats (the full unit appears in Chapter 10). Following are explanations of the categories.

Category 1: Activities Are Cognitively Undemanding, Completed with Contextual Support. During the instructional unit, the teacher read aloud an illustrated book titled *Surrounded by the Seas: Life on a New England Fishing Island* (Gibbons, 1991). Before reading the book, the teacher wrote on the chalkboard some of the jobs the people on the island perform: repairing sails, loading equipment, bringing in the catch, and unloading the fish for processing. The photographs in the book are excellent and make it easy for all children to see what is involved in

Figure 2.1 Social Studies Activities: Cognitive Demand and Contextual Support

CATEGORY 1
Activities are cognitively undemanding, completed with contextual support.
- The topic is simple and easily understood.
- Students are asked to do things that require relatively simple thinking (e.g., recalling and summarizing).
- Completion of the activity is supported by cooperative learning, visual aids, real things, and hands-on experience. Materials that students read or view are easy to understand.
- These are the "easiest" activities to complete. All students should be successful.
- Example from a third-grade unit on boats: Pantomime—Life on a New England fishing island.

CATEGORY 2
Activities are cognitively undemanding, completed with little, if any, contextual support.
- The topic is simple and easily understood.
- Students are asked to do things that require relatively simple thinking (e.g., recalling and summarizing).
- Students complete the activity individually, with little support of any kind.
- Even though the topic is easy and the required thinking is simple, the lack of contextual support will make it difficult for some students to be successful.
- Example from a third-grade unit on boats: Independent reading of picture books.

CATEGORY 3
Activities are cognitively demanding, completed with contextual support.
- The topic is complicated and difficult to understand.
- Activities in this category require complex thinking (e.g., analyzing, synthesizing, and evaluating).
- Completion of the activity is supported by cooperative learning, visual aids, real things, and hands-on experience. Materials that students read or view are easy to understand.
- The topic and level of thinking will challenge students, but the contextual support will help them be successful.
- Example from a third-grade unit on boats: Lesson on the history of boats.

CATEGORY 4
Activities are cognitively demanding, completed with little, if any, contextual support.
- The topic is complicated and difficult to understand.
- Activities in this category require complex thinking (e.g., analyzing, synthesizing, and evaluating).
- Students complete the activity individually, with little support of any kind.
- These are the most difficult activities to complete successfully.
- Example from a third-grade unit on boats: Student-authored encyclopedia.

each task. Also, the teacher modeled each job through a slow and somewhat exaggerated pantomime. Finally, the children joined their teacher in pretending to do each job through a group pantomime experience. The teacher's objective was simple and appropriate: She wanted her students to have a basic understanding of the work the people on the island do as a part of an economy based on fishing.

This activity is a good example of those falling in category 1 because the information the students were expected to learn (the different jobs related to island fishing) was relatively simple, and the behavior expected of students (to listen and to pantomime) was easy, fun, and performed in a group. The photographs and the modeling provided by the teacher provided a great deal of support. If, on the other hand, students were expected to complete a chart, answer questions, or work independently, then the level of cognitive demand would increase, and the activity would belong in category 3.

Category 2: Activities Are Cognitively Undemanding, Completed with Little, if Any, Contextual Support.   Few instructional activities fall into category 2. Here, the topic or material requires simple thinking (cognitively undemanding), and little, if any, help is provided for children (which makes it context reduced). During the unit, children read picture books independently. Each story was related to the unit's topic, boats. The stories were simple, so cognitive demand was minimal. Because the children read on their own, the level of contextual support was reduced.

Category 3: Activities Are Cognitively Demanding, Completed with Contextual Support.   In category 3, I have placed a lesson the teacher presented on the history of boats, emphasizing how methods of propulsion have changed over the years (sails, oars, and engines). The specific learning objective was that "students will learn that though the functions of boats have remained constant, their design and capacity (e.g., speed and size) changed radically." This was cognitively demanding material, especially because most of the third graders knew very little about boats when the unit began. So it was important that the teacher provide contextual support for her students. Following is a description of how she designed the lesson to provide the support for her English learners (in Cummins's words, how the activity became more "contextually embedded"):

1. Early in the unit, the students participated in a field trip to a harbor to see boats in action. This gave them a "firsthand" experience. This activity provided a knowledge base for all the lessons that followed.
2. When selecting her materials, the teacher chose books with excellent illustrations: *The Book of Fantastic Boats* (Bernard, 1974), *Oars, Sails, and Steam* (Tunis, 1952), and *Ships, Sailors, and the Sea* (Humble, 1991). The English learners in this classroom would not have been able to read any of these books. It was not necessary because the content could be presented through the illustrations.
3. The teacher made good use of maps and charts. The lesson was supported with a timeline and a map that showed when and where the following boats were built and used: a Roman trireme (powered by sail and oar),

a Haida canoe (sail and oar), "Old Ironsides" (the *Constitution*, sail), the *Great Eastern* (sail and steam engines), the *Queen Mary* (engines), and the *Nautilus* (first atomic-powered submarine).

4. During the lesson, the teacher modified the way she talked so that her presentation was comprehensible. She slowed down, watched her choice of words, and repeated certain descriptions and explanations. At no time, however, did her speech sound artificial.

5. At the end of the lesson, the teacher and the students completed a large data retrieval chart as a summary of the material that had been presented. The chart listed each boat in the presentation, the source of power for each boat, and when and where each boat was built. It is important to provide clear summaries of essential material for English learners.

6. The children worked in cooperative groups to answer three questions: (a) What are the advantages of ships that have engines? (b) If a ship had oars and sails, what conditions would make it difficult for the ship to move in the water? (c) Many people today buy boats with sails because they enjoy sailing. Why might it be more fun to sail than to go on a boat with an engine? It is unlikely that the English learners could complete this task individually. To use Vygotsky's words, working in groups allowed the students to move into a "zone of proximal development."

7. After the lesson was over, the Spanish-speaking aide worked with children who needed primary language support. The aide reviewed the essential information in the lesson and answered any questions the students asked.

Category 4: Activities Are Cognitively Demanding, Completed with Little, if Any, Contextual Support.   Activities that fall under category 4 are the most difficult for students to complete successfully. Cummins claims that one reason English learners have difficulty in school is that teachers ask them to do category 4 activities before their level of English proficiency is adequately developed. Category 4 has a high level of cognitive demand because the topic is challenging, the material is new, or the activity requires complex thinking. It is important that English learners be confronted with this type of intellectual challenge. The problem is that in category 4, the task lacks contextual support. The student is left to do the most difficult type of activity with the least amount of help! In the unit on boats, some students chose to compile a small encyclopedia on boats. They wrote and illustrated several "entries," each summarizing what they knew about the entry (such as "submarine," "clipper," or "starboard.") The task for a third grader was challenging because the students could not simply copy information from an encyclopedia. They had to synthesize and condense what they knew about each item to fit the restricted space available on each page of the homemade "encyclopedia." Most social studies lessons using the textbook, unless they make use of other resources, fall into category 4 and will be frustrating experiences for your second-language learners.

Effective Instruction with English Learners: A Summary.   The perspectives of Krashen and Cummins lead to some simple conclusions: (a) Teachers must present social studies content so that it is comprehensible to their English learners; (b) the classroom environment must be as free as possible of anxiety and fear so that the comprehensible input can be received; and (c) social studies activities for our English learners should be those that have a great deal of contextual support (those that fall into categories 1 and 3). This type of teaching, where the teacher uses a variety of strategies to help support students as they learn social studies, science, and math, is called *different things.* The most popular descriptor is "sheltered instruction;" though in California the phrase "Specially Designed Academic Instruction in English" is used (Diaz-Rico & Weed, 2005; Echevarria & Graves, 2006). Echevarria, Vogt, and Short (2003) developed the SIOP model as a means of evaluating the effectiveness of content teaching with English learners (SIOP stands for "Sheltered Instruction Observation Protocol"). Drawing on the ideas of Krashen and Cummins and from the SIOP model, Figure 2.2 summarizes the key things to remember about good social studies teaching with English learners.

◆ Cultural Diversity

In addition to differences in native language, our classrooms are culturally diverse. Remember that native language and cultural identity are not synonymous. Among our Spanish-speaking students, we could have Ecuadoran Americans, Nicaraugan Americans, and Mexican Americans. African American and Native American children come to our schools with rich cultural identities. The challenge of educating children from many backgrounds has always been a facet of American public schooling. The fact is that schools in the United States have done a poor job of educating Native Americans, African Americans, children of poverty, and immigrant students (see, e.g., the results of the National Assessment of Educational Progress at the U.S. Department of Education Website, www.nces.ed.gov). All too frequently, culture and native language have been ignored, with the unfortunate results of lower achievement and high dropout rates (Banks & Banks, 2003; Garcia, 1994). Our goal should be to practice "culturally responsive pedagogy." There are two aspects to culturally responsive pedagogy. The first aspect is the focus of this section of this chapter, how we align our teaching to the cultural identities of our students. The second aspect will be covered in the next chapter, how we incorporate the cultural identities of our students in our social studies curriculum (Gay, 2000; Hollins & Oliver, 1999).

Definitions of Key Words and Descriptors

It would probably be a good idea to first clarify some terms regarding culture because they will be used throughout this book. I prefer to use an anthropological definition of *culture:* the shared behaviors, beliefs, and values of a group of people (Ember & Ember, 2006). Thus, culture is commonly shared and learned by a group of people. Remember, though, that people are not members of a culture. Each person belongs to a *cultural group;* the group shares a culture.

Figure 2.2   **Effective Social Studies Teaching with English Learners**

(1) Clear and Reasonable Objectives
- Content objectives for lessons are well defined
- The amount of material students are expected to learn is reasonable

(2) Materials Supplement the Textbook
- "Visual" resources (graphs, charts, and illustrations)
- Information books written at many reading levels
- Adapted, simplified version of textbook pages
- Materials in the students' first language

(3) Effective Vocabulary Teaching
- In addition to the words taught to all students, those that might confuse English learners are taught

(4) Comprehensible Input
- Teacher modifies his or her speech
- Variety of materials are used
- Instruction takes place in a low-anxiety environment

(5) English Learners Get Help
- Teacher frequently checks for level of understanding and provides corrective feedback
- When possible, introductions and summaries are provided in the English learner's first language (preview/review)
- Extra help provided in one-to-one or small-group tutorials

(6) Multiple Grouping Patterns
- Small group experience utilizes cooperative learning
- English learners work with their monolingual English-speaking peers
- English learners are sometimes grouped together for extra help
- Whole-group, partnerships (two-student groups), and individualized activities are used

(7) Firsthand and Hands-On Experiences
- Field trips are planned
- Hands-on experiences allow students to examine objects and make things

(8) Experiences of Students Used to Enrich Instruction
- When possible, cultural identity of students is incorporated in units
- Everyday experiences of students used as a basis to learn about other people

The NCSS Task Force on Ethnic Studies produced its *Curriculum Guidelines for Multicultural Education* (1992). This document considers an *ethnic group* to be a special kind of cultural group. Authors of the guidelines believe that some ethnic groups are defined by different things, like religion (Jewish Americans) or national origin (Polish Americans). James Banks (Banks & Banks, 2003) believes there is a "core" culture in the United States that includes things almost all Americans share, such as baseball and income taxes. Thus, every American is a member of a core U.S. cultural group and an ethnic group. This gets even more complicated because each person also identifies with other types of groups (e.g., gender: woman, social class: upper, religion: Unitarian). Finally, every individual adopts certain behaviors, beliefs, and values that are the result of personal decisions, rather than of culture, gender, religion, or social class.

In this book, I will use *cultural group* and always try to be absolutely clear as to the identity of the group (e.g., Vietnamese Americans). I will also use the phrase *minority groups,* which includes African Americans, Asian Americans, Hispanic Americans, and Native Americans. As I have noted previously in the text, the combined total of "minority" groups will constitute the *majority* of the K–12 student population in the United States sometime early in this century, so the use of "minority" and "majority" is problematic. One other point is tricky: I will refer to those of us who are "white" or "Anglo" or "mainstream" or "majority" as European Americans. I acknowledge there are problems with this descriptor (Kleg, 1993).

How Culture Shapes Learning

A great deal of research has been conducted on the different styles of learning, communication, and participation of minority students (Gay, 1991; Ladson-Billings, 1995; Losey, 1995; Stone, 1991). For example, studies have been conducted with African Americans (Boykin, 1982; Ladson-Billings, 1995; Shade, 1986), Native Hawaiians (Au, 1980; Boggs, Watson-Gegeo, & McMillen, 1985), Mexican Americans (Heath, 1986; Losey, 1995; Ramirez & Castaneda, 1974), the larger Hispanic community (Grossman, 1984), and Native Americans (Greenbaum, 1985; Phillips, 1972). These studies indicate that there are differences in the way children of different cultural groups communicate, learn, and interact. Our goal as teachers should be to create a "cultural congruence" between our classroom and the homes of our students (Au & Kawakami, 1994).

Before proceeding, one important caution is in order. Although researchers can describe a norm—a typical way of thinking or behaving among the members of a cultural group—these are generalizations. For some individuals within the group, they will not be accurate. Kurtz-Costes and Pungello (2000) stressed this point when providing recommendations for teachers working with immigrant students: "Successful educators recognize that each child deserves to be treated as an individual with his or her own unique gifts" (p. 122). Let me provide an example from an observation I made while supervising two university students who were participating in a second-grade bilingual (Spanish–English) classroom. All the children were Hispanic. Research has shown that Hispanic students have a preference for social learning, for working in groups (Losey, 1995). The children in this classroom decided to stay indoors during recess since the temperature had climbed to 100. All the children were drawing pictures of the fire station they visited earlier in the week. The children were free to work where they wished. Of the 28 children, 20 worked in small groups, chatting happily as they drew. This was consistent with the research. Eight children, however, did not follow the norm, choosing to work individually. My afternoon in that classroom provided a good example of how a cultural norm will not define the behavior of every member of a cultural group.

It would be impossible in a book of this size to summarize all the conclusions reached on each cultural group, but here are some examples of these cultural differences:

- How children understand the history we attempt to teach them will be influenced greatly by their cultural identity. In fact, after reviewing the research on social identity and the teaching and learning of history, Epstein and Shiller (2005) concluded that what children will learn from their textbooks and their teachers will be limited when there is a conflict with what they learned at home. Specific studies have shown differences in what African American and European American children "see" in the same photograph and differences in the way Northern Irish and American children explain the events in the past.

- *European American* teachers and parents will expect students to ask questions and express personal opinions. However, many *Korean American* children will be hesitant to demonstrate these classroom behaviors. In traditional Korean culture, student behavior of this sort is considered rude; it shows disrespect for the teacher. In Korea, children refrain from asking questions because it indicates that the teacher did a poor job. It is not appropriate for a child to express an opinion to an adult (California Department of Education, 1992).

- *Native Hawaiians* have a strong tradition of group storytelling called "talk-story." It is no wonder, then, that many of these students thrive in activities that require cooperation and a lot of talking. Many native Hawaiian students become frustrated with activities that ask for silence and that are completed individually (Au, 1993).

- Some teachers claim that their *African American* students give no answer, give single-word answers, or give short, flippant answers to questions asked in front of the whole class. The same students on the playground talk in an animated manner and speak at great length when explaining things and describing events. Shade and New (1993) note this is because "in the traditional African American community, children are not usually expected to be information givers and are infrequently asked direct questions" (p. 320). Communication among African Americans is passionate and less formal than among European Americans. Teachers should expect their African American students to differ from European American children in each of the following aspects of language use: (a) turn taking (when people speak, European Americans follow a more rigid structure during a conversation), (b) tone (European Americans speak in less audible tones), (c) gestures (most European Americans use few gestures), and (d) pace (European American speech is slower). Research shows that African American students do better in school when (a) teachers plan participatory learning experiences where students move around, like dramatic role play; (b) students have many opportunities to talk with classmates in informal, conversational settings; (c) students have a chance to think out loud and work in small groups; and (d) teachers present material auditorily through music, rhymes, and chants (Hollins, Smiler, & Spencer, 1994; Ladson-Billings, 1995).

- Prior to coming to school, *Native American* children learn by observation and direct experience. This stands in stark contrast to European American children, whose caretakers spent a great dealing of time talking to and with children. Native American children have learned not to respond quickly to questions because such a response is disrespectful. This hesitance to respond is often misinterpreted by teachers from other cultural groups (Gilliland, 1992; Stokes, 1997).

- In the aftermath of the horrific events of September 11, 2001, *Arab American* and *Muslim American* children frequently are stereotyped and find themselves on the receiving end of considerable anger (Alvi, 2001; Seikaly, 2001). Like all students, Arab American and Muslim American children should feel safe and secure in our classrooms. Many American teachers know little accurate information about these two groups and most American students either know little about the Middle East or have inaccurate views influenced only by stereotypes and distortions (Jaffee, 2004) . For example, how many of us are aware that some Arab Americans are Christians (typically of the Maronite, Melkite, Chaldean, and Coptic denominations)? At the same time, not all Muslim Americans are Arab Americans; in the United States, there are Muslims from many ethnic groups. The nation with the most Muslim citizens is not an Arab nation, it is Indonesia.

- Teachers should understand the unique challenges faced by Muslim girls in American schools (Elnour & Bahir-Ali, 2003). First of all, many teachers have a stereotypical image of Muslim girls, especially in regard to clothing. In fact, how Muslim girls dress will depend on their families' interpretation of Islam. Some may wear jeans and blouses, typical of many American teenagers, while others will wear clothing that covers their entire bodies except for the faces and hands. The authors point out that many Muslim families do not allow their daughters to participate in extracurricular activies (but then again, many do). Conservative Muslim girls follow norms of behavior that severely restrict their actions with boys and men. Some Muslim girls will avert their gaze so as not to look directly into the eyes of their male teachers, and some Muslim girls will avoid situations which involve direct interaction with males, such as being the only girl in an otherwise all-boy group working together on a project.

Good teachers respect the diversity of their students. We should use the resources of our local community to learn about the cultural identities of our students. We should understand the level of English proficiency of our English learners. We should get to know our students as individuals, and have a good sense of each student's interests and abilities. The methodology for today's classroom must reflect the diversity of our students, must be multidimensional, and must include a wide variety of instructional resources and strategies. This book describes that culturally responsive methodology.

One way to "celebrate" the cultural diversity of our students is to use their experiences as a basis for social studies teaching. At the end of the chaper, you will find a mini-unit does just that.

◆ Exceptionality

Our discussion on exceptionality will focus on children with mild learning disabilities and children who are gifted. Educators have struggled with how to label children with disabilities, and some choices include "challenging condition," "exceptional," or "special needs." Turnbull and her coauthors make a good point when they argue that we should avoid labels unless they are absolutely necessary. If we need to refer to a child we should use her or his name (Turnbull, Turnbull, & Wehmeyer, 2007). The scope of our discussion dictates that I use the broad descriptor "exceptionality" and the specific descriptors "learning disability" and "gifted." Note that there are many other categories of exceptionality that we will not address here, such as emotional/behavioral disorders and communication impairments.

Differentiating Instruction for Children with Learning Disabilities

There are a number of instructional interventions that will help children with learning disabilities learn social studies content and master social studies processes (Lewis & Doorlag, 2006; Sheehan & Sibit, 2005; Steele, 2005; Tomlinson, 2001; 2003; Turnbull, Turnbull, & Wehmeyer, 2007). Children with learning disabilities have difficulty in basic psychological processes as evidenced by problems with listening, thinking, speaking, reading, writing, spelling, and mathematical calculations. The primary manifestations of a learning disability are problems with reading and any of a number of other characteristics that may include memory deficits or difficulty with fine motor coordination (Sheehan & Sibit, 2005). Our discussion is limited to children with *mild* disabilities who are able to function in a "general education" classroom along with children who do not have disabilities. As noted previously, differentiated instruction for children with learning disabilities involves three categories of modifications in how we teach: (a) content, (b) instructional processes, or (c) work products. (Figure 2.3)

Modifications in Curricular Content.   One option for teachers working with children with learning disabilties is to make changes in the content such students are expected to learn. Caution is in order here. We are not talking about "watering down" the curriculum, our goal is to have children with learning disabilities meet the same standards as other students. Two interventions will help. These are as follows:

**Figure 2.3 Effective Social Studies Teaching with Children with Mild
Learning Disabilities**

> **(1) Modifications in Curricular Content**
> - Divide material into small, manageable units
> - Present material in a systematic fashion
>
> **(2) Modifications in Instructional Processes**
> - Adapt materials
> - Additional presentations and practice
> - Increased use of graphs and charts
> - Use of instructional prompts and cues
> - Active student involvement
>
> **(3) Modifications in Student Work Product**
> - Adapt task characteristics/requirements
> - Change task criteria
> - Change task modality

Divide material into small, manageable units.   Teachers can look at what we expect students to learn and consider presenting it in smaller units or "chunks." In this section, all instructional examples come from a fifth-grade unit on the American Revolution of 1775. In such a unit, a single lesson could cover the three causes of the Revolution (results of the Seven Years' War, oppressive taxation, and colonial unity). This topic could be broken into small units, and for children with learning disabilities, the teacher could plan additional, separate "mini-lessons" on each cause.

Present material in a systematic fashion.   While teachers should always accomplish this task, it is very important for children with learning disabilities. When starting a unit of study, it is important to present an overview, showing all the topics that will be covered. When moving from one topic to another, we should review what has been learned before and highlight the relationship between each day's lesson and what immediately preceded it.

Modifications in Instructional Processes.   Good news! There are several ways to change how we teach to enable children with learning disabilities. Note that no teacher would implement every option with every lesson; rather, successful teachers choose wisely from the following menu items.

Adapt materials.   Our goal is to have children learn content. How they acquire that knowledge should vary depending on each child's strengths and needs. In other words, our objective should not be to "get through the textbook"; it is to have children learn the content specified in our state or district social studies standards. For a unit on the American Revolution of 1775, the textbook could be supplemented or replaced by easier-to-read information books selected from the school or community library. Another useful adaptation is to have audiotapes of chapters in the grade-level social studies textbook. Children who have trouble reading would then have an auditory presentation of the material to supplement the visual. All instructional units and as many lessons as possible should use materials and activities in *multiple modalities:* visual, auditory, kinesthetic, and tactile. Kinesthetics means "bodily movement." A kinesthetic activity would require students to move. A teacher might plan a dramatic role play of the Boston Tea Party and ask students to work in groups of four to throw imaginary chests of tea off a ship and into Boston Harbor. Tactile means "touch." Tactile activities are very important for our youngest students. For our fifth-grade unit on the American Revolution, students hand-mixed flour and water to make "firecakes," a common, but not very tasty, meal for George Washington's soldiers.

Additional presentations and practice.   Children with learning disabilities may need more than one chance to learn content or master a process. After an instructional activity involving the whole class, we could plan an additional presentation for those children who need it. We might present content at a slower pace, use simpler materials, or introduce new supporting resources, like photographs, maps, charts, or diagrams. For a process, like learning to use a scale of miles on a map to calculate distance between two cities, children with learning disabilities will need additional guided practice with close supervision.

Increased use of graphs and charts.   Teachers should consider using graphs and charts to support both oral presentations and reading assignments. Graphs and charts simultaneously simplify material, highlight the most important words and phrases, and visually reveal the relationships between subtopics. In Chapter 9, you will find examples of several graphs and charts, including a graphic organizer, a semantic map, expository text structures, and a data retrieval chart.

Use of instructional prompts and cues.   A very useful strategy is to emphasize essential bits of information, words, and phrases by prompts and cues. This can be done with written material by highlighting, underlining, or color coding. For example, in a lesson on how the Colonists responded to the taxes imposed by the British Parliament between 1765 and 1773, one of the teacher's content objectives was for the children to understand a boycott, a practice used successfully by the Colonists to protest the import taxes known as the Townshend Duties. The teacher prepared a poster with the definition of a boycott, "an organized plan to not buy things." The key words in the definition were *not buy.* The teacher used a red marking pen to write those words, the rest of the definition was written in black. Prompts and cues can be used in oral presentations as well. A common prompt is "remember to." One assignment in the American Revolution unit asked the fifth graders to write newspaper headlines for important events. After giving instructions to the whole group, the teacher might end with "Again, remember to keep your headline short, under six words." Other cues include repeating words and phrases and clapping hands two times before and after an important phrase or sentence. Some teachers use their hands very effectively when they are talking to their students by showing numbers (holding up one finger when stating "first") or pointing to places on maps or charts to focus student attention.

Active student involvement.   It is important that as many social studies lessons as possible keep all children actively involved. Elementary school teachers should avoid the instructional method used most frequently at the college level and far too frequently at the high school, "lecture/discussion." The teacher makes an oral presentation and, at certain times, students are asked to respond to questions. While some material may be presented to children in oral presentations by elementary teachers, these lectures should be brief and supported by other materials, such as charts, diagrams, maps, illustrations, and real objects. For children with learning disabilities, it is very important that instructional activities that typically require relatively little student involvement, like oral presenations and silent reading assignments, be modified. At different points in the lesson, students need to be asked to *do* something. One choice is for a mass response using colored cards. Each student has a red card and a blue card. The teacher asks a question and poses two possible answers, one to be signaled by the red card, the other by the blue card. The teacher restates the question and the possible answer and then says, "Without looking at your neighbor, please show me your answer." All students show the teacher one of the cards. This also is an excellent way to check to see if the students understand the material presented. Another good choice is to pose a question and ask the students to discuss possible answers with a partner. This technique is called "Think-Pair-Share" and is described in Chapter 5.

Modifications in Student Work Product.   There are three ways teachers can differentiate instruction for children with learning disabilities by changing the tasks, or work products, they are asked to complete. These three ways are as follows.

Adapt task characterisitics/requirements.   An example of adapting task characteristics used for many years for older students is to make an examination "open book," and allow students to refer to a textbook when answering test questions. For elementary school children with learning disabilities, we can modify the characteristics of almost every task we pose to students. By fifth grade, it is appropriate to ask students to answer any questions that appear at the end of a textbook chapter. After students have tried to answer the questions on their own, the teacher may want to help children with learning disabilities, by modifying the task characteristics by providing two possible page numbers where each answer can be found. One of the unit projects challenged students to find out what types of food do not spoil easily, a major consideration for both the Colonial and British armies. Children who would not be able to complete this assignment on their own could be helped in several ways. The teacher could provide reference resources, like appropriate volumes of a hard-copy encyclopedia and Websites. Or the teacher could give a child a list of foods to research. Finally, a very important way to change task characteristics for children with learning disabilities is to allow tasks to be completed while *working in groups* (see Chapter 5 on cooperative learning).

Change task criteria.   Another way to differentiate instruction is to change the criteria for "success" for students. Usually, changes are made in the criteria of speed and accuracy. Teachers have to be careful here because there are some school tasks where speed and accuracy are essential and cannot be compromised, especially in reading and mathematics. For many other tasks, though, the path to ultimately finishing a type of task promptly and correctly requires adjusting criteria in early efforts. This is common sense; initially all of us took longer to do things that we now do in half of the time. Think of how long it takes you to look up a word in a dictionary now, as an adult, and how long it took you when you were 10 years old. One activity in the American Revolution unit challenged the fifth graders to make a propaganda poster, which could either encourage Colonists to joint Washington's Colonial army or it could take the other side and encourage Colonists to join Loyalist regiments and fight with the British. Although most students had five days to complete the project, additional time was given to children who would find the task difficult. Accuracy cannot be sacrificed for "literal comprehension" questions where there is a correct answer (see Chapter 9). On the other hand, open-ended questions with no one correct answer can allow teachers to accept responses that are, at least, partially justifiable. For example, after the lesson on the Colonial boycott of British goods following the imposition of the taxes on goods imported from Britain, the teacher asked students to write a response to the following question: "Some colonists boycotted British goods for several years. What do you think were some of the effects the boycott had on their everyday lives?" A child with learning disabilities answered, "People would have to learn to live without certain things. Maybe they would drink coffee instead of tea." This is a reasonable response, though it only mentions a single effect and neglects two other effects a complete answer would mention: merchants selling those items would suffer losses and the Colonists could start growing or producing their own products and stop importing items from Britain. Although a more able student might be challenged by the teacher to come up with at least one more effect, this child's response should be considered acceptable.

Change task modality.   The third modification in task characteristics involves changing the modality of an assignment. In this sense, modality refers to whether the task is written, presented orally, completed through the arts (drawing, singing, acting, etc.), or some combination of modalities. A common modality change is to allow students with difficulty writing an opportunity to complete the same assignment through an oral presentation. For example, one project in the American Revolution unit was a summary report on how the Revolution changed the lives of children living at the time. A student with a learning disability could be allowed to make an oral presentation to the class rather than write a report. In some cases, students can use the visual arts to show what they have learned (see Chapter 9). Teachers must be cautious here, however. Children will not learn to write if they are never challenged to do so. Thus, on some assignments, children with learning disabilities must be required to produce a written product.

Gifted Children

It is worth pondering the definition of "giftedness" found in federal law:

> [Gifted children] possess demonstrated or potential abilities that give evidence of high performance capability in areas such as intellectual, creative, specific academic or leadership ability or in the performing and visual arts (Public Law 95-561, Title XIV, section 902).

Perhaps the key words are "high performance capability." Gifted children can have high, general intellect; the ability to think creatively and critically; the ability to lead; and extraordinary talent in the visual or performing arts. Currently 29 states have laws or policies requiring "gifted and talented" eduation (Lewis & Doorlag, 2006; Tomlinson, 2001; 2003; Turnbull, Turnbull, & Wehmeyer, 2007; see also the Website of the National Association for Gifted Children, www.nagc.org). Our concern is differentiating instruction for the gifted children who are in our elementary classrooms. Again, we will organize our discussion by the three categories of modifications teachers can implement: Changes in content, changes in instructional processes, and changes in work product.

Modifications in Curricular Content. In many instructional units, gifted students are challenged to learn more social studies content than their peers. This can be done by adding "depth," so that students learn more information about a topic; or by "breadth," by adding new topics. Here is an example of a "depth" modification. All students in our American Revolution unit would be expected to know the main ideas Jefferson expressed in the Declaration of Independence. Gifted students, however, might be asked to find out more about the 27 specific "abuses and usurpations" described in the middle part of the Declaration. Jefferson claims that the British were guilty of "transporting us beyond Seas to be tried for pretended offenses." What did this mean? What crimes could result in Colonists being taking to Britain for trial? Why did Jefferson label them "pretended"? An example of a "breadth" modification would be: While all students would be expected to know about Paul Revere, some gifted students could learn about two other Colonists, in two different contexts, who rode through the night to warn that the "British were coming," Sybil Ludington and Jack Jouett.

I must share one anecdote here from my own teaching experience. I spent five wonderful years teaching at Joaquin Miller Elementary School in Burbank, California. Our fourth-grade social studies curriculum focused on the history of California. One year, I differentiated instruction for one gifted student by modifying the curriculum through a "breadth" project. I asked this student to write a biography about the man our school was named for, the American poet, Joaquin Miller. Miller had a somewhat nefarious past and when the student finished her biography she told me, "Quite frankly, Mr. Zarrillo, I think it was a big mistake to name our school after that guy!"

Two techniques used to allow gifted children to learn additional content are "compacting the curriculum" and "tiering assignments." Compacting the curriculum is a process in which students are allowed to show what they know at the beginning of a unit. This is typically done with a pretest. Children are not asked to learn what they already know; rather, they are asked to learn extra content while the rest of the class works on the topics they have mastered. Tiering assignments involves creating several activities that all lead to the achievement of a single standard. Some "core" activities are required of all students. There are, however, several other activities at various levels of difficulty. Children with learning disabilities might be asked to complete the simpler ones while gifted students pursue the most difficult. You will see an example of tiered assignments in the unit on boats in Chapter 4.

Modifications in Instructional Processes. Differentiation in instructional processes involves using more challenging materials, providing more critical thinking activities, and planning more creative activities. Just as children with learning disabilities need simpler, easier-to-read materials; gifted children can be asked to read more difficult books. Also, gifted students can be asked to explore a wider range of reference materials, especially Websites. Teachers, however, should practice all the cautions listed in Chapter 7.

Gifted children typically thrive on activities that require critical and creative thinking. Such activities, fully described in Chapter 6, involve solving problems that are open-ended and interdisciplinary. Critical thinking activities allow gifted children to enhance their abilities to locate, analyze, and present information. In our unit on the American Revoultion, one critical thinking activity planned for gifted students asked them to answer the question, "What would have happened if the British had won the Revolutionary War?" The focus would be on the political, economic, and social history of the American Colonies with this revised scenario. Students would need to study the history of parts of the 18th century British empire that did not become independent until later, like Canada or Jamaica.

Modifications in Student Work Product. The most notable modification in this category is the increased autonomy teachers should afford gifted students. Two aspects of autonomy to consider here are iniative and direction. One way to accomplish this is to allow student initiative. At times, gifted students should be encouraged to choose the extra topics they pursue. For example, a student who is talented in music may want to learn more about and eventually perform the songs of the best-known American composer of the era, William Billings (who, interestingly enough, had one blind eye, a crippled leg, and a crippled arm!). Another student, more interested in the visual arts, may want to analyze Emanuel Leutze's famous painting *Washington Crossing the Delaware* and create a more realistic depiction of the event (perhaps General Washington should be seated, not standing; and did Leutze paint the appropriate American flag?).

Autonomy should also be accomplished by providing gifted children less direction. On many tasks, gifted children will be impatient to begin and the instructions offered to the rest of the class will be unnecessary to them. One format for "tiering" the directions for a task is to provide a "core" set of instructions for all students. Then allow those students who want to get to work to do so while at the same time asking students who would like more direction to gather with the teacher in one of the corners of the classroom.

◆ Summary of Key Points

- Students will differ in gender, age, language status, cultural identity, challenging condition, psychosocial status, family income, ability, interest, and physical characteristics.
- English learners will be learning social studies at the same time they are acquiring a second language.
- Social studies teaching should present comprehensible input to your students in a low-anxiety environment.
- Most social studies activities, especially those planned for a diverse class, should have a great deal of contextual support.
- Cultural identity shapes learning. Methodology must account for the learning styles, ways of communicating, and participation preferences of several cultural groups.
- To meet the needs of students with learning disabilities and gifted students, teachers should differentiate instruction by modifying curricular content, instructional processes, or work product.

FOR FURTHER READING

Linguistic Diversity

- The best summary of Krashen's ideas are in his book *Explorations in Language Acquisition and Use* (2003). Cummins's is most accessible in his chapter in the book *The Multicultural Classroom: Readings for Content-Area Teachers* (Richard-Amato & Snow, 1992).
- An excellent and overdue book on teaching social studies to English learners is by Barbara Cruz, Joyce Nutta, Jason O'Brien, Carine Feyten, and Jane Govoni (2003). (I thought I would break bibliographic protocol and cite the full names of each author because this book is full of wonderful teaching ideas!). An older book by Mohan (1986) is very good, with an excellent description of how language is used in the classroom.
- Rodriguez, Salinas, & Guberman (2005) discussed how teachers can provide opportunities for historical analysis with English learners.

Cultural Diversity

- All teachers should understand our African American students. There are several insightful chapters in *Teaching Diverse Populations* (Hollins, King, & Hayman, 1994). I also recommend books by Hale-Benson (1986), Kochman (1981), Paley (1979), and Smitherman (1977). Gay (1991) reported that surprisingly little research has been conducted on the social studies achievement of minority children. One interesting study showed that African American students were greatly influenced by their teachers—so much so that many identified their favorite school subject as the one taught by their favorite teacher (Hollins et al., 1994).
- The educational achievement of immigrant children is a primary concern for public school educators. Caplan, Choy, and Whitmore (1991) wrote a book about the success of the children of Southeast Asian boat people. An ongoing process called "democratic dialogues" was very successful with ninth-grade immigrant students, and it certainly could be used with upper-elementary students, too (Pezone & Singer, 1997). The November/ December 1998 issue of *Social Education* includes several articles on teaching about immigration and meeting the needs of recent immigrants (Rong & Hickey, 1998).
- A good place for teachers to learn more about Muslim Americans is the Council on Islamic Education Website, www.cie.org.

Exceptionality

- If you want to know more about social studies and challenged students, read the excellent article by Taylor and Larson (2000). See also Curtis's (1991) review of the literature. For gifted children, see Delisle (1991).

China

- At the end of this chapter there is a mini-unit on teaching fourth graders how to write in Chinese. Two participants in the Fulbright-Hays program, which funds American teachers and scholars' visits to other nations, Stephanie Wasta and Margaret Scott (1998), wrote about a third-grade unit on China they developed called "Building Bridges to China."
- The Schools of California Online Resources in Education (SCORE) Website is an excellent resource for teachers (www.score.k12.ca.us). Resources are organized by California's curriculum framework. Excellent resources and activities on China can be found by clicking on "Grade 6."
- In addition to the reproductions of Chinese writing produced by masters from the 10th century to the present, the "China Is Beautiful" site has a good essay that will provide the background information a teacher would need to know (www.chinapage.com).

LESSON PLANS AND INSTRUCTIONAL ACTIVITIES

This chapter concludes with a mini-unit for fourth graders on "Chinese Writing." It is offered as an example of how a teacher can use the cultural diversity of her or his students as a basis for instructional activities.

Laura Dwight/Laura Dwight Photography

The world's people share certain basic needs, like communication. Your students should learn that cultural groups develop unique ways of meeting those needs. Students here experience the challenge of writing in Chinese.

Grade Four: Chinese Writing

MINI-
UNIT

This mini-unit was planned for a fourth-grade class in which the majority of students were English learners. One girl in the class, Chimei, was learning to write Chinese. Chimei's mother was teaching her. During a time when students could "show and tell," she talked about what she had learned. Other students expressed interest when Chimei showed them the beautiful examples of Chinese writing she had produced. The teacher saw Chinese writing as an excellent opportunity for a mini-unit and used the NCSS standards for social studies as an organizing framework for unit objectives.

Part I: Organizing Framework

Standard: From *Expectations of Excellence,* NCSS Thematic Strand I: Culture. Performance Expectation (a) for the middle grades: "The learner can compare similarities and differences in the ways groups, societies, and cultures meet human needs and concerns" (NCSS, 1994, p. 33). The common need is to communicate.

This mini-unit answers one question:

> Unit Question: How Is Chinese Writing Like English Writing, and How Is It Different?

Part II: Instructional Activities

Resources and Materials: (a) children's books: *Chinese Writing: An Introduction* (Wolf, 1975) and *Lóng Is a Dragon* (Goldstein, 1991) and *Chinese Calligraphy* (Wong & Miran, 2002); (b) "China the Beautiful" Website (www.chinapage.com); (c) a member of the community who can write and speak Chinese (not absolutely necessary but a real plus); (d) blank paper, fine-tipped paintbrushes, and black tempera paint.

Content Objectives: Students will learn that the English system of written language differs from the Chinese system in two ways: form and number of characters. They will also learn that the function of the Chinese writing system is the same as English.

Process Objectives: After students *listen* to their teacher read aloud *Lóng Is a Dragon,* they will observe the logographic system of Chinese writing, *compare* the Chinese characters to English letter forms, *reproduce* the basic strokes of Chinese writing, *recognize* the tonal system of Chinese oral language, and *write* five Chinese characters.

Values Objectives: Students will develop an appreciation for the beauty and sophistication of the Chinese system of writing. It is hoped that students will abandon ethnocentric attitudes they might have toward languages other than English and see that other languages are neither better nor worse than English, just different.

Day I

1. Read aloud *Lóng Is a Dragon: Chinese Writing for Children.* Be sure that students understand that Chinese writing is logographic. Each character represents something (a thing, a person, a place, or an idea). A good way to do this is to compare the English representation of a word (e.g., *water*) with the single symbol in Chinese. Note the origins of the characters as pictographs (pp. 4–8 of *Lóng Is a Dragon*). Stress the artistic, almost spiritual, side of writing in Chinese.
2. Display computer-based images of certain Chinese characters produced by Chinese grand masters of calligraphy (You may need to define *calligraphy* for your students.) The Website titled "China the Beautiful" has excellent descriptions and examples of Chinese calligraphy from A.D. 900 to the present (www.chinapage.com). You may want to point out to students that there are really five styles of Chinese calligraphy and that within each style is room for artistic expression. The samples of Chinese writing

available on the Website identified here dramatically illustrate the artistry of the calligrapher.

3. Begin instruction in the basic strokes (pp. 9–10 of *Lóng Is a Dragon*). The ideal situation is to have a person who is familiar with writing Chinese demonstrate these strokes for the class. (Chimei's mother could not visit this class, but the mother of another child in the class, Zhou, was able to participate.) Any teacher, however, can demonstrate the basic strokes with practice (true mastery takes time). Stress the importance of moving the brush in the correct direction. The children should begin to understand that drawing the Chinese characters takes considerable skill and practice.

Day 2

1. Read aloud parts of *Chinese Writing: An Introduction* or have a class visit from a person who speaks a Chinese dialect. Although Chinese has many spoken dialects, it has only one written form. This is one advantage of a logographic writing system: Speakers of different dialects are able to understand the same system of writing. Students are fascinated to learn that spoken Northern Chinese has four "tones" (other dialects have as many as nine tones) and that each tone gives an utterance a different meaning. Thus, *tung* can mean "to succeed," "together," "to govern," or "painful," depending on the vocal pitch of the speaker (see p. 13 of *Chinese Writing*).

2. Teach the children how to make five characters (see pp. 11–26 of *Lóng Is a Dragon*). The children should first draw the character in pencil and then, if you think they are ready, trace with fine-tipped paintbrushes and black tempera paint.

Day 3

1. Stress again the mental state of the calligrapher (pp. 23–24 of *Chinese Writing*).

2. Continue to work on painting the characters. Today try a sentence (p. 27 of *Lóng Is a Dragon;* p. 18 of *Chinese Writing*)!

3. Ask the class the unit question: "How is Chinese writing like English writing, and how is it different?" Place the children with partners to answer the question using the cooperative learning structure called Think-Pair-Share (see Chapter 5). If students have trouble with the question, help them by suggesting two categories of comparison: (a) function—the language serves the same function; they are used to communicate; and (b) form—the written languages look different.

Day 4 and Beyond

The mini-unit will be just the beginning! Depending on students' responses, the entire class might benefit from a longer unit that looks at other aspects of

China, such as the visual arts, music, and religions of the Chinese people. Perhaps small groups of students will want to learn more about the history, geography, and current political status of China. They could share what they have learned with their classmates.

Evaluation: You can use two sources of data to assess your students. First, keep a record of the Think-Pair-Share activity on day 3. It might be a good idea to make a chart listing each set of partners with space to write comments next to each name. Circulate around the room as students figure out how Chinese writing and English writing are the same and different. Note the level of success students have in answering the question. Another alternative is to have each student write an answer after the Think-Pair-Share experience concludes. These written answers could serve as a simple test.

Second, it is important to keep anecdotal notes during the first 2 days of the unit. The notes should record some of the questions students ask and summarize your assessment of which students seem to grasp the similarities and differences between the two language systems. The comments students make as they work during the unit should give you an idea of whether they have adopted the values you proposed in the objectives sections of the mini-unit. Interestingly enough, the samples of Chinese writing painted by each student would have little value in assessment; this writing experience, though essential to achieve the mini-unit's objectives, provides little evidence to determine whether students understand the differences between the two writing systems (e.g., a student could make an elegant copy of a Chinese character yet not understand the logographic nature of that character).

 Effective Teaching in Today's Diverse Classroom: The mini-unit was a great success and a good example of culturally responsive teaching. It was a perfect chance to raise the self-esteem of Chimei and the five other Chinese American students in the classroom. The mini-unit is a good example of what can happen when a teacher chooses to avoid a "deficit" model of teaching in a diverse classroom. Rather than viewing cultural diversity as a hurdle that must be overcome, this teacher used the cultural identity of one of her students to enrich the curriculum. Also of note, even though many children were in the beginning stages of acquiring English, all were successful. The unit made strong use of visual aids (the illustrations in the books and the demonstrations by Zhou's mother). Full participation did not require the use of English.

For children with mild learning disabilities, the intervention of *additional presentations and practice* could be appropriate. It may be necessary to have an extra small group lesson that reteaches the difference between Chinese writing, which is logographic, and English writing, which is alphabetic. This is a difficult difference for children to understand. You would not, of course, use those descriptors. Instead, you might focus on the example of "water," which is represented by a single Chinese symbol, but takes five English letters to spell. Some children, both those with learning disabilities and those without, will need one-on-one help to make the strokes correctly when writing Chinese. This additional practice will be essential for some children. For your gifted students, this mini-unit would be a good opportunity to provide some curricular *breadth*. Gifted students could be challenged to learn about another form of writing, ancient Egyptian hieroglyphics (a good Website is the one created by art teacher and amateur Egyptologist, Mark Milmore, www.eyelid.co.uk).

Chapter 3

The Transformed Curriculum: Infusing Multicultural Perspectives

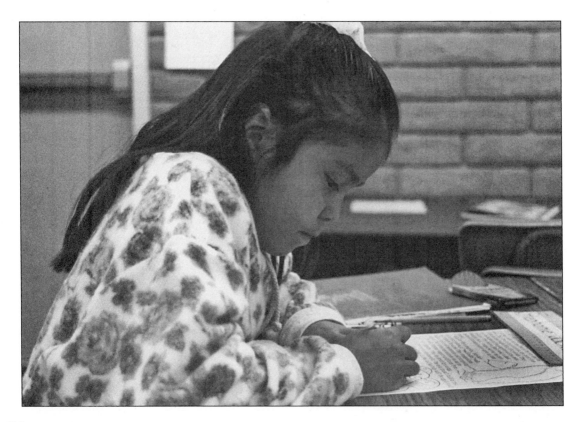

Sara's letter read:

November 22, 1778

Dear Patricia,

My dear cousin, I can't believe your last letter. I don't know how to tell you this, but you are a traitor. Your brother Andrew has made a big mistake by joining Washington's army. When Andrew is caught, he will be hanged. My father has gone to join the British army, and they will win! God save our wonderful King George III.

Your loving cousin,
Sara

P.S. Is it cold in Virginia? It is freezing in South Carolina.

Sara and Patricia were fifth-grade classmates. They were studying the American Revolution, and during one of the unit's projects, they participated in a writing simulation. The class divided into pairs; Sara pretended to be a colonial child whose family remained loyal to the British King George III, and Patricia pretended to be her cousin from Virginia whose family fought for the rebel cause. The girls exchanged letters after participating in multiple lessons that identified the political differences between loyalists and rebels. The letter exchange in Sara and Patricia's classroom was an activity designed to help them see how the same set of events can be viewed from different perspectives and make history more personally relevant for students.

In the previous chapter our focus was on *how* we teach, specific teaching strategies that differentiate instruction and are culturally responsive. In this chapter, the focus shifts to the curriculum, *what* we teach. As I noted in Chapter 1, your social studies curriculum will be dictated by your state standards. Almost any topic you study, however, can be "transformed" to include both (a) multiple perspectives on historical and current events and (b) information on the contributions of women, children, and people from several cultural groups. At the same time, getting students to become more actively engaged in social studies lessons "transforms" learning for them. Thus, the social studies curriculum of a truly multicultural classroom is transformed when students are made aware that historical events affect more than those people who are traditionally identified as participants. Social studies comes alive in classrooms where activities illustrate that there is no single view of any historical event or a current issue. Sara and Patricia's teacher included the letter exchange activity as part of an American Revolution unit developed to include objectives for learning about the roles of colonial women and children, Native Americans, African Americans, common soldiers, and the loyalists in addition to content about events leading to and during the Revolutionary War. The objectives and activities were designed to capture the interests of students and their various diverse backgrounds.

• • •

In this chapter, you will read about

- James Banks's perspectives on how to transform the teaching of social studies to incorporate more pluralistic concepts and generalizations
- Three considerations for transforming social studies units of study, including scope, geographic boundaries, and people
- Available resources that help present multicultural perspectives
- Teaching students to use oral histories to appreciate significant events and to connect more personally to family and community history

◆ The Dimensions of Multicultural Education

Multicultural education is probably a familiar topic to you. I would guess you have either taken a course titled "Multicultural Education" or have had discussions of multiculturalism in several of your college courses. Our concern here is how to transform the elementary social studies curriculum so that it may accurately be described as multicultural. As so often is the case with school-related words and phrases, *multicultural education* has many aspects and, thus, many definitions (Banks & Banks, 2003). There are really two interrelated dimensions:

1. *The curricular dimension.* In multicultural education, students learn about many cultural groups, both those that compose the pluralistic society in the United States and those that live in other countries. A multicultural social studies curriculum provides children with opportunities to learn about other cultures as they learn about themselves. Students should study both the current status of cultural groups and the history that led to the present. The personal experiences of each child should be considered valuable and worthy of inclusion in the social studies curriculum. A multicultural curriculum does not limit itself to presenting information about a wide range of people; it provides the perspectives of people who frequently have been silenced or relegated to the margins in traditional social studies programs (Banks et al., 2005; Burstein & Hutton, 2005).
2. *The equity dimension.* Multicultural education is the reform process that creates classrooms where all students have equal educational opportunity. This means that teachers take positive steps to ensure that students of both genders, of every ethnicity, with non-English native languages, with challenging conditions, and from all social classes reach their full potential (Banks & Banks, 2003; Gay, 2000).

Levels of Curricular Integration

Banks (Banks & Banks, 2003) has described four levels of integration for incorporating multicultural perspectives into the curriculum. These are as follows.

The Contributions Approach.   The contributions approach is sometimes called the "heroes and holidays" approach. The social studies curriculum remains the same because the only things added are a few lessons on Martin Luther King Jr. during January, a dance festival for Cinco de Mayo, and a Multicultural Day, on which parents bring to school the foods of their homelands. The key element missing is a lack of depth: No comprehensive study of other cultural groups is undertaken, nor is any attempt made to look at topics from a full range of perspectives.

The Additive Approach.   In an additive approach, the units of study change only in that content is added to include multicultural perspectives. For example, in a fifth-grade social studies curriculum on the United States, two units of study are added: "The Civil Rights Movement" and "The Immigrant Experience." The additive approach is an improvement over the contributions approach, but the problem is that experiences and perspectives of minority groups in the United States and people in foreign countries appear as an afterthought.

The Transformation Approach.   In the transformation approach, the social studies curriculum has undergone a significant revision. The key element of a transformed social studies curriculum is that it allows students to consider more than one perspective on a concept, topic, or issue. An excellent example of a curriculum that provides multiple perspectives is "Land and Landscape: Views of America's History and Culture," which was developed by the National Museum of American Art of the Smithsonian Institution (Powe, 1998). Students view a series of historic photos and then compare and contrast the Native American and European American ideas of the ownership of land. A transformed curriculum is essential in a society that values diversity and is part of the foundation on which effective social studies teaching is built.

The Social Action Approach.   The social action approach includes all the elements of the transformation approach but goes further and asks students to make decisions and take action. This action is often in the form of service learning. For example, if a class of elementary students were to study their city, they would learn about problems the city faces. If the teacher had adopted the social action approach, then students would not only talk about issues but also prepare a simple "position paper" and present it to the city council. Not all units present the possibility for social action, and some actions are appropriate only for middle and high school students. In this chapter, our discussion covers the "how to" process of transforming the curriculum, and in Chapter 10 we provide a more complete examination of social studies service learning and social action projects.

The Transformation Process

Transforming social studies curriculum to make it multicultural is an evolutionary process and includes the following steps:

1. *Reconsider the scope of the social studies curriculum.*   This is a task that, in most cases, should be undertaken by a committee of teachers. Units of study should be analyzed for their content. Do they reflect only the

perspectives of the mainstream, European American majority? Should some units be eliminated? Should new ones be created? For example, most fourth graders study their state. Virginians study Virginia, Californians study California, and so on. The curriculum is almost always chronological. In the study of Virginia, for example, the units of study would be "The Natives," "Colonial Virginia," "Virginia in the New Republic," "Virginia in the Civil War," "Reconstruction in Virginia," "Virginia in the Twentieth Century," and "Virginia Today and Tomorrow." The transformed curriculum would include information on African Americans, Native Americans, immigrants to Virginia, women, and children. Units need not be based on historical periods. Instead, issues or themes could be used as the focus. Examples are as follows:

- "People and the Natural Resources of Virginia." What are the resources of Virginia? How have the natives, colonists, and subsequent inhabitants of the state used these resources? What must be done to preserve the natural resources of the state? Throughout the history of the state, why have different groups taken opposing positions on the use of the state's resources? Are the resources that are recognized to be important to Virginians today the same as those recognized to be important in colonial times? How have the resources of Virginia shaped the economy and jobs of the people of Virginia? What natural resources in Virginia are threatened today, and what can be done to save them?

- "The Struggle to Be Free." At the same time that prominent Virginians led the American Revolution, what was the status of Native Americans, African Americans, women, and poor European Americans? How did laws in Virginia maintain a system of slavery and indentured servitude? How might a slave, an indentured servant, a shopkeeper, and a plantation owner have reacted differently to the Declaration of Independence and the adoption of the U.S. Constitution? During the period of segregation (1870–1965), what was life like for African Americans living in Virginia? How did people gain civil rights in Virginia? What else should be done to create a just society? (Often in fourth grade, the study of state history stops shortly after the Civil War. In a transformed curriculum, the civil rights movement of the 20th century will receive the same attention as the colonial period.)

- "Technology and Life in Virginia." How have the tools and machines used by Virginians changed over the years? How did the industrial revolution of the 19th century change the way people lived in Virginia? What does the information age mean for the citizens of Virginia? Will technology close the gaps between the rich and the poor or exacerbate the differences?

- "Production, Distribution, and Consumption." What have Virginians produced? How have goods and services been distributed? What has been imported and exported? How did a slave-based economy function? How did the economy of Virginia change after the Civil War? How do Virginians earn their livings today?

2. *Expand the geographic boundaries of your units of study.*   Take a global perspective and look for cross-cultural comparisons. For example, first graders should not only study their school and neighborhood but also compare them to schools and neighborhoods in other states or countries. If third graders are learning about what characterizes a city, they could explore how their city compares to other cities.

3. *Introduce your students to a mosaic of people.*   This is the *who* of the transformed curriculum. Whatever the topic, consider the contributions of, and the impact on, African Americans, Asian Americans, Native Americans, Hispanic Americans, women, and children. This should be a process of inclusion, not exclusion. For example, the addition of Revolutionary War hero Sybil Ludington, who warned the residents of Danbury, Connecticut, of an impending British raid, does not mean that you eliminate coverage of Paul Revere. The transformed curriculum should continue to present information that has traditionally been a part of social studies.

◆ In Their Own Words: Children's Books

To transform the curriculum, children must hear the voices of a wide range of people. It is one thing to read secondhand descriptions of the experiences of other people; it is another to read firsthand accounts, written or dictated by people who were participants in the events. After many years of neglect, there currently are a large number of books that share the perspectives of African Americans, Asian Americans, Hispanic Americans, Native Americans, members of religious minorities, children, and people from outside the United States. Some of the accounts are autobiographical; others are anthologies of oral histories.

For example, in *Voices from the Fields: Children of Migrant Farmworkers Tell Their Stories,* editor Beth Atkin (1993) interviewed and photographed nine children of migrant workers. Perspectives of children usually are overlooked in elementary social studies, so Atkin's book is an important addition to our reservoir of instructional resources. Other edited books can provide your students with the words of enslaved people (*To Be a Slave,* Lester, 1968), teenage civil rights activists (*Freedom's Children: Young Civil Rights Activists Tell Their Own Stories,* Levine, 1993), African Americans throughout U.S. history (*The Black Americans: A History in Their Own Words,* Melzer, 1984), and Native Americans who came in contact with European Americans (*Native American Testimony: An Anthology of Indian and White Relations,* Nabakov, 1978).

Autobiographical accounts provide an essential level of authenticity to social studies teaching. This transforms your curriculum. For example, students can expand their knowledge of Asian Americans by reading about the following topics:

Conditions in North Korea during the 1940s and 1950s (*Year of Impossible Goodbyes,* Choi, 1991)

A childhood in Vietnam (*The Land I Lost: Adventures of a Boy in Vietnam,* Huynh, 1982)

Figure 3.1 Books for Children: First-Person Accounts

Atkin, S. Beth (editor). *Voices from the Fields: Children of Migrant Farmworkers Tell Their Stories.* Atkin interviewed and photographed nine children.

Choi, Sook Nyul. *The Year of Impossible Goodbyes.* The author tells of her childhood in North Korea during the 1940s, the Japanese occupation, and escape to South Korea.

Crews, Donald. *Bigmama's.* African American author-illustrator Crews reminisces about summer trips to his grandparents' farm. Easy-to-read picture book.

de Paola, Tomie. *26 Fairmount Avenue.* Popular author/Illustrator recounts his year in kindergarten, 1938.

Frank, Anne. *The Diary of a Young Girl.* More able fifth and sixth graders can read this well-known diary of a Dutch Jewish girl in World War II.

Garza, Carmen Lomas. *Family Pictures.* This Mexican American painter tells of growing up in a small town in Texas. Easy-to-read picture book; the text is in Spanish and English.

Hautzig, Esther. *The Endless Steppe.* The author, who was born to wealthy Jewish parents in Poland, provides an account of growing up in a slave labor camp in Siberia.

Huynh, Quang Nhuoug. *The Land I Lost: Adventures of a Boy in Vietnam.* The author remembers incidents from his childhood in Vietnam.

Lester, Julius (editor). *To Be a Slave.* Anthology of autobiographical narratives told by several former slaves.

Levine, Ellen (editor). *Freedom's Children: Young Civil Rights Activists Tell Their Own Stories.* Thirty African Americans who were children or teenagers during the 1950s and 1960s describe their experiences.

Lord, Bette Bao. *In the Year of the Boar and Jackie Robinson.* Fictionalized account of the author's immigration from China to Brooklyn in 1947.

McKissack, Patricia. *Goin' Someplace Special.* Author of children's books tells her own story of growing up in Nashville.

Meltzer, Milton (editor). *The Black Americans: A History in Their Own Words.* Testimony of African Americans from the early 1600s to the 1970s.

Myers, Walter Dean. *Bad Boy: A Memoir.* Noted author tells of growing up in Harlem in the 1950s.

Nabakov, Peter (editor). *Native American Testimony: An Anthology of Indian and White Relations.* This books contains 200 years of Native American commentary and is an excellent teaching resource. Almost all entries can be read by fourth- or fifth-grade students.

Reiss, Johanna. *The Upstairs Room.* Author's experience when she and her sister were hidden by a farm family during World War II.

Say, Allen. *The Bicycle Man.* Author-illustrator Say, who grew up in Japan, tells the story of the day when two American soldiers visited his school.

Uchida, Yoshiko. *Journey to Topaz.* Fictionalized account of the author's family's evacuation and internment during World War II. The sequel is *Journey Home,* where Uchida and her family are released from the camp in Topaz, Utah, and return to California.

A Chinese girl's immigration to Brooklyn (*In the Year of the Boar and Jackie Robinson,* Lord, 1984)

Life in Japan immediately after World War II (*The Bicycle Man,* Say, 1982)

The internment of Japanese Americans during World War II (*Journey to Topaz,* Uchida, 1971).

Figure 3.1 lists some of the children's books that are first-person accounts. At the end of the chapter is a lesson plan based on the narratives of enslaved people found in *To Be a Slave.*

◆ In Their Own Words: Oral History

All people have interesting stories to tell. Children should never consider social studies to be a dry subject that tells the stories only of other people living in other places. Our families and communities can be rich sources of information. Oral histories collected by your students will help you transform the curriculum. *Oral history* is a method of gathering spoken, first-person accounts of past events (Ritchie, 1995). Oral histories collected by adult historians are tape recorded, carefully indexed, and placed in an accessible archive. Several authors have written about how students can collect and use oral histories (Anand et al., 2002; Hickey, 1991; Huerta & Flemmer, 2001; Mehaffy, Sitton, & Davis, 1979; Olmedo, 1996; Walbert, 2004). Oral history projects conducted by students can be relatively simple. For example, Miller (2000) described how fifth-grade students wrote biographies after each fifth grader conducted an interview of a second grader in the same school. On the other hand, some oral history projects will challenge both students and teachers. Alibrandi, Beal, Thompson, and Wilson (2000) provided a report of a project conducted by middle school students that incorporated oral history, field trips, historical maps, and data from the computer-based GIS (geographic information systems).

The Benefits of Oral History

The process of collecting, analyzing, and reporting oral histories is a wonderful experience for our students for many reasons:

- Oral history allows students to become historians; they will learn how historians work and will have firsthand knowledge of one important source of historical evidence.
- Oral history transforms the curriculum in that it inevitably increases the sources of information available to our students. If we limit social studies to sources that are in print, then we ignore the history that is most immediate, relevant, and comprehensible to our students: their history, the history of their families, and the history of their immediate communities. Hickey and Kolterman (2006) showed how oral history can be used in a social studies unit that helps children learn about the roles of women in history.

- Oral history is an excellent language arts activity. In the process of gathering, analyzing, and reporting oral histories, students will listen, speak, read, and write.
- Olmedo (1996) explained why oral history projects work well with English learners. These projects are relevant to their experiences, they teach social science inquiry processes, and they allow English learners to use both their languages. Oral histories can be collected in any language, so we can encourage our bilingual students to gather oral histories in their native languages.
- Oral history makes any subject more interesting. Hirshfield (1991) notes, "Oral history attaches emotion to events that can be provided only by the person who has lived through them, the young interviewer inevitably develops a deeper understanding of the recent past" (p. 111).

Guidelines for Oral History Projects

Oral history projects require thorough planning. The following guidelines will help us prepare for the use of oral histories and help children successfully complete an oral history project.

1. *Determine the focus of the oral history project.*   Choose one of two possibilities for the project focus. First, oral histories can *supplement* other resources. For example, a group of fourth graders studying the recent history of their state will read about recent immigrants in their textbooks and in children's books. Add oral histories to the print and other media resources. Second, oral histories can be the *sole source* of information for a lesson. A fifth-grade class did a project on how their grandparents met. In this project, the only source of data for a Website the students created were the oral histories they gathered.

2. *Identify the project's outcomes for students.*   It is important that students understand the entire process of gathering data from interviews, analyzing the data, and creating a final product. They should know about how long each phase of the process will take. Perhaps most important, they should understand what they will ultimately produce, and there are several possibilities: a Website, a CD-ROM, a written report, a bulletin board display, or an oral presentation.

3. *Engage students in doing some background work.*   The more your students know about the time, places, people, and events that are the substance of the interview, the better. They will need this knowledge to make sense of what they hear and to ask follow-up questions. This is easier in some projects than in others.

4. *Direct students to plan their interviews.*   After the topic has been defined and students have acquired background knowledge, ask the class to make a list of people they could interview. Discuss with students why thinking carefully about how the person(s) they choose to interview will inform

Anthony Magnacca/Merrill

Effective teachers work with their students in a variety
of instructional settings. All children benefit from
individualized instruction.

their own knowledge base and contribute to their oral history project.
Explain how being a good communicator can help them better reach their
goal. Determine as a group that the value of any interview is directly
related to the quality of the questions asked.

5. *Create a list of questions to be asked during the interview.*   In some projects, a standardized set of questions should be asked of all interviewees.
In other projects, each interviewee will have a different set of questions.
Questions should be open ended; questions that can be answered with
one word or a short phrase should be avoided. For example, a group of
sixth graders compiled an oral history of playground games as part of a
large project on "Kids at Play: A History from Ancient Egypt to Today."
Rather than ask senior citizens, "Did you play with jump ropes when you
were in elementary school?" students should ask, "Tell me about the
games you remember playing at recess when you were in elementary
school." Generate with your class samples of open-ended questions, such
as the following:

What do you remember about _____?
How old were you when _____ happened? How do you know that
     the event happened when you were _____?
How did this event affect (change) your life?
What did you do when _____?
What else was going on during the same time?

6. *Help students understand how to "go beyond" previously determined
questions.*   As Gail Hickey (1991) states, predetermined questions should
be "a guide rather than a strict script" (p. 217). We might even have our
students interview us. Interviewing is difficult for students to master, but

the ability to ask a good follow-up question is essential for the oral historian. When students hear something unusual, they should ask additional questions, even though it means deviating from the standardized list of questions. Remember, too, your students should be interested in interviewing people who have *firsthand* knowledge. It is inevitable that some interviewees will repeat things they have heard. Family stories that have been passed down for generations will be told and are interesting to hear. From a historical sense, however, the real value of oral history is in recording eyewitness accounts.

7. *Hold the interviews in a controlled setting.* A significant challenge in an oral history project is the logistics of the interviews. In many cases, the teacher will contact informants and arrange for them to come to school for their interviews. In other projects, the students make contacts with letters and follow-up telephone calls. If interviews take place outside of school, students must be accompanied by their parents. Hirshfield (1991) lists two essential features of the interview setting. First, the interview should be one on one. Second, the interview should be in a quiet place with no distractions. Be sure that interviews are conducted only after an appointment has been made and confirmed.

8. *Help your students be good interviewers.* Students should ask one question at a time. If students use a tape recorder, they should know how to operate it. If students write down the answers provided by the interviewee, they should be trained to write fast and accurately. My experience has been that the vast majority of students cannot write fast enough to record what the interviewee is saying. Tape recorders are a much better tool for the interviewer to use. Students should be sure that they have the correct spelling of names and places. They should ask follow-up questions to be sure that dates, places, and names are stated (and recorded) clearly. It is a good idea to role-play oral history interviews beforehand so that students become comfortable with the process and efficient in getting information (one student plays the informant, the other the interviewer). To help students while they role-play the act of interviewing or to help them feel more confident when they conduct their interviews, consider providing some kind of planning form, such as the one displayed in Figure 3.2. Students can use this form to think critically before they conduct any interviews and to hold them accountable for getting their interview plan in motion.

9. *Request that interviewees sign a release form.* A release form authorizes the interviewer to share what he or she has heard from the interviewee. The form can be simple (a sample is shown in Figure 3.3) and should be approved by the school principal. The important thing is that people who are interviewed know that other people will hear or read what they have said and that their comments "belong" to the school (in the unlikely event that they are published, the copyright and any money generated by the publication they appear in belong to the school).

Figure 3.2 Planning the Interview

Interviewer _____ Date _____

Whom will you interview?

_____

What is the purpose of your interview? _____

_____

When will you conduct the interview? _____

_____

Date _____ Time _____

What questions do you intend to ask and in what order?

1. _____

_____

2. _____

_____

3. _____

_____

4. _____

_____

5. _____

_____

Remember, answers you hear to your questions may change any follow-up
questions you may ask. Be flexible!

Figure 3.3 Permission Form for Oral History Interviews

Please complete the following before or after your interview. Thank you.

I agree to be interviewed by _____ _____

I understand that what I say will be shared as part of a classroom project. I also
understand that my comments may be published for school use and that if the
school decides this interview project is important enough to be shared beyond the
use of _____ that I will be

                                                    School name

contacted for further permission.

_____   _____
            Signature of Interviewee   Date

10. *Support interviews with documents and artifacts.*   Many times, an interview will lead a person to "dig out" old clothing, photographs, letters, souvenirs, gifts, or other items. Usually, these are too valuable to take to class. Under some circumstances, they can be borrowed, photographed, or photocopied. These documents and other artifacts are important historical sources and can provide illustration for the text of a report based on the interviews.

11. *Analyze interviews.*   After students have completed their oral interviews, their work has just begun. First, students should do what real historians do: make an index (list) of the interviews. Second, they should meet in groups and attempt to make sense of what they heard. The simplest form of analysis is to edit out irrelevant comments and compile an anthology of the interviews. This would work if all the interviewees responded to one broadly stated question (e.g., "What do you remember about the teachers' strike in 1980?"). Students will learn more if they compare and contrast the interviews. Some projects lend themselves to a chronological review; events described in several interviews can be arranged in the order they took place. Typically, though, the analysis will look for similarities and differences.

At the end of the chapter is a description of an oral history project completed by third graders on the history of their elementary school.

Incorporating the Personal Experiences of Your Students

Firsthand accounts of events, including both those found in children's books and those recorded as oral history, are two ways to transform the curriculum. Equally essential is using the personal experiences of your students as a basis for social studies teaching and learning (Alleman & Brophy, 1994a). Virtually everyone who writes about social studies and minority students stresses the importance of incorporating the personal experiences of students into the curriculum (e.g., Banks & Banks, 2003; Garcia, 1994; Short et al., 1994). This is a venerable idea, advocated in the late 1800s by Francis Parker, John Dewey, and other Progressive educators (Cremin, 1961). By "personal experience," I mean the daily existence of students outside of school. Here are some ways to connect social studies to the personal experiences of students.

Cultural Universals.   All people share basic needs, such as food, clothing, shelter, and transportation. These "cultural universals" can be used to transform social studies teaching and learning by linking the lives of your students to people from other places and times (Alleman & Brophy, 2000; 2004). Units and lessons can begin by having students consider their own existence, proceed to a middle section where information is presented about people living in other places or in other times, and conclude with cross-cultural comparisons. For example, a unit on the Pilgrims might include an activity on "Lunch with the Pilgrims, Plymouth, 1622." First, the students would answer these questions:

- When do we eat lunch at school?
- Does your family have a "lunch" at home on the weekends? (Many cultural groups eat their main meal at midday.)
- What types of foods do we eat for lunch at school? How are they different from breakfast and dinner?
- Whom do you eat lunch with at school? (Do adults eat with children?) Whom do you eat lunch with at home?
- How does lunch begin at home? (Some students might begin with a prayer or other ritual.)
- What beverages do we drink with lunch at school? What do you drink with meals at home?

Students would learn that the first Pilgrims ate with their fingers, drank a low-alcohol beer with their midday meal, and consumed incredible amounts of food each day (a half pound of butter, a half pound of meat, and a pound of bread). Several children's books would serve as resources: *Giving Thanks: The 1621 Harvest Feast* (Waters, 2001), *Colonial Living* (Tunis, 1957), *Meet the Real Pilgrims* (Loeb, 1979), *Eating the Plates* (Penner, 1991), and *Sarah Morton's Day* (Waters, 1989). Students could then make comparisons and observe the similarities and differences between lunch today and the midday meal of the Pilgrims. Finally, there should be an examination of how the coming of European Americans changed the food sources and meal customs of the Native Americans living in Massachusetts during the 17th century. A small group of students could prepare a presentation for their classmates.

The Experiences of Childhood.   When we are teaching about another cultural group or about people who lived in the past, one effective way to link subject matter to the personal experiences of your students is to focus on the experiences of children. All too often in social studies, the curriculum seems to ignore the existence of children. I think the status of children is highly relevant and an interesting avenue to understanding other cultural groups. Today almost all children go to school and participate in some form of recreational activity. School and play are perfect topics to include in any study of another group of people, whether they lived long ago or are living today. Comparisons based on school and play will provide information about many other topics you wish to cover, such as the roles of men, women, and children; the values of the group; and the technology of the group of people being studied.

For example, consider a second-grade unit on "Our Grandparents." The teacher calculated an "average age" for her second graders' grandparents. (The year was 2007, so most of her second graders were born in 2000. She figured that their parents were 30 when the children were born: 2000 − 30 = 1970. She then figured that the grandparents were 25 years old when the parents were born: 1970 − 25 = 1945. Thus, the grandparents, on average, had been born in 1945 and turned 7 in 1952.) What games did the grandparents play when they were in second grade? What books did their teachers read aloud to them in 1952? How did their grandparents dress when they went to second grade? The unit provided answers to all these questions as the class looked at what it was like to be a second grader in 1952.

A Child's Life History.   The life histories of our students can be used in a variety of ways as part of the social studies program:

- Some students may have participated in events you are studying. For example, in California the experiences of immigrants are part of the social studies curriculum in grades 2 to 5. Students in our rooms who are immigrants can tell about their immigration; these oral histories can supplement other resources. (One important note: Some students may have fled their native countries under horrible conditions; if these students do not want to recount their experiences, then that wish should be respected.)
- Students can learn how historians work by writing *documented* histories of themselves (autobiographies) and their families (Czartoski & Hickey, 1999; Schwartz, 2000). There is value in having students write from memory. Memories can be combined with a historical record; however, old photographs, report cards, and birth certificates should be consulted and referenced. Students should interview their parents, siblings, former teachers, and other people who have known them. The addition of the documentation will show students how historians gather data to support their texts.
- Students should learn about their communities, and as they do, they can combine their personal experiences with field trips, oral history, and the examination of documents, like old newspapers (Hickey, 1999). Many school districts make a study of the local community the focus of third-grade social studies. It is important that your curriculum incorporate the people and places your students know well. For example, children walk and drive by many buildings with historical significance every day. Children can take "walking field trips" to visit these buildings. They can learn when a building was built and who has occupied it.

Current Events.   The events of the day can also be used to provide a link between personal experiences and social studies. Three general strategies come to mind:

- Of greatest value are events that your students experience firsthand. Although the content may not fit with the curriculum guide or the textbook you are following, it makes sense to break away and explore significant events. For example, students who have coped with earthquakes and floods should be challenged to consider the social aspects of those natural disasters (e.g., public agencies that address emergencies, private organizations that assist, the role of individual citizens in helping out, and the possible future consequences of the event).
- Primarily through television but also through the Internet, other media, and daily conversation, your students vicariously experience important events as they happen. Students will have considerable curiosity about significant events, and the social studies curriculum should respond to their questions. In the aftermath of

September 11, 2001, for example, a great deal was written about how teachers should teach about what transpired on the day itself, what preceded it, and what has happened since (Berson & Berson, 2001; Mehlinger, 2002; Simpson, 2001a; Singleton, 2001; Stevens, 2002; Webeck, Black, Davis, & Field, 2002).

• Students could look at newspapers to find events that parallel those they are studying. For example, Short, Mahrer, Elfin, Liten-Tejada, and Montone (1994), in their junior high school unit on the American Revolution, ask students to search newspapers for articles about current political unrest in a lesson about colonial protests to British policies.

Consumer Goods.   Articles of clothing, toys, cans of food, and other consumer goods can be the starting point for lessons in geography and economics. Students will see that the goods they use every day come from many countries. For example, several children in a second-grade classroom had shirts made in Sri Lanka (they found this information on the labels sewn into the collars). This led to a mini-unit on that nation. Where is Sri Lanka? What resources does it have? What is life like for the workers who made the shirts? How do the shirts arrive in the United States? Why is it less expensive to make the shirts in Sri Lanka than in the United States?

Adapting a Traditional Unit of Study

Almost all fifth graders study the history of the United States. An important unit of study during the year is the American Revolution. How could a standard unit be transformed so that the scope of the unit, its geographic boundaries, and the people discussed become more multiculturally focused?

First, the activities in the unit should go beyond those suggested in a traditional teacher's edition of a basal social studies textbook series. We need to gather ideas and information from other sources, like a middle school unit on the American Revolution prepared at the Center for Applied Linguistics (Short et al., 1994). Designed for English learners, this material is a good example of a curriculum that relates to today's diverse classrooms. This material and others can help fifth graders see the perspectives of people often left out of traditional units of study, such as children and teenagers, women, Native Americans, African Americans, and, in this case, colonial loyalists. Review the following examples.

Expand the Resources Found in Traditional Units.   Additional resources, beyond the textbook, can be added to a traditional unit to enhance information and descriptions of people, events, and ideas. McCormick (2004) showed how primary source material, written in 1776, could be used successfully to teach fifth graders about the Battle of Trenton. Also, earlier in this chapter, I noted that a lesson on Paul Revere could be expanded to introduce Sybil Ludington. In 1777, 14-year-old Ludington warned the militia in Danbury, Connecticut, of the movements of a British raiding party. Good sources of information on Ludington are (a) a children's book, *Sybil's Night Ride* (Winnick, 2000); (b) two simple picture books, one by Drollene Brown (1985), *Sybil Rides for Independence,* and the other by Marsha Amster (2000), *Sybil*

Ludington's Midnight Ride; (c) a poem by Cindy Mahrer, located in a unit published by the Center for Applied Linguistics (Short et al., 1994); and (d) Internet sites, like the site for the museum of the town of Patterson, New York, www.historicpatterson.org.

The Internet continues to grow as a significant resource for a transformed social studies. For example, the best source of information on the experiences of African Americans during the Revolutionary War is "Revolution," a Website created by the Public Broadcasting System as part of the "Africans in America" television series (www.pbs.org/wgbh/aia/tguide). Many fifth graders can read the text on this Website, which also includes reproductions of historical documents. Students could read about Prince Hall and Colonel Tye, African Americans who fought on opposing sites during the war.

Provide More Than One Perspective on Historical Events.   A transformed curriculum can help students understand a wider range of perspectives. Several activities could accomplish this goal. For example, students could use a Venn diagram to compare and contrast the political views of the colonists who remained loyal to the British king (loyalists) with those of the rebels. The students will see that while these two groups differed fundamentally on some issues, there were some areas of agreement (e.g., both groups in the South supported slavery). Otherwise, the class can divide into two groups of equal number—one group being loyalists, the other group being rebels—and each loyalist can pair up with a rebel. Throughout the unit, the "two cousins" of each pair can write one another—the loyalist urging fidelity to the crown, the rebel advocating revolution. Sara's letter at the beginning of the chapter was completed as part of this unit. A unique children's book that shows multiple perspectives on the same events compares the views of King George III and George Washington, *George vs. George: The Revolutionary War as Seen by Both Sides* (Schanzer, 2004).

Most units on the Revolution fail to present the perspectives of the common, ordinary foot soldiers in the colonial army. Some of these soldiers, however, were not much older than today's fifth graders. To provide the perspectives of these young people, use Milton Meltzer's (1987) *The American Revolutionaries: A History in Their Own Words, 1750–1800.* Two passages that I suggest for inclusion are those written by 16-year-old colonial soldiers James Collins and Thomas Young. They describe the bloody battle of Kings Mountain, where a rebel army defeated an army of colonial loyalists. A good activity is to have students participate in a readers' theater project, with students reading aloud in dramatic fashion excerpts from the passages dictated by Collins and Young. A more elaborate readers' theater presentation could use a script taken from many of the oral histories and documents preserved in Meltzer's book.

Include a Wider Spectrum of Biographies.   Our students should learn about a wide spectrum of Revolutionary War personalities including:

- Deborah Sampson, who fought in the Revolutionary War disguised as a male soldier. See the children's books *I'm Deborah Sampson: A Soldier in the War of Revolution,* by Clapp (1977); *The Secret Soldier: The Story of*

Deborah Sampson, by McGovern (1975); and *Deborah Sampson Goes to War,* by Stephens (1984);
- Prominent colonial women, such as Abigail Adams (see the biographies by St. George, 2001 & Wallner, 2001) and Mercy Otis Warren;
- Margaret Corbin and Molly Pitcher (see the biography by Rockwell, 2002), who participated in Revolutionary battles;
- African Americans like James Armistead, Austin Dabney, Saul Matthews, and Salem Poor, who all served in the colonial army (see the children's book, *Come All You Brave Soldiers: Blacks in the Revolutionary War,* by Cox, 1999);
- British military leaders, such as John Burgoyne, Lord Cornwallis, and Banastre Tarleton; and
- Native American leader Thayendanegea (Joseph Brant), who sided with the British.

Students could create biographies, complete with clipped portraits, and post them on a unit Website.

Reveal a Wider Range of Events. Traditional social studies units on the American Revolution are, for the most part, limited to political and military events. Again, no good unit can ignore the signing of the Declaration of Independence or the battle of Yorktown. A unit on the American Revolution, however, also could include information that most adults, much less elementary children, do not know. How many of us, for example, are aware that the central problem for those who remained at home during the war was runaway inflation, or knew that women at home assumed new roles, such as running the businesses their husbands left behind when they went to war? To embellish textbook coverage of the home front, I suggest four excellent children's books: Brandon Miller's (2005) *Declaring Independence: Life During the American Revolution;* Kay Moore's (1998) *If You Lived in the Time of the American Revolution;* Barbara Brenner's (1994) *If You Were There in 1776;* and John Loeper's (1973) *Going to School in 1776.*

Encourage the Reading of Juvenile Novels. Students should be encouraged to read fiction with characters who are young people, loyalists, or African Americans. For example, James Lincoln Collier and Christopher Collier have written a trilogy that tells of the wartime and postwar experiences of African Americans in the North (*Jump Ship to Freedom* [1981], *War Comes to Willy Freeman* [1983], and *Who Is Carrie?* [1984]). Another book by the same authors, *My Brother Sam Is Dead* (1974), tells the story of Sam, the only rebel in a family led by a loyalist father. Two juvenile novels written by well-known authors also focus on the tension between loyalists and rebels (*Early Thunder* by Jean Fritz [1967] and *Johnny Treegate's Musket* by Leonard Wibberly [1959]).

Expand the Study of Prominent People and Events. Even people, events, and ideas covered traditionally in a unit on the American Revolution can be transformed by offering a different perspective. George Washington, for example, is usually presented as a political and military leader. To many children, I suspect, he seems as lifeless as his image on a dollar bill. I suggest two children's books to help students see the "human" side of Washington. Miriam Anne Bourne's (1983)

The transformed curriculum connects students with a wide spectrum of cultural groups. Here, a gifted storyteller introduces children to a trickster tale from the Ashanti of West Africa.

Uncle George Washington and Harriet's Guitar is based on the Washington family letters written from 1790 to 1795. We see Washington from the perspective of his nieces and nephews. *George Washington's Teeth* by Deborah Chandra and Madeline Comora (2003) does more than cover his dental problems, it provides insight on the daily routines of his life. Finally, while all units should emphasize Washington's unique contributions to U.S. history and his rightful status as "father of our country," students also should examine Washington's economic interests as a slaveholder and the consistent criticism of his leadership of the Continental army (see the children's books *George Washington: An Illustrated Biography* [Adler, 2004] and *George Washington and the Birth of Our Nation* by Meltzer [1986]).

◆ Summary of Key Points

- James Banks described four levels of integration of multicultural content: contributions, additive, transformation, and social action.
- To transform the curriculum, reconsider the scope of what we teach, introduce our students to a wide variety of people and to their experiences and perspectives, and expand the geographic boundaries of our instructional units.
- To have a curriculum that is truly multicultural, we should be sure our students are exposed to firsthand accounts of events written by African

Americans, Asian Americans, Hispanic Americans, Native Americans, members of religious minorities, women, children, and people living outside the United States.

- Another way to transform the curriculum is to have students collect oral histories. Oral history expands the social studies curriculum by incorporating the histories of the students themselves, their families, and their communities.

- The transformed curriculum incorporates the personal experiences of our students.

FOR FURTHER READING

- Though the tragedy of 9–11 is no longer a "current" event, the advice that authorities in the field of social studies gave to elementary teachers is important reading. These articles provide guidance on how to teach any major event and should continue to guide teachers on how to deal with the aftermath of 9–11. Articles written soon after the event address three main topics: dealing with tragedy, searching for facts, and responding as citizens. The article by Mehlinger (2002) did an excellent job of summarizing four approaches teachers could have used in dealing with September 11 and its aftermath. Webeck et al. (2002) reviewed how elementary teachers responded. Berson and Berson (2001) discussed the psychological and emotional health of children in the wake of September 11. Three more recent articles are Jaffee (2004) on resources for teaching about the Middle East and Elinour and Bashir-Ali (2003) on the challenges faced by Muslim girls in American schools; and Chick (2004) on children's books about 9–11.

- Hickey and Kolterman (2006) described several activities, including a family history project, that teach children about the roles of women in personal, local, national, and international history. With the same goal, Sincero and Woyshner (2003) provided good ideas for teaching women's history to upper-grade elementary school students. See also the January/February 2003 theme issue of *Social Education*, "Women of the World" (Merryfield & Crocco, 2003, and Tyson & Hinton-Johnson, 2003, for children's books about women and social justice.

- Many journal articles provide examples of how a topic can be transformed so that a variety of perspectives and experiences are incorporated. For example, Fertig (2005) described a unit of study that challenged children to write letters from the perspective of 19th century homesteaders on the Great Plains. Dever, Sorenson, & Broderick (2005) and Sandmann (2004) wrote about children's books that promote social justice. Warren (2006) offered suggestions for incorporating the voices of Native Americans. VanFossen (2003b) discussed how to use children's literature to teach about the experiences of immigrants to the United States.

- The October 1998 issue of *Social Education* has several excellent articles on the African American experience in the United States, including important background information, Internet resources, and teaching ideas (Barss, 1998).

• I mentioned interviewing grandparents as part of an oral history project. Hittleman and Hittleman (1998) provided a unit on "Bringing Grandparents into Social Studies." On teaching the American Revolution I mentioned McCormick's (2004) excellent article on how to use primary sources to teach about the battle of Trenton (when Washington crossed the Delaware on Christmas night, 1776). It has many valuable suggestions for using primary source material with elementary school children.

LESSON PLANS AND INSTRUCTIONAL ACTIVITIES

This chapter concludes with a lesson plan and a group project that are good examples of a transformed curriculum and culturally responsive teaching: (a) A lesson plan for fifth graders using the narratives of enslaved people found in *To Be A Slave*; and (b) An oral history project for a third-grade classroom on the history of their elementary school.

LESSON PLAN

Grade Five: From *To Be a Slave*

Overview: This lesson is a part of a fifth-grade unit on the southern colonies and uses a book, *To Be a Slave,* to identify first-person accounts of life as a slave. Working with a modification of Jigsaw (a cooperative learning structure discussed in Chapter 5), all 30 students will take part in reading and responding to narratives dictated by enslaved people in the 19th century.

Resources and Materials: (a) copy of *To Be a Slave;* (b) copies of the following narratives: (1) Moses Grandy (p. 43), (2) Anonymous (pp. 44–45), (3) Josiah Henson (pp. 48–49), (4) Charles Ball (p. 54), (5) Sis Shackelford (p. 56); (c) time line for the unit; (d) map of the United States in 1859. Note: This lesson can be done with any collection of narratives from enslaved people. For example, portions of Charles Ball's narrative are included in a Website called "Excerpts from Slave Narratives" (http://xroads.virginia.edu/~hyper/wpa/wpahome.html).

Standard: From the *National Standards for History,* grades 5 to 12, Era 4 (Expansion and Reform, 1801–1861), Standard 2d: "The student understands the rapid growth of the 'peculiar institution' after 1800 and the varied experiences of African Americans under slavery. Therefore, the student is able to describe the plantation system and the roles of their owners, their families, hired white workers, and the enslaved African Americans" (National Center for History in the Schools, 1996, p. 95).

Content Objectives: Students will understand the history and economics of slavery. They should reach the generalization that African American slaves in the United States were bought and sold like other "goods." Facts presented in the lesson will include that (a) slaves were transported from Africa in inhuman conditions; (b) slaves were bought and sold without regard to the status of other members of their families; (c) some slaves were sold privately, from neighbor to neighbor; (d) many slaves were auctioned; and (e) slaveholders would give extra food to slaves about to be auctioned.

Process Objectives: Students will (a) *listen* to their teacher read the background information, (b) work in groups to *analyze* one of the slave narratives, (c) *answer* three questions about the narrative, and (d) *compare and contrast* their answers with those of groups who analyzed different narratives. A member of each group will report to the whole group.

Values Objectives: Your students should believe that all people have fundamental human rights, such as liberty. In this lesson, they will learn more about a period in U.S. history when human rights were denied to enslaved African Americans.

Teaching Sequence:

1. Be sure all teaching resources are in place. You will need six copies of each of the five narratives.
2. A few days before the lesson, select one child from each group to be a "reader." The reader will read the narrative to the rest of the group. The readers should have 2 or 3 days to rehearse their oral reading. If you prefer, you can have your readers record their readings of the narratives on audiotape.
3. Start the lesson by referring to the time line and the map. This lesson should be preceded by others on (a) the cultures of West African tribal groups and (b) the "middle passage" from Africa to colonial America. Subsequent lessons would cover the working and living conditions of enslaved people in the American South.
4. Tell the class that today they will learn about how slaves were bought and sold. Read to the whole class Lester's explanatory comments from Chapter 2. It is not necessary to read all his commentary, but be sure to include the text on pages 39, 40, 43, 44, and 46. Some of the slave narratives include the defamatory "n" word. Discuss the historical context of this word and emphasize that it is insulting and should never be used today. You might also check to see if your school district has a policy in place regarding the use of that and other inflammatory words.
5. Write the following questions on the chalkboard:

   1. Who dictated the narrative you read? Was the slave a man or a woman, a grown-up or a child?
   2. In your narrative, what happened to the slaves?
   3. If a slave master is mentioned in your narrative, what did he or she do?

Explain that each group is to answer these three questions for the narrative they have read. Distribute the copies of the narratives to the group. Allow time for the readers to read the narratives to other members of their groups. Then have each group select a reporter to share their answers with the class.

6. For each of the five narratives, first have the reader read the narrative to the whole class, then have the reporter share the group's answers to the three questions.

Evaluation: Take notes as you circulate among the groups, recording the names of students who do a good job of answering the questions. Takes notes as well on the oral reading performance of each of the readers. This type of anecdotal record keeping will provide useful information if you gather data on an ongoing basis over the course of the year.

Effective Teaching in Today's Diverse Classroom: Small-group work is essential in a diverse classroom. Research shows that regular experiences in cooperative learning improve intercultural relations. Students from different cultural groups will get along better if they work together to accomplish common goals (see Chapter 5 for a review of the research). One other note: If the class were homogeneous in reading ability, then you could have each student read the narratives on his or her own rather than using a group reader. On the other, the use of a "reader," who has practiced reading the narrative aloud in advance, will be of great assistance to children with mild learning disabilities. It is an example of *adapting instructional materials*. This allows students to access the narratives not just by reading, but through the auditory modality as well.

GROUP PROJECT

Grade Three: An Oral History Project—The History of Our School

Project Description: A third-grade teacher decided to have her class write a history of their school, Theodore Roosevelt Elementary School. The children used old photographs, school records, and newspaper articles as sources, but they needed more information. Oral history seemed essential to provide a more complete story. The class made a list of people who might provide oral histories. When two children showed the list to the principal, she steered them toward specific people with whom they would want to talk. The roster of interviewees included the following:

- The superintendent of schools at the time the school was built (1965). Though in his 80s, the superintendent still lived in the community.
- Three teachers who were on the first faculty. These teachers could share the memories of the first year of Roosevelt School.

- One teacher who had taught at the school from 1970 to 1992. Her longevity would make her an important source for "longitudinal" data on changes over time at the school.
- A school board member at the time the school was built. In his 80s, he would be a valuable source because there was a heated debate over the naming of the school. One faction wanted to name the school after a former mayor who had just died, and another faction wanted to name the school after a famous baseball player who had grown up in the community. Roosevelt was chosen as a compromise.
- Two principals in the school district, one at a junior high and the other at the local high school. Both had gone to Roosevelt School as children and could offer a "child's-eye view" of Roosevelt in previous decades.
- A member of the school board and her brother, the city attorney. These two prominent members of the community were among the first African American students to attend Roosevelt in 1974.
- A group of current sixth graders. These students at Roosevelt could provide information on the more recent history of the school.
- Five current faculty members, each of whom had taught at the school for at least 10 years. Like the sixth graders, members of the current faculty could comment on recent events at the school, and the interviews would be easy to arrange.

Project Activities

1. The children developed questions for the interviews. Each person was asked a very broad opening question: "What is the first thing that comes to your mind about Roosevelt Elementary School?" Then more specific questions were written for each interviewee.
2. The interviews were scheduled. Some of the interviews took place outside of school. These had to be approved by the principal, and each student was accompanied by a parent.
3. The interviews revealed fascinating details. For example, the African American students and the teachers who were at the school at the time remembered both acts of kindness and resentment when the African American students first attended. The superintendent told of how difficult it was to decide on the design of the school. The teacher who taught at Roosevelt commented on how different the students have dressed over the years.
4. In addition to personal interviews, some children researched old newspaper articles that provided more specific historical details. School records revealed the number of students who had attended the school at various times and the number of classrooms.
5. The children gathered all this information and wrote a book about their school, illustrated with copies of old photographs. The oral histories brought the book to life through the stories that people told.

Effective Teaching in Today's Diverse Classroom: This project is a good example of a transformed social studies curriculum. In learning about their school, the students learned a great deal about the social history of their city and our nation, and they learned it by listening to voices that would never be included in a textbook. Although some members of the community would have preferred to ignore the racism that greeted the first African American residents of this city, the book written by this group of students tackled the issue head on.

This would be a difficult project for children with mild learning disabilities. It would help them if the interviews were conducted by a small group of students. Redesigning tasks that might otherwise be completed individually so that they are completed in *small groups* is an important strategy to help students with challenging conditions. The children would definitely need to tape record the interview, and children with disabilities might well need to listen to the interview more than once. Then, the members of the group can work together to analyze the results of the interview.

Part II

The Fundamentals of Social Studies Teaching

Chapter 4 Lesson and Unit Plans: Organizing Instruction

Chapter 5 Cooperative Learning: Enhancing Skills and Knowledge Through Group Activities

Chapter 6 Inquiry and Critical Thinking: Challenging Students with the Complex and the Controversial

Chapter 7 Technology: Teaching with Computer-Based Resources

Chapter 8 Assessment: Acquiring and Analyzing Data on Student Achievement

Chapter 9 The Integrated Curriculum: Incorporating the Language Arts, the Performing Arts, and the Visual Arts

Chapter 4

Lesson and Unit Plans: Organizing Instruction

The students in Donna Richard's fifth-grade classroom took part in a 6-week instructional unit on Native Americans. They studied the cultures of five tribes—the Mohawk, the Seminole, the Oglala Sioux, the Tlingit, and the Navajo—before the arrival of Europeans to North America. Mrs. Richard decided to do this unit so that her students could learn about the diversity and history of Native Americans and to see for themselves the problems of stereotyping a cultural group. By allowing students to compare the historical diversity of multiple Native American groups, they would find out that not all Native Americans lived in tipis, hunted buffalo, or wore feathers. Further, students would learn where and how "Indians" live in the United States today.

To initiate this unit of study, Mrs. Richard started with a study of the Sioux of the mid-19th century. Using an LCD (liquid crystal display) overhead projector, Mrs. Richard projected an image of a painting by George Catlin, *Buffalo Chase, Upper Missouri,* onto a movie screen positioned at the front of the classroom. The painting, also called *Buffalo Chase, Bulls Making Battle with Men and Horses,* is part of a collection stored at the Smithsonian Institution (it is also on the Smithsonian's Website, www.si.edu). A copy of the painting can be found at the end of this chapter as Figure 4.6. Providing black-and-white copies of the painting to student groups, Mrs. Richard asked students to study the painting and to answer a series of eight guided-response directives. The next-to-last query was, "Pretend you are one of the Sioux. Write down what you are thinking, feeling, hearing, or seeing." Answers to this request led to several lively discussions. In one group, Darlene started off by saying that if she were a Sioux in the painting, she would be scared. She wanted to know why one Sioux was jumping on a buffalo. In response, Jerome speculated that the Sioux wanted to pull one of his arrows out of the buffalo and use it again. Mrs. Richard noted that Jerome's guess was a good one because the book *Buffalo Hunt,* by Russell Freedman (1988), related how sometimes arrows would barely penetrate the buffalo's hide and the Natives would try to pull them out to use again.

Dontray said that he was going to write about shooting the buffalo with arrows. Before she left the group to allow them to start writing, Mrs. Richard asked about things the Sioux might have heard during the hunt. Andrew stated that it was loud because that is the way it was in the buffalo hunt in the film *Dances with Wolves.* Darlene added that one thing the Sioux would have heard was the horse screaming. Mrs. Richard asked whether anybody had anything else to say in response to directive number 7. No hands went up, so the five students started writing their responses. After about 10 minutes, members of each group shared their work.

The final query in the study guide led to the second half of the lesson. That directive was, "Think back to what we learned about the Mohawk. Think what the Mohawk ate and how they got their food. Think about what we have learned about the Sioux. All people need some way of getting food. What is the same and what is different about these two tribes?" Mrs. Richard encouraged each group to make a simple comparison chart by folding a sheet of paper in half lengthwise and on one side writing details they remembered about the Mohawk and on the other side writing what they learned about the Sioux. Mrs. Richard had information books and encyclopedias ready as help for students who could not recall information about the Mohawk. Fortunately, though, at least one member of each group noted that the Mohawk had fields and raised crops of squash, corn, and beans. After all the groups reconvened, Darlene stated an accurate conclusion: "The Mohawk had a lot more ways of getting food. They farmed, they fished, they gathered berries. The Sioux just hunted and gathered." Matt added that both groups hunted but that they hunted different things: The Sioux hunted buffalo, whereas the Mohawk hunted deer and turkeys and other birds. Jerome made another comparison: The Sioux hunted while riding horses, whereas the Mohawk hunted on foot. Mrs. Richard then asked the class why the food-getting practices of the two groups were different. Students first considered this question in their groups. All the groups quickly stated that the Mohawk could not hunt buffalo because no buffalo lived where the Mohawk lived and that the Sioux could not fish because the Plains did not have enough rivers and streams. By the time the lesson ended, most students could not come up with a good explanation of why the Mohawk farmed and the Sioux did not, so Mrs. Richard decided to plan a lesson on that topic.

This lesson is noteworthy for two reasons. First, the lesson was an important component in Mrs. Richard's attempt to help her students take a comprehensive look at Native Americans. The final directive, comparing the food-getting practices of the Sioux and the Mohawk, helped students understand that, before the coming of European Americans, there were significant cultural differences among the Native American tribes of North America. The diversity among Native American tribes, unfortunately, is rarely taught in elementary schools (Finchum, 2006; Brophy, 1999). Second, the success of this lesson, like almost all lessons that go well, was the product of Mrs. Richard's thoughtful and thorough planning. This chapter is about planning lessons and instructional units. It will introduce a variety of formats for preparing exciting, challenging, and effective social studies lessons and units.

• • •

In this chapter, you will read about

- Simple guidelines to help in planning effective social studies lessons
- Instructions on writing instructional objectives
- Perspectives on using two kinds of lesson sequences—Hunter's seven-step model and the concept attainment model
- Five principles to consider when planning units of study
- A third-grade sample unit on boats

◆ General Guidelines for Planning Social Studies Lessons

The concept of "lesson" should be broad and include each of the following:

- Lessons that are teacher directed and involve the entire class (often called "whole-group" lessons)
- Lessons that are designed for small groups or individuals
- Lessons that place the teacher in a less central role as the teacher serves as facilitator, tutor, and provider of resources

Regardless of the specific lesson format we use, we should follow two guidelines when planning an effective lesson. These two guidelines are

1. *Decide precisely what we expect students to do.* This guideline seems obvious. I have seen hundreds of people teach; some were student teachers I supervised, others were veteran teachers participating in research projects. When a lesson is unsuccessful, more times than not it is because the teacher does not have a clear idea of what the students are supposed to do *from the beginning of the activity to the end*. Some lessons go poorly because the teacher knows exactly what the students are to do at the *end* of the lesson but has not really thought about what they should do before then. This does not mean that we should choreograph every step so that all our students behave like members of a chorus line. Many lessons will have some students do one thing while their classmates do another. Other lessons will have time for students to be creative. Still other lessons should have times when students can choose what activity they pursue. The point is that we should plan for each of these situations. Before we teach a lesson to the whole class, before we work with a small group, before we hold a conference with one student, we should be sure we know what we expect the student(s) to do. I suggest that, before we write a lesson plan, we should make a simple list. For example, for her lesson on *Buffalo Chase, Upper Missouri,* Mrs. Richard wrote

   1. I want the students to look closely at the painting.
   2. I want them to answer questions about the painting while working in small groups.
   3. I want them to compare and contrast the food-getting practices of the Sioux and the Mohawk.

2. *Decide what we, the teachers, must do in order for our students to achieve what we expect of them.* After we have a clear idea of what we expect our students to do during the lesson, we must think of ourselves. If our students are to be successful, what must we do? We have much to consider here: What materials must we gather? Will the classroom furniture need to be rearranged? What visual aids will we need? What must we say and when? What problems should we anticipate? Again, I suggest that before we make a formal lesson plan, we should jot down a list of things we must do. Mrs. Richard wrote

   1. Get the LCD projector.
   2. Write the study guide and run 32 copies.
   3. Make sure the time line and the map are ready.

◆ Lesson Plan Formats

I distinguish two general formats for lesson planning: the *comprehensive* lesson plan and the *abbreviated* lesson plan. Comprehensive lesson plans are detailed and quite time consuming to prepare. The lesson plan at the end of Chapter 1 was a comprehensive lesson plan (for *A Chair for My Mother*). Abbreviated lesson plans are much less detailed and take less time to prepare, but still require care and thought in their preparation.

The Comprehensive Lesson Plan

The comprehensive type of thorough lesson planning has several forms. As you have no doubt discovered, it seems as if each person who teaches a methods course has a preferred form. Relatively few times during our careers do we prepare comprehensive plans: We write them during our methods courses and field experience (internship or student teaching) as part of learning to teach. We write them during our teaching years mainly for two reasons: (a) When we are being evaluated by a principal, the process usually includes the preparation of comprehensive lesson plans, and (b) when we are doing a complex or innovative activity, it is a good idea to write a comprehensive plan. It would be impossible for us to write a comprehensive plan for each instructional activity we teach because there simply is not enough time to do so. These lengthy, detailed plans are important because their preparation is part of learning to teach. They require attention to each aspect of a lesson and ensure that lessons are logically sequenced. Figure 4.1 is an outline of the comprehensive lesson plan format I use throughout this book.

Let's take a closer look at each part of this format.

1. *Overview.*   The overview places the lesson in context. In this section, state the grade level and number of students who will participate in the activity. Provide the title of the instructional unit the lesson is from.
2. *Resources and materials.*   Instructional resources are things like Websites on the Internet, textbooks, CD-ROMs, children's books, and audiovisual items. Materials are things like paint, glue, and construction paper.
3. *Standards.*   Since most of us teach from a standards-based social studies curriculum, our comprehensive lesson plans should clearly state which standard(s) the lesson addresses.

Figure 4.1   Comprehensive Lesson Plan Format

1. Overview
2. Resources and materials
3. Standards
4. Content objectives
5. Process objectives
6. Values objectives
7. Teaching sequence
8. Evaluation

4. *Content objectives.* I prefer a simple form for writing objectives. This section is a list of the content—the subject matter we expect our students to learn in our lesson.

5. *Process objectives.* This is a list of what we expect our students to accomplish during the lesson. Whereas content objectives list the "what" of the lesson, process objectives focus on the activity of students, both mental and physical.

6. *Values objectives.* Not all lessons will include this section. Here we list any values the lesson will help our students acquire.

7. *Teaching sequence.* At this point in preparing a comprehensive lesson plan, we shift our focus and make a list of things that we ourselves will do. Considerable controversy surrounds the topic of teaching sequences. Many authorities have advocated sets of teaching steps that are usually called teaching "models" (Joyce, Weil, & Calhoun, 2003). Some teaching models are discussed in a subsequent section of this chapter. My approach is pragmatic and situation specific because the things we as teachers do and the order in which we do them depend on what we expect our students to do. We should tailor our teaching sequence to fit the needs of our students, the resources we use, and the objectives of our lesson. Our teaching sequence should start with the things we will do before we begin teaching, such as preparing materials and gathering resources.

8. *Evaluation.* You can collect several types of data to help you determine whether students achieved the lesson's objectives. In Chapter 8, you will read about the many ways you can evaluate your students.

Figure 4.1 summarizes the steps in my Comprehensive Lesson Plan format. At the end of this chapter you will find an example of a comprehensive plan, this one for Mrs. Richard's lesson with *Buffalo Chase, Missouri.*

The Abbreviated Lesson Plan

When we assume responsibility for teaching all day, either as student teachers or as first-time teachers, we will not have time to prepare comprehensive lesson plans for each activity that takes place. We will use an *abbreviated* form and save comprehensive planning for those lessons that require extra attention. We should, of course, continue to think about all the elements that are part of a good lesson.

The Plan Book Grid. The most common form of abbreviated planning is done in a planning book. Several companies produce these plan books, although each is in a unique format. Almost all, however, are spiral bound. A week is spread across two pages; along the left side are the days of the week, and along the top are blocks of time. In each square, about 2 inches on each side, we write what we will do that day in that block of time (the blocks usually represent 1 hour). Figure 4.2 shows what Donna Richard wrote in her plan book for the lesson with the painting *Buffalo Chase, Upper Missouri.*

Figure 4.2   Teacher's Plan Book: *Buffalo Chase, Upper Missouri*

12:45 to 1:50

SOCIAL STUDIES
  Day 3 of mini-unit on Sioux
  ▶ *View Buffalo Chase, Upper Missouri*
  ▶ *Complete study guide in groups*
  ▶ *Introduce follow-up projects*
Resources Smithsonian Website, LCD projector, time line, map, 32 copies of study guide, related books, books on Mohawk

Three-Column, Single-Sheet.   Another form of an abbreviated plan is completed on a sheet of paper with three columns. The useful outline format requires a separate sheet of paper for each lesson. Table 4.1 provides an example of this format, again with the *Buffalo Chase* lesson.

Table 4.1   Three-Column, Single-Sheet Lesson Plan
Lesson: Painting—*Buffalo Chase, Upper Missouri*
Date: Tuesday, October 11
Time: 12:45–1:50

Objectives	Teaching Sequence	Materials/Resources
CONCEPT: Human–environment interaction GENERALIZATIONS— (1) The buffalo was the essential resource for the Sioux (2) The Sioux and the Mohawk had different food-getting practices FACTS— (1) Use of bows, arrows, lances to hunt (2) Sioux hunted in groups (3) Horses increased efficiency (4) Danger	(1) Use LCD projector to show the painting (2) Time line, map (3) Show painting again, students comment (4) Work in groups on study guide, questions 1–7 (5) Reconvene as a whole group, discuss questions 1–7 (6) In groups, discuss question 8 (Mohawk–Sioux comparison) (7) Reconvene as a whole group—question 8 (8) Introduce related projects and books	(1) Smithsonian Website, www.si.edu (2) LCD projector (3) 32 copies of study guide (4) Time line (5) Map (6) Related books

◆ Writing Lesson Objectives

An essential element of lesson planning is the writing of instructional objectives. These objectives delineate the expectations we have for our students in any given lesson. I shared with you in Chapter 2 that social studies lessons can be broken down into considerations for content, process, and values objectives. The standards documents (discussed in Chapter 1) and our curriculum course guides (provided by local school districts) will help us in determining our needs for content objectives. To establish how to write more meaningful process and values objectives, I want to introduce you to considerations that curriculum developers often make.

Making Objectives More Meaningful

One key to making objectives more meaningful is to write objectives that identify specific and observable performances by students. According to Ralph Mager, author of *Preparing Instructional Objectives* (1997), effectively written objectives identify what students are expected to do and demonstrates how they do it. Using Mager's standards, we can differentiate a poor objective from richer ones with these examples. "To be able to develop an appreciation of music" is an inadequate statement of performance. It does not tell what the student is to do, and it is not observable. However, both "To build a model of the Parthenon" or "To list three reasons why the American Colonists declared independence from Great Britain" can provide more meaningful structure to lesson planning. Instructional objectives that provide focus and direction for both teachers and learners are essential to planning more effective lessons.

One simple component of objectives that can help focus expectations for students is the verb that describes the desired performance. Action verbs, as discreet as possible, can better pinpoint what we want students to do. For example, if, after watching a film on the economy of Mexico, students are expected to identify the correct answers to questions on a worksheet, then the instructional objective could be "Students will circle each product that is exported from the Republic of Mexico."

Raising the Levels of Performance: Objectives in the Cognitive Domain

In his *Taxomony of Educational Objectives* (Bloom, 1956; Gronlund, 2000), Benjamin Bloom created a framework for writing objectives at many cognitive levels. Bloom's taxonomy remains a useful tool for teachers, especially because it provides a basis for planning activities that require complex, critical thinking. In his taxonomy, Bloom categorizes mental activities into six sequential levels: knowledge, comprehension, application, analysis, synthesis, and evaluation. Social studies activities should include objectives in each level, especially the last three, which require students to use higher-level thinking processes.

1. *Knowledge.* Bloom (1956) stated the following definition for the knowledge category: "Knowledge involves the recall of specifics and universals,

the recall of methods and processes, or the recall of a pattern, structure, or setting" (p. 201). This is the mental process of remembering. As conceived by Bloom and his associates, this is a broad category involving knowledge of facts, terminology, sequences, categories, processes, principles, and theories.

2. *Comprehension.*   To Bloom (1956), comprehension "refers to a type of understanding . . . such that the individual knows what is being communicated and can make use of the material . . . without necessarily relating to other material or seeing its fullest implications" (p. 204). The ability to restate or summarize is evidence of comprehension, as is the ability to state the main idea in something.

3. *Application.*   At the application level, the student begins to use what he or she knows and understands. Application is "the use of abstractions in particular and concrete situations" (p. 205). An objective in this category would ask a student to apply a law or theory. Another example is the ability to apply a process learned in one context to another context.

4. *Analysis.*   The analysis category refers to the ability to identify the component parts of something and to describe their relationship. It includes distinguishing one thing that is closely related to another and comparing and contrasting things. Bloom noted that distinguishing fact from hypothesis is an analytic operation.

5. *Synthesis.*   In the synthesis category, the learner creates something new as the parts of something are rearranged into an original configuration. This category includes the activities of speculating and hypothesizing. Students who develop a plan to solve a current social problem are engaged in this category of cognitive activity.

6. *Evaluation.*   The last category of the cognitive domain involves "making judgements" (Bloom, 1956, p. 207). This includes rating a list of things in priority order or judging things according to a set of criteria.

Objectives for the lesson with *Buffalo Chase, Upper Missouri* could be written using Bloom's taxonomy. Notice that, to have objectives in each of the six categories of the cognitive domain, some activities would have to be added to the lesson:

1. *Knowledge.*   List the weapons the Sioux used to kill buffalo.
2. *Comprehension.*   Describe the dangers to the Natives' horses during a buffalo hunt.
3. *Application.*   Dramatize the buffalo hunt by pretending you are a hunter who is telling his children about the day's hunt.
4. *Analysis.*   Compare the food-getting practices of the Sioux and the Mohawk.
5. *Synthesis.*   Speculate on the sounds of the buffalo hunt and write about what the Sioux would have heard.
6. *Evaluation.*   Make a list ranking the most important qualities and characteristics of an effective buffalo hunter.

Figure 4.3 provides a list of verbs, arranged by category within the cognitive domain, that could be used in writing objectives.

Figure 4.3   Taxonomy of Educational Objectives: Cognitive Domain—Suggested Verbs to Use When Writing Objectives

1. Knowledge	3. Application	5. Synthesis
define	demonstrate	compose
identify	dramatize	design
list	illustrate	hypothesize
match	sequence	invent
recall	show how to	speculate
2. Comprehension	4. Analysis	6. Evaluation
describe	compare	criticize
explain	classify	judge
paraphrase	diagram	justify
restate	distinguish	prioritize
summarize	verify	rate

◆ Perspectives on the Teaching Sequence

As I noted earlier, many authorities have developed step-by-step teaching sequences. In this section, I describe two of these teaching models.

Hunter's Seven-Step Model: Direct Instruction

Madeline Hunter, former principal of the University Elementary School at UCLA, developed a generic, seven-step teaching sequence that she believed can be applied to any subject at any grade level (Hunter, 1984). At one time, the Hunter model was officially adopted by hundreds of school districts, and many state departments of education endorsed or mandated it (Kirp, 1990). I chose to discuss the Hunter model because it is an example of "direct instruction," where the teacher provides information and tightly controls the activities of the children (Marchand-Martella, Slocum, & Martella, 2003). It should be noted that there is research on the Hunter Model that questions its effectiveness in boosting student achievement (Mandeville & Rivers, 1988–1989; Slavin, 1989; Stallings & Krasavage, 1986). The Hunter model is a teaching sequence of seven steps:

1. *Anticipatory set.*   During the first step, the teacher directs student attention to the lesson. The goal here is to get students who will participate in the activity to stop thinking about other things and start thinking about the lesson. For example, Mrs. Richard began by asking students to look at the projected image of the painting. This focused students' attention on the task at hand.

2. *Objective and purpose.*   Next, the teacher states the purpose of the lesson. Hunter (1984) suggests that this include "what will be learned and how it will be useful" (p. 175). For example, "Today we are going to look at a painting of the buffalo hunt, an important aspect in the lives of the Plains tribes. This will help us better understand how these Native Americans lived."

3. *Input.*   Hunter (1984) states that "students must acquire new information about the knowledge, process, or skill they are to achieve . . . from discovery, discussion, reading, listening, observing, or being told" (p. 176). This can be a selection from a textbook, a demonstration, a film, or a lecture.

4. *Modeling.*   In the fourth step, the teacher, another adult, an older student, or a member of the class demonstrates what all the students will be expected to do. This may involve showing a range of options and then having students choose one to complete.

5. *Check for understanding.*   Before allowing students to work independently, Hunter suggests, teachers should find out whether the students know what they are supposed to do. This can be determined by asking questions or by taking a quick look at the initial efforts of a few of the students.

6. *Guided practice.*   The students work, the teacher circulates. The teacher gives help on request and looks for students who are having difficulty.

7. *Independent practice.*   The final step does not appear in every lesson. This is a time when students complete tasks without help from the teacher.

At the end of the chapter, you will find an example of how the lesson on *Buffalo Chase, Upper Missouri* could be written using the Hunter format.

Direct Instruction and the Hunter Model: An Appraisal.   I take the perspective that no one teaching sequence can be applied to every teaching situation. *How* we teach should depend on *what* we teach and *whom* we teach. One problem with the Hunter model, like other models of direct instruction, is that some educators think this type of teaching works for all subjects and at all grades—this, despite what Hunter (1984) wrote: "Because making a basic lesson design explicit was 'welcome news' to so many educators, it has unfortunately become a rigid measuring stick of 'correctness' in teaching. That was never its intent" (p. 175). Direct instruction is one of the many models we can use in social studies; it should never be the only teaching sequence we follow.

The Concept Attainment Model

Authorities recommend other teaching sequences, and I use many of them in this book (e.g., in Chapter 5, the Three-Step Interview and Jigsaw). These teaching sequences are designed for specific purposes, not as generic models (like the Hunter model). To provide one example for comparison, here I describe the teaching

Lessons often begin with a whole class activity to motivate learning or provide procedural directions.

Anne Vega / Merrill

Some lessons require planning for small-group work, guiding concept development, or teaching students how to review what they have learned.

Anthony Magnacca / Merrill

Daily lessons should include time for students to become engaged in critical thinking activities or independent practice. Teachers can then answer individual questions about a project or assignment.

Anne Vega / Merrill

sequence developed by Joyce et al. (2003) to help children acquire concepts. It is based on the research of Jerome Bruner and his colleagues (Bruner, Goodnow, & Austin, 1956). It is called the *concept attainment model,* and it is frequently used in social studies. I have found that it works better with older children than with younger ones and that it should be used at the end of an instructional unit. The concept attainment model has three variations. I describe the reception form, which has the greatest level of teacher direction. It has three phases, each with three parts:

1. *Presentation of Data and Identification of Concept.*
   1.1 The concept attainment model is like a game. It begins with the teacher explaining the purpose of the activity, which is to help students better understand a concept. The first phase starts with the teacher presenting students with examples and nonexamples of a concept. The examples and nonexamples can be the names of people or places, things, or events. The teacher tells the students whether each item is an example or a nonexample of the concept.
   1.2 Next, the teacher encourages students to compare the examples and nonexamples: What makes them different? What do all the examples have in common?
   1.3 At this point, students should be ready to state a definition for the concept. The definition is a hypothesis that will be refined in the second and third phases.
2. *Testing Attainment of Concept.*
   2.1 In the second phase, the teacher presents items that are *not* labeled as "examples" or "nonexamples." Students state whether each item is an example of the concept. The definition may be revised because of the characteristics of the items.
   2.2 The teacher now comments on the definition the students have developed. If necessary, the teacher may restate the definition of the concept.
   2.3 The final part of this phase is a challenge. Now the teacher asks students to generate examples of the concept. This will test whether they can apply the definition they have learned.
3. *Analysis of Thinking Strategy.* The third phase need not be included each time the concept attainment model is used. This phase asks students to reflect on the first two phases of the model.
   3.1 Students describe how they reached their conclusions about the status of each item. What were they thinking when they decided that something was or was not an example?
   3.2 Students then talk about how they changed their definitions. Why did they have to change their early definitions?
   3.3 Finally, students talk about the characteristics of the concept and consider the process of hypothesis testing.

At the end of the chapter you will find an example of how the concept attainment model could be used at the conclusion of the unit "19th-Century Native Americans."

♦ Principles for Planning Instructional Units

Social studies lessons should be organized into well-designed units of instruction. An *instructional unit* is a set of related activities with a unifying element, something that serves as a focus for the unit. Although some units are brief and include only three or four lessons (I refer to these as "mini-units"), most social studies units are more ambitious and run for several days. The idea of the unit is an old one. In fact, some of the finest instructional units in social studies are almost 100 years old and were developed during the era of Progressive Education at places like the Laboratory School of the University of Chicago and the Lincoln School in New York City (Cremin, 1961; Mayhew & Edwards, 1936). A good place to start our discussion is with five principles for planning instructional units in the social studies:

1. Units should be integrated.
2. The scope of each unit should be clearly defined.
3. Activities in a unit should follow a logical sequence.
4. Units should feature a variety of instructional resources.
5. Units should include whole-group, small-group, and individual activities.

Units Should Be Integrated

Social studies units can be integrated through content or by process. *Content integration* occurs when a unit goes beyond history and geography to include concepts from other social sciences (political science, anthropology, economics, and sociology), the arts (literature, the visual arts, and the performing arts), science, mathematics, and physical education. *Process integration* is the result of planning activities that make a social studies unit a vehicle for teaching the language arts (speaking, reading, listening, and writing), the performing arts, the visual arts, and technology skills (see Chapter 9 which discusses the integrated curriculum).

The Scope of Each Unit Should Be Clearly Defined

All units should have a clearly defined scope. In the jargon of curriculum development, *scope* refers to the limits of the content covered in a lesson, unit, or academic year. Generally, most social studies units attempt to cover too much material. The NCSS Task Force on Standards for Teaching and Learning in the Social Studies (1993) noted that "the most effective teachers do not diffuse their efforts by covering too many topics superficially" (p. 216). For example, rather than planning the unit "Ancient Civilizations of the Americas," it would make more sense to plan the unit "The Aztec." During this unit, comparisons could be made with the Inca and Maya, but the focus would be the Aztec.

The unifying element, or topic, of the unit will define the unit's scope, and fortunately there is no shortage of topics that can serve as the unifying elements for social studies units. Following are some possibilities:

- *Historical focus (when).*   With the current emphasis on history in the social studies curriculum, units that focus on a particular time and place are very popular. Examples are "Life in the Young Republic: The United States from 1790 to 1850," "The Early Days of Our City," or "Ancient China."
- *Person or people (who).*   It is also possible to develop units that examine a cultural group—for example, "The Navajo: Yesterday and Today." Excellent units can be constructed around one person—for example, "Dr. Martin Luther King Jr."
- *Location (where).*   Sometimes called "area studies," location units have as a unifying element a place—for example, "Japan" or "Hawaii." Units that look at places should also be limited by time. For example, the unit on Japan could avoid superficial coverage by being redesigned to become "Modern Japan: 1945 to the Present."
- *Question or problem.*   Some of the most intriguing social studies units have questions as their unifying elements. Activities in a unit help students develop a complete answer to the unit's unifying question. Examples are "How Does a Person Become President of the United States?" or "Why Is Gold Valuable?"
- *Things.*   Things, both human made and natural, can be the focus of a social studies unit. The unit on boats in this chapter is an example of this type of unit. Other examples are "Rivers" or "Calendars." The idea here is to show how different people in different times and places developed or used the object.
- *Concept or theme.*   An example of a unit based on a concept is "Immigration: Coming to the United States." Broad concepts can be the unifying elements of units. I have seen units on "Change," "Conflict," and "Shelter" that were fascinating. One advantage of conceptual and thematic units is that they allow us to take a global perspective and incorporate content covering several times, places, and peoples.

The process of developing units varies from school district to school district. Most elementary teachers work in school districts that supply curriculum guides for social studies. A curriculum guide typically is written by a committee of teachers and administrators and includes a list of units to be taught at each grade level. The best guides have units that are fully developed, aligned with a set of standards, and complete with clear learning objectives, lists of available resources, and practical lesson plans. Working with the guidelines of the curriculum approved for our school districts, we should customize the instructional units to fit the needs of our students. All our units should allow students to pursue related topics of personal interest.

Activities in a Unit Should Follow a Logical Sequence

Planning effective units of instruction in social studies requires us to think about the sequence of activities in each unit. Which lessons should be planned for the first few days of the unit? Which activities should serve as a culmination to the unit? As I explain later in the chapter, a unit should consist of activities that involve all students in the classroom (whole group), activities that are completed by only some students in the room and are cooperative efforts (small group), and activities that are completed individually (individual). As a general rule, the unit should begin with whole-group activities. As the unit progresses, more and more small-group and individual projects get started, and by the last third of the unit, few whole-group activities may take place as the concluding days of the unit are devoted to small-group and individual projects.

We should meet two goals at the start of a unit: (a) determine what our students know about the topic we will be studying and (b) find out whether our students would like to investigate anything in particular. Here are some techniques for accomplishing these goals:

- *The K–W–L chart.*   An example of a K–W–L chart (Ogle, 1986) appears later in this chapter in the unit on boats. K–W–L charts can be used to assess student knowledge of a topic and to discover special areas of student interest (see Chapter 9 for a description of this instructional strategy).
- *Open-ended journal prompts.*   A simple way to find out what students know about a topic is to have them write a response to "Write what you know about _____." A simple way to learn what is of special interest to them is to say to them, "Write any questions you have about _____." The advantage of open-ended prompts is that they provide information from each student in the classroom. Many of us have our students write responses in journals, which are used throughout the unit.
- *Discussion.*   An informal discussion on the first day of the unit can be used to assess student knowledge and interest. We can take notes, or we can record on chart paper what our students say.

It is usually best to start a unit with activities that establish time and place because students need to know the context of what they will be studying. Time lines and chronologies are good ways to establish time, and maps and globes of many kinds can be used to give students a sense of place (see Chapter 12). Also, at the beginning of a unit, it is a good idea to use resources that provide an overview of what students will be studying. I suggest starting the unit with videos, films, and the chapter from the textbook. Constructivist learning theory states that it is best to move from the whole to the parts, and I think this is essential in social studies. These initial activities will help students acquire essential "core" understandings, content we expect all students to know.

For the middle of a unit, we should plan a mixture of whole-group, small-group, and individual activities. We should devote the social studies period on some days to small-group and individual work. Students should have begun to study topics of personal interest. Cooperative learning is important as small groups work on projects that involve writing, the visual arts, and the performing arts. The content that students acquire will be more detailed and will vary from student to student.

For the conclusion of a unit, it is a good idea to plan activities that introduce the next unit of study. I call these "segue" activities. A *segue activity* shows students the relationship between one unit and another. These relationships include the following:

- *Chronology.*   Time is a frequent source for segue activities. For example, if we were studying the history of our state, then a unit on the Native Americans who inhabited our state would be followed by a unit on the first European settlers. The link between the two units is chronological, of course, in that one set of events follows the other.
- *Geography.*   A fifth-grade teacher could teach separate units on the New England colonies, the Middle colonies, and the Southern colonies. The units cover the same period of time. The relationship of one to the others is geographical (in this case, moving from north to south).
- *Culture.*   A unit on West African cultural groups (e.g., the Minde) could be followed by a unit on the enslavement of Africans in the Americas. The segue activities examine how some aspects of these cultures survived in the Americas, how others were changed, and how some cultural characteristics were lost.
- *Theme.*   Frequently, in the early grades (K–2), the social studies curriculum is linked by theme. For example, first graders might learn about cooperation. A unit on helping each other at school could be followed with a unit on how members of a neighborhood can benefit from working together. Activities should be planned that show how the same spirit of cooperation is embodied by different peoples.

Many units end with culminating activities. Such activities can take many forms, but they usually involve the performing arts. Students act in plays, produce films, and present material they have written. Other culminating activities can be simulations. For example, "A Day with the Ingalls" could be the culminating activity for the unit "The Prairie Pioneers." Several children's books could serve as resources: Wilder's *Little House* books, of course; *The Laura Ingalls Wilder Songbook* (Garson, 1968); *Skillet Bread, Sourdough, and Vinegar Pie: Cooking in Pioneer Days* (Ichord, 2003); *Frontier Living* (Tunis, 1961); and *My Prairie Year: Based on the Diary of Elinor Plaisted* (Harvey, 1986). Students would sing, play, eat, study, and work in historically authentic ways. Part of the day could be devoted to a simulation of the one-room schoolhouse of the late 19th century. In any case, the culminating activity should be a project that students have worked on for some time.

Figure 4.4 presents a summary of the principles for the sequence of activities in a unit.

Units Should Feature a Variety of Instructional Resources

There are two good reasons for using a variety of instructional resources in each social studies unit we teach: (a) The units will be enriched and more appealing to students in our classrooms, and (b) we will have a better chance of meeting

Figure 4.4   Sequence of Activities in a Social Studies Unit

Beginning (First one-third)	• Assess student knowledge and Interest • Establish context (time and place) • Whole-group activities: Provide overview and core content • Begin small-group projects, individual activities
Middle (Middle one-third)	• Students learn more specific information • Fewer whole-group activities, more small-group and individual activities
End (Last one-third)	• Small-group, individual projects completed • Culminating activity • Segue activities

the needs of our highly diverse students. Although many students do quite well with units that rely on the social studies textbook, other students will need films, photographs, and other visual media to learn the content we present. In addition to the social studies textbook, we can choose from both hard-copy and CD-ROM reference materials (encyclopedias, atlases, and almanacs); children's literature (fiction and information books); charts, graphs, and maps; videos and films; film-strips, study prints, and listening media (audiotapes and compact discs); realia (real things); community resources (people who visit our classes, places we visit); and computer-based resources (software programs, hypermedia, and the Internet).

Units Should Include Whole-Group, Small-Group, and Individual Activities

Good social studies units of instruction include activities that require students to work in several grouping formats. All three types of grouping should be a part of a social studies unit. A unit that relies heavily on lessons during which all students are expected to do the same thing at the same time will not meet the needs of a diverse student population. Differences in ability, language status, and cultural identity require frequent use of small-group work and individualized activities.

I distinguish whole-group, small-group, and individual activities as follows:

• *Whole group.*   A whole-group activity is an activity that involves participation by all students in the classroom. During some whole-group activities, such as watching a film or listening to a guest speaker, all students participate in the activity at the same time and in the same place. Other whole-group activities include a teacher making a presentation and then students completing an assignment while working in small groups. In others, the teacher may pose a question, and then the students break into groups to discuss the question. Another format for a whole-group activity is a learning center. Students might visit the center in groups of six,

Each child is special, wonderfully unique, and capable of thriving under your guidance. As you create instructional units, be sure to include activities that allow each child to be successful.

Anne Vega / Merrill

one group a day. Again, from my perspective, a whole-group activity is assigned to all students in the room.

- *Small group.* A small-group activity has two characteristics: (a) Only a part of the class takes part, and (b) the participants work together. Small-group activities are projects, usually in writing, the visual arts, or the performing arts. Many of these small-group activities use a cooperative learning structure.

- *Individual.* Individual activities may be voluntary or assigned. Like small-group activities, they do not involve the whole class; rather, a student works independently, typically on a project of personal interest.

Many different formats can be used in planning instructional units in social studies. Elsewhere in the book (Chapters 2, 11, and 12) are examples of shorter "mini-units," which can be completed in less than a week. At the end of this chapter is a longer unit on boats, designed for a highly diverse group of 25 to 30 third graders.

◆ Summary of Key Points

- Lesson plans are of two general types. Comprehensive lesson plans are detailed and lengthy. Abbreviated plans are written in outline form.
- Instructional objectives focus the direction and expectations of teachers. When they are well written, these objectives provide specific and observable expectations of student performance.
- Bloom's taxonomy of cognitive objectives describes levels of thinking processes. Instructional objectives can be written to require students to use higher-level mental activities.

- Direct instruction models, like Madeline Hunter's seven-step lesson plan, follow a teacher-directed format. The concept attainment model is less well-known.

- Units should be cross curricular and integrate the social science disciplines, language arts, the visual arts, the performing arts, science, mathematics, and physical education.

- Units should have a clearly defined scope. Each unit has a unifying element, which may be a period of history, a person or group of people, a location, a question, a thing, or a concept.

- Activities in a unit should follow a logical sequence. Activities at the beginning of a unit determine what your students know about the topic you will be covering and establish what subtopics they would like to investigate. Segue activities at the end of a unit introduce the next unit of study.

- Units should use a variety of instructional resources and feature whole-group, small-group, and individual activities.

- You may use many different formats for planning units, including detailed (comprehensive) unit plans and mini-units.

FOR FURTHER READING

Lesson Plans

- The books by Eggen and Kauchak (2001); Gunter, Estes, and Mintz (2006); and Joyce et al. (2003) are the best sources for models of teaching. I think the clearest statement of Madeline Hunter's teaching model is her chapter in *Using What We Know About Teaching* (1984) from the Association for Supervision and Curriculum Development. Books by Gronlund (2000) and Mager (1997) are a must for anyone who has to write behavioral objectives.

- You probably have had your fill of lesson models and formats. This chapter, of course, has only scratched the surface. For example, Yeich (2002) proposed a lesson plan format for using newspapers to teach about elections. Engle and Ochoa (1988) defined a model for reflective teaching in issues-centered social studies programs; their model has five steps. Felton and Allen (1990) developed an eight-step lesson format for using visual materials, such as photographs and paintings, in social studies.

Native Americans

- The Internet, the ERIC system, and social studies journals have too many good resources on teaching about Native Americans to list all of them here. I think that Donna Richard's unit is appropriately named ("19th-Century Native Americans"). It is important that children realize that Native Americans do not live today as they did in the past. The March/April 2006 issue of *Social Studies and the Young Learner* (vol. 18, no. 4) was devoted to teaching Native American culture and history. The January 1999 issue (vol. 63, no. 1) of *Social Education* has several good articles on teaching about Native Americans and includes a list of tribal Websites. One topic often overlooked in lessons and units about Native Americans is the governmental systems created by the Iroquois League, the Lakota Nation, the Muskogee Nation, and the Pueblo (Sahr, 1997). The article I mentioned by Powe (1998) in the previous chapter presents a curriculum that uses other paintings by George Catlin.

- By all means, look at the children's books that Donna Richard brought to class for her lesson. *Buffalo Hunt* (Freedman, 1988) is the best book on the topic for children. It is illustrated with paintings by Catlin and Karl Bodmer, another artist who visited the Plains before the Civil War. *Buffalo Woman* (Goble, 1984) is a folktale told in similar versions by several tribes. *Indians of the Plains* (Rachlis, 1960) is an older book but a good one and is part of the American Heritage Junior Library. It contains a chapter ("Indian Cattle") on buffalo hunting. *Where the Buffaloes Begin* (Baker, 1981) is a story collected and retold by Olaf Baker, an Englishman who came to the United States in 1902. An excellent essay on a related topic was written by Jennifer Turan Rothwell (1997). She discusses how a variety of visual images can be used to teach about the Plains Indians.
- Many Websites are available about the Sioux. One good one is part of the site for the Glenbow Museum in Calgary, Canada (www.glenbow.org).

Instructional Units

- Do not reinvent the wheel. Excellent social studies units are available from a variety of sources. Units are available on the Internet. I suggest you start with three Websites: the site for the NCSS, www.ncss.org; the "History/Social Science for K–12 Teachers" site, http://k-12historysocialstudies.com/boals.html; and the "Schools of California Online Resources for Education" (SCORE) site, www.score.k12.ca.us. The ERIC system includes hundreds of social studies units for elementary students; most were developed under the auspices of state departments of education and school district curriculum committees. The material in social studies textbooks for children is organized in units. Check the teacher's edition at your grade level and be willing to expand the unit to include resources and activities beyond those provided by the publisher of the textbook.
- Of particular interest are the units on cultural universals developed by Janet Alleman and Jere Brophy (2001a, 2001b, 2002b, 2002c). There are units on food, clothing, shelter, communication, transportation, family living, childhood, money, and government. The units are based on the authors' extensive research on the understanding K–3 children possess on these topics.
- If you want a historical perspective that still works, read how social studies units were developed at the Dewey School in the early 1900s (Mayhew & Edwards, 1936). Taba's (1967) thoughtful approach to unit development still makes a great deal of sense.

LESSON PLANS AND INSTRUCTIONAL ACTIVITIES

At the end of this chapter, you will find three lesson plans, all for fifth graders. The first two lessons are based on the same instructional resource, George Catlin's painting, *Buffalo Chase, Upper Missouri*. The purpose here is to show how one resource can be used for lesson following different formats. The third lesson, also focusing on the Sioux of the Plains, is an example of the Concept Attainment Model. Finally, you have an example of a lengthy, complete instructional unit for third graders on "Boats." Presented here are

1. A lesson plan in the "comprehensive format" for fifth graders based on the painting, *Buffalo Chase, Upper Missouri;*
2. A lesson plan using the same painting, *Buffalo Chase, Upper Missouri*, but this time using the "Hunter format;"
3. A third lesson plan based on *Buffalo Chase, Upper Missouri*, in this case based on the "Concept Attainment Model format;" and
4. A comprehensive unit plan for a third grade unit on "Boats."

Grade Five: Comprehensive Format: *Buffalo Chase, Upper Missouri*

LESSON PLAN

Overview: For a lesson in a mini-unit on the Oglala Sioux, a part of a unit on 19th-century Native Americans, students will work in groups to discuss a historical painting depicting a buffalo hunt, an important aspect of Sioux life.

Resources and Materials: (a) study guide, one per student (see Figure 4.5); (b) time line for the unit; (c) map of the United States; (d) children's books: *Buffalo Hunt* (Freedman, 1988), *Buffalo Woman* (Goble, 1984), *Indians of the Plains* (Rachlis, 1960), and *Where the Buffaloes Begin* (Baker, 1981); (e) sources to help students recall what they learned about the Mohawk (e.g., information books, encyclopedias, and charts the students completed).

The essential resource for the lesson is a copy of George Catlin's painting *Buffalo Chase, Upper Missouri* (also called *Buffalo Chase, Bulls Making Battle With Men and Horses*). You could use either of two formats:

1. *With a computer.* A copy of the painting is available on the Smithsonian Institution's Website, www.si.edu . The painting is part of the collection of the National Museum of American Art in the Smithsonian.
2. *Without a computer.* A copy of the painting can be found in most books on the work of George Catlin, such as *George Catlin and the Old Frontier* (McCracken, 1959, p. 146).

Figure 4.5   Study Guide: *Buffalo Chase, Upper Missouri*

Name _____

Date _____

Look closely at the painting. Talk about each question with the members of your group. Then write your answer. You do not have to write the same answer as the other members of your group.

1. How would you describe the land where the action takes place?

2. How many Sioux can you see?

3. What weapons are the Sioux using to kill the buffalo?

4. What is happening to the horses in the painting?

5. In the middle of the painting, we see one hunter who is not on a horse. Why?

6. Imagine hunting buffalo without horses. Why would it be more difficult?

7. Pretend you are one of the Sioux. Write down what you are thinking, feeling, hearing, and seeing.

8. Think back to what we learned about the Mohawk. Think what the Mohawk ate and how they got their food. Think what we have learned about the Sioux. All people need some way of getting food. What is the same and what is different about these two tribes?

Standard: From *Geography for Life,* the national geography standards, Standard 15: How Physical Systems Affect Human Systems. Knowledge Statement 2: The student knows and understand how the characteristics of different physical environments provide opportunities or place constraints on human activities (Geographic Education Standards Project, 1994, p. 173).

Content Objectives: Students will grasp the concept of human-environment interaction as they see an example of how resources influence the food-getting practices of a cultural group. They will learn that the buffalo (American bison) was the essential resource of the Sioux and other Natives of the Plains. Specifically, the lesson teaches that the Sioux used bows, arrows, and lances to hunt buffalo; the Sioux hunted in groups; the use of horses increased the Sioux's efficiency; and the buffalo hunt was dangerous to both the Sioux and their horses. The comparison of the Sioux and the Mohawk will help students understand two concepts: (a) There were great differences in how Native Americans lived prior to the coming of Europeans, and (b) the resources of a region play a central role in determining how groups of people obtain food.

Process Objectives: Students will (a) *observe* the painting; (b) *respond* to the teacher's open-ended question; (c) *describe* the physical setting and the action taking place in the setting; (d) *speculate* on why one hunter is not riding a horse; (e) *compare* hunting buffalo with and without horses; (f) *speculate* on what the hunters thought, felt, heard, and saw; (g) *compare and contrast* the food-getting practices of the Sioux and the Mohawk; and (h) *state* why the practices of the two groups differed.

Values Objectives: Students will acquire the values of cultural understanding and respect as they learn more about the Sioux.

Teaching Sequence:

1. Prepare the resources for the lesson: Website, projector, books, study guide, time line, map, and materials for review of the Mohawk.
2. Ask the students to look at the painting. Show it for a brief time and identify your expectations for the lesson: You will ask students to examine the painting to learn more about how the Sioux hunted buffalo.
3. Point to the relevant dates on the time line: (a) 1680, the earliest probable date that Natives of the southern Plains had horses; (b) 1730, the date that the Blackfoot, a northern Plains tribe, had horses; and (c) 1885, the approximate date by which buffalo had virtually disappeared from the Plains.
4. Use the map to show the region of the United States where Natives hunted buffalo.
5. Again, show the slide. Ask an open-ended question: "Would anyone like to say anything about this painting?" Use students' responses as a basis for discussion.
6. Divide the class into groups of four to work on the study guide. Distribute the study guides. Tell students that before they write, they should discuss each question. Circulate among the groups and help students share ideas.
7. Call the groups together and have the students return to their seats. Ask for volunteers to share their answers.

8. Use the last query in the study guide to stimulate a comparison of the food-getting practices of the Sioux and the Mohawk. Have students answer the query in groups and then share conclusions with the whole group. Finally, ask each group to explain what factors caused the two tribes to use different ways to get food.
9. Introduce related books to the class. Discuss each one and encourage the students to read them.

Evaluation: Collect the study guides. This would be a good source of information to place in the students' portfolios. You could also take notes as you circulate among the groups.

Effective Teaching in Today's Diverse Classroom: In the 21st century, all our students will need to know how to use resources on the Internet. This lesson could be extended so that students use the Internet. The National Museum of American Art in the Smithsonian Institution has an extensive collection of George Catlin's paintings, including 10 depicting Natives of the Great Plains hunting buffalo. A small group of students could complete a project using the Smithsonian's Website as an instructional resource (www.si.edu). The quality of the color and the specificity of the detail in the paintings will depend on the quality of your hardware (computer, monitor, and liquid crystal display). I was particularly interested in his two paintings of Natives hunting buffalo in deep snow. One other point: As I noted in the description of the lesson, it is important that students learn about the great diversity among Native American tribes. That is why lessons about the Natives of the Great Plains must be part of a broader study of other tribes. It is also important to have students learn about how Native Americans live today.

It is absolutely essential that all our students learn how to access information on the Internet. Children with mild disabilities need to meet these challenges, and teachers would be wise to consider a modification in curricular content to assist them by breaking the task *into small manageable units.* For example, the task of locating information on a Website could include lessons on each of the following: (a) typing in the URL, (b) using the links on the site's main page, often displayed in a vertical or horizontal "bar," (c) finding information using the site's internal search system, and (d) scanning a location for the specific information you need.

Also, in this lesson, children with learning disabilities may need help in completing the study guide (Figure 4.5). One intervention a teacher could consider here is to *change the task criteria.* A teacher might well ask the more able students to complete their responses to the eight questions in 20 minutes. Children with disabilities could be given extra time.

Finally, an important intervention to meet the needs of our gifted students is to pose tasks that require complex thinking, like making inferences. After students understand that not all Native tribes hunted buffalo and that some, like the Mohawk, had agriculture, gifted students could be asked to speculate on the implications for a native tribe that depended on migrating buffalo as a primary food source. Gifted children could be asked what this meant for the tribe's shelter (had to be portable, like a tipi), the implications for what tools and animals would be valuable (accurate bows and

Figure 4.6   **George Catlin toured the American Great Plains in the 1830s. He painted what he saw. This painting, completed in 1833, is known by two descriptive titles: *Buffalo Chase, Upper Missouri,* and *Buffalo Chase, Bulls Making Battle With Men and Horses.***

Smithsonian American Art Museum, Washington, DC/Art Resource, NY

arrows, swift horses), and what talents would be prized by members of the tribe (the ability to find and kill buffalos).

Figure 4.5 is the study guide Mrs. Richard developed for the lesson; Figure 4.6 shows the painting *Buffalo Chase, Upper Missouri.*

Grade Five: The Hunter Format: *Buffalo Chase, Upper Missouri*

LESSON PLAN

1. *Anticipatory set.*   Show the painting. Ask students to look closely at it.
2. *Objective and purpose.*   Say, "Today, we are going to learn about how the Sioux and other Native Americans who lived on the Great Plains hunted buffalo. We will look closely at this painting, and then you will work in groups to answer

some questions about the painting. Then I will ask you to think about the similarities and differences between the Sioux and the Mohawk."

3. *Input.* Use a time line to show students the historical period when Natives hunted buffalo on horseback. Use a map to show them the region of the United States where buffalo roamed and the location where the artist George Catlin observed the buffalo hunt depicted in the painting. Then ask the class to break into groups. Distribute the study guides and explain how the students are to work in groups. Turn the projector on again so that all students can see the painting.

4. *Modeling.*   Read aloud the first query and work with one group on the response. Stress the importance of listening to what each member of the group has to say before writing a response. Also point out that the students should talk just loudly enough so that other members of the group can hear them but not so loudly that other groups can hear.

5. *Check for understanding.*   Ask each student to write a response for the first query and then to work on the second query. Move from group to group to be sure that students write responses in the appropriate places and that each group discusses before writing.

6. *Guided practice.*   As the groups work on queries 3, 4, 5, 6, and 7, circulate among the groups. Try to maximize the number of students who talk in each group. Help groups fully explore queries 6 and 7. After discussing the first seven queries, have each group respond to the last query, which asks students to compare the Sioux and the Mohawk.

7. *Independent practice.*   Ask for volunteers for projects. One group of students could use the Smithsonian Website to create a CD-ROM scrapbook on George Catlin's paintings. Another group could look at other books, especially *Buffalo Hunt* (Freedman, 1988) and *Indians of the Plains* (Rachlis, 1960), for pictures showing other techniques used to hunt buffalo; then that group can write their own book, *How to Hunt a Buffalo.* A third group could make a large chart comparing the cultures of the Sioux and the Mohawk.

LESSON PLAN

Grade Five: The Concept Attainment Model: The Sioux of the Plains

Concept: The Sioux (Dakota); more specifically, the culture of this tribal group of Native Americans who lived on the Great Plains (sometimes called the "Western Sioux")

1. Explain to students that you will present some sentences to them. Each sentence will be either an example of something or a nonexample. (You might have to use other words to explain this distinction, like "This fits but this does not fit.")

Here each sentence will be labeled as a "Yes" or a "No." Write the following sentences on sentence strips, number them, and display them on a pocket chart:

  a. No: They made boats out of driftwood and tar.
  b. Yes: They hunted buffalo for food, clothing, and shelter.
  c. Yes: They lived in tipis.
  d. No: They lived in longhouses in villages surrounded by a fence.
  e. Yes: The most important ceremony was the Sun Dance.
  f. No: They trapped beaver.
  g. Yes: The men wore their hair long.
  h. Yes: Men paid for desirable things with horses.
  i. No: They farmed corn.
  j. No: For the most part, they lived peacefully and did not fight with other tribes.

2. Ask students to compare the two groups of sentences. What do the "Yes" sentences have in common? What makes the "No" sentences different from the "Yes" sentences?
3. Ask students to write a definition or description for all the "Yes" sentences. They should come up with something like "Things we know about the Sioux."
4. Now you present five more sentences to the students (see the following numbered list). This time, the sentences are not labeled "Yes" or "No." The students must decide whether each is a "Yes" or a "No":

  a. They communicated with a written language.
  b. Women owned property; daughters inherited it.
  c. The goal of a warrior was to "count coup" by touching an enemy.
  d. The wealthy were expected to give feasts and offer presents to the poor.
  e. They made beautiful clay pottery.

5. Comment on the definition the students have developed. If necessary, restate the definition of the concept.
6. Finally, ask the students whether they can generate examples of the concept. Ask, "Who can say something else about the Sioux that would be a 'Yes' sentence?"

Grade Three: Boats

Part I: Organizing Framework

UNIT

This unit is organized by performance standards taken from the NCSS *Expectations of Excellence* (for the early grades; 1994). Standards provide useful tools for the adults who are planning social studies units, but you must clearly communicate your expectations to the children. To achieve this purpose, this unit uses a simple format: a set of four questions phrased in words that third graders can understand. The unit takes about 3 weeks to complete.

Unit Question 1: What are the different types of boats, and why are they different?

Standard: Thematic Strand 1, Culture. Performance Expectation (a): The learner can explore and describe similarities and differences in the ways groups, societies, and cultures address similar human needs and concerns.

In this unit of study, children will learn that all people share certain needs that boats help them meet: finding food, exchanging goods, traveling to achieve personal goals, and defending themselves. The focus in this unit is on the different designs and functions of boats.

Unit Question 2: Where in our state, country, and world would you find people using boats?

Standard: Thematic Strand 3, People, Places, and Environments. Performance Expectation (b): The learner can interpret, use, and distinguish various representations of the earth, such as maps, globes, and photographs.

The unit of study on boats will require children to interpret several maps as they learn about the commercial, recreational, and military uses of boats.

Unit Question 3: What types of jobs do people perform on boats, and how have those jobs changed over time?

Standard: Thematic Strand 7, Production, Distribution, and Consumption. Performance Expectation (e): The learner can describe how we depend upon workers with specialized jobs and the ways in which they contribute to the production and exchange of goods and services.

The division of labor on a boat depends on its purpose and complexity. Children will learn that two factors have increased the number of specialized jobs on boats: size and technical sophistication.

Unit Question 4: How have boats changed over time?

Standard: Thematic Strand 8, Science, Technology, and Society. Performance Expectation (a): The learner can identify and describe examples in which science and technology have changed the lives of people, such as homemaking, child care, work, transportation, and communication.

Technology has changed the design of boats, especially in regard to propulsion, to make them more efficient. These changes have modified both the lives of people who work on boats and the lives of people who use them.

Part II: Instructional Activities

(1) Introductory Activities

Please note that the instructional activities in the unit will be presented in two formats. In the first, you will find both content and process objectives, which provides a full description of the activity. In the second, briefer format, the activity is described in a few sentences.

Unit Introduction: K–W–L Chart

Content Objectives: Children will be presented with the four questions they will be expected to answer during the unit (the unit questions). Because it is impossible to predict what any group of children will say when asked, "What do you know about boats?" other content objectives cannot really be listed.

Process Objectives: Children will *recall* what they know about boats, *ask* questions they would like to have answered, and *discuss* the unit's four questions.

1. With the children, start a K–W–L chart on boats. Divide a sheet of chart paper into three columns, one with the heading "What We *K*now About Boats," the second with the heading "What We *W*ant to Learn About Boats," and the third with "What We *L*earned About Boats." The first two columns will be completed on the first day of the unit. The third column will be filled as the unit progresses. Items under the "W" column should be written as questions. If the children do not ask questions that cover the subtopics you planned to cover, add them (in this unit, the four unit questions must be written down). If members of the class show an interest in something you were not planning to include, I suggest you modify your unit plan. Add resources and activities to fit the children's interests.
2. Begin by asking, "What do you know about boats?" Record what the children say under the "K" column. I like to have the four unit questions written on strips of paper so that they can be placed under the "W" column along with the questions the children ask. Be sure to have a brief discussion about each question so that the children have a clear understanding of what they will be expected to learn. See Figure 4.7 for an example of a K–W–L chart for this unit.

Field Trip to Los Angeles Harbor

Everyone loves a field trip. The class will travel to the harbor to observe first hand several types of boats, including purse seiners (fishing boats), tugboats, oil tankers, freighters, cruise ships, and the fireboat. Each child will complete a data retrieval chart summarizing what they have learned about each type of boat.

(2) Unit Question 1: What are the different types of boats, and why are they different?

Teacher Read-Aloud: Boats on the River

Content Objectives: Children will expand their knowledge of the different types of boats and focus on the different designs and functions of the following: ferryboat, paddlewheel, ocean liner, tugboat, motorboat, sailboat, rowboat, freighter, submarine, and battleship.

Figure 4.7   K–W–L Chart for a Unit on Boats: First Day of Unit

K	W	L
What we <u>K</u>now about boats	What we <u>W</u>ant to learn about boats	What we <u>L</u>earned about boats
• Lots of us have visited the <u>Queen Mary</u> • Some boats have sails, others don't • Pedro, Leshana, Juan—their dads work at the harbor, and so does Donna's mom • <u>Titanic</u> was a movie about a boat that sank	*Our Questions* A. How much does it cost to buy a boat? B. How fast can boats go? C. How can a big boat like the <u>Queen Mary</u> move? *Unit questions* 1. What are the different types of boats, and why are they different? 2. Where in our state, country, and world would you find people using boats? 3. What types of jobs do people perform on boats, and how have those jobs changed over time? 4. How have boats changed over time?	

(Chart header: BOATS)

Process Objectives: Children will *listen* to the book being read aloud, *share* their personal responses, *identify* and *differentiate* the design and function of each boat, and *classify* the boats by function.

1. Read aloud the wonderful book *Boats on the River* (Flack, 1946). Afterward, ask the children whether they would like to say anything about the book.
2. Write the following words on the chalkboard: *ferryboat, paddlewheel, ocean liner, tugboat, motorboat, sailboat, rowboat, freighter, submarine,* and *battleship.* Go through the book a second time and discuss with the class Jay Barnum's paintings of the boats, focusing on what each boat is used for (its function or purpose). Focus on the following principle: that design serves function. Organize the boats under the following categories on the chalkboard: "Used to Move People," "Used to Move Products," "Used for War," "Used for Fishing," and "Used for Fun" (Note: Some boats should be placed under more than one category).

To adapt this activity for a group of English learners, you might consider photocopying the illustrations of the boats so that there is one, large image of each boat. Then, label the illustrations so that there is both a written and a visual connection for each type of boat. This will help remind students of what each type of boat looks like.

Jigsaw: Modern Warships

Children will learn about the design and military function of five types of modern warships: aircraft carriers, battleships, submarines, transport ships, and search-and-rescue ships. For each type of warship, the teacher will prepare a data file, with descriptions and illustrations. The class will be divided into five groups. Have each member of one group pick a different type of warship; he or she will become an "expert" about that warship and share his or her expertise with the remaining members of the group.

Bulletin Board Display: Voyages

This display will reveal what one group of children learned about the different types of boats used to transport people, both historical and contemporary. The bulletin board display will include images of Chumash canoes (the Chumash were a tribe of Native Americans in California who built oceangoing canoes), the Pilgrims' *Mayflower,* the ill-fated *Titanic,* and a dozen other boats used to transport people (e.g.,ferries, ocean liners, recreational craft). The group will use CD-ROM encyclopedias, Internet resources, hard-copy encyclopedias, and information books as resources. Each of their paintings will have a caption listing the type of boat and, if the boat has a name, the boat's name. After the bulletin board is finished, the children who painted and wrote about the *Mayflower* and the *Titanic* will make a presentation to their classmates, challenging them to explain why one ship sank and the other successfully completed a transatlantic voyage.

This should be an activity that will work for your students with learning disabilities. The students could, of course, be asked to write a report of their findings. Instead, here the final product has two parts: (1) the paintings of the boats displayed on the bulletin board and (2) the oral report on the *Mayflower* and the *Titanic.* Other than the brief captions, there is no written product. This is an example of *changing the task modality* to allow children with disabilities to show what they know.

Inquiry: The Voyage to Hawaii

Content Objectives: Children will learn about the migration of people from Tahiti to Hawaii in about C.E. 1200. They will understand that the Polynesians accomplished incredible feats of navigation, sailing with the resources they possessed. They will locate Tahiti and Hawaii on a world map. The inquiry will ask them to decide what supplies the Tahitians should take on their canoes as they prepare for their voyage to Hawaii.

Process Objectives: Children will *listen* to the historical overview provided by their teacher, *view* pictures of Polynesian catamarans, *locate* Tahiti and Hawaii on a world map, *examine* a list of resources available to the Tahitians, and *identify* the items they would take with them if they were making the voyage.

1. All the information you need for this lesson is available on the Website of the Polynesian Voyaging Society (www.pvs.hawaii.org). The site has excellent

illustrations of the double-hulled canoes the Polynesians used, maps of the journey from Tahiti to Hawaii, and background information on all aspects of Polynesian shipbuilding, navigation, and migration. Present the background information the children will need to complete this inquiry activity. Explain that historians think a group of people from Tahiti emigrated to Hawaii in C.E. 1200 (an earlier group of Polynesians settled Hawaii many years earlier, but little is known about the original settlers). Display illustrations of the Polynesian canoes the Tahitians used for the voyage. You may want to take the class onto the playground and draw an outline of a Polynesian double-hulled canoe so that the children have some idea of the size of these boats. Share that the catamarans could hold as many as 50 people. Show that storage space would be limited.

2. Use the maps to show the distance from Tahiti to Hawaii. Members of the Polynesian Voyaging Society built a replica of a 13th-century canoe and sailed from Hawaii to Tahiti and back in 1976. The journey from Tahiti to Hawaii took 25 days. Explain the problem the sailors must solve: What should be taken on the voyage? Point out that the Tahitians did not know what they would find when they arrived in Hawaii, so they had to pack for both a long ocean voyage and an uncertain future. Present the children with a list of things the Tahitians could have taken with them: taro, coconuts, breadfruit, pigs, dogs, tools to repair the ship, weapons, extra sails, extra paddles, extra clothes, water, line and hooks for fishing, buckets, and shell jewelry. Have each group of five children generate a prioritized list of the items they would take with them if they were on the first voyage to Hawaii.

Your English learners will need some "sheltering" on the task requiring them to prioritize the items the Polynesians would select for an exploratory voyage. Working with your English learners in a small group, take some extra time to analyze each possible item, first being sure the purpose of the item (e.g., for *sails*, be sure they understand that wind powered the catamarans). Then, talk about the possible consequences of including or not including the item on the voyage.

(3) Unit Question 2: Where in our state, nation, and world would you find people using boats?

Map-Reading Activity

The children will identify port cities on coasts, rivers, and lakes. They will understand that not all port cities are located on ocean or gulf coasts; some are far inland (like Duluth, Cincinnati, and Kansas City).

Teacher Read-Aloud: Freighters

The teacher reads aloud the book, *Freighters: Cargo Ships and the People Who Work Them* (Ancona, 1985). The children will listen to their teacher read aloud, compare and contrast the design and function of a freighter with an ocean liner and a fishing boat, recognize the purpose of a canal, identify the locations of the Suez and Panama

Canals, and examine a world map to determine the most direct international trade routes between seven port cities.

(4) Unit Question 3: What types of jobs do people do on boats?

Pantomime: Working on a New England Fishing Boat

Content Objectives: Children will learn the tasks that must be completed by people who live in a New England fishing village.

Process Objectives: Children will *listen* to their teacher read a book aloud, *ask* questions about the content of the book, *identify* the tasks that people in the village must complete, and *dramatize* five of those tasks.

1. Read aloud *Surrounded by Sea: Life on a New England Fishing Island* (Gibbons, 1991). Afterward, ask the children whether they have questions or comments about the book.
2. Then focus on the different activities that take place on the island from season to season. On the chalkboard, make a list of the work that must be done: mending nets, repairing sails, loading equipment, bringing in the catch, and unloading the fish for processing. Have the children pretend to do each job.

Videocassette: Ships

The class will view the video, *Ships*, and learn about the different jobs on an ocean liner, focusing on the responsibilities of the cruise director, the engineer, the captain, the stewards, and the radio officer.

(5) Unit Question 4: How have boats changed over time?

History of Boats Lesson

Content Objectives: Children will learn that although the functions of boats have remained constant, their design and capacity (e.g., speed and size) have changed radically. They will learn about the design and function of seven famous boats.

Process Objectives: Children will *listen* to information presented by the teacher, *examine* illustrations of each boat, *distinguish* the differences among the boats, and *predict* how boats might be different in the future.
   The lesson will ask the children to examine each of the following boats:

- A Roman trireme
- A Haida canoe (the Haida are a Native tribe living in British Columbia and Alaska)
- The *Constitution* ("Old Ironsides")
- The *Great Eastern* (a ship powered by sail and steam)
- The *Queen Mary* (powered by engines)
- The *Nautilus* (first atomic-powered submarine)

1. Examples of historical boats can be taken from four books with excellent illustrations: *Into the Wind: Sailboats Then and Now* (Ofinoski, 1997), *The Book of Fantastic Boats* (Bernard, 1974), *Oars, Sails, and Steam: A Picture Book of Ships* (Tunis, 1952), and *Ships, Sailors, and the Sea* (Humble, 1991). For an illustration of the Haida canoe, use the Website of the Canadian Museum of Civilization (www.civilization.ca).
2. Prepare a time line that shows when each kind of boat was used; also prepare an illustration of each boat.
3. Display an illustration of each boat and discuss two features: (a) how the boat was powered and (b) how the boat was used. Ask questions that will help children see how each boat is alike and different from the one that preceded it.
4. Finally, have children predict how boats might be different in the future.

For children with learning disabilities, this would be a good opportunity to meet their needs by *dividing material into small, manageable units*. The important thing for teachers in this lesson is to keep focused on the content objective: To learn that although the functions of boats have remained constant, their design and capacity (e.g., speed and size) have changed over time. While this is shown most clearly by examining seven boats used at different chronological points, the objective can be achieved by looking at just the *Constitution,* which was powered by sails, and the *Queen Mary,* powered by powerful engines. This narrowed focus should help children with learning disabilities.

Song: "The Erie Canal"

Time for a song! Teach the class the American folk song "The Erie Canal." First, read aloud Peter Spier's picture book about the song, *The Erie Canal* (1970). Spier's illustrations show the horse- and mule-drawn barges that were used on the canal. Have the children look closely at selected illustrations of the barges. Discuss why the barges were pulled along by horses and mules. Speculate how the design of the barges could have been improved and what alternative power sources could have been used.

(6) Concluding Activities

Suchman Inquiry: What Makes Things Float?

Content Objectives: Children will learn why some things float and others do not. They will see that almost anything will float, regardless of weight, if it is supported by a large enough platform.

Process Objectives: Children will *observe* items of various weights placed in a tank of water, *predict* which items from a second set will float, *ask* questions attempting to resolve the paradox of why some heavy things float and some light things do not, and *propose* a rule that defines why things float.

1. This inquiry activity provides a cross-curricular link to science. Fill an aquarium with water. Then present this puzzler to the class: "Explain why incredibly heavy ships like ocean liners and aircraft carriers float."

2. First, show the class a lightweight item that will float in the tank (a paper clip). Ask the children whether the paper clip will float (they typically think it will). Then place the item into the tank (the item will float if you set it on top of the water horizontally rather than put it in vertically). Next, show a heavier item that will sink (a large nail) and ask the children whether the item will float (they will predict it will sink). Then place the item into the tank (the item will sink). Ask the class whether they can state a rule explaining why some things float and others sink. (Usually, children will conclude that heavy things sink and light things float.) Ask, "How can heavy ships like an ocean liner or an aircraft carrier stay afloat?" Tell the class to ask you yes/no questions as you continue the demonstration. Float plastic plates and trays in the tank as supports under items of differing weights. The children will eventually see that heavy items can float if the surface area of water underneath them is expanded (a heavy wrench will float in the tank if it is placed on a cafeteria-style tray).

Concept Attainment/Assessment

This activity will assess and reinforce children's understanding of the different functions of boats. The children will classify 10 boats into four functional categories: (a) Used to Move People, (b) Used to Move Things, (c) Used for Fishing, and (d) Used for War. The students will examine copies of illustrations of 10 boats (found from Websites, books, and encyclopedias).

Unit Test

The third graders will take a simple end-of-unit test. It is important to remember that any test designed for third graders must be brief and should fit the abilities of the children. This test should ask the children to respond to the following: Choose one boat that we have learned about during the past few weeks. Answer each of the following questions:

a. Which boat did you choose?
b. What makes the boat go?
c. What is the boat used for?
d. Is the boat a modern boat or an old boat?
e. Where does the boat go?
f. What jobs do people perform on this boat?

To help children choose, allow them to look at the illustrations of boats you used for the concept attainment lesson. Answer questions the children ask about how to complete the assignment. Give children plenty of time to finish writing their answers.

Permit your English-language learners to complete the test orally in either English or their first language if they cannot write simple phrases or sentences in English. For children with learning disabilities, this might be an opportunity to challenge them to expand their abilities to write sentences. The "test" will be difficult for a student with a disability. You might let such students respond first orally, allow them to write their answers, and then guide them to more correct form (spelling, sentence structure), This would be an example of *changing the criteria for success on a task.*

Segue Activity: Think-Pair-Share on Boats and Planes

Let's suppose the next unit for this class of third graders will be on airplanes. A simple segue activity is for you to pose these questions: "How are ships and airplanes alike? How are they different? The children will learn that despite the obvious differences between airplanes and boats, these serve the same functions (transport people, transport goods, or warfare). They will understand the significant differences between airplanes and boats (speed, size, and utility). Have each child work with a partner. First, each child thinks about the questions. Then the partners discuss their responses. Finally, the children share their responses with their classmates.

(7) Enrichment Activities

In Chapter 2, I wrote about several instructional modifications that could be used to meet the needs of gifted students. One technique is called *tiering assignments.* In such an approach, each unit has certain "core" assignments that all children complete. Every unit, however, should include opportunities for all children to explore topics of personal interest. Gifted students need chances to either examine additional topics (*breadth approach*) or examine topics previously covered at a deeper level (*depth approach*). At the same time, enrichment activities will allow you to help children who have special needs. For example, children who are having difficulty using a CD-ROM encyclopedia can be assigned to an activity that will give them an opportunity to become more proficient. Each child in the class should choose (or be assigned to) at least one enrichment activity.

Construction: Paper Boats

Using the directions in *Toy Boats to Make at Home* (Leeming, 1946) or *Let's Make a Toy Sailboat* (Stokes, 1978), show the children how to make one of three types of paper boats.

Oral Presentation on Semaphore

Have a group of children teach their classmates some of the semaphore alphabet (a system of visual signaling by two flags, held one in each hand, and each flag being a square constructed of one white triangle and one black triangle). The group can construct semaphore flags from black and white construction paper and dowel rods and then teach their classmates the first letters of the semaphore alphabet. This would be an example of a breadth activity in that it introduces a new topic not covered in the unit's core assignments.

Independent Reading

Children may choose to read one of the unit-related books you have brought to class. Each book should be displayed on a table or in a special bookshelf. Figure 4.10, at the end of this chapter, is a list of books that could be used for this unit. A student choosing to read *Ship* by David Macauley would be an example of a depth activity, allowing the student to learn a great deal more about sailing ships, a topic previously covered in the unit's core assignments.

Design a Fantastic Boat

Allow any child who wants to draw a picture of a fantastic boat. Encourage children to use their imaginations. Each boat should be different and unusual. *The Book of Fantastic Boats* (Bernard, 1974) could serve as inspiration. This would be a good activity for gifted students.

Encyclopedia of Boats

Some children may choose to create a class "encyclopedia" of boats. You will have to provide a booklet that has 10 photocopied pages like the sample in Figure 4.8. Two pieces of 9- by 12-inch construction paper can serve as the cover. Each page has a

Figure 4.8 Form for an Encyclopedia Entry, Grade 3

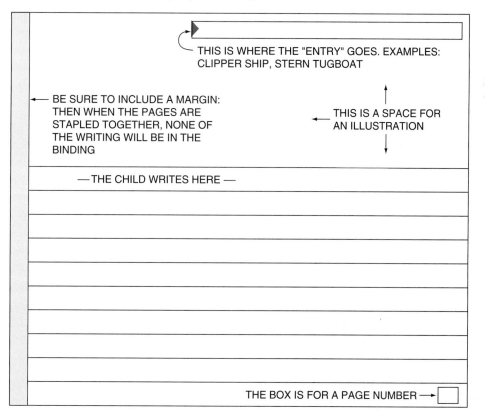

place for a title, an illustration, and a brief description. When finished, the children can arrange the entries in alphabetical order and then complete a title page and a table of contents. Help the children bind the booklet together.

Writing: My Voyage

Children who have taken a ride or trip on a boat can write simple autobiographical essays about it.

Part III: Unit Support Plans

Outline of Daily Plans: Unit Grid

The easiest way to make an outline of what will happen each day during the unit is with a unit grid. Figure 4.9 shows a grid for this unit.

Assessment Plan for Unit

The assessment plan for this unit is presented as Figure 8.5 in Chapter 8. All activities in the unit will generate behaviors and products that can be used for assessment. Certain activities, however, are particularly important for assessment purposes. You need to know to what extent each child has mastered the objectives for the unit and

Figure 4.9   Unit Grid for Boats

DAY 1	DAY 2	DAY 3	DAY 4	DAY 5
1. K–W–L chart 2. Field trip	1. Read aloud *Boats on the River* 2. Introduce independent reading	1. Jigsaw: Modern warships	1. Continue Jigsaw: Modern warships 2. Introduce Encyclopedia of Boats Project	1. Map-reading activity 2. Introduce Semaphore Project
DAY 6	DAY 7	DAY 8	DAY 9	DAY 10
1. Read aloud *Freighters* 2. Song: "The Erie Canal"	1. Video: *Ships* 2. Introduce Bulletin Board Project	1. Life on a New England fishing island 2. Introduce "My Voyage" writing	1. Inquiry: The Voyage to Hawaii	1. History of boats lesson 2. Introduce boat construction and design a fantastic boat
DAY 11	DAY 12	DAY 13	DAY 14	DAY 15
1. Sing "The Erie Canal" again 2. What makes things float?	Individual and small-group work	Student presentations on semaphore and the bulletin board	1. Individual and small-group work 2. Concept attainment lesson	1. Unit test 2. Segue-Boats Planes

met the standards the unit addresses. Here, again, is a summary of the assessment plan for the unit:

Objective 1: What are the different types of boats, and why are they different? Activities used for assessment:
- Field trip to harbor
- Concept attainment lesson
- Unit test

Objective 2: Where in our state, country, and world would you find people using boats? Activities used for assessment:
- Map reading
- Inquiry—"Voyage to Hawaii"
- Unit test

Objective 3: What types of jobs do people perform on boats, and how have those jobs changed over time? Activities used for assessment:
- Bulletin board display
- Videocassette—*Ships*
- Unit test

Objective 4: How have boats changed over time? Activities used for assessment:
- Bulletin board display
- History of boats lesson
- Unit test

Figure 4.10   Children's Books: Grade 3 Unit on Boats

INFORMATION BOOKS

Ancona, George. *Freighters: Cargo Ships and the People Who Work Them.* This book is too difficult for most third graders to read. The photographs, however, are a good source of information.

Barton, Bryon. *Boats.* Illustrated by the author, this is a very easy reading book, within the capabilities of almost every third grader. Barton's illustrations are a problem: They are cartoonlike and lack the realism a good information book requires.

Bernard, Christine. *The Book of Fantastic Boats.* Illustrated by Roy Coombs's brilliant, full-color illustrations of boats through the ages, this book includes novelties such as the first submarine (the *Turtle,* 1776) and the *Popoffka,* a 19th-century Russian warship that was round! More able third-grade readers can understand the text.

Carter, Katherine. *Ships and Seaports.* Illustrated with photographs, this book is very easy reading.

Cook, Nick. *The World's Fastest Boats.* Illustrated with photographs. This book, which can be read by most third graders, shows catamarans, hydrofoils, and several types of jet engines.

Freeman, Marcia. *Fire Boats.* Illustrated with photographs. This is a very easy-to-read book.

(continued)

Figure 4.10 **Continued**

Gibbons, Gail. *Surrounded by Sea: Life on a New England Fishing Island.* This book tells of one year, season by season, on an island off the coast of Maine. Most third graders could read this book.

Hartford, John. *Steamboat in a Cornfield.* Illustrated with historical photographs, this is a picture book about an incident in 1910. The steamboat *Virginia* went aground while traveling on the Ohio River. An excellent book, the period photographs are fascinating. A good choice to read aloud.

Humble, Richard. *Ships, Sailors, and the Sea.* Illustrated by several artists, this book is part of the superb "Timelines" series. Although it is difficult for third graders to read, the detailed, full-color illustrations of historical ships are an excellent resource.

Kalman, Maira. *Fireboat: The Heroic Adventures of the John J. Harvey.* Author/illustrator Kalman tells the story of a New York City fireboat, launched in 1931, retired many years later, and then called into service on September 11, 2001. Almost all third graders can read this book.

Kentley, Eric. *Boat.* Illustrated with photos and drawings. Part of the excellent "Eyewitness Books" series.

Lasky, Kathryn. *Born in the Breezes: The Seafaring Life of Joshua Slocum.* Illustrated by Walter Lyon Krudop. This is the story of the 19th century mariner who tried to sail around the world on his own. Able third graders can read it.

Lasky, Kathryn. *Tall Ships.* Illustrated with Christopher G. Knight's photographs, this book is too difficult for third graders to read, but the photographs are a useful teaching resource.

Lasky, Kathryn. *Tugboats Never Sleep.* Illustrated with Christopher G. Knight's photographs, this book can be read by most third graders.

Macauley, David. *Ship.* This is a fascinating book in two parts. In the first, archaeologists discover a 15th-century caravel. In the second, how the caravel was built is described. As with all his books, Macauley's drawings are great. Third graders will need help with the text.

Ofinoski, Steven. *Into the Wind: Sailboats Then and Now.* Illustrated with photographs and drawings. Easy reading, the book shows many boats, including a jangada, a one-sailed Brazilian fishing boat.

Olney, Ross R. *Ocean-Going Giants.* Illustrated with photographs, this book can be read by most third graders.

Rand, Gloria. *Sailing Home: A Story of a Childhood at Sea.* Illustrated by Ted Rand. This book is based on the journal of Captain Masden, who sailed with his four children around the Hawaiian Islands between 1896 and 1910.

Rosenblum, Richard. *Tugboats.* Illustrated with the author's excellent drawings, this book is for more able readers.

Scarry, Huck. *Life on a Barge: A Sketchbook.* Illustrated by the author, this is a wonderful book about the author's trip on a barge in the Netherlands.

Scott, Geoffrey. *Egyptian Boats.* Illustrated by Nancy L.Carlson, this is a nicely done book that is easy to read.

Stetson, Emily. *Knots to Know: Hitches, Loops, Bends, and Bindings.* Illustrated by Marc Nadel and Sarah Rakitin. Throughout the years, sailors have known how to tie several unique knots in ropes. This excellent book teaches children to tie more than 50 different types of knots, though third graders will need help with the text.

Sullivan, George. *The Civil War at Sea.* Illustrated with photographs. Excellent photos of ships used in the American Civil War.

Tunis, Edwin. *Oars, Sails, and Steam: A Picture Book of Ships.* The text is written for older children, but the author's artwork is one of the best sources on the history of boats.

Van Tol, Robert. *Submarines.* Illustrated with photographs, this is a book that most third graders can read.

Wormfield, Hope Herman. *Boatbuilder.* Illustrated with photographs, this is a good book to read aloud. It is about Ralph Stanley, a sailboat maker who lives and works in Maine.

Zeck, Pam, and Zeck, Gerry. *Mississippi Steamwheelers.* Some third-grade readers can handle this book, which is illustrated by George Overlie.

FICTION

Brown, Marcia. *Henry-Fisherman.* Illustrated by the author, this book was a Caldecott Honor book in 1950. It is within the reading ability of most third graders and tells the story of a boy living in the Virgin Islands.

Fisher, Leonard Everett. *Sailboat Lost.* This is a wordless picture book with wonderful illustrations by the author. In the story, high tide takes a boat out to sea.

Flack, Marjorie. *Boats on the River.* Illustrated by Jay Hyde Barnum, this 1947 Caldecott Honor Book is a perfect book for this unit. Flack's poetry describes a ferryboat, a paddlewheel riverboat, an ocean liner, a tugboat, a motorboat, a sailboat, a rowboat, a freighter, a submarine, and a battleship. The illustrations are bright and accurate, although the book does show its age.

Kay, Verla. *Tattered Sails.* Illustrated by Dan Adreasen. Kay's verses describe the journey of one family from England to America in the 1600s.

Molloy, Anne Stearns. *Shaun and the Boat: An Irish Story.* Illustrated by Barbara Cooney, this book is for more able third-grade readers.

Spier, Peter. *The Erie Canal.* Illustrator Spier has taken the lyrics to this folk song for his text. His illustrations have accurate historical detail. For the teacher, background on the canal is provided.

Van Allsburg, Chris. *The Wreck of the Zephyr.* Illustrated by the author, this is a picture book fantasy about a sailboat that could fly. Most third graders can read it.

Effective Teaching in Today's Diverse Classroom: The unit on boats includes several features that make it appropriate for children with learning disabilities. First, the unit uses a *wide range of resources:* books with excellent illustrations, Websites, children's books, encyclopedias, a video, a field trip, and maps. This will help children who are not proficient readers learn the content the unit presents. The K–W–L activity will help children *activate their background knowledge* about boats. As children hear their classmates talk about boats, they will recall things they know. For our English learners, this unit has a great deal of "*comprehensible input.*" The picture books read aloud by the teacher have simple texts and excellent illustrations. Lessons are supported with the use of illustrations. Many activities, like the inquiry on the voyage to Hawaii, feature *cooperative learning*. Group work will push children into their zones of proximal development and provide the *contextual support* English-language learners need to succeed. Many children learn best through *the arts*. This unit provides learning experiences in the performing arts (the pantomime and singing of "The Erie Canal") and the visual arts (bulletin board display and design a fantastic boat). *Firsthand experiences* make it easier for all children to learn new things. Many children will see real boats for the first time on the field trip. The mixture of *whole-group, small-group,* and *individual* activities allows more able children to be challenged and permits children who are particularly interested in boats to satisfy their curiosity.

Chapter 5

Cooperative Learning: Enhancing Skills and Knowledge Through Group Activities

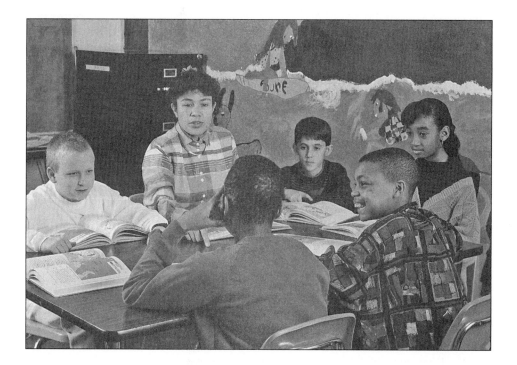

This was the last day of Rosa Navarro's third-grade social studies unit on boats. For 13 days, the children had participated in a variety of activities. The third-grade teachers at Ms. Navarro's school chose transportation as an organizing theme for the first half of the school year (the second half would be devoted to the history of their community). After the unit on boats, Ms. Navarro planned on teaching a unit on airplanes. Today, the final lesson on boats would be a "segue" activity, one that led the class to the unit on airplanes. This simple activity would use a cooperative learning structure called *Think–Pair–Share.*

On a sheet of chart paper, Ms. Navarro had written the following questions:

- How are boats and airplanes alike?
- How are they different?

In the first phase of the activity, she asked the children to think quietly about each question. She encouraged them to write down any answers they had to either question. She then asked the children to sit next to their "buddies." (Ms. Navarro assigned each child a different buddy each week so that, during the year, every child in the room would get a chance to work with every other child.) After each set of buddies was "paired up" and ready to share their answers, Ms. Navarro asked one member of each duo to give an answer and then the other. She allowed time for partners to chat casually about the similarities and differences of their responses. Finally, Ms. Navarro called the class back to their seats. It was time to share responses with the whole class. Tiffany and Maria volunteered to go first. Tiffany stated that they made a list of the many ways boats and airplanes were alike ("They carry people around," "They go faster than walking," "They come in many sizes"). Roger noted two differences: Boats only travel on water, but airplanes travel in the air, and the fastest airplanes were "a lot faster than the fastest boats." The sharing continued for another 10 minutes.

This was a good social studies activity for two reasons. First, it accomplished the goal of forming a bridge from one unit of study to another as Ms. Navarro's class started thinking about the content of their next unit—airplanes. Second, every child in the room had the opportunity to express his or her ideas. In most class discussions, only a few children talk; most children spend their time listening. In Think–Pair–Share, all 28 children in the room had an opportunity to express their perspectives.

• • •

In this chapter, you will read about

- The fundamental reasons why cooperative learning is a powerful instructional tool for teaching social studies
- Several cooperative learning structures, including Group Projects, Jigsaw, Think–Pair–Share, Three-Step Interview, and Student Teams–Achievement Divisions (STAD)
- Factors that affect the success of cooperative group learning; the development of group goals, individual accountability, social skills, and effective planning

- Decisions teachers make to organize cooperative groups; how to place students in groups, when to use ability and interclass grouping, how long members of groups should work together, and when to change group dynamics

◆ Introduction to Cooperative Learning

Collaboration and cooperation among students have been essential parts of social studies for more than 100 years. During the Progressive era (about 1890–1940), students in elementary schools frequently worked on projects with their classmates. One of the greatest Progressive thinkers, William H. Kilpatrick (1918, 1925), proposed that social studies consist almost entirely of students working on projects they selected and planned. This was the ultimate "child-centered" approach: Children would study what they found interesting. Although students could work on projects individually, Kilpatrick encouraged group work. His three characteristics of a successful project are worth remembering in the broader context of cooperative learning: Children should be involved in "purposeful activity" conducted in a "hearty fashion" in a "social surrounding" (1918, p. 321). Recently, educators have shown intense interest in instructional formats that require students to work together in groups. New models for group work have been developed, and hundreds of studies have been conducted. Today, when educators talk about cooperative learning, they usually refer to the contributions of Spencer Kagan, Robert Slavin, David Johnson, and Roger Johnson.

Let's look at two definitions of cooperative learning that epitomize these models:

> It involves students working together as equals to accomplish something of importance to all of them. (Slavin, 1990, p. 34)
> Cooperative learning means instructionally using small groups so that students work together to maximize their own and each other's learning. (Johnson & Johnson, 1992a, p. 45)

Spencer Kagan (1989–1990; 1997) has written about over a dozen cooperative learning *structures*. These structures are "content-free ways of organizing social interaction in the classroom" (1989–1990, p. 12). Kagan distinguishes cooperative "structures" and "activities":

> Teachers can design many excellent cooperative *activities,* such as making a team mural or a quilt. . . . In contrast *structures* may be used repeatedly with almost any subject matter, at a wide range of grade levels, and at various points in a lesson plan. (1989–1990, p. 12)

Robert Slavin (1990) prefers to call these structures "systematic and practical cooperative learning methods" (p. 21). I refer to them as either "models" or "structures" and describe five models of cooperative learning. First, though, let's take a look at the research that supports the use of cooperative learning.

◆ A Research-Based Rationale for Cooperative Learning

Research on cooperative learning shows that it can have positive results (Johnson & Johnson, 1998, Johnson & F. P. Johnson, 2005; Johnson, Maruyama, Johnson, Nelson, & Skon, 1981; Slavin, 1980, 1994a). Cooperative learning can boost student achievement, but we must keep two things in mind. First, almost all the studies have focused on learning basic skills in reading and mathematics. Second, to be effective, cooperative learning must involve *group goals* and *individual account-ability* (Slavin, 1992). Group goals exist when students work toward some reward for their group. Individual accountability means that each member of the group must demonstrate what she or he has accomplished. After reviewing 46 studies, Qin, Johnson, and Johnson (1995) concluded that cooperative effort produces higher-quality problem solving than does individual effort. This is an important finding because problem solving is an essential part of social studies. When confronted with a problem, students working in groups are able to exchange information, share insights, and compare the worth of various solutions.

Virtually none of the best research on cooperative learning has looked at elementary social studies (Slavin, 1989–1990, 1994a). It seems safe to say that on the basis of research on cooperative learning in other areas of the curriculum and with older students, cooperative learning should be a part of our social studies program. Remember, too, the social studies curriculum is concerned with more than content. We also teach processes and values. Among the values we want students to adopt are a respect for diversity and a reverence for democracy. A good K–6 social studies program emphasizes social processes, which include working cooperatively toward a common goal.

A classroom of diverse students should have many opportunities for cooperative learning because research shows that the use of cooperative learning improves intergroup relations. Cooperative learning helps students of different cultural groups respect each other. It promotes positive feelings toward students with disabilities. Slavin (1989–1990) summarized the results of several studies:

> When students of different racial or ethnic backgrounds work together toward a common goal, they gain in liking and respect for one another. Cooperative learning also improves the social acceptance of mainstreamed academically handicapped students by their classmates . . . as well as increasing friendships among students in general. (pp. 53–54)

In addition to the research base, a theoretical argument can be made for using cooperative learning. Our common sense would tell us that "two heads are better than one." Interaction with other people exposes us to different perspectives and helps us clarify what we know. A compelling theoretical argument for cooperative learning was presented by the Russian psychologist Lev Vygotsky. He believed a gap exists between what children can learn and do independently and what they *could* learn and do if they had help. This assistance could be collaboration with an adult or peers (Vygotsky considered the best situation to be one where a child works with more capable peers). Vygotsky's ideas place great emphasis on the social aspects of learning. Fifty years before cooperative learning became part of the conventional wisdom, Vygotsky had already explained why it helps children learn (Vygotsky, 1962).

As with any instructional technique or resource, moderation in cooperative learning seems like a reasonable attitude. Teachers would make a mistake if we never used cooperative learning, and we would make a mistake if we used only it and excluded whole-group and individual activity. Let's take a look at five cooperative learning structures (a sixth structure, Group Investigation, is one of the models of inquiry presented in Chapter 6).

Group Projects

In the Group Projects cooperative learning structure, two or more students work together to produce something. In social studies, Group Projects fall into five categories:

1. *Inquiry projects,* in which students work together to solve a problem (they "produce" an answer)
2. *Written projects,* in which students work together to produce a written product, like a book or a script
3. *Visual arts projects,* in which students work together as they paint, draw, sculpt, or use another media to produce a work of art
4. *Performing arts projects,* in which students work together to act, dance, or sing in a performance
5. *"Combination" projects,* in which students are asked to use more than one format (e.g., some projects require students to do things in both the visual and the performing arts); a written product often results from an inquiry

Group Projects work best if students volunteer to participate. Once students volunteer, these become "interest" groups because the members have expressed an interest in the project. Sometimes, though, we as their teachers assign students to work on a project. We might want to create a group that is heterogeneous and has a mixture of genders, ability levels, and ethnicities. Or we might decide that some students need to participate in a project because they have not chosen previously to do so. Some students, for example, never choose to participate in a performing arts project unless it is a requirement.

The big issue in planning a Group Project is what role each student will play in the common task of finishing the project. In some cases, the students themselves will decide what each member of the group will do. In others, we will assign the tasks. On some projects, students work together throughout the project, whereas on others, group members complete tasks individually, and their efforts are reassembled at some later point.

Here is an outline of the steps in a Group Project in the social studies. They are written from the teacher's point of view, but notice how, in each step, student autonomy can be increased:

1. *Form the group.*   For greater student autonomy, we should ask for volunteers.
2. *Provide an overview of the project.*   In some situations, students themselves will define precisely what they will produce. In every case, teachers should listen to the interests, ideas, and needs of the group members and make adjustments accordingly.
3. *Decide what each student will do.*   In performing arts projects, this means assigning roles. In writing projects, it means listing what will be written and by whom. If we wish to increase the level of student control over the project, then we should allow students to decide what roles they will play.
4. *Make a list of materials and resources.*   We should be sure that all materials and resources will be available when they are needed.
5. *Establish a timetable.*   The timetable for completing the project should include times when the entire group will meet again. In some projects, it may be best to let members of the student group establish the timetable.
6. *Work with individuals, subgroups, and the full group.*   We should have a schedule indicating when we will provide guidance and assistance to members of the group. To increase student autonomy, we should encourage them to help each other before they turn to us.

John Paul Endress/Silver Burdett Ginn

For over 100 years, groups of elementary school students have worked together on social studies projects. One member of a group puts the final touches on a mural.

At the end of the chapter is a description of a Group Project that produced a chronological mural.

Student Teams–Achievement Divisions (STAD)

Robert Slavin (1989, 1992, 1994a) has been an effective advocate of cooperative learning. He and his colleagues at Johns Hopkins University developed several cooperative learning structures. One of the most popular is Student Teams–Achievement Divisions (STAD; Slavin, 1978, 1994b). According to Slavin, STAD is "most appropriate for teaching well-defined objectives with single right answers, such as specific locational characteristics in geography and some map skills, knowledge of events in history, and principles of economics or government" (1992, p. 21). Thus, STAD should be limited to teaching students basic information. STAD is not a method of teaching; it is an *alternative* to independent seat work (during which, at the conclusion of a lesson, students work alone on follow-up assignments).

The teacher places students in four-member heterogeneous teams that are a cross section of the whole class—boys and girls, a mix of ethnicities, and high-achieving, mid-achieving, and low-achieving students. The teacher presents a lesson or group of lessons to the whole group, and then the students work together to learn the material. This "team study" may take from a half hour to several days. Slavin recommends that the teacher prepare worksheets for the students to complete together. STAD works only if all members of the team accept that it is their responsibility to help their teammates learn all the material the teacher presents. The teacher then gives a quiz that students take individually. The teacher compares each student's quiz score with that student's performance on earlier social studies quizzes and gives each student a score that reflects how much that student exceeded her or his average previous performance. The four scores for each team are added to create a team score, and the teams with the highest scores are given points, certificates, or some other reward. Following are some examples of instructional objectives that would lend themselves to units using STAD:

- *Grade 2.* Explain what role each of the following plays in keeping our community safe: firefighters, police officers, public health inspectors, public works crews, school crossing guards.
- *Grade 3.* Identify the following places on a map of our city: Miller Elementary School, City Hall, Olive Park, Verdugo Park, McCambridge Park, St. Joseph's Hospital, Bob Hope Airport, Media City Mall, NBC Studios, Warner Brothers Studios, Golden State Freeway, Ventura Freeway.
- *Grade 5.* List and describe three examples of "checks and balances" in the U.S. Constitution.
- *Grade 6.* Compare and contrast the Aztec and Inca systems of government, economic production and distribution, religion, and social organization.

Jigsaw

Jigsaw was developed by Elliott Aronson and his colleagues (Aronson, Blaney, Stephen, Sikes, & Knapp, 1978). Here is how it works: The teacher places students in six-member groups, also called "home teams" (a class of 30 students would have five home teams). The teacher then breaks down a topic or unit into six subtopics. For example, if a class of students were to do a unit titled "City Workers," the six subtopics might be (a) police officers, (b) firefighters, (c) recreation leaders, (d) sanitation workers, (e) librarians, and (f) animal control officers. Each member of a home team is assigned a subtopic and is expected to become an expert on that subtopic.

Students then learn about their subtopics. Aronson describes Jigsaws in which students would be able to read a section of a text to find out what they needed to know. (I think Jigsaw works well when students learn from a variety of sources, including videos, computer-based resources, audiotapes, and lessons taught by the teacher.) Once students learn information about their topics, they then meet in "expert teams." For example, the six students who all had learned about firefighters would meet together, the six who had learned about recreation leaders would meet, and so on. In these expert team meetings, students can compare what they found out and decide on how they wish to present what they learned to the other members of their home team. Students then return to their home teams. Each student is an expert who has information to share. The students take turns teaching the other members of their home teams all they have learned.

Landorf and Lowenstein (2004) provided an excellent example of how Jigsaw can be used in an elementary school classroom. They described how a third-grade teacher in Florida, Jennifer Morrow, used Jigsaw to help her students investigate the "Rosa Parks Myth." Ms. Morrow followed a classic Jigsaw design, with five home teams. Each member of each home team was assigned to one of five expert teams. Each expert team, with one member from each home team, examined a different children's book about Rosa Parks. Ms. Morrow strictly defined the roles of the members of the expert teams. Each group had a *facilitator,* who made sure each person had a chance to speak; a *scribe,* who recorded the conclusions of the team; a *manager,* who kept the team members on task; a *conductor;* who kept track of time; and a *communicator;* who talked to the teacher if the team had questions.

Think–Pair–Share

Think–Pair–Share is a simple cooperative learning structure that works well in social studies (Lyman, 1992; Lyman, Foyle, & Azwell, 1993). Think–Pair–Share greatly increases the number of students who actually say something during a class discussion. If a teacher leads a discussion in front of the whole class, few students actually make contributions. Rarely do more than a quarter of the class do anything but listen; it is not unusual for three or four students to dominate. In Think–Pair–Share, every student in the class will have an opportunity to express her or his perspective. This cooperative learning structure has three phases:

1. *Think.* The teacher poses a question that should stimulate a discussion. The question cannot be too difficult or too simple. If the question is too difficult, then students will have nothing to say. If the question is too simple, then all that can be said will be over quickly. I think the question should be written either on the chalkboard or on a sheet of chart paper. All students then think about possible answers. Depending on the complexity of the question, the teacher might want students to write their answers on paper. For a third-grade unit on the future of their city, a teacher could ask her students to answer any of the following questions through Think–Pair–Share:

   • What challenges would our city face if its population increased significantly in the next 20 years?
   • Which of the city's businesses will grow in the next 20 years? Which of the city's businesses might have a difficult time?
   • What will the schools in our city be like in the next 20 years? How might they be different from the way they are today?

2. *Pair.* Each student then works with a partner. The partners explain the rationale that led to their answers. During this phase, each student in the class will have an opportunity to talk.

3. *Share.* Now the whole class reconvenes. The floor is open; students may share their answers with their classmates. If partners have arrived at a shared answer, then each partner may talk a bit about how the duo arrived at their answer.

Three-Step Interview

Like Think–Pair–Share, Three-Step Interview is a cooperative learning structure that maximizes student participation (Kagan, 1989–1990, 1997). Three-Step Interview is simple and can be used repeatedly during a social studies unit:

1. During the first step, the teacher asks a question (or questions). Again, the questions should be written on the board or chart paper, and they should be thought provoking. The class then separates into groups of four. Within each group, each student works with a partner. One partner is the interviewer and the other is the interviewee. For example, Ahmed, Ashah, Keiko, and Hideo are the members of a group. During this first step, Ahmed asks Ashah questions; Keiko asks Hideo to give his answers to the questions.

2. In the second step, students reverse roles. This time, Ashah interviews Ahmed while Hideo interviews Keiko. The Three-Step Interview works best when students learn how to ask follow-up questions, much like a good newspaper reporter: "Why do you think that is the answer?" "What

makes you think that?" Follow-up questions should be asked with respect, but they can be challenging: "Are you sure? What about _____ (some fact or idea the interviewee had not considered)?"

3. In the third and final step, the group of four reconvenes. In round-robin fashion, each student shares her or his answer.

◆ Making Cooperative Learning Work

Four features must be present for cooperative learning to be effective: (a) group goals, (b) individual accountability, (c) social skills, and (d) effective planning.

Group Goals

As Johnson and Johnson (1992a) note, "Students must believe that they sink or swim together" (p. 47). The Johnsons call this *positive interdependence*. The group must have a clear sense of what they are supposed to accomplish, and this goal must be shared and understood by all members of the group. Sometimes the group goal is simple. For example, in Think–Pair–Share, the partners have the goal of listening to each other and exchanging ideas. In a Group Project, the goal is to produce something. The Johnsons and Slavin believe that there must be tangible rewards for groups that accomplish their goals. I am not sure. I have seen many groups work together beautifully, and their only reward was their joy in creating something they were proud of. Tangible rewards include points (which can be redeemed for rewards) and certificates. I have seen rewards as diverse as popsicles and the opportunity to be first in line for lunch. If tangible rewards are given, then they must be given to each member of the group.

Individual Accountability

As Johnson and Johnson (1992a) explain, "Students learn together so that they can subsequently perform better as individuals. To ensure that each member is strengthened, teachers hold students individually accountable to do their share of the work" (p. 48). It is essential that each student's performance be evaluated. This does not necessarily mean assigning a score or grade to each student. It does mean keeping some sort of record that describes two things: (a) the student's performance in the process of working in a group and (b) the student's level of achievement in the *product* the group created. I describe ways of keeping evaluative records in Chapter 8, including an example from the chronological mural project described earlier in this chapter.

Social Skills

Johnson and Johnson (1989–1990, Johnson & F. P. Johnson, 2005) have discussed at great length the social skills students must master to be successful in cooperative learning. Students must "get to know and trust one another, communicate accurately and unambiguously, accept and support one another, and resolve conflicts constructively" (1989–1990, p. 30). Here are the four steps in teaching these social skills:

1. *Students must see the need for the skill.* For example, we can explain to our students how resolving conflicts quickly and fairly will help a group finish its assignment.

2. *Students must understand the skill.* Unfortunately, this book does not have enough space to describe fully the social skills of trust, communication, support, and resolution. I recommend the books the Johnsons and their colleagues have written (Johnson & Johnson, 1998; Johnson & F. P. Johnson, 2005; Johnson, Johnso1n, & Holubec, 1994). One simple method is to describe the words that are used in the social skill. For example, to support the other members of their group, students can say things like, "That looks great!" "Tell me more about where you found that out," "Let's be sure that idea is in our report," and "I haven't thought about that; thanks for bringing it up."

3. *Students must have many opportunities to practice these social skills.* Students must have frequent chances to work in groups, and teachers must monitor and support those students who work well together.

4. *Students must evaluate how well they are doing.* The Johnsons call this *group processing.* The group needs to talk about their successes and frustrations. Rather than focus on individual behavior, the group processing should bring clarity to the behaviors that make group work easy and pleasant.

Effective Planning

Some cooperative learning structures require minimal planning (Think–Pair–Share, Three-Step Interview). Other structures will work only if they have been thoroughly planned (Jigsaw, Group Project, Group Investigation, and STAD). For all cooperative activities, each of the following must be accomplished:

- *Be sure the goal is clear.* If a group is to perform a play, then the members of the group must know what the play will look like when it is performed. Will costumes be worn? How long will the play be? Where will the performances take place?

- *Be sure the goal is attainable.* That is, given the best of circumstances, will the group achieve the goal? If a group is given a task that is beyond their level of ability, expect lots of problems.

- *Be sure that roles are clearly and reasonably defined.* Each student must know what he or she is expected to do. If some students have to do a great deal of work and others little, this must be decided at the beginning of the activity and accepted by the members of the group.

- *Be sure the group has adequate materials and resources to finish their task.* Nothing will stop a group from being effective faster than a lack of books, paper, maps, or other essential resources.

- *Be sure that time lines are set and that members of the group adhere to them.*

◆ Other Issues in Grouping

What Is the Proper Place of Cooperative Learning in Social Studies?

In their overview of cooperative learning in social studies, Stahl and VanSickle (1992a) state that "cooperative learning strategies should not replace all other teaching strategies in the social studies classroom" (p. 4). Some activities will involve the whole class. Individual work has its place as children go about exploring topics of personal interest. Cooperative learning, however, helps make social studies social. It provides children with the opportunity to "learn and practice the knowledge, abilities, and attitudes necessary to function effectively within the social group and as part of the social community" (p. 4).

What Criteria Should Be Used to Place Students in Groups?

Most groups should be formed on the basis of either *interest* or *proximity*. Group Projects and Group Investigations work best when students volunteer to take part (thus, the basis for forming the group is interest in the topic or project). Simple cooperative learning structures, like Think–Pair–Share, lend themselves to proximity grouping; students work with whomever is seated near them. Almost all groups should be *heterogeneous:* Each group should be a microcosm of the class, with boys and girls from all ethnic groups. Each group should have students at a range of abilities. This is not to say that occasionally a group of girls (or boys) might be the only volunteers for a project. The point is that if segregation gets to be a pattern, then we should intervene and modify the composition of the group. For some cooperative learning structures, like Three-Step Interview, Jigsaw, and STAD, we will assign students to groups.

Ability Grouping.   The National Council for the Social Studies (NCSS) has issued a policy statement on ability grouping (NCSS Ad Hoc Committee on Ability Grouping, 1992). *Ability grouping* is the practice of placing students in groups on the basis of their level of academic achievement. It tends to happen more in elementary language arts and mathematics than in social studies. The research on ability grouping is voluminous and contradictory (Kerckhoff, 1986; Lou et al., 1996; Oakes, 1985; Slavin, 1987, 1989–1990). Although grouping students by ability can work in some subject areas if done properly (mathematics and reading), educators agree that students should not be placed in "permanent" ability-based groups. Ability grouping, unfortunately, often leads to the segregation of the least able, the challenged, the poor, and the linguistically different. Some activities during the year we plan just for our most able or least able students, but for the most part we should design our units so that students work in several different groups and with classmates of every ability.

Interclass Grouping.   Some schools use a form of interclass grouping for social studies, although this is more prevalent in language arts and mathematics. In a *departmentalized* elementary school, a fifth-grade teacher might teach three 2-hour social studies/language arts blocks each day. Other teachers would teach a mathematics/science block and the arts/PE block.

Team teaching has many forms. For example, two third-grade teachers may decide to rotate their students each day from 12:45 to 3:05 P.M. From 12:45 to 1:50, Teacher A teaches social studies while Teacher B teaches art. Then students change rooms, and from 2:00 to 3:05 P.M., Teacher A repeats her social studies lesson, and Teacher B repeats her art lesson. In a purer form of team teaching, three second-grade teachers may work together and share responsibility for the 90 second graders in their school. Together, they plan the week's activities for all the second graders. At different times during the year, each teacher would take the lead in planning a social studies unit. The other teachers would play a supporting role, helping fulfill the planning teacher's ideas.

How Long Should Students Stay in a Group?

The amount of time students should spend working in the same group varies. For some models of team learning, the teams should be kept together for several months (Vermette, 1998). Most other groups, however, will not exist for that long. Most groups should be ad hoc; they should exist until they achieve their goal, which may take from a few minutes to 4 or 5 weeks. A Group Project, for example, may take a month to complete, whereas a Think–Pair–Share group activity may last only a few minutes. Ideally, each student in a class should work with every other student in that class in a cooperative group sometime during the school year.

◆ Summary of Key Points

- Group work has a long history in social studies. For more than 100 years, elementary school children have worked together as part of social studies.
- Recently, cooperative learning structures have been used widely in elementary classrooms. Structures are models for organizing group work.
- Research shows that the use of cooperative learning improves intergroup relations.
- Cooperative learning structures include Group Projects, Jigsaw, Think–Pair–Share, Three-Step Interview, and Student Teams–Achievement Divisions.
- The following features increase the chances that cooperative learning experiences will be positive: group goals, individual accountability, social skills, and effective planning.

FOR FURTHER READING

- Much was written about cooperative learning during the 1990s, there have been fewer publications on the topic during the last five years. Most relevant to social studies is the fine little book *Cooperative Learning in the Social Studies: An Introduction to Social Study* (Stahl & VanSickle, 1992b). An excellent place to start your reading is the special edition of *Educational Leadership* devoted to cooperative learning (vol. 47, no. 4, December 1989/January 1990). It has articles by Kagan, Slavin, the Sharans, and the Johnsons. There are many books available on cooperative learning. I like Johnson and Johnson's *Learning Together and Alone: Cooperative, Competitive, and Individualistic Learning* (1998), Slavin's *Cooperative Learning: Theory, Research, and Practice* (1994a), and Vermette's *Making Cooperative Learning Work: Student Teams in K–12 Classrooms* (1998). If you want to know how to teach students the social skills necessary for successful group work, then read the books and articles by David and Roger Johnson cited in the text. For more on cooperative learning structures, try Kagan's book.

- As I have stated repeatedly, group work and cooperation have always been a part of social studies. The work of Alice Miel, a true giant in the field of social studies, has a great deal to say to all teachers, no matter where, when, or whom we teach. I recommend her book *Cooperative Procedures in Learning* (1952). Another old book I like is Ruth Strang's (1958) *Group Work in Education*.

- Also of interest: Edward De Avila, Sharon Duncan, and Cecelia Navarrete developed a curriculum based on cooperative learning to teach science to bilingual students. It is called *Finding Out/Descubrimiento* (De Avila, Duncan, & Navarrete, 1987a, 1987b). It is a good example of how to use cooperative learning to teach content to English learners. The Johnsons have proposed a cooperative learning model called "constructive controversy" that promotes critical thinking and the analysis of different perspectives on a single issue (Johnson & Johnson, 1992b). Taylor and Larson (1998) explain the advantages of using cooperative learning with students who have attention-deficit learning disorder. An excellent research review on grouping and social studies written by Nancy Winitzkey (1991) is found in *Handbook of Research on Social Studies Teaching and Learning*.

- A couple of good classroom applications: Shafer et al. (2006) describes a geography project where children worked in groups. Foncault (2000) explains how lessons on conflict management improved the cooperative learning experiences of her students.

LESSON PLANS AND INSTRUCTIONAL ACTIVITIES

Group projects have long been an important part of elementary social studies. Here you will read about one that integrates social studies and the visual arts: a group project for third graders, a chronological mural, revealing 10 periods of time in the history of their community.

Grade Three: Chronological Mural

Al Braccio's third graders spent the second half of the school year studying their city. Now Mr. Braccio thought it might be worthwhile to have a group of children create a *chronological mural* of the history of their city. A chronological mural shows several scenes in the order they took place. Previously, I listed the six steps in completing a Group Project like this one.

Step 1: Form the Group
Mr. Braccio asked for volunteers. Privately, he encouraged his two English-language learners (Sara and Ben) and his two lowest-achieving students (Cliff and Dan) to take part. All four said they would like to work on the mural. Six other children volunteered. It was a diverse group in gender, ethnicity, and ability (the group included high-achieving students, too).

Step 2: Provide an Overview of the Project
The next day, Mr. Braccio met with the group. He showed the children photographs of a mural that fifth graders had completed depicting scenes from U.S. history. Mr. Braccio told the group their mural would be similar and suggested eight possible scenes from their city's past:

- Morning at a Gabrielino village (the Gabrielino were the Native tribe that lived where their city now stood)
- Mission San Fernando Rey de España (actually a few miles from their city but very important)
- A wedding at the rancho that covered most of the land the city now occupied
- The house of the dentist who founded the city
- The teacher and her students at the first public school
- Workers entering the aircraft plant, which was the city's largest employer
- Actors, camera operators, and a director making a movie, another of the city's important industries
- Airplanes at the city's regional airport, which opened for commercial passenger service in 1975

The group discussed these scenes. Someone suggested they add a drawing of city hall. The other children agreed; this was not surprising because the old city hall was one of the places the children visited on their field trip of the city. Mr. Braccio suggested they add some buildings damaged in the earthquake of 1994. All agreed this would be a dramatic addition to the mural.

The group decided that, for each of the 10 scenes, they would provide an illustration, title, and a brief caption. The illustrations would be on large sheets of construction paper. When finished, the illustrations would be stapled to a large bulletin board. For example, for the earthquake scene, the title was "1994: Earthquake!" The caption read, "On January 17, 1994, a big earthquake shook our city; 750 buildings were damaged, and 47 people were hurt."

Step 3: Decide What Each Student Will Do

When the group met again, Mr. Braccio made a chart identifying the 10 scenes in their mural. He suggested that the group divide into five subgroups of two children each. Each pair would draw and describe two scenes. Mr. Braccio wanted to be sure Sara and Ben did not work together; he also wanted to separate Cliff and Dan. He made a list of the five subgroups and presented it to the group. Then each subgroup selected the scenes they would depict. Mr. Braccio made a chart showing the assignments:

Scene 1: A Gabrielino village—Sara, Debbie
Scene 2: Mission San Fernando—Ben, Denise
Scene 3: The rancho adobe—Sara, Debbie
Scene 4: The dentist's house—Brad, Claudia
Scene 5: The first school—Brad, Claudia
Scene 6: Old city hall—Cliff, Tina
Scene 7: Aircraft plant—Ben, Denise
Scene 8: Making a movie—Cliff, Tina
Scene 9: New airport—Dan, Amber
Scene 10: Earthquake—Dan, Amber

Step 4: Make a List of Materials and Resources

Mr. Braccio and the group decided they would need the following materials:

- Colored marking pens and crayons
- Large white construction paper (18 × 24 inches)
- Websites, including the site for the city of Burbank, California (www.ci. burbank.ca.us); the site for the Bob Hope Airport (www.burbankairport.com); and one for the San Fernando mission (www.californiamissions.com/cahistory/ sanfernando.html)
- Study prints (large photo reproductions) of the history of their city
- 10 copies of the softcover social studies textbook on the history of their city, which included other photographs

Photographs Mr. Braccio took while he and the class were on their field trip. (He had good photographs of city hall, the mission, the dentist's house, the first school, the airport, the aircraft plant, and buildings damaged by the earthquake.)

Step 5: Establish a Timetable

Mr. Braccio and the group met the next day to begin work. The 10 children agreed on the following timetable:

May 10: Pencil drawings finished for each scene
May 16: Final illustrations
May 17: Rough drafts for titles and captions completed
May 18: Titles and captions completed
May 19: Bulletin board "backed" with powder blue paper, title of mural stapled to board, illustrations and captions stapled to the board

Step 6: Work With Individuals, Subgroups, and the Full Group

This project was completed during the final social studies unit of the year, "Our City Today and Tomorrow." Of the 10 children who worked on the mural, only one set of partners had some problems communicating. Dan and Amber had some trouble working together; Dan wanted to draw both scenes, which gave Amber nothing to do but the captions. Mr. Braccio helped them resolve their differences by leading them to discuss their scenes and agree on the composition of each one. Then they were directed to draw and color both scenes together.

The students did a good job adhering to the timetable, although one group fell behind because they had trouble getting started. Once Mr. Braccio helped them "block out" their drawings, they moved along fine. After the mural was finished and displayed for all to see, each student was proud of what he or she had created.

Note: While these 10 students were working on the chronological mural, other students were engaged in different projects in groups or independently. One class group looked at what the city might look like in the year 2100 and illustrated a book to share their ideas. Another group conducted a Group Investigation to determine why people might immigrate to their city.

Effective Teaching in Today's Diverse Classroom: Group Projects like this one and all other forms of cooperative learning will enrich the educational experiences of all children. Kagan's research shows how consistent use of cooperative learning can improve intergroup relations. Cooperative learning has great appeal to students who thrive in instructional formats requiring social learning (see Chapter 2).

Cooperative learning is also essential for English learners. Children have the ability to provide comprehensible input to their classmates who are English learners. A student often can explain a difficult idea to someone his or her own age with more clarity than an adult can. Cooperative learning, if done properly, creates an environment free of anxiety because students relax when working with their classmates. Sometimes you will want your English learners to work together under your guidance (so it is easier for you to provide comprehensible input). Usually, though, you should disperse your English learners so that they gain the benefits from working with their English-only classmates.

Chapter 6

Inquiry and Critical Thinking: Challenging Students with the Complex and the Controversial

et me begin this chapter with a memory from my own teaching experience. An important part of the fourth-grade curriculum in Burbank, California, was the study of California history. Each year, my fourth graders viewed a filmstrip on the California missions, which were built under the direction of Franciscan missionaries between 1769 and 1823. I remember this filmstrip because it featured excellent photographs of the missions (today, filmstrips have been replaced by computer-based delivery systems). I preferred showing filmstrips without their accompanying narration so the class and I could linger on interesting images and discuss them.

In the middle of this filmstrip was an old drawing of a group of Natives attacking a mission clergyman (padre). The padre was bound with ropes, and the Natives were beating him with clubs. In previous years, when my classes viewed the same filmstrip, this image did not generate any interest. This time, Susan, one of the students in my class, raised her hand and asked, "Mr. Zarrillo, did that really happen? I don't think anybody would attack a priest." Instead of answering the question, which would have been impossible because I did not know the answer, I decided that the question would make an excellent inquiry. It also would be a wonderful opportunity to challenge the students to think critically. I responded by saying I did not know the answer but that a small group of students could work with me to find an answer. We worked for a month to answer Susan's question. It was an exciting and challenging experience for the students who participated. This inquiry project provided all the students in my class with a better understanding of how California's Natives suffered during the mission era. In this chapter, I describe how to design inquiry activities and how to develop critical thinking. You will learn more about how my students found an answer to Susan's question.

• • •

In this chapter, you will read about

- Social studies instruction that is structured around inquiry-based activities
- A general teaching sequence for inquiry activities that requires teachers and students to play roles different from those they traditionally play in social studies lessons
- The Group Investigation and Suchman inquiry models
- Factors that will enable all students to participate successfully in fun and challenging inquiry activities
- *Critical thinking,* also referred to as *complex thinking* or *higher-order thinking*
- A taxonomy provided by the National Council for the Social Studies (NCSS) that can be a useful source to order the development of critical thinking skills
- Four instructional approaches that can be used to teach critical thinking skills to elementary school children
- The use of traditional, hard-copy resources and multimedia resources to use with inquiry activities and develop critical thinking

◆ Inquiry: An Overview

This chapter describes how to plan inquiry activities and how to help students engage in critical thinking. First, let us look at inquiry. *Inquiry* is a process that begins when a problem is identified either by students or by the teacher. Students then consider the problem, offer possible solutions in the form of hypotheses, gather information, and analyze what they have learned to determine whether a hypothesis is a reasonable solution to the problem. Finally, the initial hypothesis (or hypotheses) is accepted, revised, or rejected in favor of a different solution (Massialas & Cox, 1966; Wilen & White, 1991). Some social studies educators use the term *problem solving* to describe the inquiry process. The goal of inquiry activities is to help students acquire the ability to resolve problems in a rational and systematic fashion.

Inquiry, or problem solving, has a long history in elementary social studies. John Dewey, as you will recall from chapter 1, was the greatest thinker of the Progressive era of American education, which began in the late 1800s. Dewey (1933) used the term *reflective thinking* to describe the type of inquiry-based activity he thought should be at the center of Progressive schools. To Dewey, an activity requiring reflective thinking presented children with "a forked-road situation, a situation that is ambiguous, that presents a dilemma that proposes alternatives" (p. 14). Dewey thought that the social studies curriculum should give children opportunities to engage in reflective thinking and to become "versed in the methods of experimental inquiry and proof" (p. 217). In Dewey's view, inquiry should be child centered as children define problems and develop plans to gather data and reach solutions. Dewey's ideas continue to serve as the basis for many models of inquiry teaching.

The 1960s saw the introduction of the "New Social Studies" programs. Many of these programs were "inquiry based" because most lessons in a unit of study were based on problem-solving activities. These inquiry-based programs were greatly influenced by Jerome Bruner (1960, 1961). Bruner used the term *discovery learning* to describe inquiry activities. He wanted children to acquire "an attitude toward learning and inquiry, toward guessing and hunches, toward the possibility of solving problems on one's own" (1960, p. 97). Bruner thought that children should solve problems the same way as real-life social scientists and become child versions of anthropologists, sociologists, economists, and historians. Many New Social Studies inquiry-based curricula were exciting and challenging for both students and teachers.

Brophy (1990), however, noted several difficulties with these innovative programs. Many problems were too difficult for children. Some activities were based on hypothetical communities or countries, and children did not spend enough time studying real ones. Too often, inquiries were entirely teacher centered. Teachers or the textbook defined the problem and dictated how to solve it. These "problem-solving" activities were really exercises with predetermined answers. Keep these criticisms in mind as we look at how to design inquiry activities.

One factor that should encourage more teachers to plan inquiry activities with their students is the abundance of teaching resources available on the Internet. Thousands of documents, images, and other items that would have been out of reach for teachers are now easily accessed. For example, Rulli (2005) provided a list of sources relating to citizenship education that can be found on the Web. Imagine being able to use many of the resources in the Smithsonian Insitution (www.si.edu)! An excellent resource for teachers to use when planning inquiries based on Internet resources is the Web Inquiry Projects site developed at San Diego State University (Molebash, 2004).

◆ A Teaching Sequence for an Inquiry

Researchers do not agree on the exact steps an inquiry should follow. For example, Eggen and Kauchak (2001), Massialas and Cox (1966), the Sharans (Sharan & Sharan, 1989–1990; 1997), and Suchman (1962, 1966) each developed a unique sequence for an inquiry. A synthesis of their methodologies would be as follows:

1. Define the problem.
2. Speculate on possible answers.
3. Gather information.
4. Analyze the information and test hypotheses.
5. Reach a conclusion.

Let's now take a closer look at each step.

1. *Define the problem.* The social studies textbook may provide the problem, we may pose the problem, or students may generate the problem. A certain excitement accompanies questions that come from students. Recall the opening vignette to this chapter; Susan's question was a good example of the motivational power of a student-generated question. When she questioned the authenticity of the drawing, several other students agreed with her, and they were determined to find an answer! Depending on the series, textbooks can be a source of good questions for inquiries. These questions are often at the end of the chapters under subtitles like "On Your Own" or "For Further Research." When we plan a unit of study, we should be sure to look at the suggested inquiries in our textbook series.

   Inquiry questions can be placed on a continuum. The worst are those that have simple answers that can be found in a single source. A question like "What agricultural products are raised in South Africa?" is only an inquiry if the definition of that term is broad. To answer such a question, students do not need to go through the entire sequence of steps to find the answer; such questions are merely exercises in using reference materials. Better, but not perfect, are inquiry questions that have complex answers and require data from more than one source. An example is "Why do people live in our community?" Students can speculate on answers, gather data through a survey, and then reach conclusions. Another example is "How was elementary school in colonial times different from elementary school today?" This question would require students to consult several sources of information and make comparisons with their own classroom and school. The best inquiries have no single correct answers, usually because authorities in the field disagree. Examples are "What happened to the lost colony of Roanoke?" and "Who built the Easter Island monuments and for what purpose?" Questions like these require data from many sources. Because even authorities do not agree on an answer to such a question, students will reach a solution solely on the merits of the data rather than by finding verification of their hypothesis in a book. Figure 6.1 illustrates the range of inquiry questions.

2. *Speculate on possible answers.* After the inquiry question is refined and agreed on, we need to help students make *educated* guesses on possible answers. The discussion will reveal how much students know about the problem. In this sense, the hypothesis-generating discussion will help us assist students in finding information. Some inquiries are done individually, but most involve small groups of students. It is not necessary that all students agree on one possible answer; they may have several hypotheses. Sometimes students may not be able to make a realistic guess, and then we need to broaden their background knowledge before they look for answers. Hypotheses should be recorded, and as the inquiry progresses, they may be revised.

In my class's inquiry into the attack by California Natives against a mission priest, a group of five students agreed to resolve the question. Two competing hypotheses were advanced: One member of the group speculated that the picture was accurate, that the Natives had killed a

Figure 6.1 Range of Inquiry Questions

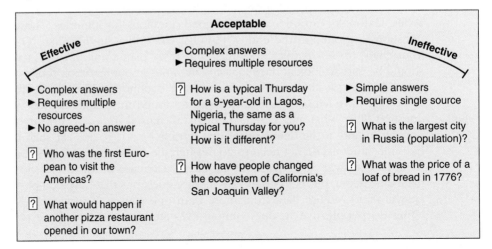

priest; the other students hypothesized that, for some unknown reason, the picture was a fake.

3. *Gather information.*   After students have speculated on possible solutions to the problem, it is time for them to gather information. We can break down our question into subtopics and assign students to look for answers in different sources (e.g., Aimee scans the Internet, Fred checks the encyclopedia, and Li looks at information books). It is best if students play a leading role in developing the "research" plan. Our role will vary, depending on the complexity of the question, the abilities of our students, and the difficulty of the sources of data. In some situations, we may only need to point students in the right direction. In others, we may need to locate materials and help students read them.

   Many sources of information can become a part of a research plan:

   - *Bibliographic and computer-based information.*   Inquiry activities provide perfect opportunities for students to master the use of both computer-based sources (e.g., the Internet and CD-ROM encyclopedias) and hard-copy references (e.g., encyclopedias and almanacs).
   - *Primary sources.*   The best inquiries ask students to look at original, historic material such as diaries and old newspapers. When an inquiry leads to a primary source, students are doing history like real historians.
   - *Surveys.*   Many inquiry-based activities can be based on contemporary issues. For example, one group of third graders was commissioned by the principal to investigate what all the school's students thought about a revised lunch schedule. Should the school move the lunch period up an hour? The third graders surveyed their schoolmates to find out the answer to this question.
   - *Miscellaneous resources.*   Just about any teaching resource can be used in an inquiry. For example, an inquiry to determine the links between ancient Egypt and ancient Greece would require an examination of maps, charts, graphs, films, videocassettes, filmstrips, audiocassettes, prints, realia, CD-ROM and hard-copy encyclopedias, the Internet, and information books. We should not limit our students; rather, we should encourage them to seek information from all appropriate sources.
   - *Direct observation.*   Although this data source is essential in the natural and physical sciences, it is more difficult to use in the social sciences, especially in the elementary grades. Many inquiries, however, can be answered through direct observation. A visit to a harbor, for example, helps students answer the inquiry "What different jobs do people perform at the harbor?"

   In my class's inquiry into the attack on the mission priest, students searched through old fourth-grade textbooks, information books in the library, and encyclopedias. In addition, at my suggestion, one student wrote to three professors of California history, each at a different campus of the California State University system. This inquiry activity took place before widespread use of the Internet; today, we could have checked many Websites. My favorite is "Spanish Missions of California" (http://library.thinkquest.org/3615/). This site was developed by two high school students in southern California, is full of useful information, and is written at a level that most fourth graders can understand.

4. *Analyze the data to test the hypothesis.*   Analysis of the information students gather is fairly simple in an inquiry: How do the data support or challenge our hypotheses? As students gather information, they will do one of three things with each of their initial hypotheses: (a) reject it as being too far from the data to be supported, (b) revise it because the information gathered supports some aspect of the hypothesis but not all of it, or (c) accept it because the information indicates that the proposed answer was accurate.

In my class's inquiry, students found that a few Native uprisings took place but not many. Interestingly enough, each professor written to wrote back, and *each gave us a different answer.* This was an eye-opener for my students, who at that point seemed stunned that "authorities" would not all give the same answer. Despite the disagreements, all the professors did support the answer the information books had given—that isolated incidents of Native rebellions against mission priests did take place.

5. *Reach a conclusion.*   In the final step of the inquiry, students state an answer and share it with the class. Although most inquiries will result in definitive answers, some will be left "dangling." In some instances, the best that can be done is to state a few possible solutions and admit that the data do not warrant a final answer. In other instances, the concluding statements may lead to a new inquiry, and the process can begin again. Whatever the results, students should share what they have learned with their classmates. Following are several possibilities for doing this:

- *Computer-based multimedia.*   Several computer-based possibilities are suitable for "reports." In many classrooms, students are posting their findings on a class or school Website. Students also can create multimedia reports on a CD-ROM through the use of a software program like Hyperstudio. Another possibility is a "virtual museum" (Ricchiuti, 1998) that becomes part of a school Website.
- *Written material.*   Students can write a book or issue a short summary of their inquiry.
- *Illustrations.*   Sometimes the answer to an inquiry can be presented visually by using illustrations or photographs displayed on a bulletin board, on an overhead projector, or via computer-based technology.
- *Charts and graphs.*   The best way to share numerical data is to communicate the results with charts or graphs.
- *Oral reports.*   Oral reports are more successful if students rehearse, if the report is brief, and if the report summarizes the process students followed to find the answer.

My fourth graders' inquiry concluded when the group made an oral presentation to their classmates. To support their presentation, they compared the three answers the professors offered.

◆ Inquiry as Cooperative Learning: Group Investigation

Group Investigation is an instructional model that combines inquiry teaching with the principles of cooperative learning. A group of students choose a question to investigate and attempt to find possible answers. To answer the question, some group members explore subquestions. Finally, the group makes a presentation to their classmates that summarizes the findings (Gallenstein, 2000). Group Investigation has its roots in the Progressive ideas of John Dewey and has been refined by the Israeli scholars Yael Sharan and Shlomo Sharan (1989–1990; 1997). The Sharans developed their model from earlier work done by Miel (1952) and Thelan (1960). Group Investigation should follow six consecutive stages:

1. *Stage 1: Identify the question to be investigated and organize the group.* Again, the best questions are asked by our students. For each unit we teach, we should develop a list of questions that could serve as the focus of a Group Investigation. Once a topic is chosen, it should be phrased as a question. The question should have more than a single simple answer, or else the Group Investigation model will not work. In this first stage, we and our students must decide whether the topic in question can be better answered by dividing the investigation into subtopics.

2. *Stage 2: Plan the investigation.* In this stage, students decide what each member of the group will do. For example, two members of the group will read nonfiction books, another will use CD-ROM encyclopedias, a fourth will surf the Internet, and a fifth member of the group will write a final report. The group decides what resources they will need. Sharan and Sharan suggest that the group write a plan describing how and when the investigation will be completed.

3. *Stage 3: Carry out the investigation.* Group members gather information, take notes, compare their findings with those other members of the group, and state possible answers to their question.

4. *Stage 4: Prepare the final report.* Quite appropriately, Sharan and Sharan have a liberal definition of *report*. Some groups will report via computer, others will construct bulletin board displays, and some will perform skits. The key, of course, is that the final presentation answer the question the group has investigated.

5. *Stage 5: Present the final report.* We should work with our students to be sure the prepared presentation is comprehensible. Because it will be presented publicly, written material should be edited, and the final draft should be in an easy-to-read display format. If the final report is oral, then students should rehearse.

6. *Stage 6: Evaluate.* Each member of the group evaluates her or his experience. Simple questions can focus this evaluation: What went well for our group? When did we have difficulty? If we were to do another investigation, what would we do differently?

A problem, usually stated as a question, will motivate students to gather the information they need to find an answer. In this classroom, the search for answers takes place in a social studies center, complete with costumes, models of historical objects, and information books.

Suchman's Inquiry Model

The first two models of inquiry teaching I presented in this chapter are quite similar. Richard Suchman, however, developed a unique teaching sequence for an inquiry activity (Eggen & Kauchak, 2001; Suchman, 1962, 1966; Joyce, Weil, & Calhoun, 2003). Suchman developed his model of inquiry teaching for the process of investigating and explaining atypical natural phenomena. Although he based his model on the work of physical scientists, Suchman's procedures have been used successfully in social studies. The Suchman teaching sequence is concise, and an activity following the model can be completed in less than an hour because we provide all the information our students require. Another advantage of this model is that it encourages students to work together toward resolving the question. This model of inquiry is also called "discrepant event inquiry" (Yell, 2002) and resembles the game of Twenty Questions (Edgington, 2001).

A Suchman inquiry has five phases:

1. *The teacher presents a puzzling situation to students.* It is essential that the situation confuse the students and lack an obvious explanation. We then might display pictures, diagrams, or maps that visually reveal the

problem. Alternatively, we might use eyewitness accounts, newspaper reports, or diary entries. We can also provide students with a fact sheet, a list of information that cannot be presented visually. Whatever the resources, we should present the problem dramatically.

2. *Students ask yes/no questions to verify data.*   This is the unique aspect of the Suchman model. After we present the problem, students ask us questions that can be answered only yes or no. If a student asks a question that cannot be answered yes or no, then the question must be restated. At this point, the questions must relate to the information that has been presented and not attempt to answer the inquiry.

3. *Students ask yes/no questions to formulate hypotheses.*   Again, students may ask only questions that can be answered yes or no. This third phase is different from the second in that students should introduce possible solutions in their questions. Their questions should seek to support those solutions.

4. *Students state their explanations and discuss them.*   Each explanation should be fully discussed in the light of the data that have been revealed. Students should acknowledge the strengths and reveal the weaknesses of each hypothesis. During this phase, we have a decision to make: Should we tell our students "the answer"? This depends. If our students have come up with an answer that is close to the correct one, then we probably should acknowledge and reward them for their success. If our students appear frustrated because their answers do not seem adequate, then we might want to explain the answer to the problem. If students appear to be interested in gathering more data on the problem, however, then we should not give an answer; instead, we should encourage them to continue to investigate.

5. *Students analyze the inquiry process.*   One purpose of the Suchman model is to help students become more proficient at solving problems. After the activity is over, we should lead a discussion about the first four phases: What questions were most effective? How must members of the group work together? What questions might have been asked that would have led to a quicker or more definitive answer?

At the end of the chapter, you will find a description of a lesson using the Suchman inquiry model.

◆ Critical Thinking: An Overview

In social studies, the desire to move students beyond rote memorization to more complex modes of thinking has been a consistent goal for educators since the early 1900s (Parker, 1991). There are many definitions of critical thinking, but for social studies teaching and learning the focus should be raising questions about statements of fact and opinion and making judgments about the validity of those statements (Beyer 1985, Brophy, 1990). Other authorities sometimes use the terms *complex thinking* or *higher-order thinking* to refer to critical thinking.

Educators cannot agree, however, on what critical thinking is or how we can help our students become proficient at it (Wilen & Phillips, 1995). The variety of perspectives on critical thinking is reflected in the number of books that have been written about the topic (e.g., Beyer, 1987; Fisher, 2001; Ruggiero, 2003; Wallace, 2005). Beyond the question of just what types of thinking are "critical thinking" are several viewpoints on the relationship of critical thinking to content. Wright (1995) describes three ways of conceptualizing critical thinking. First, some authorities believe in a set of generic critical thinking skills. Once we learn them, we can use them to think about any topic. Second, critical thinking is different from subject to subject; that is, critical thinking in economics is different from critical thinking in history. Wright prefers a third view, that some critical thinking skills are transferable from subject to subject, and some are not. On a related issue, Olsen (1995) summarizes the arguments in favor of the position that, for our students to develop critical thinking, we as teachers must cover a topic in depth. This means that we should cover fewer topics each year because it seems that in-depth coverage presents more opportunities for our students to engage in critical thinking.

What Are Critical Thinking Skills?

Beyer's (1987) definition is that critical thinking involves assessing and judging statements. Within this definition are two parts to critical thinking: (a) an analysis of the data or evidence used to support a statement and (b) an evaluation of whether the data or evidence meets some standard of sufficiency. For example, young children could think critically about the following statement: "Our city has enough parks; we don't need any more." Thus, their teacher would lead the children to gather and analyze data relevant to the statement—data that look for answers to questions such as, How many parks does the city currently have? What are they used for? How many people use them each week? Are any people and groups unable to use the parks because of insufficient time or space? Then the teacher would show the children how to analyze the data by using agreed-on criteria. Finally, the children would have to make an evaluation—verbally, in writing, or with charts and graphs—indicating whether the current park system meets the needs of the community.

Other definitions of critical thinking are broader than the one offered by Beyer. Indeed, which thinking skills are "critical" seems to be a somewhat arbitrary decision. Perhaps it would be a good idea to look at one taxonomy, or classification, of social studies thinking skills. Of particular interest is a taxonomy developed by the NCSS Task Force on Scope and Sequence (1989) that mirrors Bloom's cognitive taxonomy (see Chapter 5). The NCSS Task Force delineated activities that identify lower-level to higher-level critical thinking processes. The six categories where these skills are ordered are listed here:

- *Classify information.*

    Identify relevant information.
    Group information in categories.
    Place information in sequence.

- *Interpret information.*

  State relationships among sets of information.
  Identify cause-and-effect relationships.
  Draw inferences.

- *Analyze information.*

  Divide a topic into subtopics.
  Detect bias in information.
  Compare and contrast the credibility of different accounts of the
    same event.

- *Summarize information.*

  State the significant ideas supported by the information.
  State conclusions based on the information.
  State hypotheses for future research.

- *Synthesize information.*

  Propose a plan based on the information.
  Speculate on what might happen if the information were different.
  Propose a solution to the problem related to the information.

- *Evaluate information.*

  Judge the source of the information to determine objectivity.
  Examine the technical accuracy of the information.
  Determine the currency of the information.

The sixth category of thinking skills lists criteria students will find useful in examining and evaluating sources of information. For example, when we admonish our students to "consider the source," we are requesting that they determine whether the information is appropriate for judging data. Several factors are crucial to considering whether sources are appropriate. One of the most obvious factors is if the data that are used to support a statement come from an unreliable or, in some cases, unprofessional source. If the answer is yes, then the validity of the data would be in question. *Objectivity* is another essential factor if we are to rely on information. Information provided by sources with a bias should be questioned. Modeling for students statements that indicate an author may be biased would alert them to look for a prejudiced opinion or study. Students should also consider the *technical correctness* of what they read. If, in the critical thinking exercise about the number of parks in the city, information on the level of park use was taken from a survey that improperly defined a sample (e.g., the first week of every month), then the information may provide an inaccurate portrait. Finally, *currency* is essential in social studies. Unless we are examining historical data, the older our information is, the less likely it is to be accurate.

Developing Critical Thinking Skills

Several specific instructional strategies have been promoted as essential for developing critical thinking (see books cited earlier in the chapter). Here, I discuss (a) the application of Fred Newmann's research on critical thinking in high school to elementary social studies, (b) Hilda Taba's instructional strategies for concept formation, (c) the integrative model of teaching reasoning and content developed by Paul Eggen and Donald Kauchak, and (d) a lesson plan model for teaching critical thinking while using visual and auditory resources.

Newmann's Research on Critical Thinking in Social Studies

Fred Newmann (1990a, 1990b, 1991) has conducted interesting research on the teaching of critical thinking in high school social studies classes. His findings should help elementary teachers become more effective in developing our students' ability to think critically. Newmann (1991) concluded,

> At best, much classroom activity fails to challenge students to use their minds in any valuable way; at worst, much classroom activity is nonsensical or mindless. The more serious problem, therefore, is not the failure to teach some specific aspect of thinking, but the profound absence of thoughtfulness in classrooms. (p. 330)

Newmann (1991) identified six dimensions that are fundamental for a classroom where critical thinking can be developed:

1. *Sustained examination of a few topics is better than superficial coverage of many.* Newmann noted that "sustained concentration" on a topic is essential for in-depth thinking (p. 330). If we are in a position to shape the social studies curriculum for the grade levels we teach, then we should limit the number of topics that are covered. When it comes to the development of critical thinking, less is more.

2. *Lessons must present content in a coherent, continuous manner.* Newmann reached this conclusion after observing secondary teachers, but this dimension is also crucial to elementary teaching. The content we present to our students should be logically sequenced and well organized. In other words, the concepts we teach should build on one another and be presented in a clear, predictable manner. For example, if a teacher is introducing third-grade students to some principles of economics, then she probably would conduct activities to help students understand the difference between producers and consumers before she explains the law of supply and demand.

3. *Students should be given an appropriate amount of time to think and prepare answers to questions.* As Newmann noted, "thinking takes time" (p. 332). I have found in my observations that teachers are uncomfortable with the silence that should follow a provocative question (it is as if they were engineers of a radio program and had been trained to avoid silent

times, which are called "dead air"). Critical thinking takes time, and one test of whether a question will stimulate complex thought is that it cannot be answered quickly.

4. *Teachers must ask challenging questions or present challenging tasks.* This dimension, of course, should go without saying. Newmann calls for questions and tasks that "demand analysis, interpretation, or manipulation of information" (p. 332). It takes courage to prepare lessons that are challenging because some students will find the experience frustrating. The frustration that some students feel when they are confronted with complex tasks is essential for their development as critical thinkers.

5. *Teachers should be models of thoughtfulness.* We should show interest in our students' ideas, explore alternative approaches to problems, show how to think through a problem, and acknowledge the difficulty in answering some questions. A good way to do this is to work through a problem with students and to "think aloud" so that students can see a model of critical thinking.

6. *Students should offer explanations and reasons for their conclusions.* Newmann noted that answers to "higher order challenges are rarely self-evident" (p. 333). Students must be encouraged to explain and support their conclusions. This can be a challenge for elementary teachers, but even our youngest students can be asked to explain why they have adopted a certain perspective.

Newmann's six dimensions are important because they provide a set of fundamental characteristics for creating a classroom environment where children can grow as critical thinkers.

Taba's Strategies for Concept Formation

Hilda Taba, whose ideas on the classification of content in the social studies curriculum were discussed in Chapter 1, developed a set of instructional strategies for teaching critical thinking through social studies. In fact, Taba may have been the first to use the term *instructional strategy*. Taba developed three instructional strategies to help children reason inductively. Each instructional strategy is actually a three-step teaching sequence. The three sets are used for concept formation, interpretation of data, and application of principles (Taba, 1967, Joyce, Weil, & Calhoun, 2003).

All three strategies are important. Here I describe the strategy for concept formation because it is simple, applicable to all the elementary grades, and particularly useful for social studies. Taba (1967) thought that the strategy for concept formation should be used at the beginning of a unit. I have found, however, that it works better as a concluding activity. The three steps of the Taba strategy for concept formation are as follows:

1. *Enumeration and listing.* In the first step, we begin the activity by asking students to compile a list—for example, "What are some items we can buy at the market?" "Who were some inventors we learned about this week?" "What are some facts we have learned about Mexico?"

2. *Grouping.* In the second step, we ask students, "Do you see some things that belong together?" (Taba, 1967, p. 93). Students may be right or wrong in their groupings; the important thing is that we encourage them to think about what characteristics the items in the list share and what distinguishes the items. We should help students see many possible ways the items can be grouped. For example, students might place the things they learned about Mexico into the following categories: (a) famous Mexican men and women, (b) names of Mexican cities, (c) things that Mexico produces, (d) Mexican songs and dances, (e) Mexican folktales, and (f) life in a Mexican city.

3. *Labeling and categorizing.* In the third and final step, we help students attach labels to the groups they have created. It may be necessary to rearrange lists or to create new categories.

The concept formation teaching sequence has many possible modifications. To make the exercise easier, we can provide the list of items. It is a good idea to put each item on a separate card so that it can be moved around as students define groups. We can also tell the students how many groups they should form (e.g., "The places we have listed can be placed into five groups"). If students find this type of activity very difficult, then we can also provide the titles for each group. Each of the adjustments, however, should serve as "training wheels." They should be discarded as students become more sophisticated in the process.

An Integrative Model for Teaching Reasoning with Content

Eggen and Kauchak (2001) developed an integrative model to teach reasoning while teaching content. This model is a teaching sequence designed for content teaching, especially social studies. The sequence has four phases: (a) describe and compare, (b) explain, (c) hypothesize, and (d) generalize.

1. *Describe and compare.* We present our students with information that can be presented through charts, graphs, illustrations, or written text. One strength of this model is that it lends itself to data presented through charts and graphs. Thus, the integrative model will provide students who are not good readers a chance to practice critical thinking. We ask very specific questions about the information. The students are expected to observe and describe the information. For example, the last unit of the year for a fifth-grade class was "The United States in the 21st Century." Their teacher had prepared a lesson using the integrative model and used Table 6.1 as the basis for the lesson. Then we ask students to compare different parts of the data. The logical place to start is with the most obvious similarities and differences between two sets of data. For example, if a group of students are looking at photographs of an ocean liner and a passenger jet, then we might direct students' attention to shape and exterior design. Charts facilitate making comparisons because two sets of data can be placed side by

Table 6.1 Chart for a Lesson Using the Integrative Model for Teaching Reasoning with Content: Grade 5—Where Will Americans Live in the 21st Century?

State	State Population by Year in Millions		
	1900	1950	2000
New York	7.27	14.83	18.98
Pennsylvania	6.30	10.49	12.28
Ohio	4.16	7.95	11.35
Texas	3.05	7.71	20.85
California	1.48	10.57	33.87
Florida	0.53	2.77	15.98

(Source: U.S. Census Bureau, www.census.gov.*)*

side. Finally, teachers should challenge our students to identify any patterns that emerge after comparing and constrasting the data.

2. *Explain.* So far, students have been asked to perform relatively easy thinking skills. Now processing becomes deductive. We ask students why some parts of the data are the same and other parts different. Students must speculate, and we must ask "why" questions that students have a reasonable chance of answering. Almost any set of data will suggest questions that require too much of the students, questions they simply cannot answer. Obviously, we should avoid those questions and instead develop "why" questions that will generate reasonable speculations based on the data.

3. *Hypothesize.* This phase is closely linked to the one before and the one after. Here we ask students to extend the explanations they offered in phase 2. We do this by presenting a hypothetical situation as the students are forced to apply what they have learned. For example, if we asked the students to think about travel by ship and by airplane, then we could present them with a variety of travel scenarios and the task of identifying which mode of transportation they would choose (e.g., "You need to get to Cairo as soon as possible" or "You want to relax while you travel").

4. *Generalize.* The final phase of the integrative model is a chance to summarize. The expectation is that students will state generalizations they have learned during the activity. Many students find this a difficult chore, and primary-grade teachers may have to provide considerable assistance. For example, we could provide the first half of a generalization and ask the students to write the second half (e.g., "If you want to get someplace in a hurry, then you should _____.").

Barbara Schwartz / Merrill

To solve inquiries, students must use a variety of resources, including maps with very small print.

At the end of the chapter there is a lesson plan a first-grade teacher wrote for an activity based on Eggen and Kauchak's integrative model for teaching reasoning with content.

Using Reference Books and Multimedia to Develop Inquiry and Critical Thinking

Inquiry and critical thinking activities can use any type of instructional resource. Many inquiries will require our students to access information in hard-copy reference books. Visual media, auditory media, and realia present excellent opportunities for elementary students to engage in interpretation and analysis. As students are taught to view and listen critically, they will become more proficient in their ability to engage in complex thinking.

Traditional, Hard-Copy Reference Books.   Even with the power of computer-based resources, our students should continue to search for information in traditional, hard-copy reference books such as encyclopedias, almanacs, and atlases. Several children's encyclopedias are available for elementary-age students, such as the *World Book* and *Scholastic Children's Encyclopedia*. Almanacs have mountains of statistical information. Older elementary students can learn to use adult almanacs, such as the *Time Almanac* or the *New York Times Almanac*. Each of these is updated and published annually. An *atlas* is a book of maps. Many social studies textbooks have a mini-atlas and a "gazeteer" (a dictionary of geographic terms). Two children's atlases I suggest are the *Children's World Atlas* (DK Publishers) and the *National Geographic Our World: A Child's First Picture Atlas*. A good source for teaching ideas with reference books is the column "Into the Curriculum," which appears regularly in the *School Library Media Activities Monthly*.

Teaching Students to use Reference Books.   Our students will learn how to use reference books as they use them to complete inquiry projects. We should plan some well-designed lessons that will help our students be more proficient when they use reference books. Too often, our reference skills lessons can become boring and meaningless. We should keep these lessons simple, and those students who have demonstrated their proficiency with reference books should be excluded from activities aimed at teaching them what they already know. Here are some types of lessons that will help our students:

- Lessons on the organization of an encyclopedia. Students must understand that information is arranged by topics (called "entries"), that entries are placed in alphabetical order, and that most encyclopedias have multiple volumes.
- Lessons on how to use a table of contents, an index, page guide words, and cross-references.
- Lessons on how to scan for specific information.

Once students have received this basic instruction, give them a chance to practice what they have learned. Here are some activities:

- *For practice with encyclopedias.*   Provide the class with access to a full set of encyclopedias. Give students topics and have them figure out which specific volume has an entry for each topic. A good way to do this is to write each topic on a separate index card (e.g., "wheat," "barley," "corn," and "rye"). Have students place each card in front of the appropriate volume.
- *For practice with a volume of an encyclopedia.*   Give each student several topics and have her or him find the page where each topic begins. Encourage students to use the guide words.
- *For practice using cross-references in the entries.*   Give each student the name of an entry and have the class write the cross-references that appear in their given entries. In some encyclopedias, the additional references are boldfaced. In others, they appear at the end of the entry.
- *For practice with a single entry.*   Provide each student with a copy of the same entry. Challenge students to scan the entry to find a specific date or bit of information (e.g., for "gold," find the three countries that mine the most gold annually).
- *For practice with an atlas.*   Ask students to use the table of contents and the index to find maps of continents, nations, states of the United States, cities, rivers, lakes, oceans, mountain ranges, and deserts.
- *For practice with almanacs.*   Give students topics and have them use the index to find the appropriate page number of each topic. In an almanac, the index usually appears at the beginning of the book.

Audio and Visual Resources

Teachers have a wide variety of auditory (or listening) media to use in our class-rooms. Sound can be recorded on audiotape or compact discs. The vinyl discs, or "records," that so many of us were accustomed to disappeared in most schools. Compact discs have tremendous potential as an instructional resource. Listeners are able to choose an appropriate selection easily by entering a number in the disc player. Whatever formats are available, recordings of music, interviews, and other sounds can be a valuable social studies resource (Cooper, 1989; Turner & Hickey, 1991).

Computer technology has given us a variety of ways to present pictures. Videodiscs (or "optical disks") are a type of laser disc that can store thousands of pictures. For use with a computer, all a student has to do is insert the videodisc into the computer's disc drive; type in a request for a picture of a certain person, place, or thing; and if such an image is on the videodisc, it will appear on the computer screen. For use with an entire class of students, videodisc images can be projected onto a screen with an LCD (liquid crystal display) placed on an overhead projector. Videodiscs are an improved technology over the more traditional study prints or the illustrations found in textbooks or reference books. Visual images can also be presented through CD-ROMs and Hypermedia. Many Web sites on the Internet present excellent visual images for social studies lessons. Finally, digital cameras are an improved technology for teachers, they are more cost effective than cameras using film. Teachers and students can use digital cameras to record images within their community (Berson, 2004).

Among traditional visual media, *filmstrips* are rapidly becoming a thing of the past. Filmstrips present a sequence of visual images called frames, typically with a synchronized audiotape narration. *Prints* include photographs and reproductions of paintings. When a print is enlarged for educational use, it is typically called a *study print*. There are other ways to share visual images with students. An image can be photographed, printed on a slide, and projected on a screen. Opaque projectors can be used to display images directly from books or magazines, although they are difficult to find now that schools are using their limited resources to purchase computer hardware.

Realia refers to real things (Braun & Cook, 1985; Lankiewicz, 1987; Rule & Sunal, 1994). The use of realia in social studies is essential because it provides three-dimensional objects for students to both see and touch (the visual media, whether print or video, are of course flat). Realia can be either the real thing or human-made models. The best lessons make use of *artifacts,* real things used by people. Some school districts have collections of items they lend to other schools (e.g., a branding iron, old coins, or a butter churn): We just have to send a request, the other district ships what we need to our classrooms for use during a unit, and we ship it back after we are finished with it. Other artifacts can be viewed only at museums (e.g., Native American baskets or an ancient Egyptian mummy). When we use realia in a lesson, we can follow the same teaching sequence we would use with visual media and auditory media. The goals of the lesson are the same: We want students to look closely, to notice all the relevant details, and then to engage in critical thinking based on what they have seen (or heard). For this discussion, let's assume that students are viewing a photographic slide projected onto a large screen:

1. First, we *link* the slide to what we previously covered in the unit of study. We need to do this before we show the image (or play the tape or let students examine the artifact). We can establish in several ways the connection between the slide and what students have been learning: discussion, a review of information on a chart, or rereading parts of a textbook.

2. Next, we place the slide in *context* by establishing time and place. This usually involves using a map and a time line. For some inquiry and critical thinking activities, however, we may want to eliminate this step because the challenge for students will be to determine the time and place of the slide.

3. Then, we ask students to take a *first look* (or *listen*). We ask them what catches their attention. What about the image on the slide would they like to learn more about? What questions do they have after a first look? We can do this by having small-group discussions or by having students record their responses in writing. For discussion, the cooperative learning structures of Think–Pair–Share and Three-Step Interview work well. Although this should go without saying, we must be sure the visual image can be seen by all students participating in the activity (and if students are listening to a tape or a disc, be sure everyone can hear it). If our equipment limits how large an image can be displayed, then we should have students view it in small groups. If we are using an artifact that students can touch, we should arrange a format that permits each student some time with the object.

4. Now, we lead students to a *focused examination* of the slide. We do this by asking them either to look for specific things or to narrow their focus to a certain part of the image (or tape or artifact). This is difficult to do with an audio recording because the recording will have to be replayed.

5. Last, we help students *interpret and analyze* the slide. Here are the types of questions we could ask:

    *   Challenge students to find *relationships* between the image on the slide and other things. For historic images, recordings, and artifacts, we can help students see the connection between the old and the contemporary. If students were viewing photographs of a fifth-grade classroom of 1900, then we could ask them to compare what they see with their own experiences.

    *   Help students use the visual image to make broader *inferences* about the people, the place, and the times that produced it. Photographs of the classroom of 1900, for example, would tell us about the relationship between students and their teachers.

    *   Work with students to help them detect *bias*. In many paintings, for example, the perspective of the artist leads to distortions of reality. It is

important that we share with our students biographic information about the artist so that they can critically analyze a painting or piece of sculpture for evidence of bias.

At the end of the chapter you will find a lesson plan written by a sixth-grade teacher for an activity that requires the critical analysis of photographs of a Roman coin.

Inquiry and Critical Thinking for All Students

Every student in our classrooms can be successful and enjoy inquiry activities and the challenge of being asked to think critically. Our students with disabilities and our English learners, however, may experience difficulty. For most English learners, inquiry and critical thinking activities can be difficult because the language associated with them is not comprehensible. Problems arise because of the students' level of English proficiency. With students with disabilities, the issue is not second-language acquisition, but rather the complexity of the task that makes things tricky. Notice that I have tried to use "conditional language" throughout this paragraph because it is a mistake to underestimate our students; they will succeed at times when we may not expect it. We can help our students with inquiry and critical thinking activities:

- *Use step-by-step guidance.*   Students with disabilities will need help at each step of an inquiry or critical thinking activity. Whereas students with less severe disabilities may breeze through, some students will need considerable help during each step of the process. Explicit instructions, delivered with patience, will be necessary.

- *Present information through charts, graphs, and pictures.*   Many students with reading difficulties will be unable to participate in an inquiry or critical thinking activity if all the data are written at a level they cannot read. The alternatives are obvious: Use charts, graphs, photographs, illustrations, or films to provide the information needed to resolve the problem. In this regard, the Suchman inquiry model and the integrative model for teaching reasoning with content have particular promise because they work well when the problem and the supporting information are presented visually.

- *Allow students to work together.*   Almost any child will be able to do more with help. This help can come from us, or it can also be provided by the child's more competent classmates. Thus, inquiry activities that may seem to be beyond some students are "doable" if the students work with their fellow students.

For English learners, we should also consider the following:

- *Use the primary language.*   Those of us who are bilingual and those with bilingual aides should allow our English learners to complete inquiries and critical thinking activities in their native language. Cummins (1979, 1986a, 1992) has made a convincing case that students who learn how to gather data and solve problems in one language will easily transfer those abilities to their second language. Because some important sources of information will be available in languages other than English, the ability to use non-English resources will be an advantage for our English learners. For example, if an inquiry project requires interviews of people living in the community, our bilingual students will be able to gather information from people who speak little or no English.

- *Remember that comprehensible input is the key.* We should be sure that the English we use when leading an inquiry or critical thinking activity is understandable. We may need to slow down, repeat things, and carefully consider our choice of words. It is important, when working with our English learners, to stop from time to time and ask questions to check whether students are following our presentation.

◆ Summary of Key Points

- Inquiry is a process during which a problem is identified. Then students speculate on possible solutions, gather data, analyze the data, and reach a conclusion.
- Two specific models for inquiry activities are the cooperative learning structure called Group Investigation and the Suchman inquiry model.
- Teachers should continue to teach students to use reference books (encyclopedias, almanacs, and atlases).
- *Critical thinking* has many definitions. This type of thinking requires students to go beyond rote memorization to analyze, synthesize, speculate, challenge, verify, and generalize.
- Fred Newmann identified six dimensions that are fundamental for a classroom where critical thinking can be developed.
- Hilda Taba developed instructional strategies to help children reason inductively.
- An integrative model for teaching reasoning with content provides a format for building content knowledge while students think critically.
- Visual media, auditory media, and realia are excellent resources to use for critical thinking and inquiry activities.
- With a skillful teacher, all students can participate successfully in inquiry and critical thinking activities.

FOR FURTHER READING

- On the topic of inquiry, I suggest the books by Clements, Fielder, and Tabachnick (1966) and Massialas and Cox (1966). Although these books are more than 40 years old, the ideas they contain are still valid.
- Good descriptions of inquiry activities for elementary students: Wieseman and Cadwell (2005) reported on a problem-based unit on the history of the Gunnison Valley in Colorado. Bisland (2005) reported on a group inquiry project for sixth graders on human-made landmarks. Carlson and Holm (1999) wrote about inquiry in the context of global education, and their article includes a useful matrix for inquiry processes.

- Dozens of books and hundreds of articles have been written on critical think-ing. Parker's (1991) chapter in *Handbook of Research on Social Studies Teaching and Learning* is very good, with an emphasis on critical thinking and decision making. I also like Clarke's (1990) *Patterns of Thinking: Integrating Learning Skills in Content Teaching.* If you want to challenge yourself, try the book of readings edited by Sternberg (1994), *Thinking and Problem Solving.*
- Shiveley (2004) wrote about using Websites to develop critical thinking. Ukpodoku (2002) offers suggestions for how to infuse critical thinking into a unit based on Lynne Cherry's (1992) picture book *A River Ran Wild.* Schneider and Gregory (2000) describe a critical thinking activity based on historical interpretation with Stanley's (1996) juvenile-level biography *Leonardo da Vinci.* Drier and Lee's (1999) article "Learning About Climate" includes data that would be perfect for a lesson following the integrative model for teaching reasoning with content.
- In addition to the lesson example provided in the next section of this chap-ter with a Roman coin, there are many other possible social studies experi-ences with coins. For example, Keiper and Larson (2000) describe a project that integrates art and history and challenges students to develop a design for a quarter. This project is patterned after the 50-states commemorative quarters, the first of which appeared in 1999 and the last of which will be minted in 2008. A resource similar to coins would be political campaign memorabilia, like buttons (Potter, 2004).

LESSON PLANS AND INSTRUCTIONAL ACTIVITIES

This chapter concludes with three examples of teaching that fosters critical thinking:

1. A Suchman inquiry lesson for fifth graders that challenges the students to explain why Samoset was able to speak to the Pilgrims in English in March of 1621
2. A lesson plan for first graders, using the integrative model for teaching rea-soning with content, on the differences between summer and winter
3. A lesson plan for sixth graders that requires analysis of a Roman coin

Description of a LESSON

Grade Five: A Suchman Inquiry—Samoset Greets the Pilgrims

Mrs. Kim's fifth graders were working on a 3-week unit on the Pilgrims. The class learned about the suppression of Separatist religious groups in England, how a group of Separatists first emigrated to Holland, the voyage of the Separatists and others to New England aboard the *Mayflower,* and the establishment of the Plimoth colony during January and February 1621. Her students had taken a "virtual field trip" to the wonderful living history museum of Plimoth Plantation, which is an exact replica of the Plimoth colony of 1627 (the tour is available on the Plimoth Plantation Website, www.plimoth.org). She used the Suchman inquiry model for a lesson about the appearance of Samoset, a member of the Abenaki tribe, in Plimoth on March 16, 1621.

Step 1: The Teacher Presents a Puzzling Situation to Students

Mrs. Kim started the lesson by reviewing what the students had learned so far. After looking at several sources on the Pilgrims, including Caleb Johnson's superb Website on the *Mayflower* (www.mayflowerhistory.com), she found the best description of Samoset's visit in an old book from the wonderful American Heritage Junior Library, *The Pilgrims of Plymouth Colony* (Ziner, 1961). She wrote and read aloud the following account of an event that occurred on March 16, 1621:

> March 16 was a cool morning in Plimoth. Most of the men had gathered in the Common House for a meeting. The women and children were busy with their chores. A small number of men with guns stood guard. Many of the Pilgrims were ill from the "General Sickness" that had killed over half the people who had sailed on the *Mayflower*. So far, the Pilgrims had only seen a few Natives. Each time, the Natives ran away and hid. But on the morning of March 16, one of the guards looked up and saw a Native brave walking toward the village. He was tall, with feathers in his hair. He was smiling and waving at the Pilgrims! The guards shouldered their rifles and were about to demand that he stop. Then the Native shouted at them, "Welcome, Englishmen! My name is Samoset!" Samoset talked to the Pilgrims in English for quite some time. He told them about the region near the settlement. He talked with them well into the night. The Pilgrims were astonished that Samoset could speak English.

> Mrs. Kim then said, "It was amazing that Samoset could speak English. How did he learn English?"

Step 2: Students Ask Yes/No Questions to Verify Data

Mrs. Kim explained that the class was to figure out how Samoset learned to speak English. She explained that the students could ask her any questions they wanted, but there were two rules: (a) She could only answer yes or no, and (b) their questions should try to get more facts. Most questions the students asked were appropriate:

"Had Samoset ever been to England?" (No.)
"Was Samoset really a Native?" (Yes. Students thought Samoset might be an Englishman in disguise.)

Eventually, students asked questions that served as the basis for two possible answers to this historic riddle:

"We learned about Jamestown, in Virginia. Wasn't that before Plimoth?" (Yes. Here, Mrs. Kim went beyond the Suchman format to locate Jamestown and Plimoth on the map. She wrote the year 1607, when Jamestown was founded, on the board.)
"Were the Pilgrims the first English people to visit New England?" (No.)

Step 3: Students Ask Yes/No Questions to Formulate Hypotheses

Mrs. Kim now moved to the third step, where students asked questions that would support possible answers. One group of students thought that Samoset had lived for a time in Jamestown. This answer worked until one girl asked, "Had Samoset ever lived at Jamestown?" (No.)

"Had he ever visited the English at Jamestown?" (No.)

Now, three students focused on the English who had visited New England prior to the coming of the Pilgrims. They asked, "Did Samoset ever talk to the English who visited New England before the Pilgrims?" (Yes.)

"Did he work for them?" (The answer to this is not clear because Samoset had sailed with English captains along the Maine and Newfoundland coasts. He may have served as a guide, or he may have just been along for the ride. Again, Mrs. Kim deviated from the Suchman model by replying that Samoset had sailed with English captains who had explored the New England and Canadian coasts.)

Step 4: Students State Their Explanations and Discuss Them

At this point, it was easy for students to state an explanation: Samoset had learned to speak English when he sailed along the coast with the English explorers.

Step 5: Students Analyze the Inquiry Process

Most students said they enjoyed this activity and wanted to do more like it. Some students complained that their classmates did not ask good questions. Mrs. Kim was satisfied with the activity, although she was disappointed that more students did not participate. Next time, she decided, she would modify the teaching sequence so that students discussed the puzzling event in small groups before they started asking questions.

Mrs. Kim planned the Samoset inquiry for two reasons: (a) She wanted her students to practice the critical thinking that is part of the Suchman model, and (b) she wanted to help her students understand a historical generalization: The English had considerable contact with New England and Canada before the coming of the Pilgrims. After the Samoset inquiry, she used a time line and a map to show the following events:

1497: John Cabot landed at Cape Breton Island in Canada.

1583: Sir Humphrey Gilbert sailed to St. John's, Newfoundland, and established a temporary English settlement.

1602: Bartholomew Gosnold explored the Maine coast and sailed to Cape Cod (he named it).

1605: Sir Ferdinando Gorges and George Waymouth landed on Monhegan Island off Maine. They supposedly took another Native, Tisqauntum (Squanto), back to England.

1607: Gorges and Sir George Popham established a colony at Sagadahoc (or Popham), Maine. The colony, which was to serve as a base for fishing, failed in 1608.

1614: Captain John Smith, one of the settlers of Jamestown, sailed along the New England coast from Maine to Cape Cod. He made a map and wrote a book, *A Description of New England,* that the Pilgrims took with them on the *Mayflower.*

Effective Teaching in Today's Diverse Classroom: Let me make this point very clear: All children need to take part in inquiry and critical thinking activities. Children with learning disabilities and English learners may well find these activities challenging, but to assign them to other, more simple activities, is to deny them the opportunity to fully develop as students. In many inquiries and lessons that require critical thinking, all children can succeed if we teachers make minor modifications in how we teach.

One important component of effective instruction for English learners is "primary language support." Primary language support for English learners can be provided by a bilingual teacher, an instructional aide fluent in the student's first language, or bilingual classmates. The support can be oral as the teacher explains an activity in the primary language, or it can be written. In this lesson, the description of Samoset's visit could be translated into the primary language(s) of the English learners in the class. The English learners could read the translation, or the translation could be read to them.

Children with learning disabilities would benefit from a "pre-lesson" coaching session. The teacher would meet with a small group of children who might be overwhelmed by this activity. The teacher would use the model on something not related to the social studies curriculum. Since the Suchman model is essentially the same as playing the game of "20 Questions," the teacher might play that came with objects in the room, like the flag ("I'm thinking of something in the room, you have to guess what it is by asking questions which I can answer with a *no* or a *yes*"). The teacher would help the children learn successful strategies for a Suchman inquiry, which include narrowing the possibilities, rather than guessing the answer ("Is is something in the front of the room?").

Grade One: Using an Integrative Model—Summer and Winter

Overview: To allow for more participation, the lesson was taught three times, each time to a group of seven children. The lesson was part of the thematic unit "The Seasons," which integrated social studies, science, language arts, visual arts, and performing arts.

Resources and Materials: The lesson uses a single resource—a large chart prepared by the teacher. The chart is divided in half, one side labeled "Summer" and the other labeled "Winter." Along the left side of the chart are three categories—"Special Things to Do," "Food," and "Clothing." Each "cell" is illustrated with photographs cut from magazines. For example, under "Summer" in the "Special Things to Do" cell are photographs of people at the beach, children playing baseball, and a family having a picnic in a park. Under "Winter" in the "Special Things to Do" cell are photographs of people making a snowman, children ice skating, and a family gathered indoors around a fireplace. (A large area of the United States does not have snowy, low-temperature winters; if you are located in this area, adjust your discussions of "Winter" cells with the children accordingly.) Under "Summer" in the "Clothing" cell are photographs of people in shorts, sandals, and T-shirts. Under "Winter" in the "Clothing" cell are photographs of people in winter clothing—show heavy jackets, mufflers, knit hats, and gloves. Under "Winter" in the "Food" cell are photographs of a man placing a stuffed turkey into an oven and of a steaming cup of hot chocolate. In contrast, "Summer" "Food" depicts an outdoor barbecue and a pitcher of iced lemonade.

Standard: Standard 15 for grades K–4 of the National Geography Standards is "How physical systems affect human systems." One performance expectation of this standard is that a student is able to "describe how humans adapt to variations in the physical environment, as exemplified by being able to list ways in which people adapt to the physical environment; e.g., choices of clothing" (Geography Education Standards Project, 1994, p. 134).

Content Objectives: Children will learn that weather is one factor that determines how people live. Regarding recreational activity, food, and clothing, children will understand the differences caused by winter and summer weather.

Process Objectives: Children will *describe* the recreational activities, food, and clothing that are typical of winter and of summer; *compare and contrast* photographs of summer and winter; *explain* why people participate in different recreational activities, eat different foods, and wear different clothing during summer and winter; *speculate* on which businesses do better in the winter and which do better in the summer; and *state a generalization* summarizing the relationship of weather to the way people live.

Teaching Sequence:

1. Before the lesson, prepare the chart and make a list of the key questions to be asked during each phase.
2. Divide the class into groups of seven children. Have each group sit on the rug, with the chart displayed nearby on an easel. Follow the five-step sequence of the integrative model:

    a. *Describe.*   Introduce the lesson by saying, "Today we are going to look at photographs of things we do, things we eat, and how we dress during the summer and the winter." Direct the children to each of the six "cells" in the chart (Summer/Special Things to Do, Summer/Food, Summer/Clothing, Winter/Things to Do, Winter/Food, Winter/Clothing). For each cell, the key question is, "What do you see in this photograph?" Be sure all significant details are noted. It is best to start with the clothing cells, and you may want to pantomime the differences between summer and winter (for winter, you might have the children shiver, rub their hands together, and say things like, "It's freezing out here!").

b. *Compare and contrast.*   Help the children make comparisons between each set of photographs. Start with clothing, where the differences are most noticeable. Ask the children to look first at the clothing cell for summer and then to look at the clothing cell for winter. Then ask, "How are the clothes we wear different in summer from the ones we wear in winter?" The children should note that winter clothes cover more of our bodies, they are larger, and they are thicker. Then ask the children to note differences between summer and winter food and between special things to do in the summer and in the winter.

c. *Explain.*   Ask the first graders why we need to wear different clothes in the summer and the winter, why we eat different foods, and why we do different things. The simple answer, of course, is that it is hot in the summer and cold in the winter. Probe further by asking questions like, "Why wouldn't hot chocolate be good at the beach?" "Why is it possible to barbecue in the summer and not in the winter?"

d. *Speculate.*   This will be the most difficult part of the lesson for the first graders. On the chalkboard, write the following: "You sell beach umbrellas," "You sell mittens," and other commercial activities that have a busy season. Ask the children to identify which businesses would do better in the summer and which would probably do better in the winter. Help them offer justifications for their answers.

e. *Generalize.*   Finally, help the children understand that the information presented in the lesson supports the statement: The weather is one factor that determines how people live. With first graders, the exact wording is not important. The opening question for this step should be something like, "What have we learned today?" A more specific prompt is, "Why do people do different activities, eat different foods, and wear different clothes during the summer and the winter?" The lesson on summer and winter should lead children to a simple conclusion: that weather is one factor that determines what they do, what they eat, and how they dress.

Effective Teaching in Today's Diverse Classroom: This activity would work well with any group of children experiencing difficulty reading grade-level textbooks. Although most social studies activities require students to read—and, in fact, social studies should be an area of the curriculum that helps children become better readers—it is important that not all lessons be based on a text. The goal of this lesson is to promote critical thinking. That goal can be accomplished without the use of written material. The medium used to stimulate thinking was photographs; thus, the lesson would be effective with English learners, especially those whose level of English proficiency allows them to participate in discussions but who lack the ability to read grade-level texts.

Grade Six: A Roman Coin

Overview: This lesson would take place during a unit on ancient Rome. It is planned for a group of approximately 25 students. An excellent source of information on Roman coins is the Website "Dead Romans" (www.deadromans.com). A good source for other Websites on ancient Rome is the "Schools of California Online Resources for Teachers" (SCORE) site (www.score.k12.ca.us).

Resources and Materials: (a) wall map of the Roman Empire; (b) piece of construction paper; (c) the time line created for the unit on ancient Rome; (d) a sheet of chart paper on which are written three facts about Marcus Aurelius; (e) two photographic transparencies (slides) of a Roman coin bearing the likeness of Emperor Marcus Aurelius, one for each side of the coin; (f) slide projector; (g) a sheet of chart paper on which are written focused examination questions (see the list in the following section "Focused Examination"); (h) copies of a photograph of Abraham Lincoln from *Lincoln: A Photobiography* (Freedman, 1987) and copies of a photograph of Franklin Roosevelt from *Franklin Delano Roosevelt* (Freedman, 1990); (i) several U.S. pennies and dimes.

Standard: This lesson helps students achieve both history and economic standards. In the *National Standards for History* for grades 5–12, standard 3A is that "the student understands the causes and consequences of the unification of the Mediterranean basin under Roman rule." One of the performance expectations under this standard is that "the student is able to analyze how Roman unity contributed to the growth of trade among the lands of the Mediterranean basin" (National Center for History in the Schools, 1996, p. 151). Standard VII of the National Social Studies Standards is "production, distribution, and consumption." For the middle grades, performance expectation is that learners can "differentiate among various forms of exchange and money" (NCSS, 1994, p. 96).

Content Objectives: Students will learn introductory biographical information about Marcus Aurelius, the characteristics of Roman coins, the relationship between economic activity and the need for money, and a shared characteristic of Roman and contemporary U.S. coins (the idealized images of leaders on the coins).

Process Objectives: Students will *identify* the reign of Marcus Aurelius (C.E. 161–180) on the time line, *recall* information they learned about the geography of and economic activity in the Roman Empire, *examine* slides of the coin, *list* three things that caught their eye about the coin, *speculate* on the reasons why economic trade and the amassing of capital requires the use of money, *compare and contrast* the photographs of Lincoln and Roosevelt with their images on coins, and *speculate* on the purposes of idealized portraits that are placed on coins.

Teaching Sequence:

1. *Link.*   Using a wall map, review the geographic boundaries of the Roman Empire in the second century of the common era. Then, help students recall what they have learned about economic activity during the height of the empire.

2. *Contexts.*   Ask a group of students to help you place a piece of construction paper underneath the reign of Marcus Aurelius on the time line. Share the information about Marcus Aurelius you wrote on a sheet of chart paper (e.g., he lived from C.E. 121 to 180). I would note that Marcus Aurelius was both a political leader and a philosopher. I think students would find it interesting to discuss his stoic philosophy that emphasized forgiveness, the absence of selfishness, and the common good. That, though, would require another lesson.

3. *First look.*   For most of the activity, students will work in groups of four. Project the slides and ask the students to "look at these photographs of the front and back of a Roman coin and write down three things that catch your eye." Then use the cooperative learning structure Three-Step Interview to allow each student to share his or her response. Reconvene the group and listen to three or four students present what they wrote.

4. *Focused examination.*   Now ask each group to take another look at the slides and, working as a group, to answer the following questions, which you listed beforehand on a sheet of chart paper:

    a. What general shape is the coin?
    b. What do you think the coin is made of?
    c. Do you see any writing on the coin?
    d. Are there any numbers on the coin? Write them down.
    e. What part of Marcus Aurelius can you see?

    Reconvene the whole group and share answers to the questions.

5. *Interpret and analyze.*   Working with the whole group, see whether you can help students discern the relationship between economic activity and the need for money. (Complex trade, the division of labor, many workers engaged in "service" jobs, and the amassing of capital require money; all were present in the Roman Empire. Notice that this lesson helps students acquire Standard 11 of the *National Content Standards in Economics* [National Council on Economic Education, 1997], which reads, "Students will understand that money makes it easier to trade, borrow, save, invest, and compare the value of goods and services.") You might ask them to imagine what would happen if we did not have money. Be sure students see the connection between the complex, international system of trade and exchange used by the Romans and the need for money.

    Next, have students once again work in their groups. Distribute the copies of the photographs of Lincoln and Roosevelt, the pennies, and the dimes. Ask each group to look closely and compare and contrast the photographs and the images on the coins. How are the portraits similar, and how are they different? Students should see that the images on the coins make

Lincoln and Roosevelt look very good (to make the comparison obvious, choose photographs of Lincoln and Roosevelt near the end of their days as president). Why? Why might an artist change the way a person looked when designing a coin?

Evaluation: Collect the written responses of each student. These will provide useful information on whether individuals were able to notice details on the Roman coin. You may want to tape-record the whole-group discussions. The tape will help you identify who is talking and whether students have engaged in the type of analytic, speculative thinking the lesson requires. You certainly should take notes while the students work in small groups.

The "Dead Romans" Website mentioned in the "Overview" section of this lesson can be read by more able sixth graders. Some students could use the site as a source of information to learn more about Roman coins (e.g., how they were made, what the inscriptions on these coins mean, when the coins were minted, and how to collect them).

Effective Teaching in Today's Diverse Classroom: The lesson was planned for the entire class (assuming approximately 25 students). For much of the activity, however, students worked in small groups of four. How would you assign your English learners to these groups? You have three choices:

1. If your English learners have an advanced level of oral English proficiency, then it would make sense to spread them out and place them with students who are fully proficient in English (e.g., one English learner with three fully proficient students). Because the data for the lesson are visual and require no reading, this arrangement should work. The English learners will benefit from the comprehensible input provided by their peers who are proficient in English.
2. If you have a group of English learners with limited oral English skills, so limited that they will not be able to converse with students who are fully proficient in English, then the English learners should be grouped together and work with you or an instructional aide. If you were working with a group of English learners on this lesson, then you would need to modify your vocal register. You would speak slowly, repeat things, and limit your vocabulary so that the English learners can understand the questions written on the chart paper.
3. Finally, if you have English learners who are in the first stages of acquiring English and who would not understand you even if you used a modified vocal register, then these students can benefit from the lesson only if they are allowed to complete it in their first language. It is, unfortunately, not always possible to find the resources (materials or personnel) to allow students to use their first language. If, for example, you have in your class an Urdu-speaking student who recently emigrated from Pakistan, my guess is that you will not have materials written in Urdu or Urdu-speaking teachers or aides to help you. If you cannot provide a setting where the lesson can be completed in languages other than English, then you must do your best to help your students who speak little English understand the lesson.

Chapter 7

Technology: Teaching with Computer-Based Resources

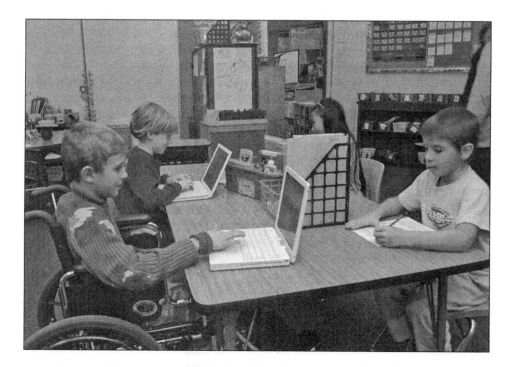

As part of a U.S. Department of Education grant, "Preparing Tomorrow's Teachers to Use Technology," I visited a fourth-grade classroom to observe students using computers. It was a valuable experience because the teacher, Dana Eaton, and his students had advanced technology skills. Mr. Eaton's classroom was equipped with seven computer stations. As part of the grant, I wrote brief summaries of my observations. All the activities I observed were designed to help students achieve California's fourth-grade History–Social Science Content Standards, which require students "to learn the story of their home state" (California Department of Education, 1998, p. 12). I saw students gather data from Websites, create their own documents and pages combining text and visual images, and use software to make time lines and plan a budget. I would like to share my summaries with you as follows:

Observation 1: While half of Dana's students worked at their seats, the other half worked in groups of two and three at the seven computer workstations. I watched his students use the Ditto.Com Website to find visual images for their reports on the California gold rush. This site has photographs, paintings, and drawings on almost every topic imaginable. There were both "content" and "process" outcomes for the students. They were becoming more skillful in "cutting and pasting" images from the Website onto their own files. At the same time, the images they saw increased their knowledge of events occurring before, during, and after the gold rush. There were challenges, though! I worked with one group who was responsible for producing a page on the Mexican War of 1846–1848. When they typed "Mexican War" into the locator on the Ditto.Com site, the first image they saw was a photograph of a 1997 funeral of a rebel soldier from Chiapas. This momentarily confused them until I explained the context of the photo. I look forward to my next visit.

Observation 2: Another eye-opening visit to Dana Eaton's classroom. This is helping me a great deal. I better understand the challenges teachers and students face while using computers. The children were doing a Martin Luther King Jr. scavenger hunt. This required the students to answer questions using a Website as a resource. The site had links to many other MLK sites. Dana's students are sophisticated Web users. They use the "bookmark" and "links" functions skillfully. Interestingly enough, some of the same old challenges remain. I worked with two students: One was very much "on task," and the other allowed anything to distract him.

Observation 3: Previously, I observed students use Websites as data sources. I asked Dana if I could observe his students working with computer software as a part of social studies. No problem! I watched Mr. Eaton teach a lesson on how to enter data into a program called TimeLiner, which allows students to create nice-looking time lines. I was surprised how easy it was for the fourth graders to cut and paste text and images from Websites into TimeLiner files. There really was nothing to it. This is a 21st-century alternative to taking notes from a hard-copy source, like an encyclopedia, and then composing a text for an annotated time line. Interestingly enough, one girl who knew very little English successfully completed this task.

Observation 4: This time, I accompanied the fourth graders to the school computer lab. Obviously, there are advantages to a lab with 30 workstations. Dana still assigned his students to work in pairs; he thinks there are significant advantages in having students share experiences on the computer. The lesson used a Website I had not visited, "Governors of California." The site had information on all of California's governors. Each pair of students gathered information on a different governor. Mr. Eaton had prepared a simple set of questions for the students to answer: What is the name of your governor? When did he serve? What was one important thing he did in office? What was happening in California while he was governor? What is one other interesting thing you read? All students were engaged in data gathering. With hard-copy resources, this would have been difficult.

Observation 5: Today I spent almost half an hour working with two fourth graders. They were on the computer using a spreadsheet to plan a budget for a hypothetical trip on the Oregon Trail in the 1840s. This was an obvious example of how software can change an experience. The spreadsheet did the math for the students—they were left with the challenge of allocating limited resources. The students dealt with a central concept of economics, scarcity.

• • •

In this chapter, you will read about

- Guidelines for keeping children safe while they use the Internet
- Suggestions for judging the accuracy of information found on a Website
- Factors that facilitate successful searches for information on the Web
- Virtual field trips and online expeditions—Web-based excursions for students
- The process of finding information in CD-ROM encyclopedias
- Computer-based resources that students can use to record and share what they have learned
- Instructional ideas that allow our students to use e-mail as part of social studies

The information age continues to bring significant changes to elementary school teaching and learning (Simpson, 2006; VanFossen, 2004a). Computer-based social studies activities occurs in almost every elementary school in the United States. Students communicate with people living in other countries via e-mail, the Internet has become the primary source of information for inquiries, and student projects are more likely to be posted on classroom Websites than on bulletin boards. There is no question, that computer-based technology can be a powerful tool for elementary school teachers, if used wisely to help students acquire social studies content, processes, and values (NCSS, 2006). In this chapter, our discussion will focus on teaching students to (a) gather information from computer-based resources, (b) record and share what they have learned in computer-based formats, and (c) use e-mail as a part of social studies activities. In each edition of this book, I have been able to make the same claim with a high level of certainty: Technology changes rapidly, and by the time you read this book, new and improved technology may well be in place.

◆ Gathering Information

The Internet and Elementary School Students

The Internet is a collection of networks made up of millions of computers. The Internet's most useful feature is the World Wide Web, which allows computer users to connect with a wide variety of resources. More and more students rely on the Web to find information. It is conceivable that the next generation of elementary school students will use the Internet to gather information and that hard-copy reference books will become obsolete. The cognitive processes involved with Internet fact-finding tasks are similar to those required for using a traditional encyclopedia or atlas. As Fitzpatrick (2000) notes, students "must be able to find information, sift out the relevant material, process it, identify patterns, and come up with meaning" (p. 33). The problem is that "in the digital universe, old constructs may not be appropriate, and students must be willing to explore paths that represent departures from the past" (p. 34). Certainly, the Internet has the potential to be the ultimate source of information for teachers and students (Berson, Cruz, Duplass, & Johnston, 2001; VanFossen, 2004a). In this section of the chapter, we look at issues relating to the process of finding information on the Web. The second section discusses what students can do with the information they have acquired.

Cybersafety: Keeping Children Safe When They Use the Web

Despite its great potential, the Internet poses significant dangers to children (Berson & Berson, 2004; Berson et al., 2001; Burgstahler and Utterback, 2000). We teachers must be sure that students do not come into contact with adults seeking face-to-face meetings with children ("cyberpredators"). We must be sure that students do not access Websites that have pornography, misinformation, or hate-based material. Federal law, the Children's Internet Protection Act (CIPA) passed in 2000, requires schools that receive federal funding for technology to take measures to protect children using the Internet. Most schools have chosen commercial filtering systems, which are problematic. Even the most reliable filtering systems can fail, and we teachers need to identify cyberthreats "as a real dilemma" and be "vigilant in responding to the needs of children for the sake of both safety and learning" (Berson, Berson, & Ralston, 1999, p. 161). The best way to protect our students is to closely supervise their Internet activities. One way to provide close supervision is to be sure that the computer screens in our classrooms face the center of the room and are easy to see. Teachers should use several tools to protect our students. In addition to close supervision, these include using effective filtering software that blocks access to inappropriate sites and implementing suggestions on Websites that address online child safety, like the CyberAngels Internet Safety Organization (www.cyberangels.org). Finally, teachers may want to consider a strategy advocated by Berson and Berson (2004): Teach children about the problems of privacy on the Internet directly. The authors propose a 12-step activity that does just that.

There are many things students should *not* do while working on the computer. Students should never give out personal information. This includes their full name, address, phone number, and name of the school. Students should never send a photograph of themselves to any location on the Web, nor should they engage in any kind of "conversation" through the Internet unless the teacher knows for sure who else is participating. Students should stop using the computer and tell their teacher if they find material that makes them uncomfortable or confused.

Accuracy of Information on Websites

No one should assume that information on the Internet is accurate, timely, clear, and important. Many adults have the perception that if something appears in print, then it must be true. Many of our students are even more gullible and are unlikely to know that any person with minimum computer skills can set up a Website. There are no restrictions on what a person can place on a site, and there are no requirements that the material be edited or reviewed. On the one hand, this has significantly broadened the range of information and ideas available to all of us. On the other, this freedom has allowed irresponsible people to disseminate misinformation for harmful purposes (Lee, 2002; Shiveley, 2004). In many teaching situations, your students will be accessing information that we teachers have recommended. Teachers must screen each site to make sure that the information presented is accurate. When our older students conduct their own searches, there is a chance they will find a site that is problematic. We should help our students evaluate Websites in the light of who provided the information and for what purpose, on the basis of how old the information is, and for the validity of the information when compared with other sources.

The following lists a number of criteria that can be used to evaluate information found on a Website (Risinger, 1998; Shively, 2004):

1. We teachers and our students should consider *who recommended* the site. A site recommended by a teacher or a librarian should be okay, assuming that person has done his or her homework. Sites recommended by authors of articles in professional journals also should be safe.
2. Second, the *source* of the information provided on the site should be evaluated. Who is the author that provided the information on the site? Is the site developed and maintained by a government agency, a university, or a private source? If the site is maintained by a private source, is it possible to contact the source to ask questions about the content of the site? Remember, a site may be the product of an individual who has an agenda that will severely bias the information presented.
3. The *timeliness* of the information should be considered. If a site is being accessed to find out more about a current event, then timeliness is a key factor. Is there evidence that the site is updated regularly?

4. Next, and this is difficult for children, the *mood* or "attitude" of the site should be analyzed. Does the site dispassionately present the information, or is there something edgy about the site that makes you feel uneasy? This is tricky, of course, because we want our students to learn about multiple perspectives on the historical past and contemporary issues. Many sites, however, that promote hate, conspiracies, and nonsense have home pages that look professional and legitimate. Once a student starts reading something that appears confusing, he or she should stop and ask for help.

5. Finally, there should be some attempt to evaluate the *accuracy* of the information on the site. Students will need help with this task. One way to judge the accuracy of the information on a Website is to determine if the site provides references, and then to check the quality of those references (many sites have no references at all). Another good question to ask is, Does the site provide data that is verifiable? Many sites offer statistics with no source or reference mentioned.

Teachers of our oldest elementary students may want to develop a set of classroom criteria for evaluating the information on a Website. The process of developing this set of criteria is an excellent opportunity to develop critical thinking skills. Figure 7.1 summarizes a set of guidelines relating to child safety and information accuracy on the Web.

Figure 7.1   Elementary School Students and the Web: Safety and Accuracy

Students should:
- Never give out personal information while working on the computer
- Not engage in any kind of "conversation" through the Internet unless the teacher knows for sure who else is participating
- Tell their teacher if they find material that makes them uncomfortable or confused

Teachers should:
- Place classroom computers so the screens are easy to see
- Closely supervise students when they work on the Internet
- Make good use of resources that protect students, like filtering software and cybersafety Websites

Teachers and students should:
- Evaluate information on a Website according to the following criteria:
  Who recommended the site?
  What is the source of information?
  How timely is the information?
  Does the site have a mood or attitude that seems biased?
  Is the information on the site verifiable and accurate?

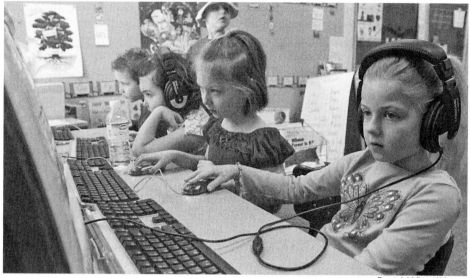

Patrick White / Merrill

Computer-based resources have transformed elementary social studies teaching and learning. Most students enjoy working on the computer.

Website Literacy

Each Website has a unique address, called a Uniform Resource Locator (URL). For example, http://www.ncss.org is the URL for the National Council for the Social Studies. Actually all Websites have a protocol, "http://," which stands for HyperText Transfer Protocol, but it is not necessary to use the protocol. Websites listed in professional journals eliminate this uniform protocol and start the URL with "www." The first aspect of Web literacy is the set of skills required to enter a site. Students can get into a Website in two ways:

1. The URL has already been provided. Then the task for the student is relatively easy: just type the URL in the location box for the browser and press Enter. The key here is for children to understand that when it comes to entering URLs, the Internet is strict! That is, even the smallest typing error will result in frustration. This is why many teachers use the bookmark or favorites feature to store frequently used URLs. There are advantages and disadvantages to providing students with the URL for a Website. The advantage is that, assuming the site has been reviewed in advance, teachers do not have to worry that our students will find a site that is inappropriate. The disadvantage is that the students will not learn how to conduct their own Internet-based searches.

2. The other way to find a relevant Website is to use a *search engine*. The option should be reserved for older students, and teachers should realize that it opens the door to every site currently on the Web.

Popular search engines include Google, Excite, About.com, and Lycos. The student types in key words, and the engine searches the Internet for sites that have those words. Each site found and displayed is called a *hit*. There are a number of simple things we should teach our students about conducting this type of search (Berson et al., 2001; Grabe & Grabe, 2000):

- You will get different results, depending on the search engine you use. Each search engine has a different system for locating Websites.
- URLs can change. Unfortunately, some URLs that once had material appropriate for children have been acquired by sites that feature pornography.
- Use singular forms, not plurals (search for *airplane,* not *airplanes*).
- The use of quotation marks results in a search for the words enclosed as a phrase; otherwise, the engine looks for each word individually (type *"George Washington"* rather than *George Washington*).
- The use of *operators* greatly facilitates your search. Operators are words like *AND, OR,* and *AND NOT* (yes, they must be capitalized). Berson (2001) points out if you type *"George Washington"* into the About.com engine, you get over 500,000 hits. *"George Washington"* AND *"Mount Vernon"* narrows the search to 3,700 hits. *AND* results in a search for sites that have both terms together, *OR* results in a search for each item separately, and *AND NOT* excludes items from the search.

Once they are on a Website and are reading the site's home page, students should be able to take advantage of both *internal links* and *external links*. One feature that Websites have that greatly facilitates information gathering is *hyperlinks*. Most Websites use hypertext to create references, or *links,* to other locations. The links are highlighted and underlined, and through the mere click of the mouse, the reader is transported to the new site. Internal links connect the reader to other locations (or "pages") within the Website. External links connect you with a different Website.

In addition to concerns about child safety and the accuracy of information, elementary teachers confront a third issue when their students use the Web. Much of the information on the Web is too difficult for our students to read. It can be quite frustrating for a student to successfully call up a Website only to find that the text is written for adults. Teachers can do a number of things to alleviate this problem. First, this readability issue is yet another reason why it is important for teachers to review as many Websites as possible before students enter them. Second, teachers should use sites that are written for children. Third, even those Websites that are too difficult for elementary school students to read can still be used for their visual images, especially photographs. Finally, the teaching suggestions in Chapter 9 on content-area reading can be applied to Websites. For example, teachers could use the text structure of a Web page to create a graphic organizer and a study guide to help students find the significant information on the page.

One more important point about gathering data from computer-based resources like the Web and CD-ROMs. When compared to hard-copy resources, it is much easier to copy text and images. Teachers must be sure that our students do not view computer-based data gathering as a process of electronic plagiarism. Sometimes, cutting and pasting is perfectly appropriate, especially for visual images but also to allow the student to read text away from a computer station. Students should be taught, however, that when they use unedited text or images in their own work, they must provide a reference.

Many teachers are connecting children with resources on the Internet by using two instructional formats developed at San Diego State University, WebQuest and Web Inquiry Project (Molebash, 2004; Molebash & Dodge, 2003; VanFossen, 2004b). At the end of the chapter is a description of a WebQuest project.

Virtual Field Trips and Online Expeditions

The Internet provides wonderful opportunities for students to experience other people and places through virtual reality. Students living in Oregon can visit the White House, and students in any state can join a group of explorers for an expedition to the Andes. A *virtual field trip* takes students to a museum or historical site through the Web (Risinger, 2005; Wilson, Rice, Bagley, & Rice, 2001). Many locations have well-planned virtual tours that are easily accessible by even our youngest students. Two good Websites with links to virtual field trips are the "Schools of California Online Resources for Educators" site (www.score.k12.ca.us) and the "History/Social Science for K–12 Teachers" site (http://k-12historysocialstudies.com/boals.html). An *online expedition,* on the other hand, allows students to share the experiences of current explorers on expeditions (Delaney & Oyler, 2001).

Like a real field trip, a virtual field trip can be either a meaningful learning experience that helps students acquire social studies content and master important processes or an excursion with little educational value. The key is teacher preparation. One issue that has emerged with virtual field trips is the tendency for students to visit a Website solely for the purpose of "cutting and pasting" either text or images from the site onto a student report of some sort. Wilson et al. (2001) correctly state that the teacher needs to structure the virtual field trip so that students "explore a site thoroughly, analyze the information critically, and present their findings in their own words" (p. 152). Here are some things teachers should do. First, either bookmark the URL of the site or begin the trip with the site's home page on the screen. There is no reason to have students struggle to find the Website since the goal of a virtual field trip is to experience a remote location, not to teach students how to find relevant Websites. Then provide the students with a study guide that will focus their attention on the most significant information in the site. Next, and this is important, write instructions on how to navigate the site. A virtual field trip does not accomplish very much if the students do not get beyond the site's home page. Once all students have completed the trip, teachers should lead a "debriefing" discussion, clarifying the information we wanted students to learn, analyzing it critically, and synthesizing it with what has been learned previously.

Students can then use what they have learned to create any of a number of projects in either hard-copy or computer-based formats.

Perhaps the best way to take part in an online expedition is through the GlobaLearn Website (Delaney and Oyler, 2001). The GlobaLearn site (www.eduserveinc.com) allows students to take part in live expeditions via the Web. For each adventure, students meet a host—a young person from 11 to 15 years old who lives in the nation or region where the expedition will take place. During an online expedition, the explorers document their experiences with digital cameras, audio and video recorders, and journal entries. All this information is transmitted to the classrooms, where students are following along (the GlobaLearn server is in Connecticut, and the information is edited and posted on their Website). Students use e-mail to communicate both with the explorers and with students in other classrooms who are participating in the expedition. Students usually keep their own journals and complete a variety of assignments related to the expedition. This could include creating an expedition page on a school Website, complete with maps, charts of geographic data (like temperature and rainfall), images pasted from the expedition Website, and written reports on any of a number of topics.

At the end of the chapter is a lesson plan for fifth graders taking a virtual field trip to Monticello, Thomas Jefferson's private residence outside of Charlottesville, Virginia.

CD-ROM Resources

CD-ROM (compact disc-read only memory) is one of the most remarkable computer-based formats. CD-ROMs have incredible storage capacity and can hold still photographs, videos, charts, graphs, text, and narration and other sounds. Many new social studies textbook series come with supporting material on CD-ROM. An entire encyclopedia can be stored on a single disc. The most popular CD-ROM encyclopedia has no hard-copy equivalent—*En Carta* (Microsoft). IBM acquired the electronic rights to the largest-selling hard-copy children's encyclopedia, *World Book,* and has produced a CD-ROM version. As CD-ROMs take more and more of the encyclopedia market away from hard-copy versions, an increasing number of CD-ROM encyclopedias will become available. Besides encyclopedias, other reference sources are becoming available on CD-ROM, like atlases (for example, the *Eyewitness 3D Atlas of the World,* a product of DK Multimedia).

Using a CD-ROM encyclopedia is similar to, yet different from, using a traditional, hard-copy encyclopedia. For example, if a student wanted to find information on Molly Pitcher, a hero of the American Revolution, using *En Carta,* here is what the student would do:

1. Assuming that *En Carta* is properly loaded, the student would review an opening menu and click the choice of "Contents."
2. The student could scroll on an alphabetic list, but it would be faster to type in "Pitcher, Molly."

3. Then, after a brief time, an entry of 65 words and an illustration of Molly Pitcher from the National Archives would appear.

4. Unlike hard-copy encyclopedias, the student would then have several options, such as (a) printing the illustration, (b) printing the text of the entry, (c) enlarging the text for easier reading, or (d) looking at related information by clicking on linked entries. Once again, teachers must be sure that any text that is cut and pasted is used as a source for analysis and that anything students write is in their own words.

At the end of the chapter, you will read a description of a second grader using *En Carta* to listen to Dr. Martin Luther King's "I Have a Dream" speech.

◆ Recording and Sharing

In the previous section, we looked at how students can gather information. We saw how computer-based resources facilitate student data-gathering from a phenomenal number of sources. The new technologies, however, also present exciting new opportunities for students to develop a range of social studies projects. Indeed, in more and more classrooms, traditional paper-and-pencil products are being supplemented by files, pages, and CD-ROMs featuring texts and images created with computers. It is beyond the scope of this book to provide a "how-to" instruction manual for each option. Rather, the focus here will be on the potential of several computer-based formats to help learn social studies content and master social studies processes.

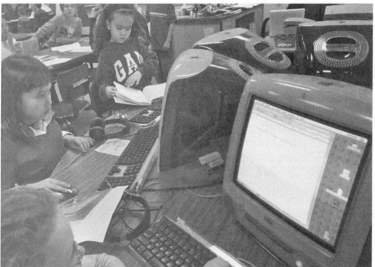

Patrick White / Merrill

Students should use computer-based resources for three purposes: to gather information, to record and share what they have learned, and to communicate with other people.

Word Processing

Once students develop some reasonable level of keyboarding skills, they will realize the advantages of using word processing software. In social studies, the results of inquiries and projects can be completed on a computer. I have seen students in grades 5 and 6 take notes on laptop computers. Teachers can facilitate note taking by creating templates that serve as data retrieval charts. Desktop publishing software allows students to include a wide range of nontextual features. Students can create books, newspapers, magazines, brochures, and many other types of documents once they master the use of desktop software. In many schools, these student-produced documents are placed in the school library. One important advantage of completing written assignments on the computer is that documents can be made available to a wide audience with relative ease. They can be added to a classroom Website, and then anyone, including a grandparent who lives far away, can have instant access to the student's effort.

Databases and Spreadsheets

Software programs like Microsoft Excel or Appleworks can be used to create databases and spreadsheets. I have seen elementary school students use both programs, though Graph Master, which is designed for children, may be a better option. Databases are collections of related information, like telephone books or library catalogs. Spreadsheets are computerized grids used with numbers. Let's take a look at a spreadsheet created in a fourth-grade classroom. One of our students at Cal State East Bay, Tatjana Ravnik, planned and implemented a project with fourth graders that made good use of spreadsheets. In the November 2002 election, California voters approved Proposition 49, an initiative that will fund after-school programs for K–12 students. As part of their study of how California government works, the fourth graders learned about the initiative process that allows voters to bypass the legislature and enact laws. Tatjana's fourth graders chose to conduct a survey of what the other fourth graders in their school thought about Proposition 49 and the issues this initiative raised. Her students came up with eight statements for their poll and then asked students in the other fourth-grade classrooms to respond to each statement. The results were tabulated using Excel and summarized in the format you see in Figure 7.2.

Linear Presentation Software

Students can use software like PowerPoint and TimeLiner to prepare presentations for their classmates. These presentations can be called "linear" because the slides always follow a "next-previous" order (Dockterman, 2002). Software like AppleWorks or PowerPoint allows students to produce high-tech slide shows, complete with text, graphics, sound, and animation. Specialized software allows students to make other types of slide shows. TimeLiner, for example, can be used to create a multimedia time line. These student-created projects teach in two ways. The students who created them learn as they collect, analyze, and reformat information. Their classmates

Figure 7.2 Citizenship Poll: Fourth-Grade California Election 2002, Proposition 49 Results Sheet

Agree	Agree (a little)	Disagree (a little)	Disagree	Series	
9	8	6	29	1	I watch television after school instead of playing with friends.
28	6	7	11	2	The after-school program helps me with my school work.
23	9	4	16	3	I have learned some really cool things in the after-school program.
14	4	5	29	4	My friends who aren't in an after-school program often get into trouble and don't do very well in school.
26	3	2	21	5	The after-school program is the best place for me to be until my parents can pick me up.
23	8	10	11	6	Cleaning up the environment is more important than after-school programs.
39	4	3	6	7	The state should give money to people who can't afford a doctor.
8	6	5	33	8	After-school programs are more important than cleaning up the environment or going to the doctor.

who view the presentations have the opportunity to learn new things in a highly appealing format.

Hypermedia

Nonlinear formats allow for the viewer to change the direction or sequence of the presentation. Hypermedia software, like HyperStudio, allows students to combine text, audio, graphics, and visual images. The difference with hypermedia is that the end product can have several paths, depending on what the viewer wants to see, so there are many possible sequences of images. Basically, students create *cards* (one "screenful" of information) that are then arranged in a *stack*. The cards can have "buttons" on them, each of which connects to a different card. For example, a hypermedia project on ancient Greece might have a card on the Olympic games. That card may have a button on "The Discus Throw." A person who wanted to know about that event could click on that button to find out how throwing the discus in the modern Olympics is different from the competitions staged by the ancient Greeks. One advantage of hypermedia is that it allows for several groups of students to work together at the same time to create the finished product. Continuing our example with ancient Greece, a "home" card could refer viewers to several other "cards," each created by a small group of students. In addition to the card on the Olympic games, there would be cards on "The Geography of Ancient Greece," "A Chronology of Important Events," "Greek Mythology," "Trade and Commerce in Ancient Greece," "Athenian Democracy," "The Spartans," "Ancient Greek Art," "The Trojan War," and "Alexander the Great."

Several technologies can be used in the process. Adding a photograph, for example, can be done by cutting and pasting the image from a Website or by using a scanner. Again, any time students take material from a site, they should provide a reference. Hypermedia projects can be saved on CD-ROMs or become pages on a school Website. I have seen children in second grade use HyperStudio successfully. The advantages are obvious: The technology of hypermedia allows students to enhance their text with charts, graphs, photographs, movies, animation, and music and provides the viewers the option of pursuing topics of special interest.

In my second year of participation in the federal technology grant, I visited Manyee Desandies's third-grade classroom. Her students completed a number of projects that were stored on the school Website. One project was a "Time-line Biography of Harriet Tubman." In the time-line biography, there were pages for 10 different years in Tubman's life. Each page had an illustration and a brief section of text, all created by the students. The site also provided links to other Websites with information about Harriet Tubman and the Underground Railroad. Figure 7.3, Figure 7.4, and Figure 7.5 are examples.

Concept Mapping

The software program Inspiration allows teachers and our more advanced students to create concept maps on the computer (the resulting product looks like the "semantic map" in Figure 9.2). The maps can center on a single word (*justice*),

Figure 7.3 Time Line Biography of Harriet Tubman

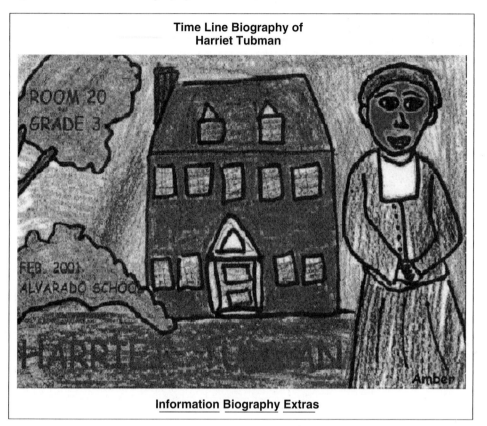

**Time Line Biography of
Harriet Tubman**

ROOM 20
GRADE 3

FEB. 2001
ALVARADO SCHOOL

HARRIET

Amber

Information Biography Extras

a book (*A Single Shard*), a person (William Lloyd Garrison), a place (Carthage), or a thing (steam engines). This type of software allows us to put things on the screen and then arrange them in several configurations. Also, Inspiration allows the user to switch back and forth from a traditional outline (e.g., with I, II, III, and A, B, C) to the emerging concept map. We can work with our students and use Inspiration to create graphic organizers, semantic maps to teach vocabulary, or summary charts.

◆ E-MAIL

E-mail has facilitated communication among people who might otherwise have very little contact with each other. Our discussion will focus on how elementary students can use e-mail in social studies to seek information, communicate with other young people, and engage in civic participation. First, it will be useful to look at the

Figure 7.4

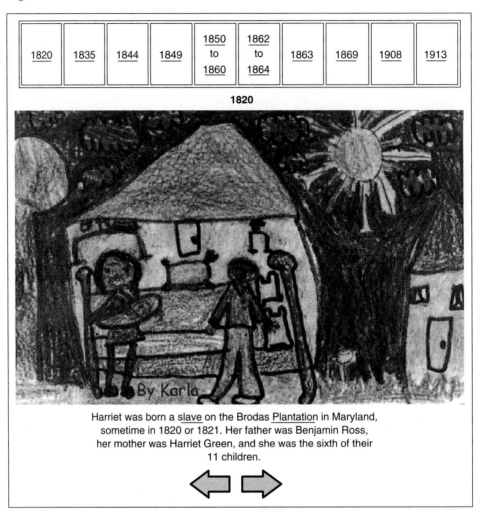

| 1820 | 1835 | 1844 | 1849 | 1850 to 1860 | 1862 to 1864 | 1863 | 1869 | 1908 | 1913 |

1820

Harriet was born a slave on the Brodas Plantation in Maryland, sometime in 1820 or 1821. Her father was Benjamin Ross, her mother was Harriet Green, and she was the sixth of their 11 children.

suggestions provided by Burgstahler and Utterback (2000) to help our students acquire what they call "netiquette," a sort of etiquette for e-mail users (p. 31). Our students should keep these suggestions in mind when sending e-mail:

- It is best to keep messages brief and stick to a single topic in a message. This allows the receiver of the message to respond to a single message. Also, longer messages are best created as word-processed documents and transmitted as an attachment to the message.
- Text features carry meaning and the message should be written using the same conventions as when composing a hard-copy text. Writing something IN ALL CAPITAL LETTERS provides emphasis and makes it look like you are shouting.

Figure 7.5

| 1820 | 1835 | 1844 | 1849 | 1850 to 1860 | 1862 to 1864 | 1863 | 1869 | 1908 | 1913 |

1869

Harriet married Nelson Davis.
Nelson Davis was a soldier in the northern army.
He used to be a slave.
Nelson Davis died in 1888.

- Children should know that sending a message through e-mail is not the same as having a conversation. The message is written, can become permanent, and may be shared with anyone. Students should write messages that they would have no objections to being made public.

Gather Information

E-mail will allow students to get information from anyone who has an e-mail address. E-mail messages constitute a new type of primary source as students come into direct contact with people who might otherwise be inaccessible. For example, Shari LaComb, a fourth-grade teacher in Georgia, designed a project that combined music and social studies. Using the Websites of symphony orchestras from around the world, students were able to find the e-mail addresses of orchestra directors and musicians. Students created a list of questions for the musicians, sent their e-mail, and received responses from New Zealand, Iceland, Australia, Greece, Canada, Florida, Illinois, Tennessee, and New York (Milson & LaComb, 2001).

E-pals (Electronic Pen Pals)

Students can become electronic pen pals with students living in other countries. The best way to locate e-pals is through the "ePALS Classroom Exchange" Website. This service began in 1996 and currently has e-pals in 191 countries with over 4.5 million students participating. This Website includes e-pals projects that integrate technology with cross-cultural understanding. For example, a project started in September 2002, designed for students ages 6 to 11, is called "The Way We Are." Students exchange information and become familiar with another student from a different culture. One of the goals of "The Way We Are" is to encourage students to reexamine their beliefs about the other cultural group.

Civic Communication

E-mail offers exciting opportunities for civic participation (Lee, 2000). E-mail provides our students with a convenient means of communicating with public officials. As with all other forms of written communication, e-mail is rapidly replacing hardcopy correspondence when citizens decide to make their perspectives known to policymakers. The power of e-mail should not be underestimated. For example, the Association of American Medical Colleges generated 17,000 e-mails to federal legislators. Three appropriate e-mail activities for our older students would be to (a) communicate with other people who have experienced a difficult time—students can express their sympathy and support for people who have suffered a natural disaster like a flood or earthquake; (b) express support or opposition to a community, state, national, or international policy; and (c) ask public officials for background information on current issues.

◆ Summary of Key Points

- We teachers need to closely supervise students when they access the Web and take steps to protect them from inappropriate contacts.
- There are no guarantees that information on the Internet will be accurate and timely; each Website must be analyzed and evaluated.
- Students will have greater success in finding relevant Websites if they use a few simple tools, like operators that narrow searches.

- Virtual field trips and online expeditions provide opportunities for students to experience people and places that are otherwise inaccessible to them.
- CD-ROM encyclopedias are rapidly replacing their hard-copy counterparts and require a different set of skills to locate information.
- Students can record and share what they have learned through word-processed documents, linear presentations using appropriate software, and nonlinear presentations using hypermedia.
- E-mail will give students opportunities to request information, communicate with people in distant lands, and participate in civic life.

FOR FURTHER READING

- The journals *Social Education, The Social Studies,* and *Social Studies and the Young Learner* frequently have articles about the instructional use of computer-based resources. All of the following were special issues on teaching with technology: almost all April issues of *Social Education* (Simpson, 2002, 2003, 2005, 2006); The March/April 2004 issue of *Social Studies and the Young Learner* (VanFossen, 2004a). Bolick and her coauthors (2005) analyzed the content of over 20 years of technology-themed issues of *Social Education,* the first such issue appeared in 1983.
- In February 1996, *Social Education* began a regular section on uses of the Internet and the World Wide Web. Through the years, these articles are a valuable source because the Websites mentioned have been carefully screened.
- You may want to look through the following computer-oriented journals: *Learning and Leading with Technology, Multimedia Schools, The Computing Teacher,* and the more scholarly *Computers in the Schools.* For those of you unfamiliar with the Internet, I suggest *Education on the Internet: A Student's Guide* (Stull & Ryder, 1999) and *Social Studies on the Internet* (Berson et al., 2001).
- Many excellent journal articles have been published in the past few years on computers and social studies. Highlights include Shafer, Stearns, & Kallo (2006), which describe a wonderfully creative project integrating geography and technology that involved each of the following: Three Beanie Baby dogs, digital cameras, thumb drives (flash drive media sticks), Global Position System Sensors (GPS) Units, a trip to Disney World, a wedding, and student-developed Websites!
- The grant I mentioned at the beginning of the chapter, Preparing Tomorrow's Teachers to Use Technology, was a collaborative effort between California State University, East Bay, and the New Haven Unified School District. The New Haven Unified School District has been a leader in integrating technology into the K–12 curriculum. You can see hundreds of computer-based projects by visiting the district Website, www.nhusd.k12.ca.us, and clicking on the various school sites.

LESSON PLANS AND INSTRUCTIONAL ACTIVITIES

Here are three examples of elementary social studies lessons and activities utilizing computer-based resources:

1. A description of a WebQuest completed by sixth graders on ancient Egypt
2. A lesson plan for fifth graders going on a virtual field trip to Monticello, Thomas Jefferson's private residence outside of Charlottesville, Virginia
3. A description of a second grader using the CD-ROM encyclopedia, *En Carta,* to listen to Dr. Martin Luther King

Description of a WEB-BASED PROJECT

Grade Six: A WebQuest on Ancient Egypt

One promising format teachers can use to help students make good use of the Internet is WebQuest (Milson & Downey, 2001). The structure of WebQuest was developed by Bernie Dodge at San Diego State University. Resources for teachers who want to build a WebQuest are available at the WebQuest site, http://webquest.sdsu.edu. For a given topic or area of study, the teacher selects relevant Websites and creates a Web page. The page leads the students through a cooperative inquiry in five stages: introduction, task, process, evaluation, and conclusion.

The WebQuest reported by Milson and Downey (2001) took place in Downey's sixth-grade classroom in Illinois. The WebQuest allowed students to use several sites to learn more about ancient Egypt. Downey selected many sites, including those developed by the Library of Congress, the National Archives, the Smithsonian Institution, the Egyptian Ministry of Tourism, and the PBS television program *Nova.* Each student created a "Time Traveler's Guidebook," consisting of information they considered most relevant for a traveler to ancient Egypt. The guidebooks were pocket pages that allowed students to insert hypertext cards with text and images. One point to note here is that teachers planning a computer-based project, like the "Time Traveler's Guidebook," can direct their students to a variety of software. The simplest option is entering text with a word processing program. The software program KidPix is great for our younger students, while more experienced students could use a hypermedia software system like HyperStudio.

Downey's WebQuest consisted of six learning stations: (a) Land and Time, (b) Daily Life, (c) People and Culture, (d) Arts, (e) Science and Technology, and (f) Mummies and Pyramids. Each station presented information in a variety of formats: books, bulletin board displays, and instruction cards. The students worked in four teams, with three teams at stations and the fourth at the six classroom computers. While at the computers, students gathered information from the Websites listed on the WebQuest page Downey had created. One interesting feature of this inquiry was that the Websites were used to support the hard-copy resources at the stations. When students had difficulty finding information at the stations, they wrote questions on index cards and brought them to the students working on the computers. Students at the computers used the links on the WebQuest page to gather information that would answer these questions.

Milson and Downey (2001), in their evaluation of this activity, found advantages to the WebQuest format. Because the teacher had built the WebQuest page with links to good Websites, students did not struggle with finding relevant sites. This activity provided an opportunity for students to sharpen their Web-based data-gathering skills. Also, Downey did not have to worry about her students ending up on inappropriate sites. Another strength was that the project worked in a classroom with a limited number of computers because the data-gathering process involved both traditional, hard-copy resources and the Web.

Effective Teaching in Today's Diverse Classroom: For our English learners, experiences with computers need to be "sheltered" so that every child can be successful. Figure 2.2 (see Chapter 2) summarized those instructional strategies that help English learners acquire social studies content. With this WebQuest project, two interventions would be important if it were tried with a classroom with English learners. First, instruction on how to move through the Websites must be carefully designed. If possible, it would be ideal to offer that instruction in the students' first language. Teachers should frequently check on the progress of English learners as they work with a Website and provide immediate corrective feedback. Second, effective vocabulary teaching would be very important. English learners would need to know key words in two categories: those relating to Web literacy (e.g., *click* and *scroll*) and those relating to ancient Egypt (e.g., *pyramid* and *agriculture*).

Grade Five: A Virtual Field Trip to Monticello

LESSON PLAN

Overview: This lesson would take place during a unit on the American Revolution and the founding of the United States. The field trip is completed by visiting the Monticello Website, www.Monticello.org, maintained by the Thomas Jefferson Foundation. Monticello, of course, was Thomas Jefferson's private residence and is located outside of Charlottesville, Virginia. Students would work in pairs to complete the lesson, following the directions and answering the questions on the study guide. The study guide is designed to allow the students to complete the virtual field trip with little teacher intervention. The lesson assumes that the students have visited several Websites and have a reasonable level of Web literacy. Students should already know about Jefferson's role in writing the Declaration of Independence. It would be a good idea to teach the meanings of a few words before the students take the tour (e.g., *ploughing* and *nailery*).

Resources and Materials: (a) access to the Website, www.Monticello.org, and (b) the study guide created by the teacher, "A Virtual Field Trip to Monticello."

Standard: From the *National Standards for History,* Grades 5–12, Era 3, "Revolution and the New Nation," Standard 1B, "The student understands the principles articulated in the Declaration of Independence," and Standard 2C, "The student understands the

Revolution's effects on different social groups" (National Center for History in the Schools, 1996, pp. 86–87).

Content Objectives: Students will learn that Monticello provides evidence that Jefferson was a product of the Enlightenment. This is reflected in his interests in learning, architecture, art, and science. Students will also learn that Jefferson owned enslaved persons who worked at both manufacturing and agriculture.

Process Objectives: Students will follow the directions provided in the study guide to *navigate* the Website; *examine* photographs, illustrations, and diagrams; *read* sections of the Website; and *answer* the questions listed on the study guide.

Teaching Sequence: The students follow the directions of the study guide provided here:

Study Guide: A Virtual Tour of Monticello

1. We are going on a trip to Thomas Jefferson's home. The house and the land around it are called Monticello. Follow all the directions in this guide. Let's go!
2. Monticello's home page should be on the screen. To get a good look at the house, scroll down to "The House" and click. Then scroll down to "Frequently Asked Questions about Monticello." Click on it.
3. We are not going to answer the questions. We just want to look at two good photographs of the house from a distance. Click on the first question, "What is the architectural style of the house?" Look at the photograph. Click on the "Back" button on the toolbar at the top of the screen. Let's look at one more photograph. Click on "Which is the front side of the house?"
4. Let's go inside the house. Scroll to the bottom of the page and click on "The House." We see a diagram of all the rooms of the house. Click on "Entrance Hall (3)." Read the section titled "Purpose of the Room" and answer questions a and b.

   a. What were the two purposes of the Entrance Hall?
   b. What types of things did the museum in the Entrance Hall have?

5. Now here comes a fun part. Scroll up and click on "Virtual Reality Panorama." Look at the photo of the room. Now click on the (+) to zoom in and get a closer look. Click on the (–) to pull back. Wow, that was like walking through the room!
6. Click on the "Back" button to get back to the Entrance Room page. Let's go visit another room. Scroll down and click on "Parlor (9)." Read the "Purpose of the Room" section. Put an (X) by every activity that took place in the room.

   a. Which of the following activities took place in Monticello's parlor?

   ___ music   ___ cooking   ___ games
   ___ reading   ___ weddings   ___ basketball
   ___ gardening   ___ dances

7. Let's take a look at Jefferson's favorite chair. Scroll down to "Furnishings of Note." Then look for the link "A Delightful Recreation." Click. Look at the illustration of the campeachy or siesta chair.

    a. Does Jefferson's siesta chair look comfortable to you? Why or why not?

8. Click on "Back" to return to the Parlor page. We only have time for one more room. Scroll down to "Library or Book Room (5)." Click. Read the section on the "Purpose of the Room." Answer two questions:

    a. How many books did Jefferson own?
    b. What happened to his books?

9. We can do a virtual reality tour of this room, too. Scroll up and click on "Virtual Reality Panorama." Again, click on the (+) to zoom in and the (−) to zoom out.

10. It is time to leave the house. Let's learn more about farming and the enslaved people at Monticello. Click on "Back" to return to the Library and Book Room main page. Scroll down to the bottom of the page and click on "The Plantation." Read the text and answer the following questions:

    a. How big was the plantation at Monticello?
    b. How many farms were there?
    c. How many enslaved people worked on the farms?

11. Scroll down and click on "Work: The Industries and Activities Pursued at Monticello." Find and click on "Ploughing. "Let's learn more about how the fields were ploughed at Monticello. Read the second and third paragraphs and answer these questions:

    a. How much did Jefferson pay for the plough he bought from George Logan?
    b. How old was the slave Robin when Jefferson wrote that Robin "works well at the plough already"?
    c. What evidence is there that women did much of the ploughing?

12. Click "Back" to return to the Work page. Scroll down and click on "Nailmaking." That's right! To make money when the farm was not producing many crops, Jefferson relied on the making of nails. Read the second paragraph and answer these questions:

    a. How many young male enslaved persons worked at the nailery?
    b. Read carefully! How old were the enslaved people who worked there?
    c. What happened to most of the enslaved people who worked at the nailery?

13. It's time to come home! Click "Back" to return to the Plantation page. Scroll down and click on the home page. The computer is now ready for someone else. Thank you.

Once all students have completed this virtual field trip, the teacher will lead a discussion. The first goal will be to review the answers to the questions on the study guide. Then the students will break into small groups to answer these questions: (a) We have learned that Jefferson, like other leaders of his time, was interested in many different topics. What evidence did we see of this in our tour? (b) We saw that Monticello was home to many enslaved people who worked in the nailery and on the plantation. From Jefferson's standpoint, what were the financial advantages of using slave labor? If slavery had been abolished, what would have happened at Monticello? From the perspective of the enslaved persons, what hardships did they experience? (c) Did the Declaration of Independence and the American Revolution change the lives of the enslaved people at Monticello?

Students may return to the Website to complete some of the projects that are part of the unit. For example, if some students are developing a "Who's Who of the American Revolution" page to be posted on the school Website, they may want to cut and paste images of Monticello to accompany their text on Jefferson. Students completing a bulletin board display on "Life in the United States, October 11, 1803" can use what they learned to create a section called "Homer Watson, Age 14, Enslaved Person at Monticello."

Effective Teaching in Today's Diverse Classroom: This activity could prove very difficult for a child with a learning disability. Sometimes it is necessary to select more than one instructional modification to help children succeed with an activity. Here, a teacher might use *instructional prompts and cues* and breaking the task into *smaller, manageable units.* For example, consider Step 11 in the activity: *Scroll down and click on "Work: The Industries and Activities Pursued at Monticello." Find and click on "Ploughing." Let's learn more about how the fields were ploughed at Monticello.* It might be necessary to print a copy of the computer screen that the children would view and highlight, with a yellow marker, *Ploughing.* This visual clue will make the task less abstract and increase the chances that all children will click on the correct link. This activity has 13 steps, which may be too many for some students with disabilities. Teachers could consider an abbreviated form of the lesson, with only six or seven steps.

Description of a Student Using a CD-ROM Encyclopedia

Grade Two: Tamika Sees and Hears Dr. Martin Luther King Jr.

In Tom Sinna's second-grade classroom, children were participating in a unit titled "People Who Made a Difference." Tamika was learning more about Dr. Martin Luther King Jr., and she had read several picture biographies of him. Mr. Sinna, however, was looking for a way to give Tamika a multimedia experience. During a visit to the school's computer lab, he decided to work with Tamika on the CD-ROM encyclopedia *En Carta.*

Together, Mr. Sinna and Tamika sat down at a Macintosh computer. Mr. Sinna clicked on "En Carta" and went to a menu and selected "Historical Audio." With Tamika operating the mouse, they scrolled a list of names, and sure enough, there was Martin Luther King Jr. Tamika recognized his name and said, "There he is!" They were in luck. *En Carta* had an audio recording of Dr. King. They clicked "Martin Luther

King Jr." and on the monitor appeared a picture of Dr. King delivering his "I Have a Dream" speech in Washington, D.C., in 1963. As the picture came into view, the recording began, and Mr. Sinna and Tamika listened. After the speech, Tamika said, "I read about this speech in some picture books I read, but this is the first time I heard it. Can I listen to it again?" This was not a problem; the audio was easily reset with a click of the mouse, and Tamika listened to the speech one more time.

Effective Teaching in Today's Diverse Classroom: The information age has the potential to improve the educational experiences of every child. Lack of access to computer-based resources, however, could exacerbate the gap between the affluent and the impoverished in our society. It is important that teachers ensure that all our students, especially those with challenging conditions and those who are English learners, spend as much time working with computer-based resources as their classmates.

Chapter 8

Assessment: Acquiring and Analyzing Data on Student Achievement

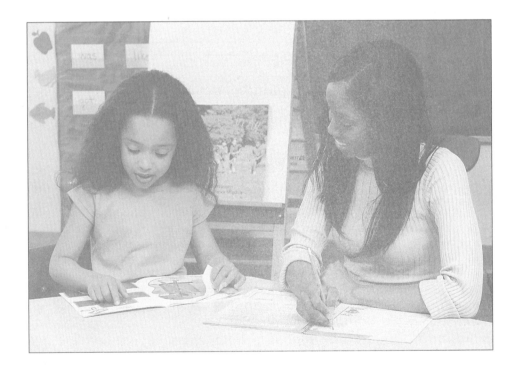

n Chapter 5, you read a description of a Group Project. While one group of students worked on the chronological mural of the city, third-grade teacher Al Braccio entered data on a Group Project Evaluation Form. The form is a kind of rating scale that enabled Mr. Braccio to document his observations of each child's performance during Group Projects. It also allowed him to make anecdotal notes for future group work planning. For example, Brad wrote an excellent caption for his part of the mural but did not complete tasks in a timely manner. Next time, Mr. Braccio will be sure that Brad works with someone who can help keep him on task. Sara, an English learner, continued to show excellent work habits and social skills. Mr. Braccio noted that the cooperative nature of the project gave her an opportunity to use her improving English skills, an excellent reason to continue to plan Group Projects for the children. All in all, the evaluation form (see Figure 8.1) proved to be a useful device for recording important data about the progress of each child working on the project.

• • •

In this chapter, you will read about

- Assessing students in a standards-based system
- The purposes and goals of both formative and summative assessment, which provide information on how much progress each student has made toward acquiring content knowledge, mastering processes, and adopting values
- Authentic assessment, an ongoing process that uses multiple sources of data—written products, nonwritten products, and multiple-form products—to evaluate student performance
- Creating and using teacher-made tests, anecdotal records, evaluation rubrics, rating scales, and checklists to evaluate students in developmentally appropriate ways
- Guidelines for analyzing data and synthesizing the contents of students' portfolios
- Sharing assessment data with students and parents

◆ Purposes and Goals of Assessment

Assessment is the process of gathering, analyzing, and sharing information on the ability and achievement of students. Although some educators have distinct definitions for *assessment* and *evaluation,* in this book the terms are synonymous. In educational settings, assessments are made for two purposes: *Formative assessment* is the process of helping students achieve more (think of a ball of clay being "formed" into a finished work of art). *Summative assessment* is the process of making judgments. In elementary social studies, summative assessment usually means completing a report card of some sort (think of "summing" things up). We as teachers must be able to fulfill both purposes of assessment. Our assessment plans for social studies must provide the data we need to make instructional

Figure 8.1   **Group Project Evaluation Form**

Title of Project: *Chronological mural of our city*

Dates: *May 6–19*

Participants: *Sara, Debbie, Ben, Denise, Cliff, Tina, Dan, Amber, Brad, Claudia*

	Social Skills	Illustration	Caption	Timetable
Sara	1	1	2	1
Debbie	1	2	1	1
Ben	2	1	2	1
Denise	1	1	1	1
Cliff	1	2	2	1
Tina	1	2	2	2
Dan	3	2	2	1
Amber	2	2	1	1
Brad	2	2	1	3
Claudia	1	2	1	3

1: Excellent   2: Good   3: Needs improvement   4: Unacceptable

Notes:

5-11   Good to see Sara & Debbie work together, Sara is making so much progress in her English.

5-12   Had to intervene with Dan and Amber. They argued. Dan has difficulty sharing. He wanted to do all the artwork.

5-13   The drawings look great. Sara and Ben are exceptional artists. Brad and Claudia needed help with their drawings.

5-15   Brad and Claudia haven't used their time wisely. They will finish a couple of days late.

5-16   I am pleased with the way Tina and Cliff helped each other.

decisions and thus increase the achievement of our students. We also need data to summarize the progress of our students and categorize their performance. Given the primary role standards are playing in almost all elementary classrooms, the ultimate goal of the assessment process is to tell us how much progress each student has made toward achieving each of our grade-level standards in social studies. To make this judgment, assessment must first reveal the extent to which students have met the objectives for a lesson or a unit.

◆ Authentic Assessment

Characteristics of Authentic Assessment

Educational assessment has undergone a revolution in the last three decades (Alleman & Brophy, 2001a; Brandt, 1992; Nickell, 1999; Nitko & Brookhart, 2006; Wiggins, 1999). Thirty years ago, almost all judgments about student achievement were based on tests. For the most part, these were tests that were part of the social studies textbook or tests developed by teachers. Assessment was the process of developing, implementing, and interpreting tests. Well-designed, developmentally appropriate tests can provide useful information and should be a part of social studies assessment, but even the best tests do not provide a complete picture of what our students know, are able to do, and value. Tests capture student performance at one point in time, limit ways of expressing knowledge, and require performance in artificial situations divorced from typical social studies activities.

The alternative to tests is generally referred to as *authentic assessment* or *performance assessment,* a process with the following characteristics:

- Data are gathered from tasks that require complex, higher-level thinking, often through inquiry and problem solving.
- The ultimate goal is to assess students' performance on tasks that correspond to the types of things people do in the "real" world rather than to make judgments on the basis of tests that people take only in school.
- Data used for evaluation can come from the everyday assignments students complete, assuming that the teacher plans a wide range of challenging social studies activities.
- The process is ongoing and longitudinal, with data gathered, analyzed, and shared throughout the school year.
- The products that students create (or records of them) are stored in portfolios.
- Students show what they know and can do in a variety of ways—through writing, speaking, art, and drama.
- The process places greater responsibility on the student in gathering and analyzing data (Alleman & Brophy, 1998, 2001a; Darling-Hammond, Ancess, & Falk, 1995; Wiggins, 1993, 1999).

Student Portfolios in a Standards-Based System

This process centers on the development of the portfolio, and sometimes the descriptor "portfolio assessment" is used instead of "authentic assessment" (Adams & Hamm, 1992). A *portfolio* is a place of storage, one for each student, and may be as simple as a manila folder. For social studies, however, the portfolio should be a larger container, something like a small box or basket. Some teachers I have known use a single portfolio for all school subjects; others have two or more portfolios for each student. In elementary school, development of the portfolio should be a joint venture as teacher and student both insert items (Stiggins, 1994). That students have some control over the sources of information used for evaluation is a significant change from traditional assessment, wherein the teacher was in complete control of the entire process. We need to be sure that each of our students understands the concept of the portfolio and the student's role in selecting items for inclusion. Many of us have begun to compile computer-based portfolios on each of our students. This is a relatively simple task. Several items can be saved on the CDs, including essays written on the computer, charts and graphs compiled with computer software, and e-mail messages from students to representatives of organizations.

In almost all public schools, a set of state-adopted standards is driving all aspects of social studies teaching and learning, including the organization of student portfolios. For this example, I will use the *National Standards for History* (National Center for History in the Schools, 1996). One way to organize each child's social studies portfolio is to have separate compartments for each standard. Let us assume, for example, that the social studies standards for fourth graders are the national standards in the category of "The History of Students' Own State or Region." There would then be five standards that all fourth graders would be expected to achieve. Thus, a fourth-grade teacher would divide each student's portfolio into five sections and have one divider for each of the five standards:

1. The student understands the history of indigenous peoples who first lived in his or her state or region.
2. The student understands the history of the first European, African, and/or Asian-Pacific explorers and settlers who came to his or her state or region.
3. The student understands the various other groups from regions throughout the world who came into the state or region over the long-ago and recent past.
4. The student understands the interactions among all these groups throughout the history of his or her state.
5. The student understands the ideas that were significant in the development of the state and that helped forge its unique identity.

As the year progresses, the teacher and each individual student share responsibility for placing evidence in the portfolio. The goal for each student is to have items in each compartment, providing enough evidence for the teacher to make a judgment about whether the standard has been met. For example, the first standard is that the student understands the history of the indigenous peoples of the state or region. Let us assume the student lives in Ventura, California, and her class has been studying the Chumash tribal group. Several items could be placed behind the first divider in the portfolio during the year: a story the student wrote titled "My Day with the Chumash," a copy of an evaluation checklist completed by the teacher on the student's minimural on Chumash food gathering, a map the student completed showing the location of Chumash villages, and the end-of-unit test.

Tests and Authentic Assessment

Too often, "testing" and "authentic assessment" are portrayed as a dichotomy. In fact, both forms of assessment have influenced each other. Tests have become more authentic; in fact, some teachers use a writing or an arts project as a test (Wiggins, 1989, 1992, 1999). For example, a teacher decides that each of her students will produce an illustrated time line of the history of South Carolina. This is a test in that all students will be required to complete the task, and the teacher will use the results to evaluate what students have learned about their state. This assignment is more authentic than most tests, however. First, the task is familiar; students have made several time lines during the year. Tests often measure student performance on tasks that are novel. Second, the task, unlike most tests, does not require students to write. Finally, the task has different "correct" versions. Although successful time lines will share common information, they will not be exactly alike. These projects used for assessment are actually a form of test and are also called *performance assessments* (Brandt, 1992). To assess the performance of our students in social studies, we should use both tests and the sources of data provided by authentic assessment (Nitko & Brookhart, 2006).

Our assessment plans for social studies, then, should have the following characteristics: (a) The overall goal will be to gather enough data to determine if each student has met grade-level standards; (b) data will be gathered from multiple sources, including tests; (c) the assessment process will be ongoing, recognizing that each day has the potential to generate useful information; (d) student work, or records of it, will be stored in portfolios; and (e) students will play a role in assessing their performance.

◆ Gathering Data

Perhaps the most useful way to go about assessment is to have the process parallel social science research, which has three components: (a) gathering data, (b) analyzing data, and (c) sharing data. Data that are gathered will be placed in students' portfolios. Analysis of these data, perhaps the most difficult part of assessment, is the process of deciding what the contents of the portfolio mean. What the portfolio reveals must be shared among the teacher, the student, and the student's parents. The components are not sequential; items will be placed in the portfolio throughout the year. Likewise, analysis of the contents of the portfolio must occur regularly. Rather than only at required parent conferences or on end-of-term report cards, the sharing of information should take place on an ongoing basis.

Each student's portfolio should contain a wide variety of items. The multiple-source approach uses the following categories of student work: (a) written products; (b) other, nonwritten products (charts, visual arts, and performing arts); (c) multiple-form products (e.g., projects that require writing, drawing, and an oral presentation); and (d) tests in a variety of formats. Whereas tests and projects completed by the whole group will be common elements in each portfolio, individual and small-group activities will yield the material that will make each portfolio unique.

Written Products.   Because most written products are an appropriate size for placement in portfolios, many end up there. (In this section, I use examples from the national *Curriculum Standards for Social Studies* (National Council for the Social Studies [NCSS], 1994).

Stories.   Stories written by students can be used as a means of evaluating what they learned. The NCSS (1994) provides the following example (p. 57): A teacher wanted her class to understand the concept of an "artifact" and how family artifacts can help people learn about how their relatives lived in the past. The teacher asked her second graders to bring something to class that their parents or grandparents owned when they were young. The children gathered things like waffle irons, newspapers, old photographs, and kitchen tools. Each child then wrote a story about her or his artifact.

Captions.   To accompany simple illustrations and as a part of bulletin board displays, students write captions. The captions can be used for assessment.

Editorials.   The editorial form of journalistic essay requires the writer to organize facts to persuade the reader and is a good project for older elementary students. Here's another example from the NCSS (1994, p. 83): An eighth-grade class examined different perspectives on the American Revolution (patriot, loyalist, and indifferent). To assess students' understanding of multiple perspectives, the teacher had students work in groups to gather information on contemporary policy issues (e.g., welfare reform). Each student then wrote a newspaper editorial advocating a position on that issue.

This example would be a good one to explore in terms of defining criteria and a scoring rubric for analysis. Although the essay could be evaluated by several criteria, let's assume the teacher decided on only one: the ability to provide factual support for the position adopted in the editorial. The teacher could develop an evaluation chart with the scoring rubric displayed in Figure 8.2. In this example, the teacher decided on three components of providing factual support in the editorial: (a) number of facts, (b) their relevance to the writer's position, and (c) the degree to which their presentation strengthened the writer's position.

Answers to Questions.   When students read from their social studies textbooks, many lessons will require them to answer questions. For assessment, the key is to ask a variety of questions, including those with answers explicitly stated in the text, those that require students to synthesize information from different parts of the text, and those that require interpretation.

Journals.   Many of us have our students write in journals. Some journals are ongoing summaries of what students think they have learned; others are change-of-perspective journals written as if the students were in a different time and place. For example, the NCSS (1994, p. 60) describes a second-grade classroom where the teacher asked the children to select a way they could make their community a better place to live. Working in groups, the children selected an organization in their

Figure 8.2 Evaluation Rubric for Newspaper Editorial

Unit: "The American Revolution"

Assignment: Newspaper editorial on contemporary policy issue

Student's Name _____

Date _____

Criterion: Ability to provide factual support for the editorial position

_____ 1. Essay cites several facts, each relevant to the topic, presented in a manner that strengthens the writer's position.

_____ 2. Essay cites few facts, each is relevant to the topic, and they are presented in a manner that strengthens the writer's position.

_____ 3. Essay cites few facts, and they are not relevant to the topic *or* they are not presented in a manner that strengthens the writer's position.

_____ 4. Essay failed to cite facts to support the writer's position.

city that could make their idea happen. The children then sent a proposal to that organization. The teacher required the children to keep journals during this activity. The teacher evaluated the journals for clarity, thoroughness, and accuracy.

Scripts.   When our students write scripts for performing arts presentations, we can save these and place them in the students' portfolios.

Summary Reports.   After our students participate in a project, we can ask them to write reports summarizing what they did and learned. The NCSS (1994, p. 65) provides an example of how this form of writing can be used for evaluation: A primary class participated in a unit on economic specialization during production. The class was divided into two groups: One group made their cookies with an assembly line; the other group made their cookies as individuals. Afterward, the class compared the two approaches in terms of productivity, pride, creativity, and quality control. Students prepared written summaries about the production process. Their teacher evaluated the summaries in terms of accuracy of description and extent to which each student used economic concepts to describe what happened.

Notes.   As students gather information from reference materials, we can ask them to take notes. Although notes usually are used as a tool to create something else (e.g., an oral presentation or a bulletin board display), the notes themselves provide evidence of the extent of each student's mastery of the process of gathering information.

Letters.   Students should write letters as part of social studies. The letters can be "real" correspondence and be mailed to other students, to local newspapers, or to government officials. Other letters can be hypothetical, written to imaginary or historical people. The NCSS (1994, p. 104) describes an eighth-grade teacher who was concerned about the stereotypes his students held about the Islamic world. The teacher had collected letters to the editor published in the local newspaper that showed a lack of respect toward women, social groups, and cultural groups. Students in his class pretended they were members of a slighted group and responded to the published letters. The teacher evaluated the letters according to clarity of purpose, accuracy of information about the target group, and effectiveness of presentation.

E-Mail.   E-mail is rapidly replacing hard-copy letters. (How many letters have you written in the past year? How many e-mails?) Just as we would save letters our students have written, we can save their e-mail transmissions. In terms of storage space, it is much more economical to save e-mail electronically on a CD-ROM than to save letters written on sheets of paper.

Essays.   We should have older students write essays that take a position and support that position with evidence. These essays are the written project most closely resembling a traditional test. For essays used for assessment at the elementary level, however, we should require students to work together to gather information, provide opportunities for discussion on what they are going to write, and create a format so that we can give our students feedback on preliminary drafts of their essays.

Nonwritten Products.   Social studies should never consist solely of paper-and-pencil tasks. Throughout this book, I present many activities in which students create things that are not "written." The collection and analysis of these products is essential as an alternative to written assessments, especially in a classroom with a diverse student population, because many students find it easier to express what they know through speaking, making charts and graphs, or producing art.

Charts.   A great deal of social science data is best presented in charts and graphs. The national *Curriculum Standards for Social Studies* provide these examples of how charts and graphs can be placed in a portfolio and used for assessment: In one classroom, students interviewed recent immigrants to the United States. Working in three groups, the students made three charts: one summarizing reasons for coming to the United States, the second the problems encountered during immigration, and the third the feelings of immigrants about leaving one place for another. Each group had to respond to questions from their classmates using the charts as a data source (NCSS, 1994, p. 53). In another classroom, students compiled charts on Native American tribes by using the following categories: geographic region, life before European contact, life after European contact, and contemporary status (p. 81). Charts are a good evaluative tool if we want to assess our students' ability to both identify and categorize relevant information.

Maria B. Vonada / Merrill

To determine if students have met grade-level standards, teachers must keep accurate records of student progress. This teacher is assessing the students' oral presentation through the use of an evaluation rubric.

Maps.   We can assess our students' knowledge of geographic information by asking them to make maps. We should use "mental maps," those drawn from memory, to assess our students' knowledge of geographic features (Wise & Kon, 1990). An example is offered in the national social studies standards: A second-grade class was studying their city, including the locations of major places. The children used a variety of maps to increase their knowledge and made pop-up maps of different areas. To evaluate what they had learned, their teacher asked them to make mental maps of the city and to include features from the area they studied while making their pop-up maps. The mental (or "sketch") maps were evaluated for accuracy (NCSS, 1994, p. 56).

Visual Arts.   We can use a variety of visual arts products for assessment. The visual arts are important because they separate knowledge from the ability to express that knowledge through writing or speaking. Murals, posters, cartoons, constructions, and any other visual art form can be used to determine what students have learned. A good example is provided by the NCSS (1994, p. 52). In a unit on their community, primary-age children each selected a topic from this list: transportation, land use, schools, people, stores, or residences. Each child then drew two illustrations: one depicting the topic as it appears today and the other as it appeared long ago. The teacher used the drawings to assess the children's understanding of the broad concept of change and their specific knowledge of how their city had changed. The checklist in Figure 8.3 could be used to analyze the illustrations.

Figure 8.3   Evaluation Checklist for Now and Then Illustrations

Unit: "Our Community: Yesterday and Today"

Assignment: Now and then illustrations

Student's Name _____

Date _____

Check all that apply:

_____   Illustrations depict the same topic or place.

_____   "Now" illustration provides three or more clearly distinguishable features.

_____   "Then" illustration provides three or more clearly distinguishable features.

_____   "Then" illustration is historically accurate.

_____   Illustrations were completed on time.

Oral Activities.   We can use a variety of speaking activities to assess our students in social studies, especially mastery of the process of civil discourse. By listening to our students, we can also judge their ability to work productively in groups. Whereas we can assess more formal oral reports in the same fashion as a written essay, discussions require us to use one of the following analytic techniques:

- *Listen to a group and assess only one objective.*   For example, we could observe three students discussing a topic and record information on the sole objective "takes turns and allows others to speak." We would assess each student in the group on her or his achievement of the objective.
- *Listen to a group and record in anecdotal form a few observations.*   We could take notes and record only those observed phenomena that "stand out" ("Heidi was able to support her position with evidence," "Vijay was patient and waited politely to speak," or "Shannon wanted to dominate and interrupted others").

For example, in a fourth-grade classroom, students took part in a simulation on international trade and the relative wealth of nations. Some groups were given considerable resources (school supplies such as glue and tape), whereas other groups were not and were considered "impoverished." After the simulation, the whole class met to discuss the experience in relation to the international economic concepts they were studying. The discussion helped the teacher assess the extent to which the students could apply those concepts to a specific situation (the simulation) (NCSS, 1994, p. 66).

Performing Arts.   If we are skilled, we can use drama, dance, and song to learn about our students. Students will provide us with much useful information for assessment in social studies prior to their performance—in the writing of the script, the creation of the setting, and the design of the costumes. Each of these components will reveal the depth of a student's knowledge of other people, places, and times. In a class studying the American Revolution, for example, children were placed in groups. Each group selected a person from the period (e.g., Mercy Otis Warren, George Washington, Elizabeth Freeman, or Patrick Henry). The group then produced a scene depicting that person's contributions before, during, or after the war. The scene had to include dialogue and a setting (backdrops and/or props). The teacher evaluated each group for the accuracy and importance of the information they presented in their scene. The teacher asked the class to place the scenes in chronological order. The teacher used this for evaluation as well (NCSS, 1994, p. 53).

Multiple-Form Products.   Many social studies activities challenge students to produce something that requires a combination of writing, the arts, charts, and speaking. In many classrooms, these multimedia products are completed with computer-based resources as students create high-tech reports on CD-ROMs with software like HyperStudio or add links to a class Website. In both cases, the finished products will feature written text, visual images (photographs taken with a digital camera or a video), and charts or graphs. Although it is possible for us to look at just one aspect of the product for evaluation (e.g., just the written part), many products should be evaluated as a whole. For example, a third-grade class was learning how humans change the environment. The children decided to undertake a whole-class project on the effects of the Styrofoam cups used in the school cafeteria. The children gathered data on the number of cups used annually and the amount of fluorocarbons released by the cups. They summarized information on the topic they found in hard-copy and computer-based reference materials. They learned about the cost of replacing the Styrofoam cups with paper cups. The class prepared a videotaped proposal for their schoolmates and, eventually, the school board.

The teacher asked each child to compile a portfolio during the project that contained all the child's work during the project, a record of daily activities, and summaries of what he or she learned. The teacher then evaluated each portfolio (NCSS, 1994, p. 68). Although no one item in a portfolio told the teacher all she needed to know, all the pieces gave her a clear picture of each child's achievement during the project. In this example, the teacher could assess each child on her or his ability to (a) understand the scientific basis for replacing the Styrofoam cups, (b) acquire mathematical data and summarize it on a chart, (c) gather and summarize data from reference sources, (d) participate productively in small-group work, (e) meet required deadlines, and (f) write a script for a videotaped presentation. Because not all children participated at the same level in each activity, the teacher will have to use the portfolio along with other data to reach a summative conclusion about each child in the class.

In another example, a seventh-grade class studied international economic interdependence. Teacher and students together constructed a survey to determine the global connections of local businesses. Members of the class used the survey to interview representatives of those businesses. Each student then prepared a poster illustrating the international aspects of the business. Each student was to prepare a short statement, similar to a news story, to use with the poster in a presentation. The teacher evaluated each student, using both the poster and the written statement, in terms of thoroughness, depth of information, and accuracy (NCSS, 1994, p. 102).

Authentic Tests.   Well-designed and developmentally appropriate tests should also be a part of our assessment plans. They will provide us with information that cannot be found in the other items in the portfolio. Tests will also provide information we can use to support conclusions we have made after we have reviewed the other items in the portfolios. As I noted previously, some teachers are developing "tests" that are "authentic" to the extent that these tests seem no different from a project typically undertaken as a part of a social studies unit. On the other hand, most states are adopting end-of-the-year standardized tests to determine if students have met the state-adopted social studies standards. These tests typically rely on multiple-choice questions.

Perhaps we should begin with a brief review of some key words and concepts relating to tests. A test should be *reliable,* which means the results of the test will be consistent when given in similar situations. A test must be *valid,* which means it measures what it is claimed to measure. With our English-language learners, test validity is a big issue because some tests do not measure the test taker's knowledge of social studies; rather, they measure the test taker's ability to read and write in English. A *standardized test* has a testing procedure that must be identical each time the test is given. Standardized tests given to a national sample of students can provide *norm-referenced* results, which report student scores in comparative numbers (e.g., grade-level equivalents and percentiles). As noted earlier, 30 states have now mandated standardized, norm-referenced tests in social studies (Burroughs, 2002). A *criterion-referenced* test establishes a criterion for each part of the test (e.g., 8 of 10 answers correct).

How do we as teachers transform our social studies tests so that they are more authentic? Here are some ways the tests have been modified:

Time.   The more traditional tests have strict, uniform time limits. Some projects used for assessment, however, should have flexible time limits; students need to be given ample time to finish the task.

Location.   Traditional tests are taken in school at the student's seat. Many of us, however, are developing tests for students to complete at home, on field trips, or in the library.

Collaboration.   In a traditional test, students work on their own. Many social studies activities, however, require students to work in groups, and some tests require group work, too. Sometimes the group work is a prelude to the performance that will be assessed. For example, each second grader must draw a picture of his or her favorite place in the community and write a brief rationale for this decision. Prior to beginning, small groups of children talk about what they will draw. The drawings and accompanying essays will be used for evaluation.

Alternatives to Reading and Writing. Most traditional tests demand a high level of literacy: The test taker reads questions and then writes answers. Some tests, however, ask students to draw, to make maps, or to talk.

We should create tests that provide information on each student's progress toward achieving our grade-level standards. Again, no teacher should rely solely on tests for social studies assessment. When used with other sources of information and more authentic tests, more traditional tests can provide useful information. *Essay tests* are particularly helpful when they ask students to compare and contrast (remember, though, we should use essay tests only when our students have well-developed writing skills). *Multiple-choice tests* have the advantage of being easy to correct and, if properly constructed, can cover a wide range of content. This type of test, along with *true/false tests,* typically fail to assess more than knowledge of facts and reveal little about students' grasp of concepts and generalizations. It takes time to prepare a good multiple-choice test. An item has a "stem" ("The city with the most people in our state is . . . ") and then three or more "options" (a. Los Angeles, b. San Francisco, c. San Diego). The options should be plausible, but only one of them should be a correct answer. Other forms of tests include *matching* (students link items in one column with items in another) and *completion* (students "fill in the blank[s]" of a partial sentence). Those of us who use these traditional forms of tests should follow the guidelines listed here:

- Plan activities that help students become familiar with the test format (practice tests or tests completed in groups).
- Be absolutely sure that the form of the test matches the developmental level of the students who will take it. Be sure that tests used with primary-age children are simple and short.
- Teach older students, especially those who will go to a middle school or junior high school in the subsequent year, how to study for tests.

Contents of Student Portfolios

The four sources of data described in the previous section will provide us with a large amount of information. The problem is that some student-produced projects will not fit into a portfolio. For example, what do we do with a mural? Other items, like a journal, are easy to save. Here is what goes into a portfolio:

- *The products themselves.* Many items that students produce can be saved "as they are" because they are small enough to fit into a portfolio (e.g., an essay, a small chart, or an illustration done on 8 1/2 × 11-inch paper).

- *Media versions of products.*   Large visual arts projects are a problem in terms of storage. One solution is to take *photographs* and place these into the portfolios of the students who created the project. *Audiotapes* can be used to record performing arts projects such as readers' theater, and they can be used to record discussions. *Videotapes* should be used for oral presentations and performing arts projects. Because most projects are group efforts, some photographs, audiotapes, and video-tapes will have to be stored separately rather than in any one student's portfolio. Multimedia projects can be saved on a CD-ROM.

- *Computer storage "devices."*   Many of us are beginning a process that undoubtedly will become routine in the future: the storage of student work on some sort of computer-based storage device. While some teachers still use diskettes, they are rapidly become passé in favor of Zip disks and CD-ROMs. Written projects, checklists, rating scales, and anecdotal notations can all be stored on easily on the computer.

- *Teacher records.*   We teachers gather a great deal of information over a period of time for each of our students. It makes sense to store anecdotal records, rubrics, checklists, and a copy of a group evaluation form or other rating scale in individual student portfolios. Keeping these records where they are easily accessed allows us and our students to better evaluate progress or lack thereof when review-ing new or ongoing projects.

Records Teachers Should Keep

In addition to the products created by students (or media versions of them), we need to keep several types of records that provide data on the performance of our students.

Anecdotal Records.   Anecdotal records can be written on sheets of paper, on "sticky," notes, or in computer files (it is not difficult to imagine a time when most teachers will use laptop computers to record their classroom observations). "Kid watching" is an essential part of evaluation, and these anecdotal notes will provide us with a great deal of important information. As we watch our students participate in social studies activities, we should write brief descriptions of noteworthy events. We should include the date, time, and context of the activity. Obviously, we will not be able to write something about each student every day, but over the course of time, our anecdotal records will show patterns. Here are two examples:

May 8, 2007

DeSean and Peyton are drawing a map of the classroom. So far, so good, and this is nice to see because Peyton usually likes "to take over" and boss class-mates around. They are working well together and their map is accurate.

May 10, 2007

Normandy is having difficulty with the scale of miles activity. The scale is 100 miles to 1 inch on the map. Instead of multiplying distances by 100, she is adding 100 to the distance.

Evaluation Rubrics and Rating Scales. An example of a rubric was shown in Figure 8.2. A *rubric* provides a scale with written descriptors to categorize student performance. A rubric should have three or more categories, and the descriptor for each category should be written with enough detail to distinguish it from the others. Reliable and valid rubrics are difficult to develop, and the best ones require a group effort and are tested in several classrooms so that the descriptors are refined. Other forms of *rating scales* may use single-word descriptors (e.g., "outstanding" and "above average"). Figure 8.4 shows an example of a rating scale for assessing a Group Project. After studying the Seven Wonders of the Ancient World, students were placed in groups and given the challenge of constructing a model of an Eighth Wonder (see NCSS, 1994, p. 100).

Checklists. Checklists allow us to record information about our students (Figures 8.3 and 8.6 are examples). Unlike rubrics or rating scales, checklists do not provide a

Figure 8.4 Rating Scale for Assessing an Eighth-Wonder Project

Unit: Europe and the Middle East in ancient days
Assignment: Group project—Construct an Eighth Wonder

Criteria	Roberto	Zella	Ned	Jiri	Winona
1. Helped group reach agreement	4	1	3	2	4
2. Supported other members of the group	4	1	3	2	4
3. Showed knowledge of characteristics of seven ancient wonders	1	1	4	1	4
4. Assisted in the design of the Eighth Wonder	4	1	1	1	4
5. Used art skills to construct Eighth Wonder	4	1	1	1	4
6. Provided a cultural context for defining Eighth Wonder	1	1	4	1	4

1: Excellent   2: Very good   3: Acceptable   4: Area of difficulty

continuum so that we can capture gradations of student performance. They are simple and typically require a yes/no judgment.

◆ Analyzing and Sharing Assessment Data

We analyze the items in our students' portfolios to determine to what extent each student has learned the content we presented in the social studies program. We can reach separate conclusions for lessons, for units, and for the school year. It is easy for those of us who work in elementary schools to reach broad conclusions because we work with the same group of children for the school year (e.g., "Caitlin knows a great deal about our city; learning social studies information is easy for her."). We should, however, be able to make more specific judgments and to base these conclusions on our objectives for lessons and units.

Verifying Acquisition of Content

For all social studies lessons, we must have some means to assess the extent to which our students achieved the objectives for the lesson. As students talk, write, draw, and act, they are providing the evidence necessary for us to judge their level of achievement. For example, Chapter 12 contains a plan for a lesson that took place during a sixth-grade unit on careers. Students completed a variety of tasks based on advertisements for jobs in the local newspaper. The content objective was that students "understand the specialized nature of jobs, how each job has unique responsibilities and requirements." Groups of students selected ads and answered questions the teacher wrote on a sheet of chart paper. The written responses indicated to what degree each group could identify the unique responsibilities and requirements of the job described in the ad they selected. The teacher also kept notes as she observed each group working.

Teachers must have evidence so that we can judge to what extent our students have achieved the content objectives established for a unit. Chapter 4 contains an example of a third-grade social studies unit on boats. The unit is organized around four questions that serve as the unit's content objectives. Although every lesson in the unit will produce either behaviors or products that can be assessed, some activities are particularly important from an assessment standpoint. The unit assessment plan in Figure 8.5 shows how the unit's activities will be used for assessment purposes.

Measuring the Understanding of Processes

Either checklists or rating scales can be used to record student progress toward mastering the processes of social studies. Here our concern is with what students can *do* (content objectives establish what we want students to *know*). We need to observe our students, keep good records, and refer frequently to the portfolios to reach

Figure 8.5   **Teacher's Assessment Plan for Unit "Boats"**

BOATS

Objective 1: What are the different types of boats, and why are they different?

Unit activities used for assessment of this objective:
Field trip to harbor
Concept attainment lesson
Unit test

Objective 2: Where in our state, country, and world would you find people using boats?

Unit activities used for assessment of this objective:
Map reading activity
Inquiry—The Voyage to Hawaii
Unit test

Objective 3: What types of jobs do people perform on boats, and how have those jobs changed over time?

Unit activities used for assessment of this objective:
Bulletin board display
Videocassette, *Ships*
Unit test

Objective 4: How have boats changed over time?

Unit activities used for assessment of this objective
Bulletin board display
History of boats lesson
Unit test

conclusions about each student's abilities. Here is an example of use of a checklist: A school district wrote objectives for the use of print encyclopedias in fourth grade. Teachers used the checklist in Figure 8.6 for assessment.

Good checklists can be used effectively, but the achievement of process objectives is a matter of degree, and checklists do not allow us to record different levels of achievement. Rating scales do, though, and are a better tool for recording each student's level of success. For example, if one third-grade social studies objective for the year is that each student "adjust his or her behavior to fit the dynamic of various groups and various situations," then it is unlikely that any students will fail to demonstrate this behavior on at least some occasions. Let's look at an example of a rating scale for achievement of process objectives.

The national geography standards established geographic skills to be learned by the end of the fourth grade (Geography Education Standards Project, 1994). These are process objectives, describing what students should be able to do, and

Figure 8.6   Checklist for Assessing Use of Print Encyclopedia

Student's Name _____

School _____

Teacher _____

Date Achieved	*Project or Assignment*	*Objective*
_____	_____	1. Uses information in encyclopedia to answer questions
_____	_____	2. Compares information in encyclopedia with other source
_____	_____	3. Uses index to locate an entry
_____	_____	4. Given a topic, locates appropriate entry(ies)
_____	_____	5. Scans for relevant details
_____	_____	6. Records information in a format that facilitates future use

are organized in five sets of skills. Figure 8.7 shows a rating scale in the form of a class profile for these geographic skills (for the complete wording of each objective, see Geography Education Standards Project, 1994, pp. 46–49).

Evaluating Development of Values

Values are standards or criteria by which behaviors, beliefs, and attitudes are judged. For example, justice is a value. That those accused of crimes are entitled to a fair trial is a belief, keeping an open mind while serving on a jury is an attitude, and speaking in favor of due process rights of people in totalitarian regimes is a behavior; each is consistent with the value of justice. This aspect of social studies is difficult to evaluate. We can make judgments about a person's values, beliefs, and attitudes only by observing her or his behavior. As teachers, we can take essentially two approaches. In the first approach, we can ask our students to express their attitudes and beliefs

Figure 8.7 Class Profile: Geographic Skills, Grade 4

Names	5.3 Apply geographic generalizations	5.2 Use geographic inquiry	5.1 Present geographic information	4.4 Use simple math	4.3 Use texts and photos	4.2 Use tables and graphs	4.1 Use maps	3.2 Construct graphs	3.1 Prepare maps	2.2 Record observations	2.1 Locate information	1.2 Distinguish geographic/non-geographic	1.1 Ask geographic questions

− Achieves objective partially and only with assistance.
+ Achieves objective partially without assistance.
* Achieves objective.
★ Achieves objective at high levels of proficiency.

through discussion and writing. The content of these discussions and written statements can be judged for consistency with the values of our social studies program.
For example, the *National Standards for Civics and Government* (Center for Civic
Education, 1994) lists equality of opportunity as a fundamental value of American
democracy. We could ask our students to establish criteria for classroom officers, and
then we could assess those criteria in terms of how inclusive they are.

In the second approach, we can observe our students' behavior to see to what
extent they have adopted the values we are trying to teach. This is somewhat trick-
ier than it might seem because of cultural differences. For example, a teacher wants
his students to adopt the value of equality of opportunity. He thinks that a behavior
demonstrating this value is when his students listen quietly and let others take turns
during group discussions. This behavior, however, will be easier for children from
some cultural groups than from others. Korean American children, especially those
whose parents were born in Korea, have learned at home a set of rules for taking
part in a discussion: Be quiet and do not talk unless the leader of the group asks
you a question. Native Hawaiian children, in contrast, who have participated in traditional "talk story" events, are accustomed to jumping into conversations in a way
that many European Americans would consider inappropriate and Korean
Americans would find shocking (Au, 1993). It is important to consider cultural influences on behavior before we make a judgment about whether a behavior was the
result of a commitment to a value.

Evaluating Achievement of Standards

Ultimately, the data gathered and analyzed through the assessment process must be
reanalyzed to determine if each student has met the social studies standards adopted
by our school districts. Many districts have created individual profiles that show each
student's progress toward achieving each grade-level standard (Figure 8.8 is an
example). As in our initial example in this chapter, Figure 8.8 assumes that a school
district has adopted the five standards in the topic "The History of Students' Own
State or Region" from the *National Standards for History*. Features of Figure 8.8
reflect basic principles in standards-based assessment:

• The evaluation process is longitudinal and ongoing. Most standards are
achieved gradually. The individual profile in Figure 8.8 requires the teacher to make
an assessment of each student in December, March, and June.

• The evaluation process acknowledges that there are gradations of achievement. The profile in Figure 8.8 allows the teacher to reach one of four conclusions
about each standard at each point in time. Some standards may not yet be
addressed. For those that have been covered, some students will have evidence in
their portfolios that the standard has been met, other students will have evidence
that leads to the conclusion that the standard has been partially met, and for some
students the evidence will indicate that the student has not met the standard.

• The evaluation process should use several sources of data. Judgments
about achievement of standards are most valid if the teacher relies on more than

Figure 8.8 **Individual Profile—Standards Assessment**

Individual Profile–Grade 4 Social Studies				

Student's Name _____

MS = meets standard PM = standard partially met NM = standard not met
NO = standard not yet addressed

December	March	June		Standard
				1. The student understands the history of indigenous peoples who first lived in his or her state.
				Sources of evidence for this standard: (a) (b) (c)
				2. The student understands the history of the first European, African, and/or Asian-Pacific explorers and settlers who came to his or her state.
				Sources of evidence for this standard: (a) (b) (c)
				3. The student understands the various other groups from regions throughout the world who came into his or her own state over the long-ago and recent past.
				Sources of evidence for this standard: (a) (b) (c)
				4. The student understands the interactions among all these groups throughout the history of his or her state.
				Sources of evidence for this standard: (a) (b) (c)
				5. The student understands the ideas that were significant in the development of the state and that helped to forge its unique identity.
				Sources of evidence for this standard: (a) (b) (c)

one source of data. Figure 8.8 requires the teacher to use at least three sources of evidence related to the standard. These could be any of the sources of data mentioned in this chapter (i.e., written products like stories or journals, nonwritten products like charts or maps, or tests).

How will we teachers know that a student has met a standard? This can be tricky because most standards are phrased with verbs that require interpretation, like "understands," "describes," "compares," and "analyzes." There are three possibilities:

1. *Rely on tests.*   This option removes, to a large extent, any subjective judgment by teachers and relies on assessment with quantifiable outcomes. For example, for the standard that "The student understands the history of indigenous peoples who first lived in his or her state," a 50-point test could be developed and administered to each student. The criterion for meeting the standard might be 80% (40 points). There are problems with this approach because it excludes many valid sources of evidence, like projects, that are more difficult to quantify. Tests that rely on multiple-choice questions cannot effectively measure critical thinking. In many states, however, this option is being implemented as standardized, norm-referenced, end-of-the-year tests in social studies are mandated and must be administered to each student.

2. *Rely on the teacher's judgment.*   This option will lead to a level of subjectivity, of course, but it does allow the teacher to consider a variety of evidence. The teacher would look at several sources of data and decide, on the basis of all the evidence, whether the student understands the history of the indigenous peoples who first lived in his or her state.

3. *Combine options 1 and 2 by establishing a criterion for each standard while placing values on several sources of evidence.*   For example, for the standard "The student understands the history of indigenous peoples who first lived in his or her state," we teachers would use a test, journal entries, a story written from the perspective of a Native American, a study guide, and a readers' theater presentation. Points would be assigned to each source of evidence for a total, say, of 100. Even with well-developed rubrics, there would be some level of subjectivity in assigning points to some sources of evidence (e.g., the story and reader's theater presentation). To meet the standard, each student would need to achieve a preset criterion, such as 80 points.

Sharing What Has Been Learned

We have gathered data from a variety of sources. We have analyzed those data to determine to what extent each student has acquired content, mastered processes, and adopted values. We have considered all the evidence and reached conclusions about the student's achievement of grade-level standards in social studies. The final component of assessment is sharing the results of our analysis. This will take place in a variety of formats, as discussed in the sections that follow.

Informal Conferences with Students.   Conversations with our students about their progress is an essential part of good teaching. These should be private and can address any aspect of the social studies program. For example, "Tony, your drawing of the Iroquois village is very good. I always look forward to your artwork, but this isn't what longhouses looked like. Where could you find more information about them?" In this case, we have commented on Tony's failure to achieve a content objective—the ability to describe accurately Native American dwellings. Our comments could focus on process: "Carmela, I looked at your map of the city, and it really shows you know how to create your own symbols." Here we are informing her that she has achieved a process objective—the ability to construct an accurate map with original symbols. Finally, the purpose of a conference could be to address a need in terms of values and beliefs: "Paul, I noticed today at recess that you called Orlando out when it was clear to everyone else he was safe. Why is it important for all of us to follow the rules when we play softball? How would you feel if you had been Orlando?"

Parent Conferences.   We should communicate with parents in a variety of formats. Schools may schedule formal conferences once or twice a year. In terms of social studies, we should be able to state our conclusions about the achievement of standards to parents *and support those conclusions with items from their child's portfolio.* The focus of the conference should be on the standards. I think it is good practice not to wait until the formal conferences to talk with parents about how their child is doing in social studies. When our students do something great, we should take the time to call their parents. All too often, we contact parents only when something wrong happens.

Report Cards.   All schools have some form for reporting student progress. These summative reports vary widely in format. "Social Studies" usually appears as a topic on the report card. More and more school districts are basing the report card on *standards.* Each standard is listed, and the teacher must indicate the level of the student's achievement of each standard (by using a rubric similar to the one provided in Figure 8.8). Some school districts use *letter grades* (e.g., A, B, C). Strong arguments can be made against using letter grades in elementary school, especially with our youngest students. If we are in a situation where we give grades, then we should be sure our students understand our criteria for making judgments. We must tell students what activities will be used to determine grades. Many school districts have report cards with *categories* or *scales*. Categories, for example, might be "area of need," "making progress," or "area of strength." Some districts have constructed summative rubrics with categories described in several sentences. Each student is then placed in the appropriate category. Finally, some report cards ask us to make *written comments*. Usually, this format is combined with either grades or a scale. Providing written comments for each student is time consuming, and rarely is there enough space to write all that we want. Whatever the format, we must be able to support our judgments with evidence from our students' portfolios.

◆ Assessment and Diversity: Final Thoughts

Our theme of diversity dictates that we use a variety of data sources to help us determine what our students know and are able to do. Diverse sources allow us to reach accurate conclusions about the achievement of our students. For too long, paper-and-pencil tests were the only assessment tool used in social studies. Both cultural and personal characteristics make it difficult for some students to show what they know on this type of test. When we shift to authentic assessment, especially when we use discussion, the visual arts, and the performing arts, we create a more equitable and accurate system for evaluation, especially for children with learning disabilities.

For our English learners, it is important that assessment be decoupled from English literacy tasks. We are on the wrong path if our assessment reveals the student's level of English proficiency rather than what he or she has learned in social studies. Quite simply, we frequently do not know whether low achievement among our English learners is the result of their not knowing social studies content or their not knowing English. To make the distinction, English learners must have the opportunity to show what they know through the performing arts and the visual arts. When possible, assessment should be done in the student's primary language. For example, if one of our standards is that students accurately describe the dwellings of four 15th-century Native American tribal groups, it does not matter if the descriptions are written in English or Spanish (note, too, that the descriptions could be drawn rather than written). Primary language assessment requires a bilingual teacher or a bilingual instructional aide and, of course, may not be possible in all schools for all children.

◆ Summary of Key Points

- The process of assessing students has undergone great changes in the past 20 years. A shift has occurred toward authentic assessment, an ongoing process in which data are gathered from everyday social studies assignments and placed in student portfolios.
- Assessment has three parts: gathering, analyzing, and sharing data.
- Assessment plans should gather data from multiple sources, including written assignments, discussions, charts and graphs, maps, the performing arts, and the visual arts.
- In addition to saving student work, teachers should use anecdotal records, evaluation rubrics, rating scales, and checklists.
- We should analyze the items in the portfolio to determine to what extent each student has acquired content, mastered processes, and adopted values. Our conclusions should be made in reference to our stated objectives for lessons, units, and the year.
- Ultimately, the data we have gathered and analyzed should allow teachers to determine whether each student has met each grade-level standard.

- We should share our conclusions with students and parents in a variety of formats including informal discussions, formal conferences, and report cards.
- For a diverse classroom, it is essential that students be allowed to show what they know and can do through discussion and the arts.

FOR FURTHER READING

- The most valuable further reading you can do is to look at the documents used for social studies assessment in a local school district. Start by looking at the report card form and the guidelines for completing it. Ask whether the district has guidelines for student portfolios. Any tests, checklists, rubrics, or rating scales would be worthwhile items to examine. How does the school district determine achievement of standards?
- For an overview of assessment in educational settings, check out Nitko & Brookhart (2006). For an introduction to authentic assessment in social studies, take a look at the 1999 special issue of *Social Education* (Nickell, 1999). There are several excellent articles in that issue.

Chapter 9

The Integrated
Curriculum: Incorporating
the Language Arts, the
Performing Arts, and
the Visual Arts

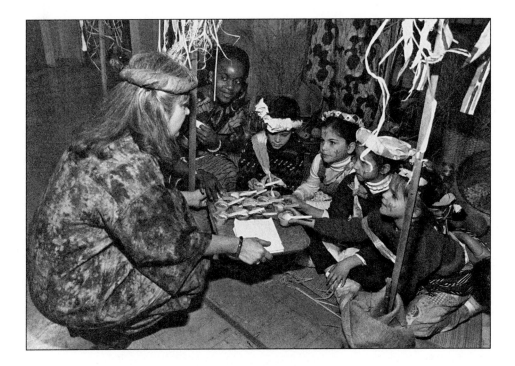

I t was time for Eugenia Potenza to update one of her favorite social studies units: "People Who Made a Difference." This unit would play an important role in helping her students meet California's second-grade *History-Social Science Content Standards* (California Department of Education, 1998). One project in the unit was a bulletin board display titled "Inventors Who Made a Difference." Ms. Potenza made frequent and effective use of the materials in the district's media center on Alexander Graham Bell, Thomas Edison, and George Washington Carver.

A few years ago, while browsing in the children's section of her local public library, she found the children's book *Shoes for Everyone: A Story About Jan Matzeliger* (Mitchell, 1986). Jan Matzeliger, an African American, invented the "lasting machine," the device that made it possible to manufacture shoes in a factory. Ms. Potenza wanted to be sure she included people of color, and she wanted to share information about inventions that had affected the lives of the children, so *Shoes for Everyone* proved to be ideal. Each year, on the day before the unit began, she backed the bulletin board with powder blue paper and then attached several sentences onto the board. Each sentence described a current condition, for example; "Millions of shoes are made every year" (for Jan Matzeliger) and "I like peanut butter and jelly sandwiches" (for George Washington Carver). As children discovered the names of the inventors and their inventions, they would write the names of the inventors on strips of paper and connect them to the appropriate sentences with colored yarn. Additional captions and illustrations would be added to complete the bulletin board.

Ms. Potenza wanted to improve the unit by including the contributions of women inventors. She was in luck! Catherine Thimmesh's (2000) picture book *Girls Think of Everything: Stories of Ingenious Inventions by Women* would be perfect. Her students could learn about the invention of products that have made everyday living easier, such as windshield wipers, invented by women. These could now be added to her display. Ms. Potenza's bulletin board project is an example of how language arts can be integrated with social studies, one topic covered in this chapter.

•   •   •

In this chapter, you will read about:

- The benefits of integrating the social studies curriculum with concepts from other academic disciplines
- The advantages and disadvantages of using social studies textbooks as an instructional resource
- Instructional strategies to help students when reading textbooks or fictional and nonfictional trade books
- Planning challenging writing activities especially suited to the social studies curriculum
- Guidelines for developing a classroom climate that promotes civil discourse
- Performing arts and visual arts activities that can be used to enhance students' social studies experiences

◆ The Integrated Curriculum

Social studies should link several areas of the curriculum. Those of us who plan and implement this type of instruction describe our teaching as "cross-curricular," "thematic," or "integrated." Although these descriptors are often used as synonyms, I use the term *integrated* in this book. Our social studies curriculum becomes integrated when we go beyond history and geography to include concepts from the other social sciences (political science, anthropology, economics, psychology, and sociology), mathematics, science, physical education, literature, and the arts. The focus of this chapter is on how to integrate the language arts, the performing arts, and the visual arts with social studies (Hinde, 2005). Chapter 10 shows how significant ideas from political science can be a part of elementary social studies, and Chapter 12 discusses the importance of teaching students concepts from anthropology, economics, psychology, and sociology.

◆ The Language Arts

The social studies curriculum should provide students with many opportunities to support literacy and become more proficient in the language arts (Camperell & Knight, 1991; Gilstrap, 1991; Irvin et al., 1995; Selwyn, 1995). The development of literacy includes teaching children to listen, read, speak, and write. Many of us, therefore, have organized our curriculum so that language arts and social studies are integrated, as social studies provides many opportunities for students to develop as readers, writers, speakers, and listeners (Roberts, 1996). The reading material most accessible for teaching social studies is the social studies basal textbook. This can be problematic, however, as I will explain.

Social Studies Textbooks

Almost every school district in the United States purchases social studies textbooks. Textbooks are part of a classroom package that usually includes a teacher's edition, student texts, worksheets, and supplemental items like videodiscs, CD-ROMs, audiotapes, maps, and charts. (Note: I distinguish *textbook* from *text*. To me, *text* has a broader meaning and includes anything that is written.) For many of us, the social studies textbook is at the center of social studies instruction. One recent national study revealed that 57% of second-grade teachers and 73% of fifth-grade teachers used a social studies textbook in the social studies lesson they taught immediately before responding to the researchers' survey (Leming, Ellington, & Schug, 2006). Despite their widespread use and popularity, social studies textbooks have been criticized (Beck & McKeown, 1991b; Wade, 1993; White, 1988). The criticisms of textbooks can be summarized as follows:

- *Social studies textbooks tend to avoid controversy and fail to present conflicting points of view.* Textbooks are marketed nationally, with particular attention to California and Texas, where state committees decide which texts will be approved for purchase for the entire state. Publishers try to produce textbooks with wide acceptability; thus, the presentation of conflicting perspectives is avoided because of the potential for alienating prospective buyers.

- *Social studies textbooks can be dull.* The writing is bland, and many textbooks ignore interesting historical incidents and people. One research study showed that if there were a "voice" to a social studies textbook, students would learn more material (Beck, McKeown, & Worthy, 1995). A passage on British taxation of the American colonists was rewritten so that it read more like fiction. The "voiced" version had more action, included quotations, and made connections to the readers' emotions.

- *Many textbooks do not always present content that is coherent.* Beck and McKeown (1988, 1991a, 1991b) studied the coherence of elementary social studies textbooks. They concluded that, in many textbooks, the main point is not emphasized, authors stray from their central point with meaningless digressions, examples and comparisons are often inadequate, the reader is given no sense of time, and many passages fail to state clearly the consequences of an event.

- *Social studies textbooks are written for a generic student.* Even if social studies textbooks were written with more panache and greater clarity, using them would still involve significant problems. Quite simply, many students cannot read their grade-level textbooks. Also, textbook-centered instruction will not be compatible with the learning styles of all students. For example, many of our students learn better from visual images other than text (e.g., charts and photographs) and through hands-on activities.

Fortunately, recent elementary social studies textbooks are an improvement over their predecessors. The illustrations and the graphics are excellent and include old paintings, cartoons, and drawings. Time lines, several types of maps, bar graphs, and summary charts present material in a form that students readily understand. Recent textbooks have broadened their coverage to include more information about minorities, women, and children. Finally, the most recent textbooks have increased the amount of primary source material they contain. Along with the chapter narrative, readers will find transcripts of oral histories, journal entries, songs, and newspaper articles. Even with these improvements, textbooks should never be the only resource we use to teach social studies. We should read the teacher's edition carefully and choose only those portions of a chapter and those instructional activities that will help our students achieve grade-level standards.

Instructional Strategies: Reading the Textbook

Effective use of instructional strategies can help our students read their textbooks (Jones & Lapham, 2004; Tierney & Readance, 2005). Our discussion looks at the following:

- Strategies that will help students recall what they know about a topic before they read
- Strategies that can be used to teach new vocabulary

- Strategies that facilitate comprehension and can be used while students read and after they have finished
- A teaching sequence that can be used with a textbook-centered lesson

Activating Background Knowledge Before Students Read.   Many teaching aids and instructional activities help our students "call to mind" what they already know about a topic. Here, we will look at K–W–L charts, PReP, and graphic organizers.

K–W–L Chart.   The K–W–L chart (Ogle, 1986) has become a popular instructional strategy to help children recall what they know about a topic. Let's assume that a group of second graders will read a selection in their textbooks about the Pledge of Allegiance. The teacher divides a sheet of chart paper into three parts: one with the heading "What We *K*now About the Pledge of Allegiance," the second column with "What We *W*ant to Learn About the Pledge of Allegiance," and the third with "What We *L*earned About the Pledge of Allegiance." The first two columns are completed during the prereading phase of the reading lesson. The third column can be completed either as the material is read or after the reading is completed. If the children do not come up with all the topics the teacher had planned to cover under the "W" portion of the chart, he or she should add them. If children in our classes show a special interest in a topic we had not planned to cover, we should modify our plans so that it is covered.

PreReading Plan.   The PreReading Plan (PReP) is another technique that will help readers recall what they know about a topic before they start reading (Langer, 1981). For example, a sixth-grade class will read about ancient Egypt. In the first phase of PReP, the teacher asks the students to express their initial associations with the topic: "What comes to mind when I say, 'Egypt'?" or "What do you think of when I say, 'Egypt'?" Next, the teacher asks the students to reflect on their initial responses: "What made you think of (whatever the students said)?" This should lead to a discussion during which students explain the sources of their knowledge. Finally, the teacher asks whether the students have any new ideas about the topic or whether they changed their perceptions: "Do any of you have new or different ideas or thoughts about Egypt?" While using PReP, the teacher will analyze the student responses. Langer (1981) suggests that individual responses can be characterized as (a) showing very little knowledge, (b) showing some prior knowledge, or (c) showing much prior knowledge. If we use PReP with a group of students, then we should adjust our plans according to student responses. Those students who have very little prior knowledge about a topic should not be asked to read the selection. Rather, they need to acquire enough background knowledge about a topic so that they can be successful.

Graphic Organizer.   An older technique that can be used in the prereading phase is the graphic organizer (Barron, 1969). A graphic organizer is a diagram that shows the structure of something—in this case, a chapter or selection in a social studies textbook or a block of text from another source. For example, first the teacher looks at the chapter and identifies the important concepts. The teacher then selects key words to represent those concepts and prepares a diagram that shows the structure of the chapter. The diagram may be placed on a chart or on an overhead transparency and is used in leading a discussion with the students before they read. The discussion may lead students to offer annotations, questions, or comments, which are placed on the graphic organizer. The whole discussion should not take a long time, just 5 to 10 minutes. Figure 9.1 is an example of a graphic organizer prepared for a class of fourth graders who will read a textbook chapter about the physical geography of their state, Connecticut.

Vocabulary. Students will learn little if they are asked to perform the task of looking up the meanings of words in a dictionary or glossary. Other instructional strategies should prove more effective. One guideline to keep in mind is that any word selected for a lesson should meet two criteria: It should be a word that students do not understand *and* it should be a word that is important in that a student who does not know what it means will have a difficult time understanding the text. There are dozens of good instructional strategies to teach social studies vocabulary. Here, we will look at (a) contextual redefinition, (b) semantic maps, and (c) a best option approach.

Figure 9.1 Graphic Organizer

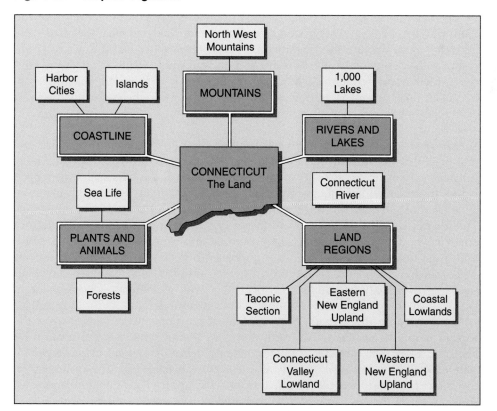

Contextual Redefinition.   For our older students, *contextual redefinition* (Cunningham, Cunningham, & Arthur, 1981) is a strategy to consider. For example, fourth graders will read the portion of a chapter on the California Gold Rush that discusses the absence of law in the mining camps. The teacher identified the following words for contextual redefinition: *bribe* and *vigilante*. Then the teacher found the first sentence in the text where each word appeared. Before the lesson, he wrote these sentences (in some cases, the sentence immediately before or after the sentence must be included) on a sheet of chart paper. For our example, these were the sentences:

1. Not all elected leaders were honest. Some took bribes.
2. In some mining camps there was so much crime that the citizens did not feel safe. They became vigilantes and punished people who had broken the law.

To begin the lesson, the teacher asked his class to come up with definitions for the words *bribe* and *vigilante* before they saw the chart with the sentences. This part of the lesson was done individually, and the teacher made it clear that it was okay to write "I don't know." In the next step, the children met in groups of four to compare what they had written. Each child then wrote a second definition, based on the discussion, for *bribe* and *vigilante*. Each group attempted to reach consensus on one definition for each word. Then the teacher showed the sentences and read them with the students. The groups reconvened and discussed what they had seen, and each child wrote a third definition. Finally, the teacher had the whole group compare the definitions in the glossary of the social studies textbook with the ones the students had written. Contextual redefinition is a powerful teaching tool because it takes advantage of both cooperative learning and the context of the word as it appears in a sentence.

Semantic Maps.   Semantic maps are diagrams that allow students to organize several pieces of information related to a single word (Heimlich & Pittelman, 1986; Johnson & Pearson, 1984; Yopp & Yopp, 1996). Much of the information generated comes from the students themselves, and semantic mapping has the advantage of simultaneously teaching word meanings and activating background knowledge. The teacher starts by writing a word inside of a circle in the middle of a piece of chart paper. The students then suggest words and phrases related to the word, which the teacher writes on the chart paper. Finally, the teacher and the students work together to organize the suggested words and phrases in "satellites" linked to the target word. My experience has been that with elementary school children, semantic webbing works better if the teacher provides descriptors for the satellites before beginning the activity. For example, if the target word was *money*, the teacher would begin the activity with the word *money* written in the center of a semantic map that includes satellites labeled *types of money, what people do with money, how people get money,* and *what money looks like.* The comments of the students would then be recorded around the appropriate satellite. Figure 9.2 shows a semantic map a group of second graders completed for the word *money*.

Figure 9.2   Semantic Map: *Money*

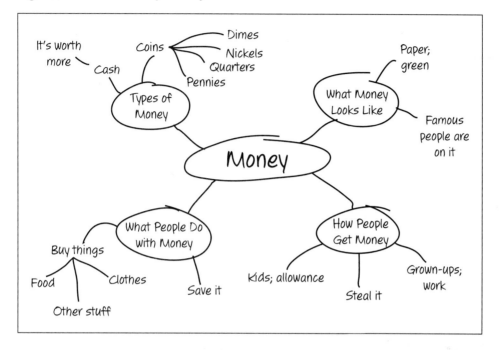

A Best Option Approach.   Again, there are literally dozens of techniques for teaching word meanings (Reutzel & Cooter, 2004; Tierney & Readance, 2005). A "best option" approach for elementary classrooms allows teachers to make choices and borrows on the Context-Structure-Sound-Reference approach first proposed by William S. Gray (Ruddell, 1997). It is based on the truth that the best way to teach the meaning of a word varies from word to word. This approach works best with small groups of children. It goes as follows:

1. *Display the word in context.* Show the children the word in a sentence, preferably the verbatim sentence from the source of the word (for our purposes, most likely, the social studies textbook). Underline the target word—for example, *Many farms in our county grow asparagus.*
2. Have the children see if they can *guess a meaning.* If they are close, you may want to add what they need to know, and you can stop right here!
3. For most words, the students will need more help. At this point, you need to make a choice. You have five good options:

   • The most effective way to convey the meaning of some words is by presenting *the thing itself or an illustration of it.* For example, if the target word is *asparagus,* your most effective teaching tool is a bunch of fresh asparagus and, not having that, a photograph of asparagus. This will not work for words that do not have a tangible referant, like *democracy.*

- Another option is to look at the *structure of the word,* focusing on prefixes, root words, and suffixes. For example, a class of third graders was studying their community, and the November election included a local antigrowth initiative. To teach *antigrowth,* the teacher could focus on the meaning of the prefix *anti-.* With older students this can involve a look at Greek and Latin roots. To teach *democracy,* a group of sixth graders studying ancient Greece would learn that the word comes from the Greek words *demos,* which means "the people," and *kratein,* meaning "to govern."
- In some cases, neither *option a* nor *option b* is the best choice because some words are best taught through *synonyms and antonyms.* The target word can be taught by displaying either words with nearly the same meaning or an opposite meaning. This works well with "big" words that have a "short" word synonym. For example, to teach *occupation,* it may take no more than displaying and discussing *job.*
- Select *some other method,* like contextual redefinition or a semantic map. Remember, not all words need to be taught the same way!
- Finally, some words are best taught by referring to a *"kid-friendly" definition.* Sometimes the glossary in a social studies book or a dictionary for children provides a simple definition that will get the job done. For other words, you may have to write one. Display the definition and discuss what it means.

Comprehension.   The ultimate goal of all reading, of course, is to understand the text. Many resources are available for those of us who want to learn more about "comprehension building" strategies (Camperell & Knight, 1991; Martorella, 1991; National Institute of Child Health and Development, 2000; Neufeld, 2006; Tierney & Readence, 2005). We will focus on (a) developing *strategic reading* through reciprocal teaching, (b) mastering the art of *question classification and answer verification* through the use of question–answer relationships, and (c) using *text structures* to focus students on the most important information in a text.

Teaching Reading Strategies Through Reciprocal Teaching.   Reciprocal teaching is a comprehension-building process that has proved effective in several studies (Lubliner, 2001; Palinscar & Brown, 1984; Rosenshine & Meister, 1994). Reciprocal teaching follows the "gradual release of responsibility" model of teaching. At first, teachers model a reading strategy. Then, students perform the strategy under the teacher's guidance. Finally, students are challenged to perform the strategy independently, and the teacher monitors their output and provides corrective feedback.

The goal is to teach students to use a set of metacognitive strategies independently while they read (*metacognitive* means thinking about our own thinking). The strategies are (a) *questioning,* as students ask questions that reflect the main idea of the text and probe for inferences; (b) *clarifying* unclear portions of a text, especially words and phrases; (c) *summarizing* the information in the text; and (d) *predicting* what might be learned next. The text is read in subparts, usually one paragraph in upper-grade texts or one page in primary texts. The teacher may focus on one strategy at a time or work on more than one. Again, at first, the teacher models the strategy, using the technique of "thinking aloud." When the teacher thinks the students can perform the strategy, the students assume that responsibility under the teacher's guidance. Thus, the teacher's role gradually diminishes as students take over more and more responsibility in the group lesson.

Question Classification and Answer Verification Through QARs. Question–answer relationships (QARs) will help students answer questions more efficiently and accurately (Raphael & Au, 2005). Our students need to classify questions by the location of their answers. This will not only make it easier to answer the questions but also help students verify their answers. The fact is that many of our students think that every question is *literal,* that is, with a clearly verifiable answer (e.g., The answer is in the second paragraph on page 73). Many questions, however, require *inferential* or *evaluative* comprehension. Inferential questions require the reader to make inferences, often through speculation, while evaluative questions ask readers to make a judgment. In each case, the answer to the question cannot be found in any one place in the text.

In the QAR format, questions and their answers can be placed into four categories according to the relationship between the question and the location of the answer. The four categories are

1. *Right there.* The answer to this type of question is explicitly stated in the text and is easy to find. These questions reflect the student's ability to perform literal comprehension tasks. For example, How long did the San Francisco earthquake of April 18, 1906, last?
2. *Think and search.* The answer is stated in the text, but the required information is in more than one place. The reader has to "put together" two or more parts of the text to come up with the answer. These are also literal comprehension tasks, but they are more complicated because the verification of the answer requires reference to at least two places in the text. For example, What three factors led to the "population boom" in southern California in the early 1900s?
3. *Author and me.* The answer is not in the text. The reader synthesizes information in the text with his or her personal knowledge or perspective. Author-and-me questions challenge the student to perform inferential and evaluative comprehension tasks. For example, We read about the first automobiles driven in California. What changes had to be made once many people began driving automobiles? (This is an inferential comprehension task because the text did not state the answer.) Now we have millions of cars in California and thousands of miles of freeways. All in all, has this been good or bad for our state? (This is an evaluative comprehension task, as students must make a judgment.)
4. *On my own.* This type of question is related to information in the text, but the reader could answer it without having the text. For example, We read about how John Muir and other conservationists worked to

create national parks in California. Have you visited a national park in California? Tell us about your visit.

The purpose of QARs is to teach students to recognize questions from each category. Once they can categorize a question, they will know what is involved in finding the answer. As social studies teachers, we can start by using QARs to write questions for a chapter in the social studies textbook. Students answer each type of question until they become proficient. Later, when students have difficulty finding an answer, we ask them to decide whether it is a(n) "right there," "think and search," "author and me," or "on my own" question.

For younger children, in grades 1 to 3, a more simple QAR taxonomy has only two categories: Is the answer to the question "In the Book", or "In My Head"? "Right There" and "Think and Search" questions have answers that can be found "In the Book." On the other hand, "On My Own" and "Author and Me" questions have answers that will be found "In My Head." I have seen teachers who use this simple categorization effectively with first graders. Before answering a question from their social studies books, the children are challenged to decide if the answer is "In the Book" or "In My Head." If the answer is "In the Book," then the teacher asks the students to find the page where the answer is located. If the answer is "In My Head," then the children close their books and think about what they have read and what they already know.

Highlighting Important Information Through the Use of Text Structures. Almost all authorities on reading social studies textbooks promote the use of expository text structures to aid reading comprehension (Reutzel & Cooter, 2004; Tierney & Readence, 2005). *Expository* text is information-based text, as opposed to the *narrative* texts, which are stories. Most chapters in social studies textbooks reflect one of the following text structures: (a) cause and effect, (b) problem and solution, (c) comparison/contrast, (d) sequence, and (e) description. Figure 9.3 shows diagrams of these text structures.

There are many possible ways to use text structures to develop comprehension, though the use of the diagrams has particular merit for social studies teaching. The diagrams can be used two ways: as a graphic organizer or a study guide. Once again, a graphic organizer is a diagram used to highlight the basic concepts in a chapter. It is somewhat "skeletal," with few words, and it is developed by the teacher. It is displayed before students begin reading. A study guide based on a text structure, on the other hand, consists of questions or fill-in-the-blank tasks that students complete during and after reading. Both structure-based graphic organizers and study guides focus student attention on the key concepts and supporting details. Figure 9.4 shows a graphic organizer based on the cause-and-effect structure for a fifth-grade social studies textbook chapter on the causes of the American Revolution. Figure 9.5 is a structure-based study on the same reading selection.

Teaching Sequence for a Textbook-centered Lesson.   For lessons using the textbook as a teaching resource, I suggest the following teaching sequence:

1. *Link* the content of the day's lesson to what we covered previously. To do this, we could look again at an important illustration in the preceding

Figure 9.3   Diagrams of Expository Text Structures

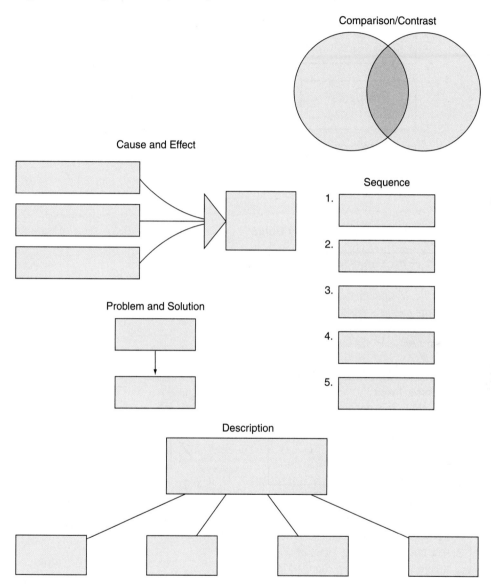

pages of the textbook, reread a chart that lists the key information students have learned, or ask questions about the topics previously presented.

2. Place the material that students are about to read in historical and geographical *context*. The best way to do this is with time lines and maps.

3. Choose a strategy that will help students activate their *background knowledge* (K–W–L, PReP, graphic organizer).

Figure 9.4   Structure-Based Graphic Organizer

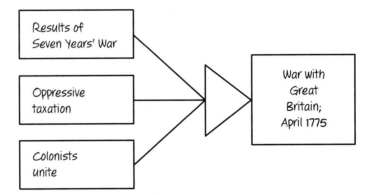

Figure 9.5   Structure-Based Study Guide

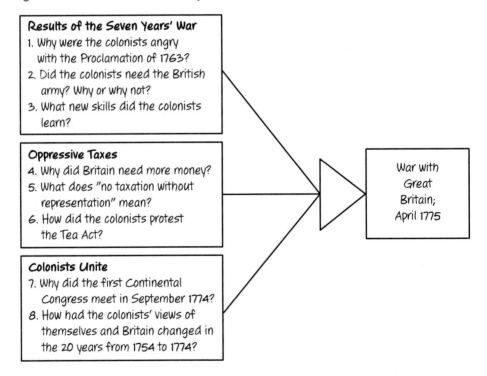

4. Teach essential *vocabulary* (see suggestions in the previous section).
5. Set a *purpose* for reading, either orally or in writing. I suggest writing the purpose on the chalkboard or on a chart paper (e.g., Today, we are going to read pages 11 to 14 to learn more about firefighters.) Another way to do this is to write three or four questions on the chalkboard that students

should be able to answer after they have done the reading. Finally, graphic organizers can provide a focus and framework before students start to read.

6. *Read the material.* We have quite a few options here. We can read aloud, students can read aloud, students can read silently, or students can listen to an audiotape. We should let students who are going to read aloud practice their reading the day before. Also, we should never have students read aloud material that is beyond their level of ability. Our goal should be to allow all students in the room to hear a fluent reading of the text.

7. *Focus on essential information.* We may want to use reciprocal teaching, QARs, or structure-based study guides to help students understand the important information in the text. To be effective, we must highlight the essential information in the block of text the students read. It is usually a good idea to summarize the important information on chart paper.

8. The reading experience often serves as a *springboard to other activities*. These follow-up activities can be for the whole group, small groups, or interested individuals.

Effective Teaching in Today's Diverse Classroom: Ten Ways to Help Children Who "Can't Read" the Textbook.   All the instructional strategies described in this section will increase the number of children in your classroom who will understand the material presented in their social studies textbooks. We all know, however, that there will be some children who will still find the textbook a mystery that cannot be solved. Some of these children will be English learners who have not acquired English literacy, whereas others will be children with disabilities who find reading a difficult chore. Here is a list of suggestions for helping such children:

1. Tape-record as many chapters in the textbook as possible (this is a great task for a dedicated parent volunteer). Let students listen to the tape before and after the chapter is covered in class.

2. Write a simplified version of a textbook chapter. Yes, I know, this is a very time-consuming task, and it will be impossible to do for all chapters. The goal is to take a chapter and cut it by two-thirds, using smaller words and shorter sentences.

3. Summarize the key points in a chapter on a set of study cards. Each card should be large: $8\frac{1}{2} \times 11$ inches, standard paper size, is about right. Prepare a limited number of cards for each chapter, approximately 5 to 10. In simplified language and with large print, restate information that is presented in the chapter. One card for a fifth-grade chapter on the causes of the American Revolution could read, "The British government made people in the Colonies pay new taxes. The people in the Colonies had no say in the decision to add these taxes."

4. Make good use of graphic organizers and data retrieval charts. Graphic organizers are effective in cueing children to what they will learn. Data

retrieval charts summarize what has been learned in a textbook chapter in a highly accessible format.

5. Make your study guides as simple as possible. For example, take a look again at Figure 9.5, the structure-based study guide. A teacher could add the page number hints to each question; for example, *4. Why did the British need more money? (see pages 104–105).*

6. Differentiate your vocabulary instruction. Try to use real objects or illustrations whenever possible. The vocabulary teaching strategies described in this chapter are effective, but they "use words to teach words." It may be necessary to provide additional instruction, typically through discussion, to teach the meanings of some words to children with reading difficulties.

7. Do a selective, second reading of a chapter with children who are struggling. This "skimming" of the chapter would consist of the following: a second look at a graphic organizer; reading and discussing the title of the chapter; reading and discussing all subtitles; reading the first paragraph and a small number of selected paragraphs; looking closely at all illustrations, charts and diagrams; reading the chapter summary.

8. Supplement the textbook with other resources. Many times the material covered in a chapter will be the topic of a children's information book written at a much simpler level. For English learners, resources written in a language other than English will be very valuable.

9. For children with learning disabilities, consider breaking the chapter down into smaller, more manageable units. After the chapter has been covered with the whole class, you may want to meet with children having difficulty and teach three, 15-minute mini-lessons on successive days, each addressing one-third of the chapter.

10. For English learners, use preview-review whenever it is feasible. Again, in preview-review, the teacher or an aide gives a preview of the contents of the chapter in the students' first language before the chapter-based lesson in English is taught. After the lesson, the teacher reviews the important information presented in the language in the students' first language. This is difficult to implement because it requires a teacher who speaks the students' first language and all the English learners in the group must have the same first language.

Children's Literature: Information Books and Biography

Information books are an essential resource for the social studies teacher (Alter, 1995b; Cullinan, 1993; Freeman & Person, 1992; McGowan, 1996; Sandmann & Ahern, 2002; Tunnell, 1993; Zarnowski & Gallagher, 1993). Books about people, places, things, ideas, and events are all information books. The best books are a blend of art and science, a combination of a vivid text, inspired illustration, and uncompromising accuracy. Why are information books so valuable for social studies teaching? Books are available on almost any topic. For example, do you know who Esther Morris was? Students who read *I Could Do That! Esther Morris Gets Women the Vote* will learn that Esther Morris worked tirelessly to get women the vote in Wyoming and was the first woman in United States history to hold political office (White, 2005). Or, want to know more about candy? *Try How Sweet It Is (and Was): A History of Candy* (Swain, 2003). Another advantage of using information books is that they are available at all reading levels, from simple picture books to books for our oldest, ablest students. For example, among the many juvenile biographies on Dr. Martin Luther King Jr. is the excellent *Martin's Big Words: The Life of Dr. Martin Luther King, Jr.* (Rappaport, 2001), a picture book for young readers. Readers with more advanced abilities could read the more challenging biography by Diane Patrick (1990), *Martin Luther King, Jr.*

Selection of Information Books. Hundreds of new information books are published each year and join the thousands that already occupy the shelves of public and school libraries. Fortunately, teachers have many good resources to help them find books that fit the social studies standards they are teaching:

- Each year, a joint committee of the National Council for the Social Studies (NCSS) and the Children's Book Council selects a list of books; the list is titled "Notable Children's Books in the Field of Social Studies." The annotated list of notable books is published annually in the journal *Social Education* (usually in the April/May issue). The NCSS also selects the Carter G. Woodson Book Awards annually. Awards go to outstanding books for young readers that treat topics related to ethnic minorities and race relations sensitively and accurately. Winning books are reviewed in the September issue of *Social Education*.
- Articles in professional journals discuss books, usually in the context of a specific topic or category of books. See, for example, Stewart's (2006) article on children's books about the life and legacy of Rosa Parks.
- Reviews of books are an excellent resource and are regularly published in the following journals: *Booklist, Children's Literature Association Quarterly, Hornbook, Interracial Books for Children Bulletin, Language Arts, School Library Journal, Social Studies and the Young Learner, The Reading Teacher, Top of the News,* and *Wilson Library Bulletin*.
- Books about children's literature can provide a great of deal help. These include large, college-level textbooks on children's literature with good discussions of information books, like Norton, Norton, and McClure's (2003) *Through the Eyes of a Child: An Introduction to Children's Literature*. A book written specifically for elementary teachers is *Transcultural Children's Literature* (Pratt & Beaty, 1999). Two books link children's literature to *Expectations of Excellence*, the NCSS social studies standards (Krey, 1998; Sandmann & Ahern, 2002).

Quality. Recommendations from the previously listed sources will give us some assurance of quality. This is an important issue because not all information books are worthy of inclusion in our classrooms. We can use two general criteria in evaluating information books:

First, *the content presented in the book should be accurate.* Accuracy, especially in biography, has been a problem in children's information books (Bigelow, 1992; Moore, 1985; Wilton, 1993; Zarnowski, 1990). Authors frequently painted heroic, mythic images of some of their subjects, ignoring or minimizing their faults and failures. Times certainly have changed, however, and more recent biographies for upper-elementary readers reveal things that had been taboo. For example, Freedman's (1993) biography of Eleanor Roosevelt has a full discussion of FDR's adulterous affair with Lucy Mercer (*Eleanor Roosevelt: A Life of Discovery*). Many authors of information books now include a list of sources. For example, Diane Stanley's (1994) picture book biography *Cleopatra* includes a "Note on Ancient Sources." Readers learn that there are no existing portraits or statues of Cleopatra and that illustrator Peter Vennema therefore based his pictures on Cleopatra's image on Egyptian coins. Some older information books lack accuracy because people of color often were presented in a biased or racist manner. To provide one example, compare two picture book biographies of Pocahontas (Lechner, 1997). One written in the 1990s, by William Accrosi (1992), is quite good (*My Name Is Pocahontas*). The book has a realistic portrayal of Pocahontas's tribal life, and no "Eurocentric" bias is evident. Compare it with an older biography written and illustrated by Ingri and Edgar Parin d'Aulaire (*Pocahontas,* published in 1946). In this book, Powhatan, Pocahontas's father, is described as a "stern old Indian chief" who "was ugly and cruel." Englishman John Smith, however, "was the handsomest man Pocahontas had ever seen" and was "hardy" and "shrewd." The bottom line was well stated by Tony Sanchez (2001) in an article about how children should learn about "heroes and heroines":

> One crucial aspect of examining the hero is to go underneath the image and myth to reveal the person's strengths and weaknesses. Only a multidimensional portrayal allows students to understand the nature of heroism. (p. 27)

The second general criterion to use in evaluating information books is that *the writing and illustration should be very good.* The books we choose should be both good social science and good literature. Again, the previously listed sources usually do an excellent job of screening information books and only recommend those that are of good quality. Some information books have won the most prestigious awards in children's literature: the Newbery Medal and the Caldecott Medal. Both are awarded by the American Library Association. The Newbery Medal goes to the author of the most distinguished contribution to American literature for children, and the Caldecott Medal is awarded to the artist of the most distinguished American picture book for children. In addition to winners of each medal, the selection committee also recognizes several "honor" books. Recent information books that have been winners include a 2006 Newbery Honor Book, *Hitler Youth: Growing Up in Hitler's Shadow* (Bartoletti, 2005), a 2005 Newbery Honor Book, *The Voice that Challenged the Nation: Marian Andersen and the Struggle for Equal Rights* (Freedman, 2004), the 2004 Caldecott Medal recipient, *The Man Who Walked*

Between the Towers (Gerstein, 2003), and the 2001 Caldecott Medal recipient, *So You Want to Be President?* (St. George, 2000).

How to Use Information Books.   Information books can be used as part of the social studies program in many ways. Usually, an information book is read in one of two ways:

1. *Read independently.*   There should be some time every day in our class-rooms for our students to read information books. Some children will choose to read information books during time devoted to silent reading (usually called either *sustained silent reading* [SSR] or *drop everything and read* [DEAR]). In addition to SSR, on some days our plan for social studies should allow students to read books independently while their classmates work on projects. Students will amass an amazing amount of content knowledge through independent reading. Think of the parallel situation among adults. Most adults realize how much a person can learn from reading fiction and biography; the potential of information books is as great for our students.

2. *Read to find specific information.*   Information books are an essential resource for students who are "hunting down" the answer to an inquiry or are looking for facts they need to complete a project. Information books provide more depth than an encyclopedia, which can either be a blessing or a curse, depending on what level of understanding a person requires. Reading to answer an inquiry or complete a project is very dif-ferent from the more casual, "kick-your-feet-up" reading done during SSR. For one thing, the reader will skip portions of the book because the only parts that matter are those that answer the inquiry. Also, information will have to be recorded, so parts of the text will be read two or three times. As students read, they take notes or write things down on a data retrieval chart.

Children's Literature: Fiction

Many authorities recommend including juvenile fiction when teaching social studies in the elementary school (Field, 1998; Sandmann & Ahern, 2002; Zarnowski & Gallagher, 1993). Three types of fiction can be used in social studies instruction:

1. *Historical novels.*   Many social studies units can be enhanced with *historical novels*. Some of the finest children's books fall into this genre, including recent Newbery Medal winners *The Midwife's Apprentice* (Cushman, 1995), *Out of the Dust* (Hesse, 1997), and *A Single Shard* (Park, 2001).

2. *Folktales.*   Folktales can be used when a unit looks at a specific cultural group. A *folktale* is a story that has been passed down through genera-tions, typically in oral form. Today, culturally authentic, beautifully illus-trated, and well-written versions of tales from cultural groups all over the

world are available. One caution is in order when using folktales in social studies. Almost all picture book folktales portray people in preindustrial settings. In folktales, Native Americans and people from Hispanic America, Africa, and Asia all wear traditional costumes and live in villages. It is important to use folktales in combination with information books that show the same group of people as they live today. If, for example, a teacher wanted to develop a mini-unit on the folktales of the Native peoples of Alaska and Northern Canada, then he or she would use the stories in books like *The Girl Who Dreamed Only Geese and Other Tales of the Far North* (Norman, 1997), *Enchanted Caribou* (Cleaver, 1985), *The White Archer* (Houston, 1967), and *Tikta Liktak: An Eskimo Legend* (Houston, 1965). It would be important to also have children become familiar with books that show the Inuit and Inupait in contemporary settings (Corriveau, 2002; Santella, 2001). Though now somewhat dated, an important book for this unit is Diane Hoyt-Goldsmith's *Arctic Hunter* (1992). This chronicles the daily life of Reggie, an Inupait boy living in Kotzebue, Alaska. Although much of Reggie's life is that of a traditional Inupait, we also see Reggie riding in a four-wheel-drive truck, living in a modern house with a television and video games, and eating hamburgers and pizza. The book is illustrated with photographs that show the combination of old and new.

3. *Contemporary realistic fiction.*   This is a broad genre of literature incorporating stories that take place during the present or recent past. For many topics in social studies, contemporary stories can be used. For example, Eve Bunting's *A Day's Work* (1994) is a fictional account of a Hispanic day laborer and his grandson. This book not only tells a good story but also will help children better understand the status of immigrants in the United States. *Too Many Tamales,* by Gary Soto (1993), is a charming Christmas story with Hispanic characters. Both books could be used to illustrate the importance of intergenerational relationships among Hispanic cultural groups (see also Cordier & Perez-Stable, 1996; Main, Wilhelm, & Cox, 1996).

Why Use Fiction?   First, fiction can help children acquire essential social studies content because a story can provide them with a sense of empathy. Books that combine thorough research with vivid writing will make children feel transported to another place. Consider Lois Lowry's *Number the Stars* (1989). Readers will share the terror of Ellen Rosen, a Danish Jew, and her best friend, Annemarie Johansen, when the girls are awakened in the night by Nazi soldiers. Also, fiction can help students acquire information about a wide range of topics. This assumes, of course, that a work of fiction is accurate—free of bias, stereotypes, and outright errors. Author-illustrator Paul Goble set a standard more authors should emulate; he cites the sources of his Native American folktales (i.e., *The Girl Who Loved Wild Horses,* 1978; *Buffalo Woman,* 1984; Goble & Goble, *Lone Bull's Horse Raid,* 1973). His stories are based on oral testimony gathered by anthropologists during the last part of the 19th century and the first decade of the 20th century. Even though authors of historical fiction are not under the same obligation as authors of information books to provide a bibliography, many list the sources of their stories or provide informative essays on the historical context of the books (e.g., Cushman provides a fine note on medieval midwifery at the end of *The Midwife's Apprentice*, 1995).

How to Use Fiction.   The same categories of activities presented in the previous section on information books can be used with fiction. The books can be read independently or to find information to complete an inquiry or a project. Unlike information books, however, fiction is not written to transmit facts and ideas. The goal of the writer of fiction is to tell a story and, in many cases, to shed light on the human condition. Therefore, the best way to use fiction is as an "adjunct" to a unit and to encourage students to read the stories independently. When we use fiction as part of social studies, a major caution is in order. Before we move to the social studies content in the book, students should first be allowed to respond to the book as a story. At the end of the chapter is a lesson plan that encourages children to appreciate a good book as literature and then learn social studies content from the story.

Writing in the Social Studies Program

A good elementary school social studies program will require students to write in a variety of formats, many unique to social studies (Beyer & Gilstrap, 1982; Firek, 2006; Gilstrap, 1991; Quigley & Bahmueller, 1991). For many years writing in elementary social studies has, for the most part, been limited to "research" reports, book reports, and filling in the blanks on worksheets (Gilstrap, 1982; Leming, Ellington, & Schug, 2006). This is unfortunate because other forms of writing are relatively easy to use and are more challenging than research and book reports. As we enter the 21st century, it should go without saying that all the forms of writing described in this section should be completed by older elementary students on computers. Our focus here is on (a) forms of writing well suited to the social studies and (b) writing as a part of civic education.

Forms of Writing Well Suited to the Social Studies

As students gather information, they will do a great deal of nonprose writing, primarily in the form of notes written on charts or graphs. Most elementary students need a great deal of help in learning how to take notes. I suggest providing students with *data retrieval charts* to record their data. Data retrieval charts provide an organizational framework for taking notes (see example in Figure 9.6).

Only after students have completed several retrieval charts should they be asked to take notes without any assistance. Taking notes is difficult because it differs from the types of narrative writing students complete during language arts (e.g., journal entries, personal narratives, and stories).

Figure 9.6   Example of a Data Retrieval Chart

Native Californians: Comparison of Four Tribes

Tribe	Region: Where did they live?	Dwellings: What type of homes did they build?	Food: What did they eat?	Other: In what other ways were they different from other tribes?
Yurok				
Yokuts				
Mohave				
Chumash				

Students enjoy projects in which they write from the perspective of a person living in the past (Firek, 2006; Selwyn, 1995). This is a written form of *role play,* wherein students assume another identity. For example, a fifth-grade class will pretend they are soldiers in the Revolutionary War. Their Valley Forge diaries are to reveal their experiences in the summer of 1777. A good way to begin this assignment is to make a chart of the contextual details students will need when they start writing. They should have a good sense of the setting for their journal entries, including the weather, the clothing people wore, and the design of buildings and other human-made objects. They should read and listen to the words and phrases people in that era used so that their written entries "sound" authentic. For another project, students could write the front page of a newspaper the *day after* an important historical event (e.g., July 5, 1776). This type of written project requires students to gather data and incorporate it into the news stories they are writing. Many students enjoy changing their "voice" as they become persons who lived long ago.

Selwyn (1995) suggests two more challenging formats for writing from the perspective of a person who lived in the past. In the first, members of the class assume complementary roles and write to each other (also described by Evans, 1995). For example, during a unit on the Civil War, one student could pretend to be an abolitionist living in Massachusetts, and a classmate could assume the role of a slave owner living in Georgia. Both could write journal entries responding to Lincoln's election in 1860. If students understand the anachronism, it would be fun for them to pretend to be on different sides of a historical issue and send e-mail to each other. Tunnell and Ammon (1996) show how children's literature can provide multiple perspectives on a historical event and help students avoid inaccurate generalizations.

What are the alternatives to the standard "research" report (Dimmitt & Van Cleaf, 1992; Koeller, 1992)? All too often, the assignment to do a report becomes an exercise in pseudowriting as students plagiarize material from the Internet and encyclopedias. Rather than assign a topic that appears as an entry in an encyclopedia (e.g., "The Navajo," "Harriet Tubman," or "Russia"), it is better to pose inquiry questions that require students to find information in more than one place. Topics that require students to gather data through surveys or interviews will eliminate the possibility of copying from encyclopedias. Finally, not all reports should be written. After gathering information on a topic or question, students can prepare multimedia presentations with software programs like HyperStudio, oral presentations, or bulletin board displays.

Writing as a Part of Civic Education.   *Civitas,* the curriculum framework for citizenship education developed by the Council for the Advancement for Citizenship and the Center for Civic Education, describes several types of "participatory writing" that should be a part of elementary social studies (Quigley & Bahmueller, 1991):

Writing to Gather Social Science Data.   Students can write surveys to be administered to their classmates, families, friends, and neighbors. They can also write to agencies for information (e.g., League of Women Voters, city council, foreign consulates, and state and federal agencies). A survey project is an excellent experience for students because they do two types of writing: composing questions on the survey and then writing a summary of their findings.

E-Mailing Public Officials.   E-mail has made it much easier for students to send written messages to public officials. They can write to congratulate candidates who win elections, to express support for a policy decision, and to complain. This type of writing will test the ability of students to adjust their writing to fit their target audience. An e-mail or letter to a member of the U.S. Congress, for example, should not sound the same as a message written to a classmate.

Writing Agendas and Minutes.   Students should take part in classroom and school meetings to understand democracy and civil discourse. These meetings should be forums for students to express perspectives and reach decisions. Meetings need agendas and minutes. Writing minutes, especially, is a difficult task. Students will have to master taking notes, pausing to clarify when they are unsure of what was said, and condensing the notes for publication.

Writing for Political Campaigns.   Political campaigns require a great deal of written material—speeches, copy for radio and television ads, posters, position papers, and brochures. Older students can write campaign materials when they run for classroom and school office. Students can also write political texts for state and federal campaigns.

Writing Laws and Rules.   The text of a law or rule requires a special type of writing; the author must be succinct and convey a precise meaning. Students can write rules for the playground, classroom, and school. Every word of a classroom rule will be important and subject to interpretation.

Speaking and Listening in the Social Studies Program

Almost every activity described in this book requires students to speak, either to each other or to their teacher. Most talk should be informal and conversational as students work in small-group formats. More formal speaking assignments are appropriate for students in the upper-elementary grades. Students should work together to report the results of an inquiry or a project. One of the best formats is several students sharing the responsibility for an oral presentation. Several things can be done to ensure that this is a worthwhile experience both for the students delivering the report and for their classmates who are listening. First, each student who is to speak should practice her or his part several times. Next, no student should speak for more than a few minutes. Finally, the oral report should be supported by visual aids, such as charts, graphs, maps, and diagrams.

As noted in Chapter 11, an essential part of citizenship education is helping students master the process of "civil discourse." Discussion should be an important part of social studies teaching and learning at every grade level (Hess, 2004; Wilen, 2004). Students should talk about controversial issues and explore multiple perspectives on events in the past. Here I will look at two perspectives on classroom discussions. First, let's review what the research reveals about classroom discussion. Then, let's look at what teachers can do to promote civil, nonthreatening, and nontheatric discussions among their students.

Diana Hess (2004) reviewed the literature on classroom discussion in social studies and identified seven characteristics of effective discussion. These are as follows:

1. The focus is on an *interpretable* topic (an issue or text). To have a good discussion, there must be more than one possible perspective. This is similar to the requirement for a good inquiry, you cannot hope to have a discussion among many participants if you start with a question that has a single, correct answer.

2. The leader of the discussion and the participants have prepared. Depending on the topic, the preparation can be informal and take only a few minutes. Other topics will take days of reading and note-taking. One teacher required students to write something down on the topic to be discussed and these initial, written thoughts became a "ticket" which allowed them to talk.

3. Most of the talk comes from the participants, not the leader. This is so important. If teachers are leading a discussion, we want to say as little as possible. If a student is facilitating a discussion, she or he must understand the limited nature of a facilitator's role.

4. There is enough time spent on a particular topic to explore it thoroughly. This is the same point raised by Newman in Chapter 6 in regard to critical thinking. Critical thinking, an important goal of discussion, is only possible if topics are explored in depth.

5. Participants feel comfortable, but disagreement is still possible. Our discussion based on Rossi's suggestions in the next paragraph will further explain how these two goals can be met. Teachers need to have an atmosphere that is nonjudgmental, and this starts with the teacher. Students need to "depersonalize" their responses by separating the content of a comment from the commentator.

6. Many people talk. This has a best chance of happening if the previous five points are implemented. Many children will talk if there is something stimulating to talk about, the children have prepared, the leader limits her or his comments, adequate time is devoted to the topic, and the children feel comfortable in expressing their perspectives.

7. Finally, the participants in the discussion ask good questions based on what has been said earlier. Being a good discussant requires students to be good listeners. Teachers should model this behavior by asking their questions in the context of previous commentary (e.g., "One idea that we heard was that we should use the PTA money to buy more computers. If we did that are there costs other than the computers that we would have to pay?")

Rossi's (1996a) article provides guidance for those of us who want to help our students learn how to express their opinions and, at the same time, listen to others in an appropriate fashion. Rossi notes that this is a challenge in the age of radio and television talk shows for which the goal is to incite, not educate, and that because "these shows demonstrate merely discussing controversial issues is not sufficient to promote civic competence and democratic attitudes" (p. 18). Rossi's five conditions for creating a civil classroom climate can serve as a framework for a description of how to have productive and polite discussions in an elementary classroom.

1. *A cooperative versus a competitive context.* We should model the attitude that when disagreements arise, the goal is not to "win" but rather to learn. We should praise students when they ask clarifying questions and make efforts to understand why their classmates have reached different conclusions. Students should learn that monopolizing the discussion is inappropriate. Personal attacks, of course, should never be tolerated in any civil discussion.

2. *Relevant information.* Discussions should be based on accurate and pertinent information. The leader of a discussion (teacher or student) should help students question in a respectful manner the accuracy of statements made by classmates. Rather than stating, "You're wrong," students should say something like, "I don't think it is accurate to say that . . ." We should record these disputes and help students find information that provides accuracy. It is important that students support their views with facts and explain why they believe the way they do.

3. *Perspective taking.* Role play can help students understand and empathize with someone else's perspective. On some issues, both historical and contemporary, students should assume the role of another person and express that person's views. This activity will help increase the amount of information presented in a discussion and will ensure that a range of opinions is presented.

4. *Disagreeing while confirming.* In discussions in which people disagree, it is essential that "somehow, participants need to be able to disagree with each others' ideas while confirming each others' personal competence" (Rossi, 1996a, p. 20). This needs to become a part of every student's listening behavior. Our youngest students should understand that interrupting others is inappropriate because they learn less when they listen less. As students grow older, they should learn to say things like, "You have done a lot of work and you know your stuff, but I don't agree with what you said" or "What you have said is making me think" or "After listening to you, I see that we agree on many things."

5. *Inclusion.* Many students are uncomfortable talking in a group discussion. We must create situations in which many students have a chance to express themselves. The cooperative learning structures discussed in Chapter 5 maximize participation, but they involve very small groups (Think–Pair–Share and Three-Step Interview). Many students who

would otherwise remain silent will speak if they have a chance to prepare and practice their comments. We could provide some students with
the discussion topic in advance, help them structure their response,
allow them a chance to practice, and provide feedback *before* the day of
the discussion.

◆ The Performing Arts and the Visual Arts

The *performing arts* are music, dance, and drama. The *visual arts* incorporate a
variety of media (e.g., crayon, clay, paint, film, video, and computer-based multimedia). The role of the arts in social studies is multifaceted (Eisner, 1991; Selwyn, 1995;
Tibbett, 2004). First, the arts provide alternatives for the presentation of social studies information. Films, paintings, live dramas, and other art forms are particularly
important resources for English-language learners. Howard Gardner's (1983, 1991)
ideas on multiple intelligences provide a strong rationale for using the arts to help
students learn about other people because some students find it difficult to learn
from written material. The arts are an alternative. As students view the visual arts
and view and listen to the performing arts, they use their senses to learn. These can
be powerful experiences because "what all of the arts have in common is their
capacity to generate emotion, to stimulate and to express the 'feel' for a situation,
individual, or object" (Eisner, 1991, p. 554).

Scott Cunningham/Merrill

To meet the needs of our diverse students, units of instruction should encourage
children to express what they know through the language arts, the performing
arts, and the visual arts. In this classroom, children have learned to use many
visual media.

Second, as Selwyn (1995) notes, "the study of the arts is part of the study of history. Music, visual arts, dance, theater, crafts, writing, and other arts are both artifacts of and a means by which to study a culture" (p. 9). As many instructional units as possible should present information through the arts. Many current social studies textbooks include illustrations of paintings, statues, ceramics, and other art forms. We can augment these resources by selecting books that display the art of a particular culture. When students view another culture's art, they will see intercultural differences and similarities. Although the specific forms of art will vary from culture to culture, students will see that certain universal themes are present. For example, forms of dance are wonderfully different among cultural groups, yet all dance can be classified as essentially social, ritual, or performance.

Third, the arts should also be used to allow students to express what they have learned. Too often, social studies tasks are limited to reading, writing, and speaking. Our students should have opportunities to display their knowledge through the performing and visual arts. In the next two sections, we look at some specific art forms that can be used with elementary students.

The Performing Arts

In Chapter 11, I describe a lesson in which kindergartners assumed the roles of a 19th-century farm family and pantomimed chores after listening to their teacher read *Ox-Cart Man* (Hall, 1979). This informal form of *role play* can be a powerful teaching tool, and it is easy to implement (Mahood, 1980; Shaftel & Shaftel, 1967). We merely ask students to pretend they are someone or something, and then the make believe begins. A more formal form of role play is the mock trial described in Chapter 11. In that activity, students assumed the roles of judge, attorneys, witnesses, and the jury. Each student performed in his or her new identity without a script. This formal role play required students to learn a great deal about their new identities, to "think on their feet," and to improvise.

Readers' theater is simple, effective, and fun (Laughlin, Black, & Loberg, 1991; Sloyer, 1982; Young & Vardell, 1993). The text of picture books, excerpts from fiction, poetry, and parts of information books all can be presented. In readers' theater, students read their lines during the performance. In *choral reading,* parts of the text are read simultaneously by two or more students. With a *nonedited* form of readers' theater, every word of the text is read. Narrators read the words outside quotation marks, and student actors read the dialogue inside quotation marks. In other presentations, the text of the book is modified for the performance. Three things help make readers' theater experiences positive. First, no student should be asked to read aloud a text that is too difficult. Second, it must be very clear to each reader when she or he is supposed to read. While performing, many students become nervous, and simple things become difficult. We could make copies of the portion of a book that is being read, provide each reader with a copy, and highlight each student's part with a colored marker. Third, even though readers' theater does not demand that students memorize their parts, students need to rehearse several times before they read in front of an audience.

Almost all children enjoy acting in *plays*. Here, of course, actors must memorize their parts. When compared with readers' theater, the production is more elaborate, with costumes, a set, and props. Plays are particularly valuable in social studies because they help students learn about people in different places and times. This assumes, of course, that the script, set, costumes, and props have a reasonable degree of historical and cultural accuracy. The first step is to write a script, which may be done by the teacher, the students, or teacher and students working together. The easiest way to produce a script is to adapt a picture book or an excerpt from a children's novel. The second step is to select the parts, and this should be done carefully. We should ensure that the same students are not always the leads, and we should guide students to roles they will be able to perform successfully. Plays, of course, require rehearsal. One form of play that has long been a part of social studies is the *historical pageant,* a multiscene play depicting the history of a place, person, idea, or event. For example, *California* could have the following scenes: (a) a vignette from a Yurok village (Native tribal life), (b) the death of Juan Cabrillo, (c) a California fiesta (during Mexican rule of California), (d) the discovery of gold, (e) the San Francisco earthquake of 1906, and (f) a conversation among migrant workers in the 1930s.

Selwyn (1995) suggests an interesting form of tableau vivante for social studies lessons—*human statues*. A group of students is given a scene to portray. The group then discusses how they should position themselves—how each person will kneel, sit, stand, or recline. All the group members come to the front

Anthony Magnacca / Merrill

Participation in dramatic presentation can help children develop a strong sense of empathy with people from other times and places.

of the class and strike their poses, each a human statue, frozen in position. Unlike true tableau, these statues can speak, and the student-statues can explain how they feel emotionally and physically. The class can ask questions, but this must happen quickly because the statues are human (and can be still for only a limited time).

Students can *dance* as a part of social studies. Some forms of pantomime blur the line between theater and dance as students convey meaning purely through body movements. Performing culturally authentic dances can be a worthwhile experience for students, but it is essential that the dances be treated with respect (such dance is typically referred to as *folk dance*). Students should see the dance performed with authenticity, either by members of the cultural group or by dancers who have studied the dance and understand its cultural context. Also, it is best to avoid sacred dances; these dances can become trivialized and their religious significance lost as the purpose of the dance, with children, shifts from ritual to social. Rather than have our students perform ritual dances, it would be better to have them observe the dance respectfully, either through a live performance or through film or video.

The Visual Arts

A group of student teachers I supervised one semester compiled the following list of media that elementary students can use to express themselves through the visual arts: crayon, paint, ink, torn paper, tissue, photography, motion picture film, videotape, clay, chalk, computer graphics, colored pencils, felt and cloth, charcoal, salt and flour, string, potatoes (to make prints), and colored sand. After a day to think about it, we were able to double the list!

Many forms of *murals* can be made as part of social studies units. *Mural* comes from the Latin word for "wall" (*murus*), and all murals are large pictures on walls, typically with several images. Because we cannot paint or draw directly on school walls, our murals are usually bulletin board displays. Even though many murals are made on sheets of "butcher paper," I think it is more practical to draw or paint images on separate sheets of paper and then staple them to the bulletin board. Many murals will involve writing, too, as students write captions to accompany their visual images. One suggestion: Do not worry about scale; it will be fine to have drawings of the Sphinx and Tutankhamen be the same size.

A *diorama* is a three-dimensional display. The simplest ones are completed in shoe boxes, which limit the perspective of the viewer. Larger dioramas, though, are more rewarding and look better. I suggest using a piece of plywood as a base. Dioramas depict scenes from the world around us, both past and present, as they incorporate student-made figures from clay and other materials and manufactured items such as toy houses and people.

Collages are combinations of images. In its simplest form, students construct a collage with cut or torn paper. Pictures from magazines and other materials, like natural objects, textiles, and manufactured items, can be used. A collage should have a clearly stated theme or idea.

Finally, we should be careful as we use the visual arts to teach social studies. Some art projects done as part of social studies actually contribute little, if anything, to student learning of the content of an instructional unit. For example, fourth graders who paint a mural of an Iroquois village will learn very little if they merely follow a prescribed process with no attempt to place the subject of their mural in historical context. In fact, many social studies art projects become nothing more than exercises in mass production. (I have seen too many first graders dutifully manufacture paper replicas of the hats the Pilgrims supposedly wore.) When done as part of social studies, visual arts activities should either help students acquire information or allow them to express what they have learned. Visual arts projects can take many forms and may be combined with the language arts.

At the end of the chapter is an example of a project that uses the visual arts to increase students' understanding of 19th-century Native Americans living on the Great Plains.

◆ Summary of Key Points

- Social studies textbooks can be used effectively in elementary classrooms. They should never, however, be the only instructional resource we use.
- We should use a variety of instructional strategies to help students (a) activate their background knowledge before they read, (b) build their vocabularies, and (c) increase their comprehension.
- As part of social studies, information books should be read independently and used to answer inquiries and complete projects.
- Fiction can provide students with a strong sense of empathy with people living in other places and times.
- Social studies provides students with many opportunities to write, often in formats they seldom use in other areas of the curriculum.
- It is essential that students learn the process of civil discourse—to listen and talk in a polite, respectful manner.
- Performing arts activities include role play, readers' theater, plays, and pageants.
- Of all the forms of the visual arts, murals, dioramas, and collages have been popular choices for social studies projects.

FOR FURTHER READING

Language Arts
- An excellent resource for teachers is *Integrating Language Arts and Social Studies for Kindergarten and Primary Children* (Roberts, 1996). Wilen (2004) provides suggestions for encouraging reticent students' participation in classroom discussions. Larson (2005) writes about online discussions for high school students—would this work with elementary school children?

- McCabe (2003) offers five suggestions for enhancing student motivation when they are asked to read their social studies textbooks. His suggestions include the use of graphic organizers, and taking advantage of format features, like bold and italicized print, type size, and the "white space" in margins and borders.
- Reciprocal teaching has a strong research base and will, if done consistently, improve the ability of our students to understand their social studies textbooks. The best "how-to" source was written by my colleague at Cal State East Bay, Shira Lubliner (2001).
- More recent journal articles on the use of fiction cover a range of topics, including children's books on the "Columbian Exchange," the long-term impact of Columbus's voyages on Native Peoples of the Americas (Field & Singer, 2006), and children's books about New York City (Groce, Groce, & Colby, 2005). Children's books that can be used as historical documents are available at the National Archives Website, www.archives.gov (Nelson, 2005). Other articles feature literature that promotes social justice (Sandmann, 2004), and teaching about women and social justice (Tyson & Hinton-Johnson, 2003).
- Alleman and Brophy (1994b) criticize how fiction is used in elementary social studies textbooks. The points they make are well taken. Teachers should select literature that matches the content objectives of the unit. Books selected should teach something worthwhile, and if an excerpt from a story is used, then the excerpt should be long enough that students will get the point being made. And, once again, the book should present information that is accurate and not stereotyped.

The Performing Arts and the Visual Arts

- Carole Cox's (2005) book is an excellent source for suggestions on how to implement the performing arts in an elementary classroom. Christensen (2006) wrote a lesson plan for elementary students based on artwork of civil rights activist Bernice Sims.
- Vardell (2003) writes about the use of poetry as part of elementary social studies, with good suggestions on how to have children perform poetry.
- Tibbett's (2004) book is about using American music to teach social studies. Milson and LaComb (2001) report on an Internet project that integrated music and social studies. La Comb's fourth graders contacted symphonic orchestra musicians from all over the world.

LESSON PLANS AND INSTRUCTIONAL ACTIVITIES

This chapter concludes with two examples of integrated social studies teaching, each based on a picture book written for children.

1. A lesson plan for a third-grade lesson using Allen Say's Caldecott-winning picture book, *Grandfather's Journey*
2. A description of a group project completed by fifth graders—a picture history depicting the events in Paul Goble's picture book *Lone Bull's Horse Raid.*

Grade Three: *Grandfather's Journey*

Overview: A third-grade class has been studying their community, and they are working on a unit called "Our City Today." Their city has many residents who are immigrants
to the United States. Allen Say's Caldecott-winning picture book *Grandfather's Journey*
(1993) will help the children understand that many immigrants to their city are
bicultural and have strong emotional attachments to both the United States and their
homelands. This lesson is for a third-grade class of 25 students.

Resources and Materials: (a) A hardcover copy of *Grandfather's Journey,* (b) chart
with response options (see the section "Teaching Sequence"), (c) wall map of the
world, (d) various information books, encyclopedias, and atlases.

Standard: In the *National Standards for History,* Standard 3C for the early grades is
"the student understands the various other groups from regions throughout the world
who came into his or her own state or region over the long-ago and recent past." A performance expectation for this standard is that "the student is able to use a variety of
visual data, fiction and nonfiction sources, and speakers to identify the groups that have
come into the state or region and to generate ideas about why they came" (National
Center for History in the Schools, 1996, p. 30).

Content Objectives: Children will learn that many immigrants retain close feelings for
their native lands. One group will identify geographic similarities and differences
between Japan and the United States.

Process Objectives: Children will *write* a response to the story and *identify* reasons
why Allen Say's grandfather felt attached to both Japan and the United States, and a
small group will *compare and contrast* the physical geography of Japan and the
United States.

Values Objective: This lesson will help children become sympathetic rather than hostile to the biculturalism of many Americans.

Teaching Sequence:

1. Prepare the chart with the response options and gather information books,
   encyclopedias, and atlases.
2. Identify for the children Japan and the United States on a wall map of the
   world. Then read aloud *Grandfather's Journey.*
3. Ask whether any of the children have anything they would like to say about
   the book. Then call attention to the three journal-writing options you wrote
   beforehand on chart paper.

Select one of the following:

a. Write anything you want about *Grandfather's Journey.*
b. Grandfather was *astonished* by the ocean, the enormous rocks, the endless fields, and the towering mountains. Write about something you have seen that is *astonishing.*
c. Why do you think Allen Say's grandfather loved both the United States and Japan?

4. Later that day or the next, bring the class together and reread the story. At the end of the story, ask question (c) to the class. Discuss possible reasons why Grandfather felt attached to both places. Help children see that Grandfather appreciated the great natural beauty, the different kinds of people, and the wide range of sites and sounds in the United States. At the same time, he could not forget his old friends and the beauty of the places he knew as a boy in Japan.
5. You might also want to go back through the story and point out to the class how Grandfather ages and changes (see illustrations on pp. 4, 5, 16, 18, 25, and 29 of *Grandfather's Journey*).
6. Ask for volunteers for a special project on the geographic similarities and differences between Japan and the United States. This group will use the reference sources to compare the two nations on (a) climate, (b) topography, (c) rivers, (d) population density, (e) cultural groups, (f) industry, and (g) agriculture. The group will decide to report to their classmates with either a bulletin board display or an oral presentation.

Evaluation: To determine whether children have achieved the lesson's content and values objectives, (a) read what they wrote in their journals, (b) listen carefully to what they said during the discussion, and (c) assess the bulletin board display or oral presentation of the children participating in the project.

Effective Teaching in Today's Diverse Classroom: This lesson provides an example of what some educators call an *additive cultural approach* to teaching. This approach calls for a curriculum that takes advantage of the cultural identities of children by using aspects of culture as the focus for lessons. Like Allen Say's grandfather, millions of our children are bicultural. Rather than ask a child to abandon his or her native culture, it makes more sense to encourage the child to add the "core" American culture to the one he or she has. For example, if you have Korean American children in your classroom, you should plan a unit that will teach all children about the history and culture of Korea. Such a unit not only would allow your Korean American children to succeed as they read and write about familiar topics but also would provide important information to all your children and help them better understand each other.

Grade Five: A Picture History of *Lone Bull's Horse Raid*

A fifth-grade class was studying Native Americans prior to the coming of the Europeans. They would learn about five tribes. The class had many English learners and others who found it difficult to read grade-level material. While the class was learning about the Sioux, the teacher asked for volunteers who wanted to complete a project that would "require a lot of artwork." This group of students read Goble and Goble's (1973) picture book *Lone Bull's Horse Raid*. The story is told from 14-year-old Lone Bull's perspective. Lone Bull is an Oglala Sioux who steals horses from the Crow. Following is a day-by-day plan for the project

Day 1

After discussing the book, explain the idea of a "picture history." Describe how the Natives of the Great Plains used picture histories, painted on their tipis or on buffalo robes, to record significant events. You can find good illustrations of picture histories painted on buffalo robes on the Website of the Glenbow Museum in Calgary, Canada (*www.glenbow.org*). You also might share illustrations of Grecian urns and Roman columns, cross-cultural examples of other forms of picture histories. Help the group make a list of the scenes from the book to illustrate (e.g., Lone Bull and his friend, Charging Bear, riding with Lone Bull's father; stalking the Crow camp; stealing the horses; fighting the Crow; and giving away the stolen horses).

Day 2

Have the group decide who will illustrate each scene. Students may work together or individually. Decide on a form for the picture history. If you are ambitious, you could construct a model tipi 4 to 5 feet high. Edwin Tunis's (1979) book *Indians* has a good set of directions on pages 90 to 94. If you decide to make a tipi, then the scenes should be painted on the outside of the tipi. A simple picture history could be painted on a strip of paper approximately 2 × 6 feet. Students should complete a sketch of their scenes.

Days 3 and 4

Bring several copies of Paul Goble's other books to class for group members to examine. They should try to use the same colors and style as Goble. If you can find books with photographs of decorated tipis, by all means bring them to class. Each scene should be blocked out so that each artist knows the space she or he has. If you are making a tipi, then the scenes from the book should be painted before the tipi is assembled.

Days 5 to 8

Once the art is done, have group members decide whether they want to tell or read the story to their classmates. The picture history, rather than the book's illustrations, should be used during the performance. Be sure the group has plenty of time to rehearse.

Effective Teaching in Today's Diverse Classroom: As I noted in Chapter 4, it is important that we help our students develop accurate knowledge about Native Americans rather than reinforce stereotypical images. This lesson supports the stereotype that all Indians lived in tipis, committed acts that European Americans considered criminal, and thrived on violence. Fortunately, this lesson was part of an in-depth study of Native Americans, with separate units of study on diverse tribes. Goble's books are historically and culturally accurate and are excellent teaching resources. The lesson is ideal for a diverse classroom because it allows students to express what they know through both the visual and the performing arts.

Part III

Sources of Content for Social Studies Teaching

Chapter 10 Democratic Citizenship: Participating in Civic Life

Chapter 11 History and Geography: Understanding People of Different Times and Places

Chapter 12 The Other Social Sciences and Topics of Special Interest: Completing the Social Studies Curriculum

Chapter 10

Democratic Citizenship: Participating in Civic Life

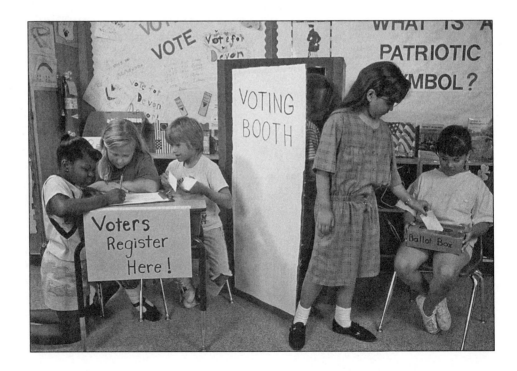

n the primary grades, citizenship can be learned through school service projects. Michiko Murayama, a third-grade teacher, provided her class with an opportunity to welcome new students to their school. Ms. Murayama's school had a significant level of transience among the students, so each year her school service project was "Welcome to Cesar Chavez School." Because each teacher at Cesar Chavez School could expect to lose several students during the year and to gain at least five, the task of welcoming new students was an important one.

The first year Ms. Murayama attempted the "Welcome to Cesar Chavez School" project, she asked her class what could be done to help new students. She had her own ideas, and so did the school principal, but her third graders came up with the following list:

- *Writing and publishing a "Guide to Cesar Chavez School."* Each year, a group of her children worked together to write and illustrate the guide, and she made enough copies for all the new students. The guide, written and illustrated by the children, included information on school rules, holidays, and the recess and lunch schedule. It contained information on special programs at the school, such as an after-school recreation program run by the city. One year, Ms. Murayama's class included a description of their favorite entrees in the school cafeteria.
- *Serving as "First Week Hosts."* Other students took part in this component of the school service project by taking new students on a tour of the school. They ate lunch with the new students and made sure they were not alone at recess.
- *Serving as translators for non-English-speaking new students at other grade levels.* Several of Ms. Murayama's third graders were bilingual. They spent some days in kindergarten and first-grade classrooms, helping teachers communicate with their new students who spoke little or no English.

School service projects like Ms. Murayama's provide children with opportunities to apply what they have learned about citizenship. Citizenship education is the topic of this chapter.

• • •

In this chapter, you will read about

- Why authorities believe that citizenship education is the primary goal of social studies programs
- Competing perspectives on citizenship education: to teach students about how government works and to follow the rules or to teach students about how to change society for the better
- The content of citizenship education as organized around five concerns posed by the *National Standards for Civics and Government* (Center for Civic Education, 1994): (a) what government is, (b) the basic values of American democracy, (c) the role of the U.S. Constitution, (d) the relationship of the United States to other nations, and (e) the roles and responsibilities of U.S. citizens

- Engle and Ochoa's teaching sequence for value-based decision making
- Forms of civic participation appropriate for elementary school students, including school service, community service, and individual service projects
- How citizenship can be developed as a part of a teacher's plan for classroom management

◆ Democratic Citizenship: The First Goal of Social Studies

Good citizenship is recognized widely as the most important goal of social studies. The definition of *social studies* adopted by the National Council for the Social Studies (NCSS) states that "the primary purpose of social studies is to help young people develop the ability to make informed and reasoned decisions for the public good as citizens of a culturally diverse, democratic society in an interdependent world" (NCSS Task Force on Standards for Teaching and Learning in the Social Studies, 1993, p. 213). Why a preeminent place for citizenship education? Knowledgeable and active citizens are essential for the survival of our democratic way of life. Consider the following statement: "Ultimately, a free society must rely on the knowledge, skills, and virtue of its citizens and those they elect to public office. Civic education, therefore, is essential to the preservation and improvement of American constitutional democracy" (Center for Civic Education, 1994, p. 1).

Citizenship education is a topic with many facets. A reading of the professional literature on the topic reveals that there is no widespread agreement on the core issue, just what "effective" or "ideal" citizenship is (Bennett, 2006; Carnegie Corporation of New York & The Center for Information and Research on Civic Learning and Engagement, 2003; Field, 1997; Patrick & Hoge, 1991; Quigley & Bahmueller, 1991; Wesheimer & Kahne, 2004). A major study conducted by Anderson and colleagues (1997) established that teachers have very different perspectives on what citizenship education should accomplish. A good place to start our discussion is with some definitions.

Engle and Ochoa (1988) note that *citizenship* "is conferred on an individual by a state or nation" (p. 16). The type of citizenship we are concerned with is broader than legal status as a citizen, so "whenever individuals make a decision or act in any way that affects others, directly or indirectly, knowingly or unknowingly, they are acting as citizens" (pp. 16–17). Simply put, citizenship is not limited to political activity; it is our public life. The *National Standards for Civics and Government* define this as "civic life," in which individuals are concerned with the "affairs of the community and nation, that is, the public realm" (Center for Civic Education, 1994, p. 7). *Democratic citizenship* refers to civic life in a free society wherein the majority rule while the rights of the minority are respected.

Civics and government are the two social science disciplines at the heart of citizenship education. *Civics* covers "the rights and responsibilities of citizens and their relationship to one another and to the government," whereas instruction in *government* focuses on "political and legal institutions" (Patrick & Hoge, 1991, p. 428). In elementary school, students should learn about how rules are made, enforced, and interpreted in families, at school, in the classroom, and at the local, state, national, and international levels. Instruction that focuses on the functioning of legal systems is called *law-related education* (LRE), and several lessons and units have been produced to accomplish the goals of LRE (Bjorklun, 1995; Hicks & Austin, 1994; Norton, 1992; Smagorinsky, 1994).

Citizenship Education and Diversity

Citizenship education must at the same time provide for unification and celebrate diversity. The values, principles, and beliefs of a democratic way of life are the unifying elements of the United States. The *National Standards for Civics and Government* (Center for Civic Education, 1994) summarize how the democratic ideal binds us as Americans: "Americans are united by the values, principles, and beliefs they share rather than by ethnicity, race, religion, class, language, gender, or national origin" (p. 25). Thus, when students become committed to our democratic system of government, democratic values and beliefs, and democratic civic life, they become Americans.

The NCSS *Curriculum Guidelines for Multicultural Education* make this same point:

> There is, after all, a set of overarching values that all groups within a society or nation endorse to maintain societal cohesion. In our nation, these core values stem from our commitment to human dignity, and include justice, equality, freedom, and due process of law. (NCSS Task Force on Ethnic Studies Curriculum Guidelines, 1992, p. 284)

In your classroom, you may have a half dozen native languages spoken, national identities that encompass all the continents, and religious affiliations of many kinds. All of our students need effective citizenship education that leads to a commitment to the democratic ideals of the United States of America and an understanding of the wonderful freedom we enjoy.

At the same time, citizenship education is education for diversity. Our units of study in social studies should help students learn about the many facets of pluralism in the United States. One of the strengths of our democratic system is that it makes diversity in language, culture, religion, nationality, and political philosophy inevitable. Students should see that diversity is not a threat to our way of life but rather a part of America that always has existed and will exist in the future. A key component of citizenship education is that students learn that our democratic ideal has not always been realized. Even though the United States was founded on values of justice and equality, public policy and private action have sometimes been unjust and unequal. For example, in California, fourth graders who study the history of their state should learn about the internment of Japanese Americans during World War II. Fifth graders who study the creation of the United States should understand that although the

Constitution was enacted by "the people," women, Native Americans, enslaved persons, and men without property could not vote in 18th-century elections.

Research on Citizenship Education

With these definitions in mind, let's take a look at the research on citizenship education. In a recent article, Janet Alleman and Jere Brophy (2006) concluded the "studies focusing on elementary students, and especially primary students, have little or nothing to say about children's ideas about democracy or democratic government" (p. 17). In an earlier review, Patrick and Hoge (1991) reached a similar conclusion as they stated "the solid findings are too few and unrelated to help practitioners make a powerful difference in how they teach government, civics, and law, and in what their students learn from them" (p. 434).

Some interesting research has been conducted on what students know and think about government and civics and how these topics are presented in textbooks. Children do understand rules and laws are a necessary part of life. They tend, however, to see government primarily as a provider of what people need, rather than as an enforcer of the rules (Alleman & Brophy, 2006; Berti, 2005). Alleman and Brophy's (2002a) study of children's understanding of the U.S. presidency revealed that K–3 students know little about the three branches of government and that their ideas about the presidency center on material items, such as a big house and a limousine, rather than on what the president does. An earlier study by Greenstein (1969) of political understanding among students in grades 4 through 8 still makes interesting reading. Greenstein found that fourth graders idealized political leaders, from their mayor to the president. By eighth grade, this reverence had diminished. Of particular interest is Greenstein's finding that elementary students did not base their feelings on political information; they knew very little about the leaders they held in high regard.

The research on how civics and government are treated in elementary school social studies textbooks is now dated. Wade and Everett (1994) examined how citizenship education was presented in four of the most popular third-grade social studies textbooks of the time. They wanted to find out whether things had changed from the 1960s and 1970s, when textbooks presented an image of a good citizen who was "passive, harmonious, and accepting" (p. 308). All four textbooks devoted several pages to citizenship. Wade and Everett concluded that the textbooks they reviewed in the early 1990s were an improvement over earlier ones. A variety of political and social acts were presented as a part of good citizenship. In addition to staying informed, voting, and running for office, good citizens were presented as also taking social action, performing community service, and lobbying public officials. The researchers thought, however, that the books did not provide enough information to help students learn the full range of civic options available to citizens of the United States. You could evaluate the social studies textbooks in your school to determine whether or not they promote "passive" citizenship, where the good citizen limits her or his activity to staying informed and voting; or an "active" citizenship, in which good citizens lobby public officials, perform community service, and, when necessary, take part in public protests.

◆ Competing Perspectives on Citizenship Education

Authorities have proffered several perspectives on precisely what citizenship education should try to accomplish. Anderson and colleagues (1997) conducted a study of how elementary and secondary teachers define citizenship education. They found "four coherent, identifiable, and separate viewpoints on citizenship education" (p. 351). A brief description of each should help us understand why this area of social studies is controversial:

- Some teachers adopt a *critical thinking* perspective. These teachers believe that citizenship education should help students question the status quo, develop critical thinking and questioning skills, and encourage open-mindedness and tolerance.
- Other teachers hold a *legalist* perspective. They believe that citizenship education should stress obedience to laws, teach the basic structure of our political system, and inform students of their rights and responsibilities.
- Teachers who have a *cultural pluralism* perspective define citizenship education as the celebration of diversity and pluralism. These teachers believe that rather than teach the basic structure of our political institutions, citizenship education should expose students to a range of ideologies.
- Finally, some teachers adhere to an *assimilationist* perspective, which is similar to the views of the legalists. Assimilationist teachers, however, explicitly reject current ideas of "political correctness" and want to transmit to students the dominant values of our society.

This summary categorizes the perspectives of teachers who, at the time, belonged to the NCSS and reveals the divergent nature of citizenship education. It should be noted, too, that some teachers hold more than one perspective. To simplify things somewhat, another way to look at the competing views on citizenship education is to examine the "transmission versus transformation" debate (Stanley, 2005). This crystallizes one of the more controversial issues in social studies. Simply, should teachers limit citizenship education to how government functions, and should their definition of a good citizen be a person who follows the rules and votes (transmission)? Or should teachers teach students how to analyze social conditions *and* then take action to bring about change (transformation)?

The *transmission model* is adopted by the legalists and assimilationists described by Anderson and colleagues (1997; see also, Leming, Ellington, & Porter-Magee, 2003). Teachers help students understand the structure and function of local, state, and federal government. Students learn about the rights and responsibilities of citizenship and are encouraged to participate in nonthreatening civic activities, such as working on political campaigns, staying informed, and voting.

The *transformation model* is endorsed by many social studies authorities (Banks & Banks, 2003; Engle & Ochoa, 1988; Jennings, Crowell, & Fernlund, 1994). It is the model used by teachers who have both the critical thinking and the cultural pluralist perspectives described by Anderson and colleagues. Advocates of this model want a curriculum that encourages students to make decisions and *take action* related to the concept, issue, or problem being studied.

Jennings and colleagues (1994) provide specific suggestions for how to implement a "transformational social studies." First, we should see our classrooms as places where students can learn about "social relationships, reciprocity, power, and community." This means that we should encourage students to analyze how things work (or do not work) and make suggestions for improvement. Second, the curriculum should present students with historical problem-solving situations that focus on historical "dilemmas of justice," such as those faced by the abolitionists and advocates for child labor laws. Third, we should encourage students to express their own opinions, not just to restate the positions of others. Fourth, the authors argue that we should teach students the dynamic relationship between pluralism and unity in our constitutional system. Fifth, argue these authors, teachers should plan for students to participate in social action projects to convince them of "the power inherent within cooperative efforts against injustice" (pp. 5–6).

You can see how controversial this could become. I think almost everyone would agree that our older students should be taught to understand and analyze a range of perspectives on important current issues. Students should learn about several forms of civic participation. Those of us who encourage students to take action, however, must be sure that we do not steer our students to any one side of a public policy issue or to a political candidate. In fact, we should encourage students to define issues rather than present an agenda to our students. Finally, we should remember we are dealing with elementary school children, and most of these "social action" projects are more appropriate for middle school and high school students.

Nonetheless, sometimes all of us can underestimate the potential of elementary school children. One of the most impressive social action projects I am aware of took place in an *elementary* school classroom. Barbara Vogel, a fifth-grade teacher in Aurora, Colorado, had completed a unit with her students on slavery in American history. Shortly thereafter, Associated Press writer Karin Davies completed a story on the slave trade existing in the late 1990s in Sudan. The story ran in a local newspaper, and one of Ms. Vogel's students, Kyle Vincent, decided that something should be done to stop slavery in Sudan. (The slave trade in Sudan was the result of civil war as local militias, who fought without pay for the Sudanese government, made captives their slaves. International organizations were able to purchase the freedom of some of the enslaved people.) Ms. Vogel's class began to raise money, originally collecting coins in jars. This social action project received national media coverage, and eventually large donations began to arrive. By the end of 1998, the project had raised more than $50,000. The money was donated to international organizations and was used to free more than 1,000 enslaved people in Sudan!

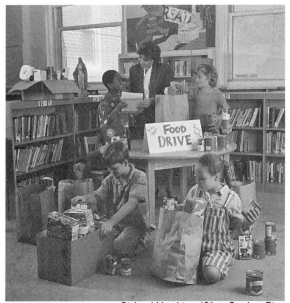

Richard Hutchings / Silver Burdett Ginn

Social studies should teach our students to be good citizens.
A key component of good citizenship is participation in
community service projects.

National Projects on Citizenship Education

Two attempts to define the scope of citizenship education are worthy of mention.
Civitas is a curriculum framework developed by the Council for the Advancement
of Citizenship and the Center for Civic Education (Quigley & Bahmueller, 1991).
Civitas is an essential document for school district committees writing instructional
units on citizenship education. The *National Standards for Civics and Government*
(Center for Civic Education, 1994) could prove to be very influential. I discuss specific sections of the national standards later in this chapter.

◆ Citizenship Education: Content

Citizenship education has three components: content, values, and processes. The
content is the knowledge students should acquire in order to be effective citizens, and
they need to know a great deal in the fields of civics and government. For most of us,
our district curriculum guide and social studies textbooks cover these topics at every
grade level. If our district's social studies program follows the expanded horizons
format, then kindergartners, first graders, and second graders focus on families, classrooms, and schools; third graders look at civic life in their cities; fourth graders study

the government of their state; fifth graders learn about the federal government; and sixth graders examine governments of ancient cultures or foreign nations.

The *National Standards for Civics and Government* (Center for Civic Education, 1994) provide a specific description of the civic knowledge our students should acquire. The standards organize content under five questions:

1. *What is government, and what should it do?*   Our students should be able to provide a basic description of government. For example, students should know how rules are made, how they are enforced, and how they are interpreted. Students should have some understanding of the types of legislatures that exist (e.g., school boards, city councils, state assemblies, and U.S. Congress). They should become familiar with courts of law. They should learn about executives, such as their principal, the mayor, and the president. It is important that students see why government is necessary and what life would be like without government. Alleman and Brophy (2006) argue that, unfortunately, "teaching about government in the elementary grades often is not as effective as it could be, either because it is confined to teaching about government leaders and symbols, or because it gets mired in the details of topics like how a bill becomes a law." They argue that the focus should be on "why governments are needed and what they do for their people" (p. 16).

   Students should learn about power and authority. Why does a city council have the power to make laws? Where did it get that power? Students should understand the authority of teachers and principals. They should also recognize examples of "power without authority," such as a robber holding up a bank or a playground bully harassing another student. Young students need to explore the purposes of rules and laws. They should recognize that rules describe the way people must behave. Again, critical analysis is necessary for good social studies lessons because the national standards expect students to evaluate laws according to criteria. Are our classroom rules understandable? Is a playground rule equitable? Is a city ordinance possible to follow and not a demand for the impossible? Finally, under this question, students should begin to understand the concept of limited government. They should see that everyone, including our most powerful elected and appointed officials, must obey the law.

   At the end of the chapter is a lesson plan for a "walking field trip." A second-grade teacher takes her students on a walk to the city library. On the way, students examine several signs that state rules of public behavior—a good way to introduce children to the purpose of laws created by government, in this case a municipal government.

2. *What are the basic values and principles of American democracy?*   As a knowledge goal, we want students to describe the important values and principles of our system of government and civic life.

3. *How does the government established by the Constitution embody the purposes, values, and principles of American democracy?*   Elementary students should know what the U.S. Constitution is and the important

ideas in it. Most social studies programs save most of this material until fifth grade. An important topic that should be explored before fifth grade is how the Constitution and the federal government protect individual rights. Students should begin to understand their First Amendment freedoms. Most fourth graders will learn about their state government and the specifics of their legislature, judiciary, and executive. Third grade has usually been the place where students study municipal government. In any case, by the end of fourth grade, the national standards state that students should know what services their local government provides, how the services are funded, and how people can participate in local government.

4. *What is the relationship of the United States to other nations and to world affairs?* Remember, a valid criticism of the expanded horizons curricular framework is the lack of global education in grades K–5. The national standards call for students in grades K–4 to develop knowledge in several international areas. Students should understand the concept of *nation*. I have found this to be difficult for young students, who frequently cannot understand the difference between a state in the United States, such as Vermont, and a sovereign nation, such as Germany. One concept that students can begin to understand is the interdependence of nations. They should be able to identify cultural exchanges (e.g., music from another nation), trade (products grown or manufactured in other nations), and military linkages (multinational military operations). Students should learn about examples of how nations solve problems peacefully.

5. *What are the roles of the citizen in American democracy?* Students are expected to know the definition of *citizenship*, how people become citizens of the United States, the rights of citizens, the responsibilities of citizens, how we select our leaders, and how U.S. citizens can participate in their government.

At the end of this chapter, you will find a mini-unit developed by a fifth-grade teacher with the goal of teaching her students about a basic right afforded us in the U.S. Constitution—a fair trial.

Teaching the Electoral Process

Children in elementary schools should learn about the electoral process in democratic societies (Gandy, 2004; Haas, 2004; Ledford & Lyon; 2004). The best way for children to learn about elections is for them to participate in a mock election. I agree with Haas (2004) that these elections should refrain from asking children to vote on actual candidates for local, state, or federal office, though many elementary schools do conduct mock elections every four years during the presidential campaign. Rather, Haas recommends that teachers should "focus instead on key concepts about . . . the voting process" (p. 340). To teach the full electoral process, it is best to have an election about a class- or school-related issue (e.g., How should we spend $100 donated by the PTA?).

After a problem has been identified, the next step is to define a small number of possible solutions. Some children then choose or are assigned to be advocates for each solution. It is probably a good idea have at least half of the class be "nonpartisan," so that the campaigners have someone to sway. A campaign manager is selected for each rival solution. The mock campaign can include campaign posters, speeches, and, in the upper grades, the development of video ads and campaign Websites. Though real political campaigns these days are poor examples, the emphasis should be on positive and accurate advocacy. Children should learn the vocabulary of free elections as they prepare for the election (e.g., poll, secret ballot, etc.). The actual election should include all the elements of real elections. The children could be asked to fill out a simple voter registration form. There should be a private polling place and, since many elementary schools serve as polling places for real elections, you might be able to use the actual polling booths used by adult voters. To ensure fairness, students from another class might be "hired" to monitor the voting and to count the ballots, with observers from each campaign on hand. Finally, the entire process should be analyzed. An important lesson would ask students to consider the key elements of a free election. Teachers should also ask the students to evaluate the effectiveness of the campaigns. If they had it to do all over again, what would they do differently?

◆ Citizenship Education: Values

Values are standards we use to judge human behavior. *Civic values* are values relevant to our public life. The *National Standards for Civics and Government* (Center for Civic Education, 1994) are a realistic statement of civic values. The standards call for students to become knowledgeable about the basic values of American democracy. This knowledge "is an essential first step in fostering a reasoned commitment to them" (p. 22). The standards offer this list of fundamental values of American democracy: (a) individual rights to life, liberty, and pursuit of happiness; (b) the public or common good; (c) justice; (d) equality of opportunity; (e) diversity; (f) truth; and (g) patriotism.

The national standards list the following principles of American government: (a) The people are sovereign and are the ultimate source of authority for government, (b) the power of government is limited, (c) the people exercise their authority directly through elections, (d) the people exercise their authority indirectly through elected representatives, and (e) decisions are based on majority rule, but minority rights are respected.

The national standards (Center for Civic Education, 1994) address the relationship of unity and diversity. They state that, by the end of fourth grade, "students should be able to explain the importance of Americans sharing and supporting certain values, principles, and beliefs" (p. 25). The United States is a place of many cultural groups, languages, and religions, and the standards correctly state that "the identity of an American is defined by shared political values, principles, and beliefs" (p. 25). At the same time, "students should be able to describe diversity in the United States and identify its benefits" (p. 26). A diverse country provides for new ideas, a range of perspectives on any issue, and choices in all aspects of life (e.g., the arts and politics). The standards call for students to understand how diversity can lead to conflict through discrimination and alienation. Social studies programs should help students see how such conflicts can be avoided and resolved.

Teaching Democratic Values

Engle and Ochoa (1988) comment that, for teachers, "the temptation is to indoctrinate children with the 'right' democratic values" (p. 66). Instead, they call for a study of values that is analytic. The national standards call for knowledge of values that will lead to a "commitment" to them. Thus, for us as teachers, it seems that our first goal should be to help students understand a value and then to analyze the issues that can arise when the value guides behavior. Finally, we want students to study controversial issues and make decisions on the basis of those values.

Engle and Ochoa (1988) define a seven-step process for value-based decision making on public issues. As an example, we will consider this process as it was used in a sixth-grade classroom. The principal of the school asked that students suggest how there could be fewer disputes over use of various areas of the playground. Younger children complained that older children monopolized the more desirable areas. Engle and Ochoa's seven steps are similar to those for the processes of inquiry and critical thinking described in Chapters 6 and 7.

Step 1: Identify and Define the Problem
In this case, the principal, acting in response to student complaints, defined the problem: How can the various areas of the playground be used so that there are fewer arguments about who should be playing where? Some sixth graders did not think this was a problem. They cited two reasons. First, when they were younger, the older students "hogged" the good areas. Second, the younger children did not know how to play some of the games that could be played only in certain areas. At this point, the teacher turned the discussion toward definitions. Engle and Ochoa note that this is an important prerequisite to value-based decision making. The teacher wanted agreement on what constituted an "area." After some discussion, the sixth graders generated a list of six playground areas (e.g., jungle gym, dodgeball circles).

Step 2: Identify Value Assumptions
Returning to the issue his sixth graders had raised, that there was no problem regarding the playground areas, the teacher decided to focus on two values: (a) justice and (b) respect for the rights of others. Engle and Ochoa (1988) wrote

that "identifying value assumptions is not limited to any one phase of the decision-making process" (p. 74). It is a good idea, though, to clarify and consider values at this stage.

The sixth graders had an extended discussion about justice, equity, and sharing. The teacher asked for definitions of *justice.* Students responded by saying it meant that people "were fair" and that "things happened according to fair rules." The value of justice would seem to require sharing the playground areas. Although all the students believed in fairness, some had difficulty with the application of this value in this case. This small group said that justice meant that because they were treated unfairly by older students when they were small, it was perfectly fair for them to treat current fourth graders the same way (fourth, fifth, and sixth graders had recess at the same time). Other students pointed out that "two wrongs don't make a right" and that "fourth graders have rights, too." The vast majority of the students agreed that, to respect the rights of all students, the playground areas would have to be shared.

Step 3: Identify Alternatives

Engle and Ochoa (1988) state that "values, previous knowledge, and experience are all involved in identifying alternatives" (p. 74). At this point, the teacher could have had his class work in small groups to maximize the number of students who could participate vigorously. He thought, though, that the whole-group discussion was progressing well. So far, this was a civil discussion. Students had not personalized comments, exchanged threatening looks, or made rude interruptions. The teacher had two students transcribe ideas as they were offered. Two "solution alternatives" survived the discussion:

- Because nine classes were at recess together (three classes each in grades 4, 5, and 6), nine areas should be designated and the classes rotate through them (the "rotation" plan).
- Students could play in any area they wanted, and two sixth-grade monitors would be assigned to each area. The monitors would ensure that all students would have a chance to play the area's game (the "monitor" plan).

Step 4: Predict Consequences

Engle and Ochoa suggest that two questions be considered: (1) What effects will follow from each alternative? and (2) What effect will each alternative have on all parties? Some students noted that the consequence of the rotation plan would be that they would be giving up their prerogative of what to play. Others noted that they would not be able to "play handball everyday, like we want to." Other students interjected the value of justice idea again at this point as they considered the second question. The strength of the rotation plan was its equity; all classes would have the same opportunity to use each area of the playground.

The monitor plan was criticized widely when the sixth graders considered its consequences. First, several sixth graders would not be playing anything; they would be acting as organizers and referees. Although many of the sixth graders would do a good job at these tasks, they would be "giving up" their chance to play. A few noted that the problem might not be solved in the monitor plan. Each area would contain fourth, fifth, and sixth graders. The younger students might continue to be pushed aside. Finally, one student commented that the younger students could not compete with them and that "some of the fourth graders" might get hurt.

Step 5: Reach Decisions

Engle and Ochoa (1988) note that reaching decisions can be filled with tension because, in most cases, no solution satisfies everyone. After considering the consequences, however, this group of sixth graders almost unanimously recommended the rotation plan.

Step 6: Justify Decisions

Once again, the discussion turned to values. When the teacher asked for reasons why the rotation plan was best, several students noted that it was "fair" and would give all classes "the same chance." This was a reliance on justice as a rationale. Other students commented that it seemed to be better than any other plan they could think of. Three students were chosen to present the class's recommendation to the principal.

Step 7: Tentativeness of Decision Making

The teacher wanted his students to understand that their suggested rotation plan seemed like a good one but that it might not work. He prompted his students to remain open-minded and to accept that they may need to revise their perspectives. In this case, it was not necessary. The principal adopted the rotation plan. It worked well and has been in place for 6 years now.

◆ Citizenship Education: Processes

The processes of effective citizenship should be practiced at home, in the classroom, on the playground, in the community, and at the state, national, and international levels. A good place to discuss the "doing" of citizenship education is with a set of attitudes, called *dispositions*, that students should adopt. The *National Standards for Civics and Government* (Center for Civic Education, 1994) argues that these dispositions will enhance "citizen effectiveness and promote the healthy functioning of American democracy" (p. 37). These dispositions are beliefs that guide behavior. They include individual responsibility, self-discipline, civility, respect for the rights of other individuals, honesty, respect for the law, open-mindedness, critical-mindedness, negotiation and compromise, persistence, civic-mindedness, compassion, and patriotism. Each of these dispositions involves a process. For example, the process of open-mindedness has many components that can be practiced and developed in the classroom. First, students can

Krista Greco/Merrill

It is important that students learn to listen, without interruption and without preconceived notions, to the opinions of their classmates.

learn to listen, without interruption and without preconceived notions, to the opinions of other students. Next, students should learn to question the perspectives of others without personalizing their comments. Finally, students should learn to accept the valid points another person makes rather than reject all of a message because some parts make little sense.

This open-mindedness is part of civil discourse, the polite way citizens in a democracy discuss public issues. Civil discourse is an essential process for students to learn (Parker, 1995, 2001, 2006). In *Civitas*, the curriculum framework developed through the Center for Civic Education, two essential components of civil discourse are defined (Quigley & Bahmueller, 1991, p. 13):

- *Addressing the issue.* Participants in a discussion focus on their contributions to the issues at hand and do not engage in personal attack.
- *Respecting the right of others to be heard.* Civil discourse requires good listening; participants in a discussion should not disrupt other speakers.

The guidelines presented in the previous chapter in the section "Speaking and Listening in the Social Studies Program" will encourage the development of appropriate civic discourse.

The national standards go on to define "the means by which citizens can influence the decisions and actions of their government" (Center for Civic Education, 1994, p. 38). These are (a) read about public issues; (b) discuss public issues; (c) communicate with public officials; (d) vote; (e) take an active role in interest groups, political parties, and organizations; and (f) attend meetings of governing agencies, work in campaigns, circulate petitions, take part in peaceful demonstrations, and contribute money to parties, candidates, and causes. Each of these can be implemented in some form in the elementary classroom:

Read About Public Issues. News magazines written for children, like *Weekly Reader,* do an excellent job of presenting national and global issues to children. Online computer resources are beginning to provide accessible information to elementary students (e.g., the online resource KidsNet). Our oldest and most able elementary students can read articles in newspapers, magazines, and on appropriate Websites on the Internet.

Discuss Public Issues. Children at all elementary levels should discuss issues that relate to their classroom, school, and community. Older elementary children who have read a variety of perspectives should be encouraged to discuss state, national, and global issues.

Communicate with Public Officials. One of the first public officials students should communicate with is their teacher. Students, at the proper time and in a respectful manner, should have the opportunity to talk with us about topics of concern. Students at all levels should learn how to speak and write to their principal on school issues. We should encourage our older students to write to their school board, city council and mayor, state legislature and governor, representatives in Congress, and the president. Our goal as teachers is to present information, to allow a range of perspectives to be heard, and to model written and oral formats of communicating.

Vote. Elementary students should take part in classroom and school elections. These elections should be as close to the real thing as possible. All elections should provide for a secret ballot, even those in the classroom. Many schools are voting places in "real" elections, and it is a good idea to let students experience a voting booth as they vote in mock state and federal elections.

Take an Active Role in Interest Groups, Political Parties, and Organizations. A variety of youth organizations encourage civic life, such as Girl Scouts, Boy Scouts, and youth groups in religious institutions. All elementary schools, however, should have student governments. Heath and Vik (1994) report how elementary school student councils allow children to exercise leadership, share ideas, resolve problems, and manage projects.

Attend Meetings of Governing Agencies, Work in Campaigns, Circulate Petitions, Take Part in Peaceful Demonstrations, and Contribute Money to Parties, Candidates, and Causes. Students should learn the petitioning process in elementary school. They can petition for changes in classroom and school policies. I know teachers who have encouraged students to consider community issues, to define a position, and to make presentations to the city council. Students can participate in fund-raising drives, but this must be done cautiously.

The cause should be noncontroversial and school related, and the process should protect those students who are unable to make a financial contribution. Students should see that they can make contributions in other ways, such as collecting things (e.g., newspapers or cans) or giving one's time.

The real test of the effect of citizenship education is whether our students become active citizens when they are older—whether they, in fact, participate when they are not directed to do so by a school assignment. The activities planned as part of the social studies curriculum should show students the range of options available to active citizens in a democratic society.

Participatory Writing

In *Civitas*, Quigley and Bahmueller (1991) provide several examples of a type of civic participation they call *participatory writing*. I discuss this more fully in Chapter 9 in the section on language arts and social studies. Examples of participatory writing are listed here:

- *Writing to fellow citizens we do not know.*   These citizens could include victims of an earthquake or a person in another state who has done something heroic.
- *Writing to public officials.*   For school children, public officials include their principal. Older students can write to their city councilors, mayor, state legislator, governor, federal representative or senator, or the president.
- *Writing to advocate positions on public issues.*   In a schoolwide referendum on a school issue (e.g., how to spend $5,000 of state lottery money awarded to the school), students could write brochures and make posters advocating their positions.
- *Writing/creating public symbols.*   Students can create classroom and school mottoes. The United States has *E pluribus unum;* each state has one (e.g., New Mexico's is *Crescit eundo* ["It grows as it goes"]); and a classroom can have a motto, too. Or students could design a flag for their classroom.

Service Learning

The NCSS position statement on service learning provides a definition, rationale, and guidelines for successful practice (NCSS Select Subcommittee, 2001). First, service learning "connects meaningful service in the school or community with academic learning and civic responsibility" (p. 240). Service learning is different from community service or voluntarism in two ways. First, the service activity is part of the curriculum and helps students acquire social studies content and civic values. Second, service learning requires reflection and, in some cases, related assignments for the students. Two of the positive features of service learning is that it provides opportunities for "intergenerational learning," as children interact with adults in their schools and communities; and it allows students to be good citizens and make their schools and communities better places since almost all service learning projects attempt to solve problems (Morris, 2003). Quality service-learning activities meet these four criteria:

1. The activity provides opportunities for both the students and representatives from other agencies to design the experience (i.e., if students participate at a senior living facility, residents of that facility help plan the scope of the students' involvement).
2. The activity includes both meaningful service and the opportunity to learn social studies content.
3. The activity requires students to reflect on their service experience and the connection between the experience and democratic values.
4. The activity should focus on how to create a better society rather than simply providing charity that perpetuates the status quo.

Proctor and Haas (1993) and Wade (1994) discuss service learning as a part of citizenship education for elementary students. Proctor and Haas argue that participation in service projects should "be a part of formal education beginning in the primary grades and continuing through graduation. The responsibilities and opportunities for community and social behaviors are present and need to begin at an early age" (p. 381). They describe a hierarchy of service projects:

- *Service projects in schools and classrooms.* These include cross-age tutoring, planting trees, raising money to buy computers for the school, and the venerable clean-campus crusade. Many of these projects can be run by the school Parent-Teacher Association. (At the end of this chapter is a description of how a second-grade teacher designed school service projects for her students.)
- *Service projects in the community.* These serve the neighborhood and the community. Proctor and Haas suggest that these begin in third grade. Community service projects typically involve cooperation with out-of-school agencies; examples are collecting food for victims of a disaster and converting a vacant lot into a park.
- *Individual service projects.* Proctor and Haas (1993) suggest that these are appropriate for middle school and high school students. These projects involve a commitment of many hours over an extended period of time, such as volunteer work at a preschool or a senior citizen center.

Service learning can involve students of every grade level. For example, Willison and Ruane (1995) describe how students in each elementary grade provided service to local senior citizens. Kindergartners made holiday cards for residents of a nursing home. First and second graders sang and performed in theatrical programs at the nursing home. Third and fourth graders had senior pen pals and visited seniors who lived on their own. Fifth and sixth graders visited their "adoptive grandparents" at the nursing home, read to them, and played games with them.

All the students studied their grandparents and the elderly to break down stereotypical images of old people.

Service learning is an excellent way to integrate the curriculum. Continuing with the specific example of providing service to seniors, Wade (1994) shows how students could prepare a survey asking seniors what services they need (language arts). A school project could require fund-raising, which entails bookkeeping (mathematics). Environmental projects, like a community garden, demand knowledge in botany and ecology (science). Finally, service learning can incorporate the use of technology. Harwood and Chang (1999) describe strategies for using the Internet to enhance service learning. Students can find information that will help them focus their project. A group concerned about a local environmental issue, for example, will find information, cataloged by ZIP code, on waste sites and other local topics in a database maintained by the Environmental Protection Agency (www.epa.gov). To provide another example of how technology can be used in service learning, e-mail can be used to communicate with people working in agencies and to share reflections on the service experience.

Citizenship and Classroom Management

A discussion of classroom management, the process of promoting and maintaining a productive environment for students, is beyond the scope of a social studies methods textbook. We should realize, however, that citizenship and classroom management are related topics (Brophy, 1985; Goodman, 1992; Hoover & Kindsvatter, 1997; Ross & Bondy, 1993; Schimmel, 1997; Wolfgang & Kelsay, 1995). Although some aspects of classroom management must be exercised by adults, our classrooms should be democratic. Ross and Bondy (1993) note that although teachers and students will never be equals, more teachers should "shift the emphasis away from controlling students' behavior to teaching students how to be responsible members of a community" (p. 328). Students at all grade levels should be allowed to do each of the following:

- *Play some role in the development of classroom and playground rules.* Teachers should establish some rules that are nonnegotiable (e.g., keep your hands and feet to yourself). Many aspects of classroom life, however, lend themselves to a variety of possible rules. Students need the experience of considering possible rules and the consequences of their implementation. Schimmel (1997) makes a persuasive argument that the development of school and classroom rules should involve everyone in the school community—students, parents, and staff.
- *Resolve problems through collaborative effort.* Students should approach us as their teachers with problems they think should be addressed. Likewise, teachers should bring some problems to our classroom community for consideration. Some problems have to be resolved only by us with the student(s) directly involved (e.g., problems that reveal private information about students); other issues should be brought before the whole class for an open and democratic discussion. Conflict resolution activities will give students a chance to practice civil discourse and value-based decision

making. One possibility teachers should explore is helping students see the relationship between interpersonal conflicts in their classroom and international conflicts between nations (Bickmore, 2002).

- *Make decisions about how they allocate their time and about what activities they pursue.* Even though we as teachers plan much of the school day, all our students should have some time when they make choices about what they will do. Likewise, we select most topics covered in class. Our students, though, should be able to choose areas of personal interest to study, especially in literature, social studies, and science. Democracy requires choices, and the elementary school day should present opportunities for students to learn how to make reasoned and informed decisions.

Schimmel (1997) makes two other important points about classroom rules and citizenship education. First, any list of classroom or school rules should include a list of student rights. Any just legal system is a balance of responsibilities and rights. Too many classroom rule systems are lists of things students may *not do;* there is no corresponding list of what students *may do.* For example, students should have the right to free expression as long as it does not interfere with teaching and learning, the right to a safe classroom environment, the right to participate in classroom activities, and the right to make their grievances known to school authorities.

Second, classroom rules should be taught like any other part of the curriculum. Schimmel (1997) correctly points out that, all too often, classroom rules are presented on the first day of class with little or no explanation. After parents and students have their chance to help create the classroom rules, the rules should be taught through small-group discussion and simulation. Lessons on classroom rules should be a part of a unit on laws in broader jurisdictions, like the school, the city, the state, and the nation. At the very least, students should understand the rationale for each classroom rule. The bottom line is that we cannot expect our students to become effective citizens in a democracy if their classroom experiences are completely undemocratic. Hoover and Kindsvatter (1997) sum it up: "What students learn from our disciplinary activities can significantly shape their future behavior as citizens in our democratic society" (p. 71).

◆ Summary of Key Points

- The development of good citizens is the most important goal of social studies.
- Controversy surrounds whether citizenship education should be limited to information on how government works with a definition of a good citizen as a person who follows the rules and votes (transmission), or whether citizenship education should teach students to analyze current issues and to take action for social change (transformation).
- The content of citizenship education is government and civics. Students should learn about what government is, what government should do, the basic principles and values of American democracy, the U.S. Constitution, the relationship of the United States to other nations, and the nature of good citizenship.

- Social studies programs should make students knowledgeable about basic American civic values. This knowledge should serve as the basis for a commitment to those values.
- A process of value-based decision making includes identifying social problems, identifying relevant values, identifying alternative courses of action, predicting consequences of actions, reaching a decision, and justifying a decision.
- Good citizens in a democracy are active. Active citizenship requires participation: reading about public issues, discussing public issues, communicating with public officials, voting, taking an active role in political organizations, and attending meetings.
- Elementary school children can participate in a variety of school and community service projects.
- We cannot expect our students to become effective citizens in a democracy if their classroom experiences are completely undemocratic; students should play some role in developing rules, resolve problems through collaborative effort, and make decisions about how they spend their time.
- Citizenship must provide for unification, as all students learn about our common core of democratic values; citizenship education must celebrate diversity as an inevitable and desirable outcome of life in a democratic society.

FOR FURTHER READING

- The Website of the Center for Civic Education has many useful links (www.civiced.org).
- The September/October 2006 issue of *Social Studies and the Young Learner* was devoted to citizenship education and has many excellent articles (Bennett, 2006). For example, Ford and Neville described their efforts to make democracy a way of life in a fifth-grade classroom. "Teaching Civics with Primary Documents" was a themed issue of *Social Education* (Potter, 2005, November/December).
- Westheimer & Kahne (2004) completed a study on citizenship education that received awards from the American Educational Research Association and the American Political Science Association. As part of the research, and based on their discussions with authorities in the field, they defined three distinct answers to the question, "What kind of citizen do we need to support an effective democratic society?" (p. 239). They found three different answers: (1) the personally responsible citizen, (2) the participatory citizen, and (3) the justice-oriented citizen.
- Koeppen (2003) describes how to promote active citizenship through an issues-centered social studies curriculum.
- Grant and Van Sledright (1996), in their well-reasoned article, dissent from the view that citizenship education is the heart of social studies. They argue that the relationship between social studies and citizenship is "tangential at best" (p. 57).

Values and Moral Education
- The teaching of values and the related topic of moral education has generated a great deal of published material. In this chapter, I have focused on civic values. On other approaches to teaching a broader set of values, I like two older works: Kirschenbaum (1977) and Raths, Harmin, and Simon (1978). Another excellent book is by Fine (1995).
- If you are interested in moral and character education, be sure to read the classic works by Gilligan (1982) and Kohlberg (1981). See also Benniga (1991) and Lickona (1991). Curtis-Seinik and her coauthors (2006) describe the character education program in the Uniondale, New York, school district. California State University, East Bay, my campus, is home to the Center for Character Education. Check the center's Website for resources: www.edschool.csueastbay.edu/services/cce/.

Law-Related Education
- Bell (2002) explains how to sue moot courts in the classroom. Bjorklun (1995) discusses how to teach personal injury law. Selwyn (1995) and Smagorinsky (1994) discuss legal simulations.

Service Learning
- The journals *Social Studies and the Young Learner* and *Social Education* publish many articles describing service-learning projects, for example, Erickson (2001), Feinberg (2002), and Keech (2002). See Wade (2000) for an argument in favor of service-learning activities reform society.

Curriculum Frameworks
- *Expectations of Excellence: Curriculum Standards for the Social Studies* (NCSS, 1994) has two themes that relate to citizenship education. Theme 9, Power, Authority, and Governance, covers the content of civics and government. Theme 10, Civic Ideals and Practices, sets standards for civic values and participation.
- Although they are lengthy, both *Civitas* (Quigley & Bahmueller, 1991) and the *National Standards for Civics and Government* (Center for Civic Education, 1994) are worthy documents full of important information.

Classroom Management and Citizenship Education
- I suggest three books: *Teaching Children to Care: Management in the Responsive Classroom* (Charney, 1993), *Democratic Discipline: Foundation and Practice* (Hoover & Kindsvatter, 1997), and *Preparing for Citizenship* (Mosher, Kenney, & Garrod, 1994).

LESSON PLANS AND INSTRUCTIONAL ACTIVITIES

Here you will find two examples of innovative social studies teaching, one focusing on the nature and purpose of laws, the other on the American concept of a fair trial: (a) A lesson plan for a "walking field trip" for a second-grade class, challenging students to understand the rules they see displayed on signs around their school; and (b) A fifth-grade mini-unit on fair trials, featuring a mock trial and an analysis of a trial depicting in the Newbery-winning novel, *The Witch of Blackbird Pond.*

LESSON PLAN

Grade Two: Walking Field Trip—Rules on Signs

A second-grade teacher took her class on a "walking field trip" to the local branch of the city library every month (for another example of a walking field trip, see Morris, 2006). They looked forward to this event because the children's librarian read aloud a picture book to them, and the children could use their library cards to check out books. The distance from the school to the library was about three-quarters of a mile. Two parent volunteers and two sixth graders accompanied the class. The teacher was in the middle of a unit called "Rules and Laws." She decided to use the walk to the library as an opportunity to show her class the many rules that are posted as signs. Her lesson plan follows:

Overview: This lesson is for second graders. It is part of a unit on rules and laws.

Resources and Materials: (a) a 35-mm camera, (b) a slide projector, (c) chart paper.

Standard: One of the *National Standards for Civics and Government* for grades K–4 is that "students should be able to explain the purposes of rules and laws and why they are important in their classroom, school, community, state, and nation" (Center for Civic Education, 1994, p. 18, Standard IE [1]).

Content Objectives: Children will understand that many rules are posted as signs, that rules describe what people may and may not do, that some rules provide for order and safety, and that other rules protect the rights of people.

Process Objectives: Children will *read* four signs during their walk to the library, *describe* how each rule displayed on a sign limits behavior, and *define* a purpose (safety or protect rights) for each sign.

Values Objectives: This lesson, along with many others, will help children understand and become committed to the democratic value of "the public good," that individual behavior must be limited to achieve an orderly and equitable society.

Teaching Sequence:

1. Explain to the children that on this walking trip to the library they will stop to look at rules written on signs. Also review the rules for a walking field trip. (Permission slips from parents would have been collected earlier.)

2. Stop at the gate of the fence surrounding the playground and grass field. The sign reads:

Public welcome to use school grounds when school is not in session. Gates are locked each night at dusk. Use of the following is strictly prohibited:

> **Golf clubs**
> **Alcoholic beverages**
> **Tobacco products**
> **Motor vehicles**
> **Bicycles, skateboards, roller skates, and in-line skates (roller blades)**

   Read the sign aloud to the children. Make sure they understand the specific items that may not be used on the playground or grass field. Photograph the sign.
3. Stop along the sidewalk to read to the children the next sign: **No Parking Monday 8–10 A.M.** Photograph the sign.
4. Stop at the speed limit sign and read it aloud: **35 mph.** Photograph the sign.
5. At the library, stop at the sign that reserves parking spaces for people with disabilities. The sign is blue and has a white logo for handicapped parking (a person in a wheelchair). Read it aloud to the children: **Reserved for Handicapped.** Photograph the sign. Tell the children that after your photographs are developed, you will talk some more about the signs.
6. After the photographs are developed as slides, continue the lesson. Make a chart with three columns: "Rule," "How It Limits Us," and "Why." Show the slide for the first sign (prohibiting the use of certain things on the playground and on the grass field). Read it aloud and discuss it. On the chart, summarize it as "Public use of playground." Help the children understand that this rule limits the items that people can use on the playground. Under the second heading, "How It Limits Us," write down the statement that the children generate; it will probably go something like "Things that can't be used on the playground." The children should understand that many people would like to use the prohibited items on the weekends and early evenings at the school. Do not be surprised if some children have seen this rule being violated. Help the children understand this is a safety rule because the use of golf clubs, alcohol, and skateboards creates many dangers. So, under "Why," write "Makes the playground and grass field safe for everyone."
7. Follow the same procedure for the no parking sign, the speed limit sign, and the handicapped parking sign. The no parking and speed limit signs also are safety signs. The handicapped parking sign is different because it protects the rights of people with disabilities. It is a good example of a rule that reflects a commitment to the common good and respect for minority rights (the majority of the population, who do not have disabilities, give up the chance to park in the reserved spots so that people with disabilities can more easily use the library).

Effective Teaching in Today's Diverse Classroom: This activity could be difficult for your English learners. In Cummins's terms, "cognitive demand" is high. Therefore, you need to "embed" the lesson "contextually" (support your English learners as they tackle a challenging lesson). What could you do? First, your English learners could have difficulty reading the sign on the playground. You might want to take them aside the day before the lesson and paraphrase the message of the sign in a simplified English they can understand. Fortunately, the other signs are easy to understand (no parking, 35 mph, and handicapped logo). Unless your English learners have a high level of oral English proficiency, they will not be able to participate in completing the chart. After your English learners listen to the class discussion that leads to completion of the chart, you should work with them in a group and discuss the chart in its final form.

MINI-UNIT

Grade Five: Fair Trials

This mini-unit is appropriate for a fifth-grade class engaged in a larger unit on the U.S. Constitution. This mini-unit looks at sections of the Fifth and Sixth Amendments, which guarantee the rights constituting the basis for a fair trial. Students will participate in a mock trial, *The State v. The Big Bad Wolf,* based on a journal article by Judith Norton (1992). This simulation is an excellent way for students to learn about the U.S. system of criminal trials. Students will analyze a fictional judicial procedure presented in the award-winning historical novel *The Witch of Blackbird Pond* (Speare, 1958).

Part I: Organizing Framework

Standard: The *National Standards for Civics and Government* (Center for Civic Education, 1994) provides the organizing framework for the mini-unit. The performance expectation is part of the national standards for grades 5 through 8 (see p. 75 of the standards):

(1) Personal Rights. Students should be able to evaluate, take, and defend positions on issues involving personal rights. To achieve this standard, students should be able to identify personal rights and identify the major documentary sources of personal rights (e.g., U.S. Constitution).

This mini-unit will teach students about the specific rights listed in the Fifth and Sixth Amendments, collectively referred to as the right to a fair trial. This mini-unit answers three questions:

Unit Question 1: What rights in the Fifth and Sixth Amendments to the U.S. Constitution guarantee a fair trial for people accused of crimes?

Unit Question 2: What happens during a trial of someone accused of a crime?

Unit Question 3: Can we identify the rights that were not respected in criminal trials conducted in the United States before the Constitution was written?

Part II: Instructional Activities

Unit Question 1: What rights in the Fifth and Sixth Amendments to the U.S. Constitution guarantee a fair trial for people accused of crimes?

Teacher-Directed Lesson on the Fifth and Sixth Amendments

Content Objectives: Students will learn the specific rights guaranteed by the Fifth and Sixth Amendments.

Process Objectives: Students will *identify* the Fifth and Sixth Amendment rights of people accused of crimes; *define* capital crime, indictment, double jeopardy, self-incrimination, jury, and witness; and *speculate* on what would happen if the rights did not exist.

1. Provide copies of the Fifth and Sixth Amendments to each student. Show the class transparencies of the amendments on the overhead projector.
2. With the class, create a chart that lists the following rights:

Rights of People Accused of Crimes from the Fifth Amendment:

1. Cannot be tried for capital crime without a grand jury indictment
2. Cannot be tried for the same crime twice (no double jeopardy)
3. Cannot be made to testify (no self-incrimination)

From the Sixth Amendment:

4. Right to a speedy trial
5. Right to a public trial
6. Right to be judged by a jury
7. Right to be informed of the nature of the crime
8. Right to confront witnesses
9. Right to summon witnesses
10. Right to be represented by a lawyer

Discuss each of these rights with the class. Be sure students understand terms such as *capital crime, indictment, double jeopardy, self-incrimination, jury,* and *witness.* Then, for each right, help students understand what would happen if that right did not exist. For example, ask, "What would happen if we did not have a right to a public trial?" (Help students understand that trials conducted in private could ignore all the rights protected by the amendments—that public trials guarantee the procedure can be evaluated for fairness.)

Unit Question 2: What happens during a trial of someone accused of a crime?

Mock Trial

Content Objectives: Students will learn the definitions of several crimes; the roles of the judge, the clerk, the defendant, attorneys, the jury, and witnesses in a criminal trial; and how the rights in the Fifth and Sixth Amendments are applied in a criminal trial.

Process Objectives: Students will *understand* the definitions of seven crimes, *identify* which crimes the wolf should be charged with, *play the role* of one of the participants in the trial, *gather and analyze* physical evidence, *participate* in the mock trial, and *distinguish* which rights were essential parts of the trial.

Note: This activity will take from 4 to 7 days.

1. Read aloud a version of the fairy tale "Little Red Riding Hood." Then present the revised set of facts on page 5 of Judith Norton's article (the wolf beats, not eats, Grandma; the wolf strikes a police officer prior to arrest; the wolf has marijuana in his pocket).

2. Distribute a copy of the "criminal code" from page 5 of Norton's article. The code defines seven crimes: battery, assault, theft, possession of marijuana, resisting arrest, disorderly conduct, and felonious restraint. Help students understand the definition of each. Then ask the class to decide the crimes with which the wolf should be charged.

3. Begin work on the mock trial. Norton's simulation has the following roles: judge, court clerk, defendant (the wolf), defense attorneys, prosecuting attorneys, the jury, and witnesses (Little Red Riding Hood, Grandma, and arresting officers). Norton suggests that you create some defense witnesses who try to provide the wolf with an alibi or vouch for his character. You can even add "expert witnesses."

4. Gather the physical evidence for the case. This can include a medical report on Grandma's beating, a blood-stained carpet, paw prints, and the police report.

5. Be sure the witnesses know what they are supposed to say. Then work with the defense attorneys on their case. What questions will they ask? Work with the prosecuting attorneys. How will they present their evidence? What should they ask each witness?

6. Meet with the judge and the clerk and discuss the conduct of the courtroom.

7. Discuss with the entire class the rules of court procedure and proper courtroom conduct (see page 6 of Norton's article).

8. Today is the trial! Norton provides excellent descriptions of how the case should proceed. The key to a good simulation is working with each student before the trial begins so that everyone is comfortable and confident.

9. After the mock trial is over, take another look at the list of rights you compiled in the first lesson (the teacher-directed lesson on the Fifth and Sixth Amendments). Which rights were evident in the mock trial? (Almost all were—public trial, jury, accused informed of nature of crime, accused able to summon and confront witnesses, and accused represented by a lawyer.)

Unit Question 3: Can we identify the rights that were not respected in criminal trials conducted before the Constitution was written?

Readers' Theater: The Trial in The Witch of Blackbird Pond

Content Objectives: Students will learn that some trials conducted in colonial America failed to protect the rights of the accused.

Process Objectives: Students will *dramatize* the trial in Chapter 19 of the book *The Witch of Blackbird Pond* and analyze the proceedings to identify which rights were denied the accused during the trial.

1. Before the other activities start and while they are progressing, read aloud to the class *The Witch of Blackbird Pond* (Speare, 1958). This is an excellent piece of historical fiction with an appealing story line. The book fits perfectly with the fifth-grade social studies curriculum in most schools—which usually includes colonial America. This is the story of 16-year-old Katherine (Kit) Tyler, who is the orphaned daughter of English royalists. She comes to live with her Puritan relatives in Connecticut in 1687 and is accused of being a witch.

2. About a week prior to the performance, select actors for a readers' theater presentation of Chapter 19. Suggest that students rehearse their parts so that this exciting chapter can be presented with appropriate characterization. Present Chapter 19 to the class through readers' theater. (In Chapter 19, Kit is tried as a witch in a judicial proceeding that is similar to a current-day preliminary hearing. The hearing is conducted by the town magistrate, who serves as judge along with two local clergymen.) After the presentation, have the class analyze the proceeding. One hundred years after this fictional event, the U.S. Constitution granted all Americans fundamental judicial rights. What rights was Kit granted? Students should see that she was informed of the charges against her; witchcraft in colonial Connecticut was a capital offense. Her hearing meets the requirement of a preliminary proceeding in capital cases (the Fifth Amendment mentions a grand jury indictment). As Chapter 19 explains, Kit was not entitled to a jury at this phase because the hearing would determine whether she would be sent to the capital of the colony for a jury trial. Kit was denied certain rights that present-day defendants have in their preliminary hearings. Students should recognize that she did not have an attorney. Also, Kit was forced to testify. Finally, Kit was not allowed to question witnesses, nor was she allowed to call her own witnesses.

3. Although this might be too complicated for fifth graders, you could point out another difference between the proceeding in *The Witch of Blackbird Pond* and present-day trials: Today, a judge decides at the preliminary hearing whether the accused must stand trial. In *The Witch,* the local judge was joined by two Puritan ministers. The 19th-century New England witch trials were one of the few times in the history of the United States that criminal proceedings were mixed with "ecclesiastical" courts. Ecclesiastical, or religious, courts were common in Europe during the Middle Ages, with full power to convict and punish people. They exist in some nations today, though no person in the United States today can be tried by a religious group unless she or he agrees to participate in the proceeding.

Effective Teaching in Today's Diverse Classroom: The mock trial is a real challenge for fifth graders. There are parts for everybody to play, but try to avoid assigning the most prominent roles only to your most able students. Although no student should be asked to perform publicly at a level beyond his or her ability, you will be surprised how most students can rise to the occasion and exceed your expectations, especially with a little extra help from you! For your gifted children, this mini-unit could be an excellent stimulus for a *depth* activity, one that allows students to learn more about a topic previously covered. Gifted students could be challenged to find out more about the qualifications for judges at the municipal, state, and federal level. Do these minimal qualifications seem adequate? Other students could look at another example of the systematic denial of fair trials in our history, the vigilante justice practiced in California's gold fields in the late 1840s and 1850s.

Chapter 11

History and Geography: Understanding People of Different Times and Places

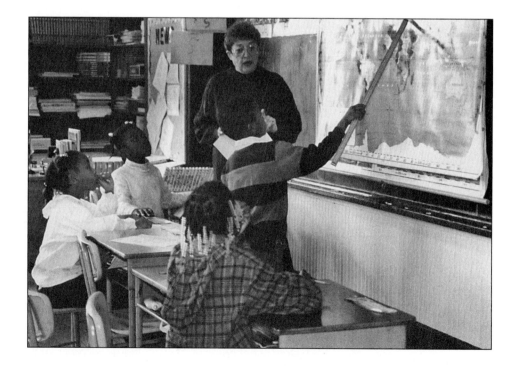

Nancy Grant's third graders were working on a unit entitled "All About Us." The children were to complete a project on a history of their families. The choices were (a) complete a family tree, (b) write a biography of one of their grandparents, and (c) make a family time line. Lourdes Delgado wanted to make a family time line. Mrs. Grant explained that Lourdes would have to be selective because it would be impossible to put every important event on the time line. The first step, then, was to compile a list of the dates that were to be charted. After talking with her mother and father, Lourdes decided on the following:

1994: The Delgado family takes a vacation to Yellowstone National Park.
1992: Maria Chacon, Lourdes's great-great-grandmother, dies at the age of 101.
1987: Lourdes Delgado is born.
1978: The first of Lourdes's three brothers is born.
1977: Lourdes's father and mother buy a house in Burbank. The family has lived there ever since.
1974: Hector Delgado and Teresa Chacon marry at Mission San Fernando.
1973: Hector Delgado (her father) and Teresa Chacon (her mother) graduate from California State University, Northridge.
1949: Lourdes's grandfather and grandmother Delgado move from Mexico City to California.
1937: Lourdes's grandfather and grandmother Chacon move from Guadalajara to California.

Next, Mrs. Grant helped Lourdes figure the time span to be covered by the time line. It would have to cover 58 years (1937 to 1995). Lourdes wanted to make her time line on a sheet of poster board 2 feet by 3 feet. If she left room for margins, she would have to place 58 years on a line 30 inches long (so each side would have a 3-inch margin). To make it easier, Mrs. Grant suggested that Lourdes have the time line cover 60 years and that each half inch would represent a year. After Mrs. Grant helped Lourdes figure the proper scale for the time line, the rest was easy. She left space at the top of the poster for her title ("The History of My Family: Lourdes Delgado"). Lourdes then drew her line and marked the 2-inch intervals. Mrs. Grant suggested that she place larger marks for the years 1940, 1950, 1960, 1970, 1980, and 1990. This confused Lourdes for a moment, before she realized she needed to measure halfway between the mark for 1939 and the mark for 1941 to find the correct location for 1940. She then wrote "1940" in bold numbers below the mark. Then Lourdes wrote the years below the marks for the designated years on her time line: 1937, 1949, 1973, 1977, 1978, 1987, 1992, 1994. She found that she had to write small and to stagger the placement of the years. Finally, she wrote brief captions under each year, explaining what happened. With great pride, Lourdes displayed her time line on a side bulletin board with projects the other children completed.

This project was valuable because Lourdes learned a great deal about her family and about the history of her community in southern California. At the same time, she experienced firsthand the "doing" of history—gathering data, organizing it chronologically, and presenting it in a format that could be understood by other people.

• • •

In this chapter, you will read about

- Research that describes the ability of students to understand historical concepts
- Using the national history standards to determine the historical content that should be taught in the elementary school
- The historical processes students should master
- Guidelines for teaching with primary sources, historical fiction, and time lines
- Research on geographic teaching and learning
- Using the national geography standards to determine the geographic content that should be taught in the elementary school
- How to teach students to use symbols, scales, grids, and direction to read maps
- How to teach students to make mental maps, relief maps, and thematic maps

◆ History in the Elementary School: Overview and Research

History has been a part of the elementary school curriculum since the United States became a nation (Brophy & Van Sledright, 1997; Downey, 1985; Downey & Levstik, 1991; Levstik, 1991). As noted in Chapter 1, controversy, however, has surrounded two issues: (a) The role history should play in the social studies curriculum and (b) the historical content that should be taught. In regard to the first issue, the argument is: Should elementary social studies focus primarily on history? Or should history assume a less central role as time is devoted to the other social sciences (anthropology, economics, and political science) and topics of special interest (environmental education and global education)? Currently, almost all of the state standards for social studies place history in the primary position. If you teach elementary school anywhere in the United States, you will teach a great deal of history. The second issue, about historical content, will always generate controversy as advocates of a "traditional" curriculum clash with people who wish to include multiple perspectives on events in the past and provide more information on women, people of color, and leaders of dissenting organizations. Almost any time someone attempts to define the history content children should learn, sparks fly as they did in Minnesota (Spies et al., 2004). There, a proposed set of K–12 social studies standards was rejected by the state legislature in favor of an alternative set of standards after a lengthy lobbying effort by the original standards' critics.

Many elementary school children, especially if their social studies curriculum follows the "expanding environments" model, receive virtually no historical content until fourth grade, when they study their state. A rationale for delaying the study of the past has been the now disproven perspective that small children are unable to understand historical concepts (Barton, 1997; Barton & Levstik, 1996; Brophy, 1996b;

Levstik, 1991; Thornton & Vukelich, 1988). One reason why educators misunderstood the capacity of children to learn history is that a previous model of the child's cognitive development and historical thinking, called the "Piaget-Peel-Hallam" model, underestimated what children can learn (Brophy, 1996b; Downey & Levstik, 1991). British scholars E. A. Peel and Roy Hallam applied Jean Piaget's stage theory of cognitive development to historical thinking. They concluded that children need to be at the "formal level" of cognitive operations to understand the past. History would have to wait until junior high school! This model is flawed because it was based on faulty experimental tasks and does not represent an accurate portrait of the abilities of children.

Jere Brophy's (1996b) excellent review of the research on the ability of children to learn history explains that children gradually develop the ability to understand the past rather than developing this capacity in Piagetian-like stages. For example, children intially fail to perceive the causal relationships of historical events. Then children take a "mechanistic view of causal determination," believing that linked events were inevitable (p. 6). Only later do young learners see that there can be multiple causes of an event and that if the causal events had not all occurred, the result would have been different. Similar developmental patterns exist for a child's ability to empathize with people from other eras and to cope with conflicting accounts of the same historical event.

One important study of children's understanding of history was completed by Keith Barton and Linda Levstik (1996). Barton and Levstik were critical of previous studies, noting that almost all earlier research on this topic suffered from one of the following flaws: (a) The researchers drew conclusions without evidence, (b) the researchers failed to consider the possibility that children younger than age 8 could understand historical concepts, and (c) the studies reflected a limited view of history, focusing solely on the sequence of dates.

Barton and Levstik (1996) asked children from kindergarten to grade 6 (a) to place in sequence nine pictures and (b) to explain their rationale for doing so (the pictures, both photographs and drawings, depicted scenes from 1772 to 1993). The results revealed the youngest students *can* make distinctions in historical time. Kindergartners and first graders were able to go beyond a simple split between pictures that belonged either in "long ago" or "close to now" categories. Most kindergartners and first graders and all the second graders identified other categories as they recognized some pictures that were older than the ones they had seen previously, whereas other pictures were identified as being newer, and some were placed between the previous pictures.

Also, for the most part, kindergartners and first and second graders have no sense of what dates signify. Not until third grade do children try to assign dates to the pictures. Beginning in fourth grade, dates are useful to children, although not until fifth or sixth grade did children in the study use dates to identify the pictures accurately. Finally, almost all children, regardless of age, seem to think that "a particular time is characterized by only one image" (Barton & Levstik, 1996, p. 440). For example, children in the study did not seem to understand that illustrations continued to be drawn after the invention of photography; thus, they thought that any drawing was automatically older than any photograph. Nor did the children understand that while pioneers were building cabins in the 1880s, large cities were being built in other geographic areas. Their rationale was "first there were pioneers, then there were cities" (p. 440). As with any study, the results of this one may later be challenged, but it seems safe to say that children at all elementary grades should have a social studies curriculum that includes historical content.

Another important body of research has examined the effects of culture, national identity, ethnicity, and gender on student's historical knowledge and beliefs. In their review, Epstein and & Shiller (2005) reached this conclusion: At every grade level, including kindergarten, what children know about history and how they view the history they are taught will be influenced by their culture, national identity, ethnicity, and gender. The authors noted that "there are limits to what and how much children or adolescents will adopt from teachers or texts, especially when school-based historical content conflicts with history accounts learned in the home" (p. 203). For example, when shown a photograph of a 1960s antiwar protest, African American fifth graders thought it was a picture of a rally against racism or a dangerous place for African Americans to be (there were armed, White soldiers in the photo). On the other hand, the European American fifth graders thought the photo showed an event in the American Civil War (Levstik & Barton, 1996).

♦ History in the Elementary School: Content

The expanding environments approach to social studies defined a curriculum with little historical content until students reached the fourth grade. Kindergarten and first- and second-grade social studies curricula have focused on social development, the school, the family, and the neighborhood. Third graders studied their community, with a small amount of local history. Not until fourth grade, when students learn about their state, was any significant historical content presented. Fifth-grade social studies, following the expanded environments framework, has always been historical, as students learned about the history of the United States. Sixth grade covered foreign regions or nations—typically Canada, Mexico, Central America, and South America. So, in the traditional scheme, global content has been covered in grade 6 but virtually not before that grade level.

Although they have generated considerable controversy, the national history standards represent the combined effort of many dedicated historians and educators. Let's take a look at the proposed topics for grades K–4 included in the *National Standards for History* (National Center for History in the Schools, 1996). The eight content standards listed will help us understand what students in grades K–4 should know:

1. *Students should understand family life now and in the recent past and family life in various places long ago.* This standard represents a shift in several states and school districts. Rather than learn only political and

Scott Cunningham/Merrill

The challenge of teaching history to children is how to make the past "come alive." This student gets a good sense of what it was like to go to school in the 19th century as she uses a fountain pen and a bottle of ink.

economic history, students should learn about their personal histories and the everyday lives of people in the past.

2. *Students should understand the history of their own local community and how communities in North America varied long ago.* Community history has traditionally been a part of elementary social studies. Students should use a variety of resources to learn about their

community, including field trips, old photographs, newspapers, and interviews with senior citizens.

3. *Students should understand the people, events, problems, and ideas that were significant in creating the history of their state.* State history, long the focus of fourth-grade social studies, should cover the Natives who first lived in the state, the early non-Native explorers of their state, and the people who have moved to their state throughout its history.

4. *Students should understand how democratic values came to be and how they have been exemplified by people, events, and symbols.* Many state and local social studies curricula delay this topic until fifth grade. This national standard bridges history and citizenship and calls for students to understand how the United States was formed through a revolution with England and to identify the basic principles in the Declaration of Independence and the U.S. Constitution. Other parts of this standard are familiar topics for the early grades: national holidays, American symbols, the Pledge of Allegiance, and the national anthem.

5. *Students should understand the causes and nature of various movements of large groups of people into the United States now and long ago.* This standard combines history and geography. Included here would be the forced relocation of Native Americans; the stories of immigrant groups who have come to the United States throughout our history; the internal migrations of African Americans, Mexican and Puerto Rican workers, and Dust Bowl families; and the 20th-century migration of Americans from farms to cities.

6. *Students should understand folklore and other cultural contributions from various regions of the United States and how they help form a national heritage.* Students should be able to describe regional folk heroes, stories, and songs; use folk literature to describe the way people lived in various sections of the United States; and describe the national influence of regional art, crafts, music, and language.

7. *Students should understand selected attributes and historical developments of societies in such places as Africa, the Americas, Asia, and Europe.* This standard represents an attempt to internationalize the social studies curriculum and is an important addition to the typical K–3 fare of family, classroom, neighborhood, and city. Students would compare and contrast different structures of family life, retell folktales and legends, describe significant historical achievements of many cultural groups, and analyze the art produced by various cultural groups.

8. *Students should understand discoveries in science and technology, some of their social and economic effects, and the major scientists and inventors responsible for them.* The content in this standard seems like a worthwhile addition to the elementary curriculum, especially as students face

technological change at an unprecedented pace. Students would examine changes in transportation and communication and learn about the technological achievements of many cultural groups, such as Chinese paper, Mayan calendars, Egyptian mummies, and English steam engines.

◆ History in the Elementary School: Processes

In addition to their acquiring historical information, we want our students to become proficient at several historical processes. This is the "doing" of history, as students begin to think and act like historians. The *National Standards for History* (National Center for History in the Schools, 1996) provides a useful categorization of the thinking and doing skills of history. These include the following:

1. *Chronological thinking.* This includes the ability to distinguish past, present, and future time; establish temporal order in constructing their own historical narratives; measure and calculate calendar time; make and interpret time lines; and explain continuity and change over time.
2. *Historical comprehension.* Students should be able to reconstruct the literal meaning of a historical passage, identify important questions in historical narratives, identify historical perspectives, use historical maps, find information in illustrations, and understand data in charts and graphs.
3. *Historical analysis and interpretation.* This is an essential set of skills for the historically literate. It includes the ability to formulate questions for inquiry, compare and contrast different ideas, distinguish fact from fiction, compare different versions of the same event, explain causes in historical events, and hypothesize how the past has influenced the present.
4. *Historical research capabilities.* Students should be able to state historical questions, locate historical data, interpret data, and use their knowledge to write a story, explanation, or narrative.
5. *Historical issues:* Analysis and decision making. These important critical thinking skills include the ability to identify issues in the past, compare the interests and values of various people, suggest alternative choices for solving a historical problem, prepare a position on an issue, and evaluate the consequences of a decision.

These historical processes usually are taught through participation in lessons that present historical content. It is possible, however, to design lessons that focus solely on historical processes.

At the end of this chapter, you will find a mini-unit that teaches students the methodology of "real" historians.

◆ Teaching History in the Elementary School

Perhaps it would be a good idea for us to review here the elements of effective social studies teaching in a classroom with a diverse student population presented in previous chapters. Because so much of teaching social studies is teaching history, the elements are worth repeating:

- For our English learners, learning history will require a great deal of contextual support (cooperative learning, visual aids, hands-on activities, modification of how the teacher talks, and primary-language support).
- For children with mild learning disabilities, teachers will need to modify curricular content, perhaps by dividing material into smaller units; modify instructional processes, which could include the use of instructional prompts and cues; and by modifying student work products, such as providing more time to finish a task.
- A variety of lesson plans and teaching sequences should be used to teach history. For some lessons, a model of direct instruction, like Hunter's seven-step plan, will work; for others, we may want to use a teaching sequence designed for inquiry, the use of artifacts, or critical thinking.
- Cooperative learning can be used effectively to teach historical content; it is essential for students to practice historical analysis and interpretation.
- Because the events of the past are subject to many interpretations, activities that require critical thinking, like the integrative model for teaching reasoning and content, are important in teaching history. Inquiry activities should be a part of every unit that has historical content (Levstik & Barton, 2005).
- History must be taught through a variety of resources: textbooks, children's literature, reference material, charts and graphs, films, realia, and computer-based resources. In the report of their study, Barton and Levstik (1996) make a persuasive case for the importance of visual images in teaching history. Pictures should be used frequently as a teaching tool, and students should be encouraged to show what they know by drawing.
- The history curriculum should be transformed so that our students learn about women, children, immigrants, African Americans, Native Americans, religious minorities, and those who have dissented from the majority. Also, history should be personalized and localized; an effective means is through oral history. Barton and Levstik (1996) argue that "the most accessible knowledge for younger children [is] related to material culture and the patterns of everyday life" (p. 442). The best way to introduce students to another time is through food, clothing, household tools, schools, play, and the other things and experiences children know firsthand.

As with other aspects of social studies, historical teaching in the elementary school has been too dependent on the textbook. Isabel Beck, Margaret McKeown, and their colleagues have published some revealing research about how history is presented in elementary social studies textbooks (Beck, McKeown, & Worthy, 1995;

McKeown, Beck, Sinatra, & Loxterman, 1991). Generally, they have found that text-books do a poor job of presenting historical material and that textbook passages can be rewritten so they are easier to understand. Children do not understand historical cause and effect and will need clarification and explanation. Also, when historical passages had a "voice" and sounded more like historical fiction, children learned more history. Textbooks should never be the sole resource for teaching historical content; rather, they should be used in concert with other resources.

Let's now look at three resources that are essential for good history teaching in an elementary classroom: (a) primary sources, (b) children's fiction, and (c) time lines.

Primary Sources

The essential resource for the professional historian is the *primary source* (Potter, 2003). A primary source is a document, work of art, or artifact produced during the period being studied. To teach history well, we must have our students work with primary sources. Teaching with primary sources has two problems: (a) We must locate sources that are relevant to the time period we are covering, and (b) the sources must be comprehensible to our young students. Actually, primary sources can be found in many places. The Internet has become an excellent resource for primary sources. I have found that the "History/Social Science for K–12 Teachers" Website is a good place to begin a search (http://k-12historysocialstudies.com/boals.html). Many Websites provide primary source material suitable for elementary students, for example try "Poetry and Music of the War Between the States" (www. civilwarpoetry. org). This site has poetry written by women on the home front, from both the North and South.

Primary source documents can be found in each issue of the journal *Social Education* in the "Teaching with Documents" feature. It should be noted, however, that some of the documents are too difficult for elementary school children to read. Nonetheless, many of the featured documents will work with students in grades 4 and up, and each article includes both a copy of the historical document and several teaching ideas.

Fortunately, the newest elementary school social studies textbooks incorporate more primary source material than textbooks published in the past. Many textbooks now include excerpts from diaries and newspapers and reproductions of old maps and paintings. When it comes to artifacts, a good museum is essential, and many cities have excellent museums of local history. Field trips to museums give students a chance to examine historical artifacts. The Internet has made it possible to take virtual tours of museums (again, I suggest using the "History/Social Science for K–12 Teachers" Website to locate virtual tours). Also, we should not forget that many of our students have old items at home that, with parental cooperation, can become a learning resource.

Although some historical documents can be read by elementary students, most are too difficult. Some of these primary sources can be adapted for young readers, and many fine children's books have done exactly that. For example, the well-known children's author Margaret Wise Brown edited a version of *Mourt's Relation* for children. *Mourt's Relation* is a journal written by several *Mayflower* pilgrims, most likely William Bradford and Edward Winslow. It was first published in 1622 and is the basis for much of what is known about the early days in Plimoth. It is far too difficult for elementary students to read. Brown's adaptation, called *Homes in the Wilderness* (1988), is delightful and well within the reading ability of most third and fourth graders. Also noteworthy are the books written by Brett Harvey, who has used the diaries of women who lived in the past as the basis of easy-to-read but historically accurate picture books. His books include *My Prairie Year: Based on the Diary of Elinore Plaisted* (1986), *Cassie's Journey: Going West in the 1860s* (1988), and *Immigrant Girl: Becky of Eldridge Street* (1987).

Songs are primary sources, too. Many old ones reveal a great deal about a time or place. Noteworthy is *The Laura Ingalls Wilder Songbook* (Garson, 1968), which includes the words and lyrics to all the songs mentioned in the *Little House* books. Most elementary music texts contain several historical songs. My favorite anthology of American folk songs is *Gonna Sing My Head Off: American Folk Songs for Children* (Krull, 1992).

Teaching Sequence for a Primary Source.   Both historical comprehension and historical analysis can be developed through work with primary sources. For lessons using primary sources, I suggest the following teaching sequence, which is similar to the one presented for realia, visual media, and auditory media in chapter 6.

1. *First, establish time and place.*   Before we share a primary source with our students, we should place it in context. This usually requires using a time line to establish time and a map to establish location. A good idea is to bring out a summary chart, a data retrieval chart, or a web we made earlier in the unit. It is important that students not have the primary source "thrown at them," absent a meaningful context.

2. *Present the primary source.*   If a primary source is written, then it should be neatly reproduced or displayed on a large screen through an LCD (liquid crystal display), an overhead projector, or a photographic slide. Even when presented in a reader-friendly fashion, many written primary sources will have to be read aloud to students. Artifacts must be presented in a way that permits every student to see them easily. Sometimes this means letting students look at the artifact in small groups. Students should then examine the primary source to "identify" it: Is it a photograph, a diary entry, a newspaper article, or something else?

3. *Start with open-ended questions.*   "Does anyone wish to make a comment?" "Who has a question about the diary entry (or letter, newspaper advertisement, coin, and so on)?"

4. *Ask very specific questions.*   These questions should require students to take a closer look at the primary source. With some written primary sources, it helps to number the lines of the text like a legal document and then ask students about specific words, phrases, and sentences. If the primary source mentions names, places, or things, students should take notice of them. With artifacts, questions we ask should narrow students' focus, such as, "What do you see in the upper-right corner of the

painting?" or "What places are mentioned in the diary entry?" The purpose of these questions is to call attention to the specifics we want our students to remember.

5. *Analyze the primary source.*   The analysis is the most important part of a lesson with a primary source because it engages students in the same type of critical thinking real historians practice, often called "source work." Van Sledright (2002a; 2002b; 2004), based on his own experience with fifth graders, provides excellent ideas on how to proceed in this stage. Students need to ask and answer questions about the person(s) who created the primary source. Once they are clear about that person, they need to ask questions about possible bias. For example, "Did the person have an agenda?" Then students assess the source against what else they know to determine the source's reliability. Does the source match what they know or does it present a different perspective? Finally, teachers should sum up what has been learned. "What new things does it show us?" "How does it change what we know [about the topic being studied]?

Several lessons and activities presented in this book use primary sources. You can find them at the end of the relevant chapter:

Chapter 3: Lesson plan based on *To Be a Slave*
Chapter 3: The oral history project "The History of Our School"
Chapter 4: The opening vignette and the lesson plans based on the
          painting *Buffalo Chase, Upper Missouri*
Chapter 6: Lesson plan examining a Roman coin

Children's Fiction: History as a Story Well Told

Fiction written for children has excellent potential as a resource for teaching history. Beck and colleagues (1995) and Levstik (1986, 1989, 1990) have written about the power of presenting history through narrative. Simply put, children learn more through stories than they do with other forms of presentation (most notably, textbook selections). A great deal has been written about how teachers can use fiction to teach history (Field, 1998; McGowan & Powell, 1996; McGowan, Erickson, & Neufeld, 1996; Zarnowski & Gallagher, 1993).

Historical fiction written for children is of two forms: (a) novels for older children and (b) picture books aimed at the youngest students. Some of the finest children's books ever written are historical fiction, including Newbery Medal winners like *Island of the Blue Dolphins* (O'Dell, 1960), *Johnny Tremain* (Forbes, 1943), *Sarah, Plain and Tall* (MacLaughlin, 1985), *The Witch of Blackbird Pond* (Speare, 1958), and *The Bronze Bow* (Speare, 1961). More recent Newbery winners include *Kira Kira* (Kadohata, 2004), *Crispin: The Cross of Lead* (Avi, 2002), and *A Single Shard* (Park, 2001). Many excellent picture books tell stories that take place in other times, like *Thy Friend, Obadiah* (Turkle, 1969), *Ox-Cart Man* (Hall, 1979), *How My Parents Learned to Eat* (Friedman, 1987), and *Follow the Drinking Gourd* (Winter, 1988).

Harms and Lettow (1994) provide a useful set of criteria for selecting picture books with historical settings. This includes

1. *Developmental appropriateness.*   The book should be written and illustrated at a level that children in your classroom can understand.
2. *Quality.*   The book should be a good book, one children will find appealing and that at least some authorities consider to be well illustrated and written.
3. *Authenticity.*   Historical accuracy extends to both text and illustration. In more and more historical picture books, authors and illustrators include a list of their sources or bibliographic notes that reveal and/or comment on the sources the author and illustrator used.
4. *Complementary text and illustration.*   This is a characteristic all good picture books share. Text and illustrations should work together rather than appear disjointed. Harms and Lettow note that this is essential in picture books with historical settings because the illustrations can enhance the level of historical understanding the reader acquires.
5. *Three-dimensional central characters.*   As noted previously, children can understand historical concepts when the past is presented as a story well told. Good stories require well-developed characters with whom children can develop a sense of empathy. This is a real challenge for authors and illustrators of picture books because of the limited space in picture books; most have fewer than 40 pages.
6. *Freedom from bias.*   As teachers, we should avoid books that present stereotypes or biased views (although older children should read such books for the purpose of detecting bias). We should seek books that show events from the perspectives of all the participants in an event. Harms and Lettow, for example, note that in Jean Fritz's *The Great Adventure of Christopher Columbus* (1992), the Natives who greet Columbus are portrayed as "uncultured and witless," unable to understand Columbus and too willing to accept trinkets in exchange for valuable information (Harms & Lettow, 1994, p. 153). It would be interesting for older children to compare this book with Jane Yolen's *Encounter* (1992) or Michael Dorris's *Morning Girl* (1992), books that present the perspectives of the Taino Natives. A story well told can provide children with a sense of empathy because fiction that is well researched and well written will make children feel transported to another place. Consider Lois Lowry's *Number the Stars* (1989). Readers will share the terror of Ellen Rosen, a Danish Jew, when she is awakened in the night by Nazi soldiers. Fiction also offers children strong images of the details of living in the past. This assumes, of course, that a work of fiction is accurate, free of bias, stereotypical images, and outright errors. After listening to their teacher read *Thy Friend, Obadiah* (Turkle, 1969), for example, children will have a sense of the clothing, buildings, and means of transportation in 19th-century Nantucket.

Children's fiction can be used in several ways. Children can read books independently. Historical novels and picture books can be read a second time to provide the specific information needed to answer inquiries and to complete projects. Fiction should be used as part of teacher-directed lessons in social studies. A word of caution is in order, however. Fiction is not written with the same purpose as a textbook; rather, the goal of the author is to tell a story. It seems reasonable that we should allow children to respond to the book as a story before they move on to a history lesson. We can do this by asking open-ended questions that encourage children to express their personal feelings, interpretations, and opinions about the story (Zarrillo, 1994).

At the end of the chapter is a lesson plan that provides an example of teaching history with a picture book.

Time Lines

Time lines are charts that show the chronological intervals among events. Time lines can be used as an instructional tool to present information to students. Students could also construct time lines as part of instructional units with a historical focus (Hoone, 1989). Students can make many types of time lines, encompassing the following characteristics:

- Time lines can be either vertical, with the earliest date at the top of the line and the most recent date at the bottom, or horizontal, with the earliest date on the reader's left and the most recent date on the reader's right.
- The standard form of a time line has a long line with intervals of time designated by short perpendicular marks (the intervals may be 1 month, 1 year, 10 years, or 100 years). Marks are added to the line at the appropriate time place to designate significant events, and each event is given a brief description in words (e.g., 1993: my little sister is born).
- Picture time lines use illustrations for historical people, places, and events. For example, a time line of the history of flight could include a drawing of Lindbergh's plane, *The Spirit of St. Louis.*
- Object time lines use real things. The activity with old buttons described earlier included an opportunity for children to make a time line with the buttons they were examining.
- Other time lines do not use paper. It is possible to make a "clothesline" time line. A string is stretched across a space, clothespins are placed on the line at appropriate points to designate historical events, and written descriptions or illustrations can be attached to the line with the clothespins.
- Finally, good news! Computer software has made it much easier to produce accurate, neat time lines. Perhaps the most popular software package is Time Liner, produced by Tom Snyder Productions. The software includes 400 historical photographs and clip art images and allows students to import images from the Internet and place them on their time lines.

♦ Geography in the Elementary School: Overview and Research on Children's Understanding of Geography

Although currently there is near-universal agreement that geography is an essential component of the school curriculum, geography has struggled to find a significant place in the schools (Douglass, 1998; Geography Education Standards Project, 1994; Gersmehl, 2005; Gregg & Leinhardt, 1994; Stoltman, 1991). In most classrooms, geographic teaching and learning are a small part of social studies, as activity is limited to memorizing the names and locations of a few geographic features, such as oceans, rivers, lakes, and capital cities (Douglass, 1998; Rallis & Rallis, 1995). A broader range view of geography is needed. A simple definition is that geography is the study of place just as history is the study of the past. The important thing is to make geography more than bits of information; it should be viewed by teachers as "a way of knowing," a process that evolves as students learn "to think in terms of spatial interactions" (Douglass, 1998, p. xvi). Gregg and Leinhardt (1994) provide a definition that we should consider:

> Geography uses the language of maps to communicate ideas about the context and distribution of phenomena and processes important for human decision making, issues of scale, the dynamic nature of phenomena, and cultural perspective. (p. 328)

This definition, though complex, provides a basis for understanding the geographic component of the social studies. Geography requires that students know how to read and make several types of *maps*. Thus, geographic understanding is a form of literacy, though in this case it is the ability to read and write maps, not words (Douglass, 1998; Gersmehl, 2005). Through geographic lessons, students should understand how people, resources, and products are *distributed* over the earth. Geographic study should provide a *context* for understanding events as students see how the *decisions* people make are influenced by their physical surroundings. Finally, students should learn how people interact with the environment and, as a result, how both people and place *change*.

Apparently, we must do a great deal to increase the level of geographic knowledge our students have. Two national assessments of geographic understanding have been completed as part of the National Assessment of Educational Progress, one in 1994, the other in 2001. The results of each study were consistent, with slight improvement occurring in 2001. The number of students at the "advanced" level is small (1994: 3%; 2001: 2%); the number at the "proficient" level in both studies was 19%. Fortunately, the percentage of students who scored at or above the basic level increased from 48% in 1994 to 53% in 2001 (the complete results are at the U.S. Department of Education Website, under "The Nation's Report Card," www.nces.ed.gov/nationsreportcard3).

Scott Cunningham/Merrill

Geography is the study of place. In this classroom, the teacher has used multicultural literature to introduce her students to several fascinating places.

Research on Geographic Learning and Teaching

Gregg and Leinhardt's (1994) article analyzing the research on geographic learning and teaching is comprehensive and will serve as the basis for the disccussion here (see also Douglass, 1998; Forsythe, 1995; Gersmehl, 2005; Rice & Cobb, 1978; Rushdoony, 1968; Stoltman, 1991). They concluded that "little research has been done on issues of learning geography outside of learning about maps" (p. 330). The relevant research has looked at the relationship between map-reading tasks and human development and the thinking processes required to read maps.

Jean Piaget investigated the map-reading abilities of children (Piaget & Inhelder, 1969). He thought that children go through three stages in their ability to see things from a different perspective, an ability that is a prerequisite to reading maps. At first, children are in a "topographical" stage, unable to use directional labels (e.g., north and south). Then children pass through a "projective" stage, when they can determine location in relation to their own position (they know what is to the right and left of them). The final stage, usually reached between ages 10 and 12, Piaget labeled as "Eucledian," as children have an accurate perception of spatial relationships. As is so often the case in developmental studies, other researchers have challenged Piaget's conclusions. Using different methods (e.g., familiar cartoon characters), researchers have shown that children are able to do more at an earlier age than Piaget thought they could.

A body of research is available on the child's ability to read symbols. Some amusing studies have shown that children tend to interpret symbols literally, stating that the urban centers colored yellow on a map were eggs or firecrackers (Liben & Downs, 1989). Children, however, can understand that symbols on maps represent things. The more difficult task for children is to see the relationships among the items represented on a map. Generally, the ability of children to understand symbols on a map is influenced by the "degree of abstractness of the symbol and the amount of detail on the map" (Gregg & Leinhardt, 1994, p. 333).

Likewise, several studies have been conducted on the ability of children to understand scale. Gregg and Leinhardt (1994) concluded that three things are necessary for a child to read and use scale. First, the child must have developed proportional reasoning; she or he must have a sense that the relationships among items remain constant even if the unit of comparison has shrunk. Second, the child must be able to measure in the units used on the map; on the simplest maps, this involves inches and miles or centimeters and kilometers. Finally, the child must have a sense of the frame of reference of the map. Maps are selective in what they reveal. No map can show everything about a place, and to understand scale the child must understand the level of detail in the map.

Research on the cognitive processes involved in map reading is complex. Researchers have investigated how the information on a map is recognized, how the images of maps are stored in memory, and how that information is recalled. Gregg and Leinhardt (1994) concluded, "From a cognitive perspective, it is not easy to make sense of the symbols and letters superimposed on the complex visual fields that are referred to as maps" (p. 343). Maps, through the use of symbol and scale, can convey large amounts of important information. Map reading is not easy; it places unique demands on the developing thinking abilities of children. Muir and Frazee (1986) noted that a significant cognitive challenge for young map readers is understanding that maps require a "bird's-eye" rather than a "ground-level" perspective. Some children, when asked to read maps, have great difficulty because they are not able to make this shift in perspective.

Unfortunately, few studies shed much light on how to teach geography. J. W. Miller (1974, 1982) did show that the design of maps makes a difference. Children find it easier to read maps with a limited number of different typefaces, clearly differentiated symbols, a compass rose, a grid system of latitude and longitude, boldly marked boundaries, and all labels in a horizontal format. Atkins (1981) found that young children can be taught to read simple maps if the instruction is presented in a clear and structured manner. In conclusion, it is important to note that at least one authority reached the same conclusion about the child's capacity to learn geography that others have reached about history. Karen Trifonoff (1997) stated that "many early geographic educators believed children to have a poorly developed sense of space. Most modern studies suggest the opposite. Students do have well-developed spatial understanding, and they continue to astound researchers with their advanced mapping behaviors" (p. 17). Although it is essential that our teaching be developmentally appropriate and not ask children to perform tasks that are beyond their abilities, it also appears that, regarding history and geography, educators have underestimated the capacity of children to learn essential concepts.

♦ Geography in the Elementary School: Content

Geography includes the physical characteristics (elevation of land and types of vegetation), geopolitical information (boundaries and capital cities), demographics (size, density, and identity of population), and economic information (type and volume of agricultural and manufactured products) of places. Students should learn the relationships among this information, especially how places change over time. Two schemes for organizing geographic content, each with considerable merit, have categorized what students should know about geography. Five fundamental themes were developed by the Geography Education National Implementation Project (GENIP) (Boehm & Petersen, 1994; GENIP, 1987, 1989): (a) Location, (b) Place, (c) Human-Environment Interactions, (d) Movement, and (e) Region. These five themes have been used as the foundation for elementary social studies textbooks, state curriculum frameworks, and school district curriculum guides. They have played a significant role in improving geographic education (Petersen, Natoli, & Boehm, 1994). The national standards for geography are organized under six elements: (a) the world in spatial terms, (b) places and regions, (c) physical systems, (d) human systems, (e) environment and society, and (f) the uses of geography (Freese, 1997; Geography Education Standards Project, 1994). Because they are more current and have the potential to shape the curriculum we teach, let's look at the elements. Eighteen standards are organized across these six elements:

1. *The world in spatial terms.* The national standards seek to develop the "geographically informed person." Such a student is expected to have basic map-reading skills and the ability to produce maps that summarize geographic information. Students should be able to read and make maps that show the spatial relationships of people, places, and environments.

2. *Places and regions.* The world's resources, both human and natural, are not evenly distributed over the earth. Each place is unique, and the earth's landmasses can be divided into regions with clearly defined characteristics. Students should learn the physical and human characteristics of places. They should know, for example, what makes Hawaii and Alaska different.

3. *Physical systems.* This is a part of social studies that overlaps science. Students should understand the physical processes that shape the earth's surface (e.g., floods, volcanoes, and earthquakes) and the concept of an ecosystem.

4. *Human systems.* This element looks at the three ways human beings relate to the surface of the earth: (a) People shape the surface of the earth by consuming resources and altering natural patterns, (b) people build structures that become a part of the surface of the earth, and (c) people compete for control of the surface of the earth.

5. *Environment and society.* People modify the physical environment of the earth. An easy example for students to understand is how the construction of a dam creates a lake. Sometimes the relationship between nature and people is the reverse as nature "strikes back" and physical systems alter those things that people have constructed. For example, a hurricane destroys buildings; over a longer period of time, persistent drought leads to mass migration.

6. *The uses of geography.* The sixth and final element states that students should know how to apply geographic knowledge to interpret the past, understand the present, and plan for the future.

◆ Geography in the Elementary School: Processes

The five sets of geographic skills proposed in *Guidelines for Geographic Education: Elementary and Secondary Schools* (Joint Committee on Geographic Education, 1984), listed next, are widely accepted as an outline of what students should be able to do in geography. The national standards in geography incorporate them.

• *Asking geographic questions.* Students must learn how to ask questions in geographic terms. "Where is something located?" "How did it get there?" "Why is it located where it is?" "How is one place different from another?" Specifically, students should be able to

- Ask geographic questions about current events
- Distinguish between questions that can be answered with geographic data and those that cannot

• *Acquiring geographic information.* As with history, geographic data can be found in both primary and secondary sources. Primary data are gathered through fieldwork as students distribute surveys, take photographs, and record their observations on field trips. Secondary data are maps, databases, and books. Specifically, students should be able to

- Make records of geographic data on field trips
- Use their mathematical skills to count and measure
- Read maps, charts, graphs, and tables with geographic data

• *Organizing information.* Geographic data can be organized in several ways. Maps, of course, are the primary tool for organizing what students learn about a place. Students should also learn how to construct charts, graphs, and tables. Specifically, students should be able to

- Prepare maps, charts, graphs, and tables with geographic data
- Write concise summaries of geographic data

- *Analyzing geographic information.* It is often difficult to distinguish the processes of gathering and analyzing geographic data. They tend to occur simultaneously. Specifically, students should be able to

    - Interpret data in maps, graphs, charts, and tables
    - Discover trends, relationships, and patterns in geographic data

- *Answering geographic questions.* Finally, students should see the relationships among the data they have gathered and analyzed. They should reach generalizations that are true across time and place. Specifically, students should be able to

    - Present oral and written reports accompanied by maps, charts, graphs, and tables
    - Apply geographic knowledge to interpret the past, understand the present, and predict the future

◆ Teaching Geography in the Elementary School

Geography presents a unique challenge to teachers, primarily because geographic information is presented in an unfamiliar format. Maps and globes require a different type of reading from the expository text students read in textbooks and encyclopedias. Further, elementary students will work with a variety of maps, each with its own category of information. For example, one type of climate map shows precipitation for South America, whereas another, historical map shows European colonies in South America during the early 19th century. Another complicating factor with world maps is the difference between conformal maps and equal area maps. The *Mercator projection* produces a *conformal map;* all the landmasses retain their appropriate shapes. Unfortunately, this type of map is distorted; Greenland appears larger than Africa. *Equal-area maps,* in contrast, show land areas with proper relative sizes. Unfortunately, this requires a distortion of the earth's landmasses. The good news is that most social studies textbooks present maps that are developmentally appropriate for the children who read them. Further, schools should have globes and maps specially designed for young learners. For example, globes at many levels of sophistication are available. The simplest ones avoid detail, include only the names of nations and their capital cities, and use bright colors to distinguish boundaries.

The Internet is rapidly replacing hard-copy atlases as the best source for teachers and students looking for maps. Excellent Websites are too numerous to mention here, but, for example, students could click on the Mapquest Website (www.mapquest.com) and request a street map for any location in the United States. This site will be a valuable resource for students studying their neighborhood and community. Maps of every sort are available on the Internet. For example, the University of Virginia's Fisher Library is home to the National Digitial Map Library, which includes several maps of all 50 states, including maps showing county boundaries, major cities, and national parks and forests (http://fisher.lib.virginia.edu).

As with many social studies processes, map-reading skills should be developed through both repeated practice and direct instruction. Students will become geographically literate if they are *repeatedly* asked to use maps; there is no substitute for practice. At the same time, teachers should plan *developmental* lessons to help our students understand the special language of maps. All geography teaching with children should move from the concrete to the abstract, from the simple to the complex. If possible, developmental map-reading activities should use the following progression:

1. First, children should participate in activities that use their bodies as points of reference.
2. Next, children should use three-dimensional maps.
3. Then children should use maps that are simplified for use in the elementary classroom.
4. Finally, children should be asked to complete activities with maps that are real and have been produced for use outside the classroom. The mini-unit presented at the end of this chapter on using a grid system follows this progression.

Symbols, Scale, Grid, and Direction

To both gather and report geographic information, elementary children must become sophisticated with four aspects of maps: symbols, scale, grid, and direction.

Symbols.　Maps use symbols to report information. Some symbols represent things with a fixed, physical presence, such as highways and rivers; others reveal patterns of data, such as levels of unemployment. Consider the challenge children face. Material that is written, such as a textbook, uses a single, unvarying set of symbols—the 26 letters of the English alphabet. Most maps, in contrast, have their own set of symbols. A red circle on one map may represent a city with a population of 100,000, whereas on another map a red circle may represent the location of a water treatment plant. The key concept for children to understand is that once a certain symbol stands for something on a map, it will always have the same meaning for that map. The *legend* on a map tells what the symbols mean.

Our youngest learners should be exposed to maps with three-dimensional symbols that look a great deal like what they represent. A three-dimensional map of the neighborhood, for example, might have milk cartons represent houses and a large shoe box, with doors and windows painted on it, represent the school. Next, students work with maps with symbols that are pictographs (or "pictorial" symbols); the symbols are drawings for what they represent. The next level of abstraction is "semi-pictorial" symbols, which look something like, or retain a single feature of, what they represent (e.g., a church is represented by a cross).

When symbols no longer "look" like what they represent (e.g., the symbol for the state capital is a star), then the maps should be simplified and include very few symbols. Following are some activities that teach children to understand map symbols:

• *Group symbols.* If students are seated in groups, have each group of students choose a symbol to represent themselves. The symbols cannot have any writing; they may be pictorial, but eventually they should be abstract—for example, blue circles or red triangles. Use the symbols in class schedules and on charts.

• *Symbols in the community.* Develop a lesson with symbols that are used in the community and in the media. Students will recognize some commercial symbols (e.g., the golden arches for McDonald's or the Nike swoosh) and others used in public places (e.g., symbols for men and women on bathroom doors or symbols for railroad tracks).

• *Matching symbols with what they represent.* Prepare simple pictorial symbols for a set of photographs. For a picture of school, the symbol could be a simple drawing of a building with a flag; for a picture of a forest, the symbol could be a triangular treetop with a narrow, rectangular trunk, like a stylized Christmas tree. Shuffle the symbols and the photographs and then have students match each symbol to its photograph.

• *Simplified maps.* If the textbook does not have them, then make some maps that (a) have few places represented (few details) and (b) use pictorial symbols. Students will need repeated practice with these simplified maps (see Figure 11.1 for an example).

Scale.   Our youngest students should work with some maps that are life size. For example, it is possible to create a life-size map of the top of a teacher's desk. Eventually, the possibilities for life-size maps are exhausted, and students will have to understand scale to use maps. My experience is that this is a very difficult concept for young children. Most maps that I have seen primary-level children produce, prior to a good unit on maps, are more illustrations than maps. The problem is that the scale on these maps produced by primary-age children is inconsistent. I recall that, when I asked them to draw a map of the neighborhood, for example, most children drew houses that were grossly out of scale and covered an area that should represent an entire block. Our older students, in contrast, should be able to calculate the exact distance between two places on a map. Following are some activities that will help children understand scale:

• Compare the furniture in a first-grade classroom with the furniture in a fifth-grade classroom. The chairs the children use will make the point dramatically. Then have the children think about the relative sizes of first graders and fifth graders. Help the children see that the furniture has been "built to scale"—smaller chairs for smaller children, larger chairs for larger children.

• Have the children draw maps of the classroom. Focus on scale. The children must represent their desks in a way that makes them smaller than the teacher's

Figure 11.1 Simplified Map to Teach Children How to Use a Grid System

desk (assuming the teacher's desk is larger than the students'). Then have the children try making maps of the school. First, you may want to measure the size of some of the buildings in the school complex. Help the children see that the smaller buildings at the school must look that way on their maps.

• When you think the children are ready, teach a series of lessons on using the scale of miles. The goal should be to have the children calculate actual distances between places by using the scale.

At the end of the chapter, you will find an example of this type of lesson, an activity in which students determine the distances between two places.

Grid.   The more detailed the map, the more important it is for the map reader to use a grid system. To locate a street on a detailed map of a city, for example, requires the map reader to find the street name in an index and then use the *coordinates* (e.g., E5) to narrow the search. Latitude and longitude constitute the grid system for maps and globes. Use of a grid system allows the map reader to find the *absolute location* of a place.

At the end of the chapter is a mini-unit designed to help third graders learn how to use grids to find places on maps.

Direction.   Children need to understand directionality to know the *relative location* of something. For example, where is San Antonio in relation to New Orleans? With our youngest students, it is a good idea to start with familiar directions of left-right and up-down before moving to the compass rose. Following are some activities that will help your students understand relative location and directionality:

• *Directions in the classroom.*   Challenge your students to describe something in the classroom by using references to other things in the room, and the other students try to guess what the item is. For example, "This thing is in the front of the room. As I look at it, it is to the left of the flag and to the right of the pencil sharpener. It is below the clock" (the item was a wall thermometer). The person describing the thing may *not* reveal physical characteristics (e.g., it is red and large).

• *Compass rose on the playground.*   Once students have been introduced to the compass rose and north, south, east, and west, take the class outdoors for a simple activity. On the playground, ask students to move according to instructions you give. Make sure all the instructions use north, south, east, and west, for example, "Take three steps north and two steps south," "Take two steps south and three steps east."

• *Relative location on a real map.*   Present to the class a simple map of the United States. Have students answer some simple questions involving relative location, for example, "Which state is north of Missouri?" "Which states border Utah?" "Which state is closer to Arizona—California or Louisiana?" "If you were going from Chicago to Seattle, in which direction would you travel?"

Reporting Geographic Data: Student-Made Maps

Reading maps is one thing; making them is another. The following sections introduce several types of maps your students should make.

Mental Maps.   The national geography standards suggest that students use
mental (or sketch) maps to answer geographic questions (Geography Education
Standards Project, 1994, pp. 146–147). A *mental map* is a map "inside your head"
and is drawn without reference to other resources. When students draw their
mental maps, these can be referred to as "sketch maps." Mental maps can be used
in several ways:

- Mental maps can be used as a diagnostic tool. They reveal what students
know about the region being mapped. More important, they reveal the mapmaker's
attitude toward the places represented. The familiar and the important tend to be
drawn larger than the less familiar and the less important.
- For some geographic tasks, a sketch map serves us well. *Sketch maps* can
help us recall the relative locations and relative sizes of places. A sketch map could
help us remember what nations a person must travel through to go from Paris to
Moscow or to show someone how to get from school to the airport.

Relief Maps.   For more than 100 years, elementary school children have made
three-dimensional relief maps. *Relief maps* reveal the topography of a region because
mountain ranges and valleys can be shown. To help your students be successful,
consider conducting the following activity:

1. Build an outline map on an inflexible surface, such as plywood (card-
   board tends to buckle, so do not use it).
2. Start with a good "outline" map. An *outline map* shows some geographic
   features but omits others. Commercially produced outline maps of the
   world, the continents, the United States, and each of the 50 states are
   available. The outline map used for a relief map must be either drawn or
   projected on the surface. Do not make the outline map too small; a relief
   map must be large enough to show the important physical features of
   the region.
3. Sketch the outline of the features in the model (e.g., mountains, rivers,
   and valleys) on the surface. Students will need an easy-to-read map to
   show the physical geography of the region they are mapping. It is essential that students have a good idea of the scale of things (e.g., how tall one
   mountain is in relation to another).
4. There are many recipes for making relief maps. The old tried-and-true
   recipe is salt and flour. Mix equal parts of salt and flour and add a minimal
   amount of water—just enough to keep the glob together. I prefer to use
   clay, but it is more expensive.

5. Have patience! It is not easy to make a mountain. Work with students to consider scale and expect some initial efforts that will need to be reshaped.

6. Relief maps look better if they are painted (e.g., mountains, brown; valleys, green; and rivers, blue). Tempera paints work fine.

Thematic Maps.   In her excellent article, Trifonoff (1997) challenges primary-level teachers to allow their students to make thematic maps. Almost all the maps that elementary students read or make are location maps, which show where things are. Thematic maps, in contrast, "illustrate a single idea, distribution, or relationship" (p. 17). An example of a thematic map is a map of the United States showing the rate of coronary-related deaths among 100 people. States are divided into four categories based on the data on coronary-related deaths. Each category is assigned a color, and on the thematic map of coronary-related deaths in the United States, each state is colored according to the data. Anyone looking at the map can easily compare the data on any two states, and, more important, regional trends (if any) are easy to spot.

To make a thematic map, start with a blank map of a region (e.g., your school, neighborhood, city, or state). The map must have clearly defined subregions (e.g., the map of the state must show counties, and the map of the school must show each classroom). Next, students need to gather data and compile it in a table. For example, students could do a survey to determine how frequently students in each classroom eat in the cafeteria. Then students would have to organize the data so that they fall into four or five categories. Each classroom must fit into one of the categories based on the average number of students who eat in the cafeteria each day. For example, on the average, (a) more than 75% of students in the classroom eat in the cafeteria, (b) 50% to 74% of students in the classroom eat in the cafeteria, (c) 25% to 49% of students in the classroom eat in the cafeteria, and (d) less than 24% of students in the classroom eat in the cafeteria. A color must be assigned to each category (e.g., over 75%, red; 50%–74%, blue; 25%–49%, green; and 24% and under, yellow). A legend must be added that explains what the colors mean, and students would have to color each classroom on the map accordingly.

◆ Summary of Key Points

- History always has been an important part of the elementary school curriculum. Publication of the national history standards generated considerable debate about what historical content students should learn.
- Children have the cognitive capacity to learn historical concepts if they receive appropriate instruction.
- Elementary students should learn about the history of their families, schools, communities, and state; the history of the United States; the history of people living in other nations; and the historical contributions of women, people of color, and common people.

- Students should develop the ability to think and act like historians; the "doing" of history is an important part of teaching history.
- Throughout the book, I have presented teaching ideas that are essential to teach history in a diverse classroom; these include contextual support, multiple lesson formats, cooperative learning, critical thinking, and a variety of resources.
- Three types of lessons are essential to teach history to children: (a) those using primary sources, (b) those incorporating children's fiction, and (c) those using time lines.
- Teachers should adopt a broad definition of geography so that our students do more than memorize geographic data.
- Maps are difficult to read because information is presented in an unfamiliar format.
- Research on the cognitive development of children and geography shows that children can learn geographic concepts, although there are developmental limits.
- Geography is the study of place, including physical characteristics, geopolitical information, demographics, and economic information.
- The processes of geography include the ability to ask and answer geographic questions by acquiring, organizing, and analyzing geographic information.
- To read maps, children must understand symbols, scale, grid, and direction.

FOR FURTHER READING

History

- Read the study by Keith Barton and Linda Levstik (1996). Unlike much published research, it is relatively easy to read and full of fascinating detail. Downey and Levstik's chapter in the *Handbook of Research on Social Studies Teaching and Learning* (1991) is a good summary of the research on the teaching and learning of history up to that point in time. The books by Brophy (1996a), Brophy and Van Sledright (1997), and Leinhardt, Beck, and Stanton (1994) are good if you want to peruse the teaching and learning of history in great depth. Keith Barton's research is helping provide a much clearer picture of the historical understandings of children. See his article on how children in the United States and Northern Ireland view the past quite differently (Barton, 2001).
- Virtually every issue of *The Social Studies, Social Education,* and *Social Studies and the Young Learner* has at least one article on teaching historical content. Some special issues devoted to teaching and learning history are Simpson (2004) and Potter (2003). The NCSS book, *A Link to the Past* by Yell, Scheurman, & Reynolds (2004) has many excellent lesson plans based on primary sources. For a full discussion of the controversy over the national history standards, see the January 1996 edition of *Social Education* and its articles by Saxe, Cohen, and Whelan.
- Many articles have been published on teaching history with children's books. See the synthesis article by McGowan and colleagues (1996) in

Social Education. Also of note are three books published by the Social Science Education Consortium: *C Is for Citizenship: Children's Literature and Civic Understanding* (Singleton, 1997), *G Is for Geography: Children's Literature and the Five Themes* (Singleton, 1993), and *H Is for History: Using Children's Literature to Develop Historical Understandings* (Singleton, 1995). Haas (2000) provides instructional ideas for a one-of-a-kind picture book *A Street Through Time* (Millard, 1998).
- One curriculum project that is worth a look is *History Alive,* developed by Teachers Curriculum Institute (1995). *History Alive* uses slides, experiential exercises, and problem solving (Bower & Lobdell, 1998).

Geography
- For anyone who wants a comprehensive look at the teaching of geography, the books by Douglass (1998) and Gersmehl (2005) are the best sources. Gregg and Leinhardt's (1994) research review is difficult reading but well worth the effort.
- The journals regularly publish many articles on geography teaching and learning. For example, Bolick (2006) writes about teaching with online historical maps; Segall (2003) provides a comprehensive look at teaching about maps; Hartman and Giorgis (2001) discuss how children can learn about maps through children's literature.

LESSON PLANS AND INSTRUCTIONAL ACTIVITIES

This chapter concludes with four examples of teaching history and geography to elementary school children:
1. For sixth graders, a mini-unit titled "The Historian as Detective," that teaches historical processes
2. A kindergarten lesson that shows how children's literature, in this case the picture book *Ox-Cart Man,* can be used to teach historical content
3. A lesson plan for fourth graders that challenges the students to use a scale of miles to calculate the distance between two places
4. A third-grade mini-unit on "Using Grid Systems to Find Places on Maps"

Description of a MINI-UNIT

Grade Six: The Historian as Detective

Gavrish (1995) describes a unit titled "The Historian as Detective." Although designed for secondary students, it could be adapted to teach historical methodology in elementary classrooms.

Part I: Organizing Framework

From the the national history standards (National Center for History in the Schools, 1996) Standard 3: Historical Analysis and Interpretation: (D) distinguish fact and fiction and (G) consider multiple perspectives.

In this mini-unit, students will be asked to think like historians as they deal with the unreliability of eyewitness accounts, work with primary sources, and challenge the accuracy of a document. This mini-unit answers three questions:

Unit Question 1: To the historian, how reliable are eyewitness accounts?

Unit Question 2: What are primary sources, and why are they more valuable than secondary sources?

Unit Question 3: How do historians challenge the accuracy of documents they read?

Part II: Instructional Activities

Unit Question 1: To the historian, how reliable are eyewitness accounts?

Activity 1

Content Objectives: Students will learn that eyewitness accounts are not always trustworthy and that this causes a problem for the historian.

Process Objectives: Students will *examine* the geographic figures on the board, *draw* what they recall, and *assess* the accuracy of their recollections.

1. Tape three diagrams to the chalkboard. Each should have an outer figure (e.g., circle or square) of one color and an inner figure of another color. Tell the students, "Look at these diagrams." Leave the diagrams on the board for a short time and then remove them. Then ask the students to draw each diagram from memory: What shape is the outer figure? What color? What shape is the inner figure? What color? This task puts students in the same place as the historian, who cannot replay events. Have the students work in small groups to determine the accuracy of their drawings.
2. Help students draw the comparison between this exercise and eyewitness accounts of historical events. Why might historical events be faulty? (With the diagrams, bias is not the issue.) Like eyewitnesses to real events, the students (a) may have faulty memory and (b) probably did not look as carefully as they would have had they known they would be asked to recall specific details.

Unit Question 2: What are primary sources, and what is their value to the historian?

Activity 2

Content Objectives: Students will learn the definition of primary sources and understand their value to the historian.

Process Objectives: Students will *list* and evaluate the value of the sources they could use to write an accurate autobiography. They will *define* primary source and *state* the value of primary sources to historians.

1. In the second activity, students consider what sources of information they would use to answer questions such as the following: Where were you born? How much did you weigh at birth? What age were you when you took your first step? What age were you when you said your first word? Read aloud the questions. Then ask the class what sources of information they would use to answer those questions. Students will probably say they would just ask their parents (or other family members). Ask the students to recall what they learned in the previous lesson about the unreliability of eyewitness accounts. Then ask them what other sources they could use besides parents or other family members. Help students see that several sources would be useful: birth certificates, baby books, and photographs. Have documents for one student (or even yourself) available to use as examples (these should be copies, and the parents and the student must approve of their use). Point out that these are all *primary sources.*

2. Tell the class that if a classmate were to write a biography of you, that biography would be a *secondary source.* Make sure the class understands the distinction between primary and secondary sources. Finally, ask the students why primary sources are so valuable to the historian.

Unit Question 3: How do historians challenge the accuracy of documents they read?

Activity 3

Content Objectives: Students will see that not all written documents are accurate.

Process Objectives: Students will *read* the historical letter prepared by the teacher and *identify* examples of historical inaccuracy.

1. In this third activity, students are told about a letter that was recently "discovered." Actually, you will have to create such a letter or use the one created by Gavrish (1995) in his article. His fake letter was supposedly written by George Washington. You could write your own as long as the letter is full of historical errors (anachronisms) that make it an obvious fake. The sample letter provided by Gavrish has many errors (it is written to Queen Victoria, it is written in Chicago, and it mentions the use of tanks in battle). Show the students the letter and challenge them to find each error.

2. I would have students work in small groups and share the errors they find. This lesson helps students learn to analyze a document. It shows that historians must view primary sources with a critical eye.

Effective Teaching in Today's Diverse Classroom: The first two activities in this mini-unit have features that would make them appropriate for a diverse student population. In the first, when students are drawing the geometric figures from memory, they do not need to be able to read grade-level texts to be successful. The second activity is based on shared, personal experience of the students—their births! One caution is in order here, though. Some students will have access to more primary source data about their births than their classmates. Whereas some students will have baby books, photographs, and birth certificates, others will not (for any of a number of reasons). Try to obtain birth-related primary source material for four or five students and use it for the lesson. The third activity is a challenging one. To find the errors in the historically inaccurate letter, students will need to know enough historical information to spot the mistakes. Because you will write the fake letter (or use the one from Gavrish, 1995), I suggest you write it so that your students will find it easy to read. Your goal is to help them see that written documents can be inaccurate, and this can be accomplished with an easy-to-read document.

Kindergarten: *Ox-Cart Man*

In a journal article, I describe history lessons that can be taught with children's literature (Zarrillo, 1989). An exciting, cross-curricular lesson can be developed with *Ox-Cart Man,* a Caldecott-winning picture book written by Donald Hall (1979) and illustrated by Barbara Cooney. This book tells the story of a New England farmer and his family, apparently in the early 19th century.

Overview: This lesson is for a kindergarten class of 25 children.

Resources and Materials: (a) a copy of the book *Ox-Cart Man* (Hall, 1979) and (b) chart paper and an easel.

Content Objectives: Children will understand that life in times past was different from life today. Specifically, they will see differences in clothing, tools, transportation, and food preparation. They will also learn about the work done on a farm many years ago.

Standard: From **The National Standards for History,** grades K–4, Standard 1, the student is able to "Compare and contrast family life now with family life over time" (National Center for History in the Schools, 1996, p. 26).

Process Objectives: Children will *listen* and *watch* as their teacher reads aloud the book and demonstrates the productive activities of the farmer, his wife, son, and daughter; *pantomime* those activities under the teacher's direction; and *distinguish* differences between how the farmer and his family lived and how we live today (clothing, transportation, and food preparation).

Teaching Sequence:

1. Before the lesson, write the following on a sheet of chart paper: carve a new yoke, saw planks for a new cart, split shingles, embroider clothing, make candles, tap syrup, shear sheep, spin yarn, plant crops.

2. Display the chart on an easel.
3. Ask the children to come to the read-aloud area and to sit cross-legged on the floor.
4. Read aloud *Ox-Cart Man.*
5. Ask the children whether they have any questions or comments about the story.
6. Read aloud each farming activity on the chart and demonstrate, through pantomime, how each would be done.
7. Ask the children to stand and, under your guidance, pantomime each activity.
8. Point to the illustrations in the book that show how the farmer and his family dressed, how they prepared food, the tools they used, and how they transported goods. Allow the children to look at each illustration closely and to talk about what they find interesting. Then ask, "What is different about how the farmer lived and how we live today?"

Evaluation: You may want to tape-record the children's responses to the question "What is different about how the farmer lived and how we live today?" The comments will reveal to what extent the children understand the lesson's content objective.

Effective Teaching in Today's Diverse Classroom: Howard Gardner has written about *multiple intelligences* (1983, 1991). This concept defies the older idea that intelligence is a single entity that can be measured and quantified (with an intelligence quotient [IQ]). It seems to make sense that some people are gifted (or challenged) in one area, like the arts, but challenged (or gifted) in another, like mathematical thinking. In any case, some children are frustrated with school because they typically have so few opportunities for learning and expression through the arts. This activity will make their day by providing an opportunity to assume the roles of the ox-cart man and his family.

LESSON PLAN

Grade Four: Using a Scale of Miles to Calculate Distance: A First Lesson

The first time students use a scale of miles to calculate the distance between two points on a map, it helps if they are not confronted with distances in fractions of inches. If 1 inch equals 100 miles, then it is easy to figure out how far apart two places are if they appear 3 inches apart on the map (3 inches × 100 miles/inch = 300 miles). It is quite another task if they are 1 3/4 inches apart.

Overview: This lesson is for a small group of fourth graders, six students.

Resources and Materials: Beforehand, make a map of either your state or the United States; cities should be placed on the map so that each city is exactly 1, 2, 3, or 4 inches from the other cities (no fractional distances). This will involve minor adjustments in placing some cities. Base the scale of miles on 1 inch (1 inch equals 50 miles or 100 miles, whichever is appropriate). Then have available (a) a plastic transparency of the map, (b) six copies of the map, (c) six sets of colored pencils, and (d) six rulers.

Standard: From the *Expectations of Excellence,* the National Council for the Social Studies (NCSS) curriculum standards, thematic strand III, "People, Places & Environments," performance expectation (d) for the middle grades: "The learner can estimate distance, calculate scale, and distinguish other geographic relationships such as population density and spatial distribution patterns" (NCSS, 1994, p. 35).

Content Objectives: Students will calculate the actual distance between two points on a map by using scale.

Process Objectives: Students will *calculate* the actual distance between cities on the map.

Teaching Sequence

1. Display the plastic transparency of the simplified map. Explain that each student will receive a copy of this map. Point out the scale of miles.
2. Using the distance between any two cities as an example, (a) draw a straight line between two cities (e.g., from Kansas City to Detroit), (b) measure the line, and (c) multiply the distance by 100 (or whatever distance is equivalent to 1 inch on this map).
3. Ask students to use their red pencils to draw a line between two other cities on their own copies of the map. Next, have students measure the line. Help them set up the multiplication problem and do the calculation.
4. Present other combinations of cities for students to calculate. For each pair of cities, have the class use a different-colored pencil. Help students with the standard process: draw the line, measure the line, and multiply to find the real distance.

Evaluation: Your observation of the students will tell you who is having difficulty using a scale of miles. Collect each student's map for further analysis.

Effective Teaching in Today's Diverse Classroom: This lesson is planned for a small group of students. I have planned this as a first lesson on using a scale of miles. Although some of your more able students will find this an easy task, most elementary students find it challenging. For children with mild learning disabilities, you may need to provide extra support through one-to-one tutoring or small group coaching. One more thing: Although you probably realize this, students cannot use a scale of miles to calculate distance on a map if they cannot perform the required multiplication (in this lesson, multiplying two-digit numbers by one-digit numbers).

<table>
<tr><td>MINI-
UNIT</td></tr>
</table>

Grade Three: Using Grid Systems to Find Places on Maps

Part I: Organizing Framework

Standard: The organizing framework for this mini-unit comes from the national geography standards (Geography Education Standards Project, 1994): Standard 1 for grades K–4, The World in Spatial Terms, performance expectation (c), "The student is able to use a map grid to answer the question—What is this location?—as applied to places chosen by the teacher and the student" (p. 107).

This mini-unit answers one question:

Unit Question: **How can we use the grid system to help us locate things on maps?**

Part II: Instructional Activities

Activity 1: The Grid Game

Content Objectives: Using the classroom as an example, children will understand how a grid system works.

Process Objectives: Children will *identify* coordinates for several locations in the room and *use* coordinates to find the absolute location of several classmates.
Arrange the classroom so that the children are seated in rows. Label each row: If you have six rows, they should be labeled A, B, C, D, E, and F. Then label the position of each chair in each row. If each row has five chairs, the first chair would be 1, the second chair would be 2, and so on. Now each child has an absolute location with a set of coordinates (e.g., the child sitting in the fourth chair in the first row would be A4). Attach large signs in front of each row with the correct label (A, B, C, and so on) and do the same for the position of the chairs (you might have to use easels so that the children can see the labels). To begin, stand next to a child and ask the class what the coordinates are ("I am standing next to José. What are his coordinates?" If José is in the last seat of the fifth row, the answer is E5). On a set of index cards, print all the possible coordinates (A1–A5, B1–B5, and so on). Shuffle the cards and pull out one at a time. Then ask, "Who is seated in D3?" (B2? A5? and so on).

Activity 2: Locating a Place on a Map of a Model City

Content Objectives: Children will understand how a grid system can be "placed" on a three-dimensional map.

Process Objectives: Children will *construct* a three-dimensional map of a hypothetical city, use yarn to *create* a grid system for the city, and *locate* places on the three-dimensional map by using the grid system.

Have the class make a three-dimensional map of a model city. This will require milk cartons, shoe boxes, and other paper containers that can be modified to resemble structures. The model should include businesses, parks, hospitals, houses, apartment buildings, and schools. After the children have finished this three-dimensional map, place a grid system "over" it with yarn. This is somewhat tricky, but be sure the spaces between the vertical and horizontal pieces of yarn are equivalent. Then label the grid. Again, the vertical rows can be labeled A, B, C, and so on and the horizontal rows 1, 2, 3, and so on. First, help children see that every place on the model city map can be identified by a set of coordinates (e.g., the hospital is in C4). Ask the children what they see in a variety of places (e.g., "What is in B3?"). Then give the class a list of places and have them identify the proper coordinates.

Activity 3: A Simplified Map

Content Objectives: Children will move from a three-dimensional map to a two-dimensional map and understand how a grid system can be used on a flat map.

Process Objectives: Children will *locate* places on a simplified map of a city by using a grid system.

Have children work with simplified grid systems. Many social studies textbooks include these. If yours does not, it is easy to develop your own. Figure 11.1 shows a simplified grid system one teacher created for his third-grade class.

First, the simplified map should have a limited number of coordinates (no more than four vertical and four horizontal). Thus, the "squares" defined by the grid system are large. Second, the map should have a limited number of places represented on the map. The simplified map in Figure 11.1 includes only seven symbols. Challenge the class to find places by using the grid system. Ask them, "Where are the two parks?" (C1 and C4). You can also ask more difficult questions, like, "Do the people who live in B4 have a church nearby?" (Yes, one is in B4). A final important activity with the simplified map: Prepare an index of locations. This should list the coordinates for the places on the map (e.g., City Hall—A4; Churches—A1 and B4; and Schools—A2, C3). Have children verify the information of the index.

Activity 4: A Real Map of Your City

Content Objectives: Children will now see how a grid system on a real map of their city can be used to locate places.

Process Objectives: Children will *locate* places on a real map of their city by using a grid system.

Third graders will appreciate the challenge of using a real city map as their parents do. Obtain several copies of a map of your city, but be sure the map has a good grid system. Have the children work in groups. Because this activity is difficult, you may want to have cross-age helpers from the sixth grade come to your room to help each group. Give children a list of 10 places to find on the map. These should include a school, a park, and a library. First, have the children use the index to find the coordinates for each place. Then ask the children to find the place by using the coordinates on the map. Finally, for a real challenge, give each group a set of cross streets to locate (e.g., Adams and Elm). They will need to find both streets on the index and then locate their intersection.

 Effective Teaching in Today's Diverse Classroom: James Cummins has described how skills learned in one language transfer to another (1979, 1986a, 1986b, 1989, 1992). Because reading maps is dependent on symbols unrelated to English, the geographic processes described in this section of the textbook can be learned in any language. If a student learns to use symbols, a scale of miles (or kilometers), and a grid system in any language, then those skills can be used to read maps written in other languages. Admittedly, most English-language learners attend schools where too few, if any, teachers and aides can provide primary-language instruction. When the possibility exists, however, it makes sense to use the primary language to teach map-reading skills to English-language learners who speak little English. For children with learning disabilities, you may need to *adapt the lesson materials* by providing *instructional cues* on the city maps they use. Rather than have the children find the appropriate page in the map book on their own, provide students with a photocopy of the correct page in the map book with the appropriate columns highlighted (e.g., if a park is located in *4G,* highlight in yellow the *4* at the top of the page and *G* on the side of the page). This will make the task much easier, while still teaching the concept of a map grid system.

Chapter 12

The Other Social Sciences and Topics of Special Interest: Completing the Social Studies Curriculum

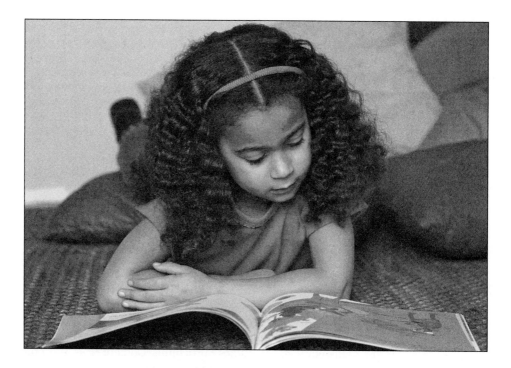

T wo years ago, a curriculum committee in Darlene Hoyer's school district decided that key concepts from psychology should be a part of the social studies curriculum. For each grade level, projects or units were designed to help students learn how to develop positive interpersonal relationships. Mrs. Hoyer engaged her fifth-grade students in an anger management project. Students in Mrs. Hoyer's classroom were expected to learn about how they could limit and control their anger. During this project, some students conducted a survey of their classmates to find out what made them angry; others interviewed the school psychologist to find out what coping mechanisms could be used to exercise control over anger; and a third group read information books and health textbooks to learn about the causes and control of anger.

The goal of the project was to produce a video that could be used with other classes. Once informed about anger management, members of Mrs. Hoyer's class would write the video script, shoot the necessary footage, and edit the tape. Students determined that they should make two versions of the video: one for children in the primary grades, and one for students in the upper elementary grades. Much of the video would be simulated scenarios, with Mrs. Hoyer's students playing the roles. The simulations would illustrate how to decrease the chances someone would get angry and, if anger did come to the surface, how to cope with the hostile feelings. This project on anger management is an example of how the social science disciplines can be used to enrich the elementary social studies curriculum.

•   •   •

In this chapter, you will read about

- How anthropology can be an important part of elementary social studies
- How our students can participate in an archaeological dig
- Integrating economic concepts into the social studies curriculum
- A six-step process our student can use when they analyze economic problems
- How concepts from psychology and sociology will help our students better understand themselves and other people
- How concepts and concerns about global education, environmental education, and current events are essential for our students to learn as we enter the 21st century

◆ Completing the Social Studies Curriculum

Citizenship education, history, and geography traditionally have been the main focus in the elementary social studies curriculum. Content from the other social sciences (anthropology, economics, sociology, psychology, and political science), however, also must be included in the elementary curriculum. Content from these areas is essential because, without it, our students will have only a partial understanding of the world they live in. In this chapter, we look at anthropology, economics, psychology, and sociology (political science was covered in Chapter 10).

It is important to note that each social science includes both a body of knowledge (content) and a way of learning about people (process). For example, the content of anthropology includes information about ancient cultural groups of the Americas, like the Maya and the Aztec. Our students should learn this information. At the same time, the social studies curriculum should help our students understand how practitioners in each discipline gather information. For example, anthropologists who study ancient cultures learn about the Maya and the Aztec through several processes, primarily by analyzing artifacts obtained through excavation. If our students understand how social scientists gather and analyze data, they will have a better sense of how these experts reached their conclusions. In this chapter, we also examine two emerging fields of study in social studies: global education and environmental education. The chapter concludes with a discussion of how to teach current events.

◆ Anthropology

Several authorities have written about how teachers can make anthropology a part of elementary social studies: Barnes (1991), Jantz and Klawitter (1991), Laney and Moseley (1990), Little Soldier (1990), Nelson and Stahl (1991), and White (1989). *Anthropology* is the study of the physical and cultural characteristics of people. Jane White (1989) stated the goal of this discipline:

> The central goal of anthropologists is to explain why groups of people are different from each other; to explain why they have different physical characteristics, speak different languages, use different technologies, and why they think, believe, and act so differently. (p. 31)

Anthropology comprises two broad fields: physical anthropology and cultural anthropology. *Physical anthropology,* which explores the evolution and physical differences of people, is rarely a part of the elementary curriculum. Some sixth-grade social studies curricula, however, do cover the origins of humankind, introducing students to the work of Mary and Richard Leakey in East Africa (human paleontology is part of physical anthropology). *Cultural anthropology,* which is the study of the culture, should be an integral part of social studies in the elementary curriculum. When we plan and present units on the Navajo or ancient Rome, we are teaching cultural anthropology. Many aspects, or "manifestations," of culture can serve as the focus of elementary social studies lessons:

• *Food getting.* How is food gathered or produced? How is food distributed? Most elementary students assume that all other people—both those living today and those who lived in the past—live the same way the students do. It may never occur to a third grader, for example, that some people do not get their food in a grocery store. Social studies should teach students about groups who depend on hunting, agriculture, or trade for food.

- *Economic systems.* What resources does the cultural group use? How are resources converted to useful things? What must they trade for? How are resources allocated? What system of money is used for exchange?
- *Social stratification.* What social groups exist within the cultural group? What advantages are reserved for members of some groups (economic, power, or prestige)? What is denied to other groups?
- *Patterns of residence.* Who lives with whom? What determines where a person lives? Although it is worthwhile to learn about different human dwellings, it is more important to consider the cultural rules that determine who resides in a home.
- *Political organization.* Who makes the laws? Who enforces the laws? How are conflicts resolved?
- *Religion.* What religions are practiced by members of the cultural group? What are the fundamental beliefs? What rituals are religious in nature?
- *Arts.* What forms of visual arts are produced and valued by members of the cultural group? What media are preferred? What types of performing arts are practiced by members of the cultural group?

Social studies units that introduce children to a cultural group do have a "bottom line," however. What is most important? *Curriculum Guidelines for Multicultural Education* (National Council for the Social Studies [NCSS] Task Force on Ethnic Studies Curriculum Guidelines, 1992) states that we want students to learn a cultural group's "ideas, ways of thinking, values, symbols" (p. 276). White (1989) summarizes this point:

> All too often, well-intentioned teachers will teach about "our neighbors across the border" by having their class, for example, break a piñata or eat tamales. They may not realize these events are the tips of a cultural iceberg . . . these isolated experiences do not really capture the more central values of how the Mexicans make meaning out of their own culture. (p. 35)

Single Group Studies

A *single group study* is a unit on one cultural group (e.g., the Kikuyu, the Nez Percé, or modern Germany). In another book, I stated some important points to consider when teaching about cultural groups (Zarrillo, 1994):

- *Don't lump groups of people together.* For example, if a teacher presents a unit on the "American Indian," students will be left with the impression that all Native groups shared a common culture. This, of course, is far from the truth. The Huron and the Hopi are as different as the Swedes and the Greeks. At the very least, a unit should cover a small group of tribes who inhabited a common physical region (e.g., "Natives of the Pacific Northwest"). A unit on a single tribe will provide depth of understanding and diminish the chances that students will learn inaccurate information about a cultural group.
- *Be specific about the historical period.* All cultural groups change over time, and so our units of study must have chronological boundaries. For example,

the Chinese of the Han dynasty (206 B.C. to A.D. 220) share many cultural traits with the Chinese of the present day, yet there are some striking differences. Thus, well-defined units should state a time span—for example, "Mexico in the 20th Century," "Medieval Japan," or "Ancient Egypt."

- *Avoid stereotyping.*   This can be difficult because anthropologists describe a norm, and it is easy for children to assume that all members of a cultural group conform to the norm. Every cultural group, however, contains variation.

- *Use as many resources as possible.*   These should include videos, CDs, the Internet, software, study prints, information books, biographies, and reference books. The more resources we use, the better the chances that our students will acquire more than a superficial understanding of the cultural group. What if a resource is guilty of bias? Biased materials should be either excluded or presented as biased. Materials created by members of the cultural group being studied are a significant addition to any unit.

- *Include lessons on many facets of the cultural group.*   For example, it should be clear to students what roles men and women fill. As I noted earlier, it is essential that students become aware of the values and beliefs of the cultural group, so lessons on religion are important. The students I taught, for example, were fascinated with the marriage and courtship rituals of other cultural groups.

- *Do some background work on the group of people to be studied.*   No one should expect us to become experts; our teaching will be more successful, however, if we take time to read about the cultural group our students will study.

One final point: Students should make comparisons among cultural groups, contrasting the way we live with the ways of other groups. The purpose of a cultural comparison is to learn about ourselves and others, not to judge whether one group of people is better or worse than another. The NCSS Task Force on Ethnic Studies (1992) states that study of different cultural groups should help students see that

> each individual and each ethnic group has worth and dignity. Students should be taught that persons from all ethnic groups have common characteristics and needs, although they are affected differently by certain social situations and may use different means to respond to their needs. (p. 286)

Doing Anthropology: A Dig

One activity that will give students some sense of how anthropologists work is a "dig." This is one way that *archaeologists,* those anthropologists investigating cultural groups from the past, gather data. During a dig, archaeologists excavate a site in search of artifacts. Several articles can help us in planning a dig with our students: Andel (1990), Carrol (1987), Hightshoe (1997), Morris (1998), Ovoian and Gregory (1991), Owen (1982), and Passe and Passe (1985). I also recommend two children's books: *Going on a Dig,* by Velma Morrison (1981), and *Digging to the Past: Excavations in Ancient Lands,* by W. John Hackwell (1986). Some Internet resources to help children understand how archaeologists conduct a dig are excellent. The "History/Social Science for K–12 Teachers" Website, through its

"Archaeology/Anthropology" link, can connect to Websites of several current projects (http://k-12historysocialstudies.com/boals.html).

Students who participate in a dig will learn how knowledge of a past culture is pieced together from the available evidence. We can plan two types of digs for our students. The first type is a *simulation*. We and a small group of our students gather old coins, pieces of inexpensive jewelry, old tools, and perhaps animal bones (e.g., from last night's roasted chicken). Then we bury these items in a sandbox on the playground. (Hightshoe, 1997, recommends constructing excavation boxes, which are 1 meter square and 15 centimeters deep.) The members of the class then conduct the excavation. They collect the items and analyze them for information on the hypothetical civilization that created them.

The other type of dig is an *excavation* of some part of the school grounds or an area in the community. It is best to conduct this type of dig with the assistance of an anthropologist. (Anthropologists are not difficult to find; almost every college has some!) The simplest example is an excavation of an area where children have played for a long time. One teacher I worked with conducted a successful dig of the bench area where children sat when their team was at bat during softball games. Other school and community digs are a more serious matter, must be conducted with an anthropologist, and commence only after receiving permission from the owners of the site. Susan Hightshoe (1997) describes a good combination of the two types of digs: Students study a local area that may have artifacts. The actual dig is a simulation, and the planted artifacts are representative of what might have been found at the actual site (this requires cooperation from a local history center or museum).

Here are some steps to consider when planning a dig for a class:

1. *Make sure students understand why archaeologists conduct excavations.* Young children do not understand why things get buried over time. Earthquakes, volcanic eruptions, and the gradual accumulation of mud, sand, and gravel bury the remains of a civilization.

2. *Provide students with an outline of the process before they start digging.* Students must understand why certain sites are selected for excavation. Explain that the actual physical act of digging must be performed with the utmost care. Students should realize that once artifacts are unearthed, their work is just beginning. The exact location of each artifact must be recorded. Once removed from their burial places, the artifacts must be cleaned, measured, and weighed. Each artifact must be analyzed to determine what it is and how it was used. Finally, artifacts should be displayed with an accompanying explanation.

3. *Prepare the excavation site.* Excavations on school grounds must be approved by the school principal before any digging begins. Excavations at off-school sites must be approved by the principal and the owner of the property. For a simulation, bury the fake artifacts ahead of time. Bury one set of artifacts at one level (e.g., 12 inches deep) and another set, belonging to an earlier culture, even deeper (e.g., 30 inches). This would approximate the layers of artifacts that archaeologists often find at a single site.

Then "square" the excavation by using wooden stakes and lengths of strings to create a grid. Make each square in the grid large enough for two or three students to work within it (at least 5 feet square). Label each square by using a grid system (make horizontal spaces A, B, C, D, and so on and vertical spaces 1, 2, 3, and so on). Thus, students will be able to determine and record the precise location of each artifact they discover.

4. *Train students in excavation techniques.*   Students must be careful. They should wear gloves for safety and use garden tools, kitchen utensils, and even whisk brooms to excavate the artifacts. Students must be cautious so that they do not break an item. When students discover something, its exact location should be recorded before the item is moved. Then it should be removed and placed into a plastic bag and labeled with the following information: date, time, coordinates of the square where it was found, approximate depth where it was found, and name of the person who found it. Students can also sift for artifacts. A simple sifter can be made by nailing an 18-inch screen to a wooden frame. Students pour dirt through the sifter so that small items are caught on the screen.

5. *Analyze each artifact in a laboratory setting.*   First, artifacts should be cleaned, usually with an old toothbrush. Then each item should be measured and weighed. Items recovered intact are easy to identify (e.g., most coins). Other items are pieces of something else (e.g., a *shard* is a broken piece of pottery). Students should identify the item, speculate on what it reveals about the people who made it or used it, and try to figure out how old the item is. The whole group needs to share findings because the discovery of any item sheds light on all others.

6. *Consider creating a classroom museum.*   An exciting way to share the results is on a "virtual" tour of a classroom museum (Ricchiuti, 1998). Students could create the tour on a school or classroom Website or on a CD-ROM. A "real" museum is fun to create and would require only a corner of a classroom. Students write descriptions of each item, listing the measurements of the item, where it was found, its age, what it is, and how it was used.

◆ Economics

Economics is the study of the production, distribution, and consumption of goods and services. Although economics has been called the "dismal science" by those who find it dull, economics can be an exciting part of an elementary social studies program (Armento, 1991; Kourilsky, 1977, 1987; Schug, 1985, 1996; Schug & Walstad, 1991; Schug & Western, 2003; VanFossen, 1998). Traditional primary-level units with an economic focus have included some elementary school classics, like "The Farm" or "The Market." In the upper grades, economics usually has been presented as a part of historical units or area studies. For example, during a unit on the American colonies, students learn about triangular trade routes; during a unit on Saudi Arabia, students learn about oil production. Recently, interest has increased in linking school and 21st-century careers so that students learn about the world of work and acquire skills they will need after they leave school. Several organizations promote economic education, including the National Council on Economic Education, the Foundation for Teaching Economics, and the National Association of Economic Educators. These three groups formed a partnership to develop national standards for economics—the voluntary *National Content Standards in Economics* (National Council on Economic Education, 1997). Our discussion of economic education examines research on the development of economic thinking, the content and processes of economics that should be included in the elementary curriculum, and some teaching ideas.

Several researchers have examined how children acquire economic concepts: Armento (1991), Berti and Bombi (1988), Brophy and Alleman (2002), Danziger (1958), Jahoda (1979), Schug (1983, 1994), and Schug and Walstad (1991). Most researchers posed economic problems to children and then interviewed them about their proposed solutions. This body of research leads to the following two conclusions:

1. *Children's economic thinking becomes more abstract and flexible with age.* Younger children are very concrete and literal in the way they view economic activity. For example, when asked to explain the exchange of money in a market, young children state that this is a form of ritual without economic meaning, that the exchange is required by law, or that the store is the place where money was produced (Armento, 1991). Young children have expressed the misconception that the price of a good is determined by the size of the price tag and that the value of money is determined by the size and color of the currency or coin (Schug, 1994).

2. *Children's mature reasoning does not emerge at the same rate for all economic concepts.* Abstract thinking comes sooner for some aspects of economics than for others. For example, although young children usually are aware of their relative poverty or affluence, they often fail to grasp the relationship between work and income. At the same time they understand that they will receive 50¢ if they perform a household chore, many children fail to comprehend that their parents' jobs are linked to the household's financial status. As children mature, the economic relationship of labor and compensation becomes clearer and is generalized to all jobs. Our oldest students can understand the relationships among the parties in an economic system (e.g., jewelry salespersons depend on goldsmiths, who depend on gold miners), provide explanations for economic phenomena (e.g., why an airline slashes fares), and state the implications of economic policies (e.g., a temporary embargo on Japanese-manufactured cars could lead to fewer jobs in U.S. automobile dealerships).

Brophy and Alleman's (2002) study examined children's understanding of the economic aspects of shelter. Their findings are consistent with the two previously stated conclusions. This study of students in grades K–3 provides us with a better understanding of what children know about "cultural universals." Cultural universals are experiences that are common to all people, like the need for shelter, food, clothing, transportation, and some sort of government. This study showed that children have "limited, disconnected, and frequently distorted ideas" about these universals, in this case, shelter (p. 464). For example, most children confused apartments and hotels and did not understand the concept of rent. This study makes a strong argument that we teachers should not assume that our students are well-informed about these cultural universals. Indeed, there is much that we will need to teach.

Economics: The Curriculum

Almost all social studies textbooks have economic content. As I noted earlier, primary texts have focused on the production and distribution of common goods, such as food available in supermarkets and clothing in department stores. Upper-grade texts have included economics as part of historical units or area studies. Two curriculum developers, however, have played a significant role in bringing economics to the elementary classroom. Lawrence Senesh (1963) and Marilyn Kourilsky (1977, 1987) have shown that basic economic concepts can be taught to young children. Senesh was the author of a popular series of texts titled *Our Working World.* Kourilsky wrote curricula based on classroom mini-societies and simulated economies in which students developed their own laws, money, and government. Eventually, each class created a unique economic system, including entrepreneurial enterprises and taxes.

One of the most influential national documents in K–12 economics education was *A Framework for Teaching Economics: Basic Concepts,* published in 1977 under the sponsorship of the Joint Council on Economic Education (Hansen, Bach, Calderwood, & Saunders, 1977). The framework defined a K–12 economic curriculum with basic concepts from *microeconomics* (the working of specific markets), *macroeconomics* (the working of the national economy), and international economics. The framework was revised in 1984 and, despite its significant contribution to the social studies curriculum, was criticized by several leading economists (Saunders, Bach, Calderwood, & Hansen, 1984).

In 1997, the voluntary *National Content Standards in Economics* were published under the leadership of the National Council on Economic Education. These standards were authorized and funded by the Goals 2000 legislation of 1994. The 20 standards are written in plain English and provide "benchmarks" at grades 4, 8, and 12. The benchmarks are objectives that state what students are expected to know and be able to do (Mezaros, 1997; Mezaros & Engstrom, 1998). Earlier, in 1994, *Expectations of Excellence: Curriculum Standards for the Social Studies,* produced by the NCSS, also attempted to define the scope of economic content that children should learn. Of the 10 strands in the NCSS standards, one (Strand 7, Production, Distribution, & Consumption) is devoted entirely to economics.

Both sets of standards expect elementary children to acquire a great deal of basic economic knowledge and to perform economic analysis. For example, Content Standard 11 in the national economic standards is "Students will understand that money makes it easier to trade, borrow, save, invest, and compare the value of goods and services." One knowledge objective in the benchmarks for this standard is that, by the completion of fourth grade, "students will know that money makes trading easier by replacing barter with transactions involving currency, coin, or checks." One performance objective for this standard is that fourth graders will be able to "decide whether they would rather have a suitcase full of money or one full of food when stranded on a deserted island" (National Council on Economic Education, 1997, pp. 20–21).

Both sets of standards expect children to know (a) that resources are limited and that people must choose to have some things and not have others; (b) that economic decisions require an analysis of costs and benefits; and (c) that economic systems are complex and involve several institutions, such as households, corporations, banks, and labor unions. In addition, children are to know (d) the nature of various economic systems; (e) how supply and demand, prices, incentives, and profits function in a market system; (f) the difference between private and public sectors of the economy; (g) how jobs become specialized; (h) various forms of exchange and money; (i) how income is determined by market conditions; (j) the nature of investment and entrepreneurship; and (k) the impact of government policy on a market system.

Both sets of standards also expect children to think critically about the economic content they learn. For example, children should be able to (a) compare economic systems according to who determines what is produced and distributed, (b) explain historical events from an economic perspective, and (c) use economic reasoning to evaluate policy proposals for contemporary issues like unemployment and pollution. Lessons with economic content should present opportunities for children to both gather and produce data in tables, charts, and graphs.

Teaching Ideas for Economics

Schug (1996) provides a framework for elementary students to use as they analyze economic problems or conditions. Use of the framework helps students grasp a fundamental concept: Economic decisions are the result of choices that people make on the basis of expected costs and expected benefits. The teacher presents a question ("Why do people save money?") or makes a statement ("We have cars in the United States that were made in many different nations"). Working in small groups or as a whole group, students then apply the six statements of Schug's framework.

1. *People choose to do things they think are best for them.*   Children need to understand that economic events are not accidental or random. A third-grade class studying their local airport must see that the decision to build the airport was a difficult choice for citizens of the community. After a long debate, the airport was approved by voters because the majority thought the airport would help them. At this point, it is important for us to help children see the rationale behind economic choices.

2. *People's choices have costs.*   The decision to build the new airport had costs. Children should realize the full range of costs beyond the money needed to acquire the land and pay for the terminal, runways, and supporting structures. Other costs included the relocation of people living

on the land purchased for the airport, the "quality of life" costs to the airport's new neighbors, and the cost of not using for other purposes the resources allocated for the airport.

3. *People choose to do things for which they are rewarded.*   Incentives encourage people to act. Wentworth and Schug (1994) note that "incentives may involve an increase in expected benefits, a decrease in expected costs, or some combination of the two" (p. 11). We might help children understand the nature of an incentive by noting some incentives that are used at school (e.g., rewards for positive behavior). To encourage people to vote for the airport, supporters offered the incentive of easier access to airline flights because the nearest other airport was 83 miles away.

4. *People create rules that affect their choices and actions.*   Economic choices can be made only within the context of the existing laws governing economic activity. Construction of the airport was possible because of federal laws that allow for the private ownership of airlines and state laws that permit local governments to purchase private land for a public purpose. For each economic condition children study, they should see that the choices people make are restricted or enabled by laws.

5. *People gain when they decide to trade freely with others.*   The key here is for children to understand that voluntary trade helps both traders. In the case of the airport, airline travel is a trade. Passengers exchange money for a ride on the airplane. Both sides benefit: The passenger reaches his or her destination, and the airline makes money. Children should understand that not all trade is voluntary. When children study the European colonization of North America and examine the economic relationships among the Native tribes and the Europeans, they will see an example of involuntary or exploitative trade in which only one side benefited.

6. *People's immediate choices today have future results.*   The construction of the new airport changed the community. New people arrived because of the jobs created by the airport. Some members of the community living near the airport, however, continued legal action because of increased noise and traffic. Speculation is an important part of economic analysis, and we should encourage children to predict what they think the future will be like if an economic decision is made. Another, simpler way to help children analyze an economic decision is to prepare a two-column chart. On one side, list the benefits that will come from the decision, and on the other side, list the costs. Challenge children to consider both short-term and long-term benefits and costs. Sometimes it is worthwhile to have children make a choice before doing the analysis and then to see how many have changed their minds after the cost–benefit analysis.

School to Career.   Recent interest has been shown in reforming the K–12 school curriculum so that students are prepared for the world of work in the emerging information age (Hembacher, Okada, & Richardson, 2004). This is sometimes called *school-to-career or workforce education.* Much of the focus at the secondary level has been on reforming the high school curriculum to fit the expectations of the contemporary workplace. At the elementary level, initiatives have expanded coverage of the requirements and responsibilities of contemporary jobs. Students are curious about "grown-up jobs," and we should plan some of the following activities for our classes:

- *Job shadowing.* Students spend time with someone while at work (e.g., a student spends a day with a dental hygienist).
- *Career inquiries.* Students find out all they can about a job: required schooling, scope of the tasks the job entails, special challenges of the job, tools used by people holding the job, and so on. Students should interview adults who currently are employed in the type of job being studied.
- *Career days.* Members of the community come to school to share information about their jobs.
- *Career opportunities.* Students use the classified section of the newspaper to learn about the jobs available in their community.
- *Simulations.* Students pretend to have a certain type of job, and then make the decisions that person would have to make. Upper-grade elementary school students can pretend to be stock brokers managing a mutual fund (Hembacher et al., 2004).
- *Children's books.* Literature written for children includes many books that can be used to teach about different careers. In addition to information books written about a specific job, other books can be used as well. For example, Hembacher (2004) and her coauthors proposed a lesson plan challenging third graders to be community planners. The lesson used *The Little House* (Burton, 1942), *The House on Maple Street* (1992), and *In My Own Backyard* (Kurjian, 1993).

At the end of the chapter is an example of this type of lesson as sixth graders analyze a classified ad for the position of controller at a furniture-manufacturing company.

Focus on the Consumer.   A variety of interesting social studies activities can be built on the economic concept of consumption. Following are examples:

- *Best buys.* Challenge older children to gather comparative price data on similar products. Most markets now include unit prices beneath items (e.g., 16¢ per oz). Students should look at several brands of a product, such as orange juice, paper plates, or ice cream. For each, they should conclude which is the "best buy." Remind students, of course, that price is only one feature a consumer considers.
- *Analysis of television advertisements.* The economic concept of distribution includes advertising and marketing. For this activity, videotape commercials that appear on television. Then challenge students to explain, for each commercial, how the advertiser has tried to make the product more appealing. Some television ads mention price or specific features of the product, but most use other factors to sell the product.
- *Budgets.* Preparation of a budget requires choices and economic analysis. Ask students to prepare proposed budgets for real situations. For example, if a

fund-raiser has provided each classroom with $100 to spend on instructional materials, what should be purchased? Young children can prepare a sample budget for a set of economic conditions. For example, you have $300 to spend on new clothes. You must purchase shoes, pants, a shirt, and a jacket. How will you spend your money? Older students can work with more complicated hypothetical budgets. For example, prepare a yearly budget for a family of five with an annual income of $50,000. This is a difficult project, requiring students to investigate the actual costs of daily living.

• *Economize.*   Students live in an era of corporate and governmental "downsizing" as families, schools, businesses, and all levels of government have made cuts in their expenditures. *Economizing* is economic analysis with the goal of saving money. Challenge students to think of ways money could be saved in the classroom, the school, their community, and state and federal governments.

◆ Psychology and Sociology

Psychology and sociology have played relatively minor roles in the elementary social studies curriculum (Nelson & Stahl, 1991). Six major areas of psychology could be included in a social studies curriculum: (a) psychological research methods, (b) growth and development, (c) cognition and learning, (d) personality, (e) mental health, and (f) social psychology (Baum & Cohen, 1989). Most of the areas related to psychology focus on the personal identity of each child and how children can deal with emotions like anger, fear, and jealously. *Sociology,* the study of human society and how individuals relate to each other, examines group behavior. Attempts to infuse sociological content into the social studies curriculum have focused on the high school (Angell, 1981; Gray, 1989; Jantz & Klawitter, 1991; Switzer, 1986). Our students should examine several aspects of group behavior and understand the roles people play in primary groups, like their families, and secondary groups, like a church choir or softball team. Attitudes toward other groups, especially stereotyping and prejudice, should be addressed in the social studies curriculum (Walsh, 1992).

Expectations of Excellence (NCSS, 1994), the national social studies standards, have incorporated important concepts from psychology and sociology in Strand IV, "Individual Development and Identity" and Strand V, "Individuals, Groups, and Institutions." Strand IV states that "social studies programs should include experiences that provide for the study of individual development and identity" (p. 57). Strand V proposes that "social studies programs should include experiences that provide for the study of interactions among individuals, groups, and institutions" (p. 57). The content of these two strands asks students to learn about the following:

• Personal changes, in terms of both physical growth and personal interests; personal connections to place, like home and school
• Unique features of families; how learning and physical development affect behavior; how families, groups, and community influence a person's daily life

- Factors that contribute to one's personal identity; how to work independently and cooperatively
- Roles people fill as members of groups
- Group and institutional influences on people and events
- Tensions between individuals and groups
- Tension between an individual's beliefs and government policies and laws
- How groups and institutions work to meet individual needs and the common good

Following are some activities that incorporate psychology and sociology:

- Suggest that students write autobiographies, using photographs of themselves as illustrations. The photographs will show how the students have changed physically. Have students complete "then and now" surveys to identify changing interests and attitudes. If your school has a Website, then the autobiographies could become part of it.
- A very interesting activity is to have students continue their autobiographies as speculative works of fiction. Ask them to write about themselves at each of the following ages: 18, 25, 35, 50, and 70. Where will they live? What jobs will they have?
- Have students make a mini-mural showing the significant places in their lives. Each student can make one by dividing a piece of 12 × 18-inch drawing paper into four or eight sections. Then the student can add to each section an illustration of the significant places in his or her life (e.g., home, classroom, baseball field, and grandma's house).
- Have students make a list of the things they can do now that they could not do when they were younger (e.g., compare age 3 and age 8). This list should include physical tasks (e.g., shoot a basket), academic performance (e.g., add large numbers), home chores (e.g., dry the dishes), and other daily activities (e.g., answer the telephone).
- Suggest that a group of students interview their classmates and make a chart with three columns of activities: those best done individually, those best done in a small group, and those best done as a whole class.
- Help students see that they belong to many groups and help them to understand their role within each group. Request that students complete a chart listing the groups to which they belong, identifying their roles in the group, and describing their responsibilities in that role. The chart should have three columns: "Group," "Role," and "Responsibilities." For example, a student would write "Group: Chavez School Student Council," "Role: representative and treasurer," and "Responsibilities: represent class, keep track of council budget." Students would make other entries for other groups, such as "Mr. Kim's class," "my family," "the East Park Rangers" (soccer team), and "Temple Beth Torah."
- Help students consider the consequences of yielding to peer pressure. Tell small groups to report on how peer pressure affects the way their classmates dress, the slang they use, and the out-of-school activities they consider worthwhile. Students should discuss the importance of maintaining a strong sense of self.

- Allow interested students to prepare a multimedia display on "America's Dissenters." The national standards state that students should be able to "identify and describe examples of tension between an individual's beliefs and government policies and laws" (NCSS, 1994, p. 60). The display could be stored on CD-ROM and could include political leaders who opposed adoption of the Constitution (e.g., Patrick Henry), early practitioners of civil disobedience (e.g., Henry David Thoreau), Native Americans who fought the expansion of the United States (e.g., Geronimo), abolitionists (e.g., Frederick Douglass), advocates of women's suffrage (e.g., Susan B. Anthony), prohibitionists (e.g., Carrie Nation), civil rights leaders (e.g., Medgar Evers), and consumer advocates (e.g., Ralph Nader).

- Invite students to go into the community to find out more about organizations that promote the common good, such as the Red Cross, service clubs, and groups that raise money to battle diseases. A group could write a book for their classmates on these groups. Or, invite the community to come to your classroom as representatives of these organizations visit your room to make presentations to your students.

Reducing Stereotyping and Prejudice

Aspects of psychology and sociology come into play when we try to reduce stereotypical and prejudicial attitudes in our classrooms. Gloria Ladson-Billings (1992) provides excellent suggestions:

1. *Assess our teaching.* Ladson-Billings asks teachers to consider what conclusions an observer would reach after spending time in our classroom. We would hope that people with overt biases never enter our profession, and I think that teachers as a group are among the most sensitive and least prejudiced people in our society. Nonetheless, many of us do things that are biased. For example, what is the seating pattern in the room? Are members of minority groups clustered together? Are boys and girls intermixed? Do we, in fact, have different discipline procedures for some students, and if so, are those students disproportionately members of a minority group? What does our room environment reveal? Are images of successful people from all groups displayed?

2. *Check our teaching materials.* Although textbooks, films, videos, children's books, and other resources have come a long way in the past 20 years to remove stereotyped and biased portrayals, it is a good idea to assess the materials we use.

3. *Transform the curriculum.* We should incorporate diverse content and perspectives.

4. *Strive for integration.* Students of both genders, of challenging conditions, of all ethnic groups, and of each social class should work together during the year. If we allow our students to select the projects they will complete, we must be sure that a pattern does not develop of some groups having only girls, only African Americans, and so on. Consistent, positive interactions through cooperative learning can improve intergroup relations (Kagan, 1985, 1989).

Anthony Magnacca/Merrill

Social studies incorporates content from all the social science disciplines, including psychology and sociology. Social studies activities should help students abandon prejudicial attitudes and form lasting friendships with their classmates.

5. *Do not ignore incidents of student prejudicial behavior.*   When some students express stereotypical or biased feelings toward other students, whether through words or actions, we should intervene. We should work with students to find the source of these attitudes and then provide information to show a better picture of the group that was disparaged. Students who use racial slurs need to know the full impact of those words. A student who says that all members of a group behave in one way should be taught about intragroup diversity. Finally, we should make it clear to our students that prejudiced behavior on campus will not be tolerated.

Families and Friendship

The traditional social studies curriculum in the early grades has devoted attention to families and friendship, two topics that can help children learn key concepts in sociology and psychology. With some political and religious groups advocating that only one type of family be promoted in the schools, discussion of the diversity of family composition has become a hot issue. My suggestion is to take an anthropological view: The definition of family varies widely from cultural group to cultural group, and any cultural group will always contain variations from the norm. Children know the other members of their nuclear family, and in the contemporary United States, families will include a variety of people other than mom and dad, brother and sister. I think the goals of family-related lessons should be to (a) show how families contribute to each child's identity and (b) help children see how the cooperative efforts among family members can serve as a model for classrooms, schools, communities, states, and nations. Remember, lessons on the family should be preceded by a letter to parents describing the activities that will take place in our classroom. Not all information should be revealed in the classroom, and parents should be aware of what we are going to cover. The focus on friendship should help children understand the challenges and rewards of being a good friend. Friendship comes easily to many children, but other children will benefit from an exploration of the characteristics and responsibilities of friends. The opening vignette in Chapter 2 described how one teacher implemented the unit "Families and Friends." Following are some other activities that could be a part of a unit on families and friends:

- *Compile family trees.*   This project requires students to interview parents, grandparents, and other family members. You will need to help students develop the survey questions and provide a model for the actual family tree that is to be completed.
- *Make a class quilt.*   The beautiful children's book *The Patchwork Quilt* (Flournoy, 1985) provides a perfect introduction to making a family quilt. In another excellent children's book, *The Secret of Freedom,* a young African American girl learns about slavery from her great aunt's quilt (Vaughn, 2001). Some elementary teachers have the expertise to help their students make real, sewn quilts. Most of us, though, will have to settle for helping our students make quilts with sections of paper pasted together. Like any quilt, each section of each student's quilt should be special and, in this case, represent something about the student's family. (McCall, 1994, discusses the use of quilts in elementary social studies. Her article focuses on the significance of quilting in people's lives and portrayals of history through quilts.)
- *Make semantic maps.*   Create a semantic map with the word *Friend* in the middle. Ask students what makes a good friend. Record what the students say, linking common characteristics.
- *Sing songs about families and friends.*   One of my favorites is "Five People in My Family" from *The Sesame Street Song* (Raposo & Moss, 1971). Another of my favorites is the song "I Live in the City," by Malvina Reynolds. This song expresses multicultural cooperation as people of many colors build a city. "I Live in the City" can be found in many kindergarten, first-grade, or second-grade music textbooks.
- *Read books about families and friends.*   Some of the best children's picture books address themes related to families and friends (Zarrillo, 1994). I provide a list of multicultural children's picture books focusing on families and friendship in Figure 12.4.
- *Tell family stories.*   Give students the opportunity to tell the stories of their families, through time lines, chronologies, murals, and biographies.

At the end of the chapter, you will find a writing project that challenges children to discover some of the special aspects of their families.

◆ Global Education, Environmental Education, and Current Events

Global Education

Revolutionary advances in technology and transportation have brought the people of the world closer together. "Global education" should be more than a slogan; the elementary social studies curriculum must be international in scope (Case, 1993; Collins, Czarra, & Smith, 1998; Hanvey, 1976; Kniep, 1985, 1986; Lamy, 1987; Massialas, 1991; Merryfield, 2004; NCSS Ad Hoc Committee on Global Education, 1987; Simpson, 1996; Tye, 1990). Global education has meant different things to different people. Robert Hanvey (1976) and Willard Kniep (1985) were early and influential advocates of global education, and each provided a definition frequently cited by other writers. Case (1993) synthesized Hanvey's and Kniep's work and argued for two dimensions to global education: a *substantive* dimension, "knowledge of various features of the world and how it works," and a *perceptual* dimension, which is "an outlook or orientation" (p. 318).

The substantive dimension includes five categories of content:

1. *Universal and cultural values and practices.* Our students should learn about the many cultural groups that inhabit the earth and discover the similarities and differences among groups.
2. *Global connections.* Our curriculum should include units and lessons that show how people are linked by global economic, political, ecological, and technological systems.
3. *Contemporary worldwide concerns and conditions.* Our students should learn about issues and problems that are global in scope and that require international solutions.
4. *Origins and past patterns of worldwide affairs.* This category requires a curriculum that helps our students understand the history of international current events.
5. *Alternative future directions in worldwide affairs.* Among the essential activities in global education are those that require speculation and that challenge our students to predict the global consequences of political and economic decisions.

Case's (1993) perceptual dimension is more difficult to define. This dimension is part of the affective domain; the goal is a social studies program that leads students to adopt a perspective that includes "open-mindedness, anticipation of complexity, resistance to stereotyping, inclination to empathize, and non-chauvinism" (p. 320). To Case, open-mindedness is crucial to global education. After all, it makes little sense to develop units of study that present global content if students will ignore the information because of previous biases or prejudices.

Social studies can help students learn about other people and places, but only if they are willing to accept that their preconceptions may be inaccurate. Global systems in economics, ecology, politics, communication, and transportation are complex.

It should go without saying that our social studies programs should help students resist stereotyping. We as teachers inadvertently lead to stereotyping by using descriptors that fail to distinguish the differences among nations, groups, and people (e.g., "The Third World"). Repeated references to "Eastern Europe," for example, can lead students to conclude that there are no differences between life in the Czech Republic and Bulgaria; in fact, the status of those two nations in the post-Soviet era is not at all alike. Likewise, lessons and units that cover a topic superficially can result in stereotyping. For example, a short unit on Egypt could lead students to think that this nation is "a museum or curiosity piece as the land of pyramids and sphinxes" (Case, 1993, p. 322).

The national social studies standards (NCSS, 1994) emphasize the importance of "internationalizing" the social studies curriculum. One of the 11 strands is "Global Connections" (Strand 10). The standards are ambitious and call for students in the upper-elementary grades to learn about a wide range of global topics and issues, such as the following:

- How aspects of culture, such as language, the arts, and belief systems, can both facilitate and impede global understanding
- Examples of conflict and cooperation among nations and cultural groups
- Effects of technology on the global community
- Causes and possible solutions of global issues, such as health, security, and environmental quality
- The relationship between national sovereignty and global interests
- Standards and concerns related to universal human rights
- The purpose and status of international organizations

Teaching Global Education

The traditional expanded environments framework leads to a social studies curriculum that lacks global content (Akenson, 1989; Larkins & Hawkins, 1990). The primary grades focus on awareness of self, primary social groups like the school and family, the neighborhood, and the community. Fourth grade focuses on the geography and history of the state. Fifth grade is a survey of U.S. history. Not until sixth grade does the curriculum become international. Alternatives, however, place greater emphasis on global education. Social studies at every grade level should include lessons and units that take a global perspective (Diaz, Massialas, & Xanthopoulos, 1999).

With global education, environmental education, and current events, we can adopt three approaches: (a) address it as a "stand-alone" component of the social studies curriculum, with separate units of study; (b) "integrate" topics into the units we teach; or (c) a combination of the stand-alone and the integration approaches. Global education units include those on other places, in both historical and contemporary context (e.g., "South Africa Today" or "The Aztec"), cross-cultural units (e.g., "Going to School in Colombia, Kenya, and Indonesia"), thematic units (e.g., "Cooperation and Conflict Among Nations"), units on events with global implications (e.g., "The Trial of Saddam Hussein"), and units on global problems (e.g., "Famines: Causes and Solutions"). Whether or not the curriculum

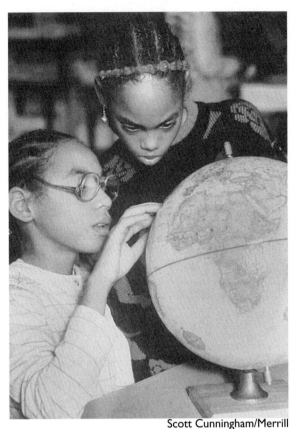

Scott Cunningham/Merrill

In the 21st century, modern technology will continue to bring the world's people closer together. Teachers should help their students understand the global implications of the topics they study.

includes separate units of study, every social studies unit should explore global connections. For example, a unit on families can introduce children to families in other nations. If the fourth-grade curriculum is the geography and history of our state, then we can incorporate considerable global content. For example, a unit on the early history of North Carolina should include information on a slave economy closely linked to Africa and the Caribbean. A unit on contemporary North Carolina should help students understand how many jobs in the state are either with foreign-owned companies or with firms dependent on foreign trade.

The following are some specific teaching ideas for global education:

• Use many topics that lend themselves to cross-cultural comparison (e.g., clothing, shelter, school, government, sports, and food). For example, if students in a third-grade class take part in a unit on transportation in Los Angeles, they should also learn about transportation systems in other places. Students in Los Angeles would learn about freeways, the metropolitan bus system, and plans for southern California's emerging light rail system. They would also become acquainted with historical means or transportation in southern California, such as horse-powered wagons, early automobiles, and the efficient system of light-rail "red cars" that was discontinued in the 1950s. To internationalize this unit, their teacher could select another large city for investigation, such as Beijing, where urban transit is not based on the automobile.

• Conduct this common global activity with your class: Have them gather data on the source of products in their homes or at school. For example, you could ask your students to select three shirts or blouses. On a data retrieval chart, the students would note where each item was produced (found on the clothing labels). Tally class totals and have students use maps to locate the places where the clothes were made. In most situations, students will see that almost everyone has clothes that were made overseas, especially in Asia and the Spanish-speaking Americas. Students should explore the economic factors that have led U.S. corporations to build factories in other nations and consider the consequences for workers here and abroad.

• Plan a unit on international organizations for your upper-grade students. This is a good Jigsaw project, as small groups gather information on different organizations and then share what they have learned with their classmates. Students could learn about the United Nations (UN), the Organization of American States (OAS), the International Red Cross, Amnesty International, the North Atlantic Treaty Organization (NATO), the World Health Organization (WHO), or the International Olympic Committee (IOC).

• Use people in your community as resources for global education. Some of your students, their parents, or grandparents are immigrants and can share information about their native lands. An increasing number of "local" businesses actually are international in scope and include employees who can talk about their work with colleagues overseas. Almost every university in the United States has faculty and students who are citizens of other countries. In addition to encyclopedias, books, films, the Internet, and other computer-based resources, people in your city with global experience can help your students with global projects.

• Teach more elementary units that look at foreign nations in a contemporary context. So often, students study places like China or Mexico only as history. Learning about life today in another nation can be important learning experiences for your students. Ensure that the resources you use are accurate. Fortunately, several excellent nonfiction children's books on other nations are available with updated information presented through well-researched text and attractive photographs. When planning these units, take time to avoid superficial coverage and misunderstandings. Topics should include economics, the arts, recreation, education, and religion.

• Challenge your students to create an atlas for a region. This is a challenging task because students will have to make several maps. These student-made books make an excellent group project. For example, an atlas on Southeast Asia would include a world map highlighting the region, a map of the region itself, a map of each nation in Southeast Asia, maps of large cities in the region, topographical maps, economic maps, and historical maps showing the political boundaries of the past.

- Suggest that your students create a "virtual tour" of a nation or region. Virtual tours can be a part of a Website or can be recorded on CD-ROM. Photographs and maps can be "clipped" from Internet sites as long as they have no copyright restriction. Students would write the text and organize the sequence of the tour.
- Assign your class a similar project, the "travel brochure." This is an old social studies favorite. Students design a document promoting a nation or a region as a travel destination. To avoid superficial coverage, I suggest that each brochure promote a tour that will last at least 15 days. Then students will have to include information about several locations in the nation. Stress to students that these brochures should highlight the places tourists would want to visit.

Environmental Education

Environmental education is highly interdisciplinary. Much of what students learn about their environment is a part of science, as they study the plants and animals and other organisms that share the planet. Many traditional elementary school learning activities, like nature study and outdoor education, are a part of environmental education. As a part of social studies, the focus is how the actions of people affect the air, water, and other living things (Charles, 1985; Simmons, 1994, 1995; Wilkie, 1993). Simmons (1995) provides a summary of the content of environmental education:

- An affective component—sensitivity and appreciation of environmental issues and topics
- Ecological knowledge—a part of the science curriculum, including the biology of plants and animals and the relationships within an ecosystem
- Sociopolitical knowledge—how human activities influence the environment
- Knowledge of current environmental issues
- Environmental skills, including the ability to use primary and secondary sources to learn about environmental topics and issues
- Environmental responsibility and citizenship—an understanding of what individuals and groups can do to preserve and protect the environment

As with the other topics covered in this chapter, environmental topics can either be integrated with existing units of study or serve as the basis for separate units. Following are some teaching ideas for the social studies part of environmental education:

- Ask students to examine the contents of school wastebaskets. This is sometimes recommended as an exercise in anthropology, as students examine the contents as artifacts that reveal aspects of our culture. With an environmental focus, students classify the items according to whether they could be reused or recycled. This task helps students see that they can play a role in conserving our natural resources.
- Plant a tree. This is an activity full of educational potential. Students will become botanists as they learn about the structure of the tree and how it lives. They will also see how people determine whether the tree survives. Initially, the tree will need to be nurtured and protected. As the tree grows stronger, both single incidents of irresponsibility and the long-term effects of human-made pollution will threaten

the tree. In addition to the science-related activities surrounding the tree planting, ask students to provide complete answers to the questions "What can we do to help the tree grow?" and "What may people do that will harm the tree?"

• Suggest reading. Many excellent children's books address environmental issues. For example, Lynn Cherry's *The Great Kapok Tree* (1990) helps students realize the full impact of cutting down a tree in the Amazon rain forest.

• Urge older students to analyze the consumption of energy at home and school. What appliances use the most energy? What use is essential? What use can be reduced? Challenge students to develop precise energy conservation plans for home, school, and classroom.

• Suggest that students share information on several endangered species. This is not only a good Jigsaw project but also a good mix of science and social studies. Assign each group of students a different species; each group is responsible for gathering information on that species and what actions by people have placed it at risk of extinction.

• See whether students can create pictorial flowcharts showing the process of converting crude oil to consumable energy. The chart should show drilling for oil, the work of an oil refinery, and the many products (e.g., gasoline and asphalt) that are ultimately produced from oil.

• Help students prepare a bulletin board display on some of the leading ecologists who have helped bring about changes in environmental policy (e.g., John Muir, Gifford Pinchot, and Rachel Carson).

• Challenge older students to analyze contemporary environmental issues and consider policy alternatives. These can be local issues, such as the construction of a highway, or national and global issues, such as toxic waste, global warming, or ozone depletion.

• Help your youngest students learn about the plants and animals that share their immediate environment at school. This can begin with a simple inventory of all the living things that either live at the school (e.g., trees, grass, and insects) or regularly visit (e.g., birds). This requires a nature walk around your school.

Current Events

Many of us can remember the dreadful chore of searching for a "current event" in the newspaper. Our time came, and we would find ourselves in front of our classmates, struggling to explain the content of our clipping. Fortunately, there are many alternatives for incorporating current events into the school day (Passe, 1988). As a separate part of social studies, one option is to schedule current events activities for a special time each week (e.g., every Friday morning). Another option is to integrate current events into our units of study; some important current events, however, will not fit into our units. A third option is a combination approach. We would be ready to modify our unit plans to include current events and, at the same time, reserve a time each week for current events activities. Current events provide an opportunity for students to apply what they have learned about citizenship, history, geography, and the other social sciences.

The exploration of current events, if done properly, can be controversial. Our goal is to increase student understanding of the event, and this requires an effort to be sure we present multiple perspectives. The material on civil discourse in Chapter 11 will help us have a fair, friendly, and thorough discussion of an event. The presentation and exploration of diverse views, however, is not as easy because attached to some topics is intense pressure to present only a popular view (Soley, 1996). We need to screen the news stories our students want to share. Some stories, such as many crimes, children are too young to discuss. For the most part, however, our students already have been exposed to major news events through television. The extra knowledge we help them acquire will often make them less anxious about troubling events.

In addition to television, radio, the Internet, and print media that are available to adults, several news resources are designed for children. Print media include *Weekly Reader, NewsCurrents,* and *Scholastic Newstime.* Technology has added software programs like World Classroom, a program that requires a modem and that links children by presenting social studies and science projects.

The following are teaching ideas for current events:

• Plan a unit or mini-unit on the news media. Writing about teaching media literacy, Passe (1994) stressed the importance of helping children understand the news they see presented in the media. Children need geographic and historical information to make sense of some events. Help students identify the major issues surrounding an event, which is often a challenge, given the amount of coverage major events receive. Also be sure that students learn to look for balance in coverage, detecting bias in the perspectives of advocates of certain positions. Involve students in news production as they make classroom or school newspapers. Work with students to produce videotaped news broadcasts, complete with news anchors, on-the-spot reporters, and commentators.

• Teach students how to use the newspaper as a data source (Rhoades, 1994). Like an encyclopedia or a Website, the newspaper is a tremendous source of information. Have older students identify the sections of a major newspaper, use the index to find a desired section, and distinguish commentary from news reporting. (By the way, the Internet provides access to all the nation's major newspapers [e.g., the *Los Angeles Times* at www.latimes.com, the *New York Times* at www.nytimes.com, and the *Washington Post* at www.washingtonpost.com].)

• As for the stand-alone approach, reserve a time for activities relating to current events. The use of student newspapers, like *Weekly Reader,* will help. Encourage, but do not require, students to bring in clippings of news stories they find interesting. Videotape portions of televised newscasts for use later in the week. Assign a small group of students to keep an "In the News" bulletin board up to date.

• Encourage small groups of interested students to "follow" a story and keep their classmates up to date. Members of the group will need to watch television newscasts and read newspapers to obtain information for their daily or weekly reports to the class. One interesting activity is to have a group of students follow each candidate during a political campaign. Each group could trace their candidate's travels on a map, follow the candidate's changing fortune as reflected in the polls, and make a display of the candidate's position on the major issues.

• Use current events as the catalyst for further study by students. Some events will stimulate students to complete written, artistic, or dramatic projects.

◆ Summary of Key Points

- Anthropology should have a prominent place in the elementary social studies curriculum, as students learn about other cultural groups and participate in anthropological data-gathering activities, like a dig.
- National standards in economics emphasize the importance of economic content and analysis in elementary social studies.
- Instructional activities drawing content from psychology and sociology will help students learn more about themselves and the people around them.
- Global education, environmental education, and current events are essential components of social studies; content from these areas should be integrated into all units of study and should serve as the focus for separate units.

FOR FURTHER READING

- Merryfield (2004) provides an excellent discussion of what teachers should do when teaching children about other cultural groups. Black (1998) describes how archaeology can be a part of the elementary social studies curriculum. She recommends the Society for American Archaeology's Website as "probably the best source of lesson plans as well as information about archaeology education programs across the United States" (p. 13). The society's Website address is www.saa.org. Yell (1998) describes a series of lessons that would help students "think like an archaeologist."
- The National Council on Economic Education's (1997) curriculum project, called "Economic America," has produced units and lessons to accompany the *National Content Standards in Economics* (contact the National Council at 1140 Avenue of the Americas, New York, NY 10036). A good Website for teaching resources is the "Economic Education" Website (http://ecedweb.unomaha.edu). Rader (1995) reflects on the innovative elementary economics curriculum that he and others developed at the University of Chicago in the 1960s.
- How about teaching economic concepts with the folktale the "Little Red Hen"? See National Council on Economic Education (2005). Van't Hooft & Kelly (2004) write about teaching fifth graders economics using handheld computers. VanFossen (2003a) provides a good summary of ideas for teaching economics to children using literature and Internet sources. Lamme (2002) explains how children's literature can be used to teach children about the barter system. Breidenstein, Butler, and Kamdar (2001) provide a description of a school–university partnership to teach economic concepts to students in elementary, middle, and high schools.
- Of the many resources on global education, consult the American Forum for Global Education (www.globaled.org) and the Global Education Network of the Association for Supervision and Curriculum Development (ASCD), whose newsletter, *Global Connections,* is a good source. The September 1998 issue of *Social Education* is devoted to global education (Collins et al., 1998).

Cangemi and Aucoin (1996) describe a third-/fourth-grade thematic unit called "It's a Small World After All," a separate unit with a global focus (I think their unit should be expanded to provide deeper coverage). My colleague at Cal State East Bay, Jean Easterly (1994), edited the book *Promoting Global Teacher Education: Seven Reports,* which has some interesting chapters.

- For resources on environmental education, see the Websites for the North American Association for Environmental Education (www.naaee.org) and the Environmental Education Network (www.envirolink.org). Imeson and Skamp (1996) describe a unit integrating environmental education and social studies; Imeson implemented it in his classroom in Australia.
- Main, Wilhelm, and Cox (1996) describe a 16-week unit on family and home culture for bilingual (Spanish/English) first graders. Morin (1997) shows how software can be used for the graphics in a primary unit on the family. Swearingen (1996) discusses how to promote tolerance among teacher credential candidates. The children's books listed in Figure 12.4 are useful resources for integrating multiculturalism.

LESSONS PLANS AND INSTRUCTIONAL ACTIVITIES

In this chapter, you will find (a) A lesson plan for sixth graders, "Jobs Offered—The Classified Ads;" which challenges the students to analyze the components of a standard employment advertisement in a newspaper; and (b) A description of a group project for second graders, "A Mini-Book on My Family," in which each student writes a small book about his or her family.

LESSON PLAN

Grade Six: Jobs Offered—The Classified Ads

This lesson was part of a sixth-grade unit on careers. The lesson examined an advertisement in the classified section of the local newspaper that read as follows:

Controller

High-energy, top-notch accounting person needed for a manufacturer of office furniture. Handle management reporting, financial analysis, and internal control. Supervise employees in payroll, payables, and receiving. Should have BA/BS degree with emphasis in accounting; CPA is a plus; heavy computer exposure, experience managing people. FAX resume and salary history.

Overview: This lesson is for a sixth-grade class of 30 students.

Resources and Materials: (a) 30 copies of the same issue of the local newspaper and (b) a chart with six focus questions you prepare ahead of time.

Standard: From the National Curriculum Standards for Social Studies, *Expectations of Excellence,* Strand VII, "Production, Distribution, & Consumption," Performance

Expectation (e) for the middle grades: "The learner can describe the role of specialization and exchange in the economic process" (NCSS, 1994, p. 41).

Content Objectives: Students will understand the specialized nature of jobs and how each job has unique requirements and responsibilities.

Process Objectives: Students will *identify* the responsibilities and requirements for the position of controller, *identify* the responsibilities and requirements for any other position advertised in the want ads, and *compose* an ad for one of the jobs at their school.

Teaching Sequence:

1. Acquire 30 copies of the same issue of the local newspaper (most newspapers will provide teachers with copies, especially day-old papers); circle the same want ad in each of the 30 newspapers. (If you cannot obtain these, make up your own or make copies of the ad for the controller shown previously.)
2. Prepare the chart with the focus questions (see step 5).
3. Review with the class the previous week's activities, all on careers, and distribute the newspapers. Tell students to open the paper to the page where the circled ad is located.
4. Explain that businesses that have open jobs often advertise them in the newspaper. The classified ads have many sections, and the section with available jobs is often called "Jobs Offered." Explain that the newspaper charges the employer to run the ad, usually by the number of words, so the text of the ads will appear "choppy" and have lots of abbreviations to keep them short.
5. Direct students to the ad for the controller. Help them answer the six questions you wrote on the chart paper:

   What is the name of the job?
   What type of business has placed the ad in the paper?
   What are the responsibilities of the person who will fill the job? What will
       the successful applicant do?
   What requirements must applicants fulfill?
   How much will the job pay?
   How do applicants contact the employer?

   You will need to explain some of the vocabulary in the ad (e.g., *internal control* and *CPA*). Also, point out that all ads do not include an answer to each question on the chart.
6. Tell students that they may work individually, with a partner, or in small groups. Tell them to select a different ad and to answer the questions on the chart. If this appears too challenging, then select simple ads for each group to examine. Circulate among the students and ask, "How are the requirements for the job you selected different from the requirements for the job of controller?"
7. Extend the lesson by presenting a project. A group of students could write an ad for one of the jobs at school (e.g., teacher, principal, custodian, or

secretary). This would require students to do some research on the requirements and responsibilities of the job. Be sure to give students a word limit; for example, each ad must not exceed 50 words.

Evaluation: Collect and review students' answers to the six questions when they selected an ad in the paper. As you circulate among the students, note how many understand the different requirements for jobs.

Effective Teaching in Today's Diverse Classroom: *Scaffolding* is a word used by many educators to describe the help teachers provide to students. The use of *scaffold* is a metaphor. Just as a scaffold helps workers reach heights they could not reach on their own, an instructional scaffold helps students accomplish things they could not do on their own. The word was first used in the area of language development as a descriptor for the ways adults helped children expand their oral language (Cazden, 1983). Now the concept has taken on a broader meaning and is often used to describe what teachers do to help English learners and children with difficulty learning succeed in mathematics, science, and social studies. To use Cummins's ideas, scaffolds provide more contextual support for the learner. The words are not important, but the concept is. The "scaffolding" you provide your English learners could be each of the following:

- In the second part of the lesson, when students select an ad and respond to the questions, be sure your English learners are in a group with someone who can help them understand the text of the ad (the help can be provided by you, an aide, or a classmate who is a good reader).
- Help English-language learners select an ad that is relatively easy to read.
- Be prepared to work with each group that has an English learner. You may have to paraphrase the content of the ad in words your English learners can understand.

Description of a GROUP PROJECT

Grade Two: A Mini-Book on My Family

As part of a unit on the family, children wrote and illustrated four-page books, including the covers, on their families.

Standard: From the *National Curriculum Standards for Social Studies, Expectations of Excellence,* Strand IV, "Individual Development & Identity," Performance Expectation (c) for the early grades, "The learner can describe the unique features of one's nuclear and extended families" (NCSS, 1994, p. 57).

Phase I

In the first phase of the project, each child surveyed her or his family by using the data retrieval chart reproduced as Figure 12.1. The chart was titled "3 Fascinating, Funny, Incredible, Wonderful, Heroic, Commendable, or Ordinary

Figure 12.1   Data Retrieval Chart: Mini-Book on My Family

---

3 Fascinating, funny, incredible, wonderful, heroic, commendable, or ordinary things someone in _my family did_.

---

1. Who, what, when?

---

2. Who, what, when?

---

3. Who, what, when?

Things Someone in My Family Did." The three cells are labeled 1, 2, and 3, and each cell contains the questions "Who, What, When?" The teachers stressed that everything recorded on the charts had to be true and that it was okay to include things that were less than extraordinary. Funny events were definitely to be included! Children took their charts home and talked with members of their families. More able children wrote the information down; other children had their parents do the writing.

In one second-grade classroom, the completed charts made great reading. One child recorded, "My grandfather met Clark Gable in a restaurant in 1938." Another student noted, "My sister, Elva, scored three goals last Saturday." A third wrote, "Uncle Luis can make a sound like a frog singing 'Happy Birthday'."

Phase 2

In the second phase of the project, teachers handed out a template for the book. Each page would be half of an 8 1/2 × 11-inch sheet of paper. Each book would be four pages, including a cover. (Templates are included as Figures 12.2 and 12.3.) The

Figure 12.2   Mini-Book on My Family: Cover and Page 1

ONE

1   1

THREE

BY

Figure 12.3 Mini-Book on My Family: Pages 2 and 3

Figure 12.4 Families and Friends: A List of Multicultural Picture Books

Baylor, Byrd. *Hawk, I Am Your Brother.* This is a story of the friendship of a boy and an animal.

Bunting, Eve. *The Wall.* A Mexican American boy and his father visit the Vietnam Veterans' War Memorial.

Choi, Yangsook. *The Name Jar.* A Korean American child is embarrassed by her name. A friend helps.

Clifton, Lucille. *My Friend Jacob.* This is the story of a friendship between an African American boy and another who is mentally challenged.

Crews, Donald. *Bigmama's.* African American author-illustrator Crews reminisces about trips to his grandparents' farm.

Dorros, Arthur. *Abuela.* A Latina girl and her grandmother fly above New York; some text is in Spanish.

Flournoy, Valerie. *The Patchwork Quilt.* An African American girl helps her mother make a quilt.

Friedman, Ina. *How My Parents Learned to Eat.* The book tells how a boy's father, a U.S. sailor, and his Japanese mother met.

Garza, Carmen Lomas. *Family Pictures.* This book, with text in English and Spanish, tells about growing up in a small Texas town.

Grifalconi, Ann. *Osa's Pride.* An African girl alienates friends with stories about her dead father.

Havill, Juanita. *Jamaica Tag-Along.* An African American brother thinks his little sister is a nuisance.

Keats, Ezra Jack. *Peter's Chair.* An African American boy decides to run away because of the arrival of his new sister.

Kerley, Barbara. *You and Me Together: Moms, Dads, and Kids Around the World.* Illustrated with photographs, this book shows a wide range of cultural groups.

Miller, Montazalee. *My Grandmother's Cookie Jar.* A Navajo girl and her grandmother eat cookies and share stories.

Monk, Isabel. *Family.* Mom is Black, Dad is White.

Morris, Ann. *Loving.* This is an information book that shows parents, friends, siblings, and pets from all over the world.

Polacco, Patricia. *Chicken Sunday.* A European American girl and her African American friends figure out a way to get a hat for Grandma Eula.

San Souci, Robert. *The Faithful Friend.* A retelling of a folktale from the island of Martinique, two friends break the spell of a wizard.

Say, Allen. *The Lost Lake.* A Japanese American boy and his father go backpacking.

Soto, Gary. *Too Many Tamales.* A Mexican American girl loses her mother's diamond ring on Christmas Eve.

Steptoe, John. *Stevie.* An African American boy deals with his foster brother.

Turkle, Brinton. *Thy Friend, Obadiah.* This book is a good introduction to religious minorities. A Quaker boy befriends a duck.

Uchida, Yoshiko. *Sumi's Special Happening.* A Japanese girl must find a gift for a 99-year-old relative.

Updike, John. *A Child's Calendar.* Trina Schart Hyman's illustrations accompany Updike's poems, describing a biracial family's experiences.

Williams, Sherley Anne. *Working Cotton.* The author recalls her African American family's life as migrant workers in California's central valley.

Williams, Vera. *A Chair for My Mother.* (See the lesson plan in Chapter 1.)

Woodson, Jacqueline. *The Other Side.* Two girls from different ethnic groups fight barriers to become friends.

children colored the numeral 3 at the top of their covers and then added, in their own writing the title "Fascinating, Funny, Incredible, Wonderful, Heroic, Commendable, or Ordinary Things Someone in My Family Did." On each page, children provided an illustration and a description of the noteworthy event.

Effective Teaching in Today's Diverse Classroom: This would be a good opportunity to use a variation of the *language experience approach* (LEA) for children with learning disabilities. The LEA is a method of teaching children to read. The child tells the story of a personal experience to an adult, who writes down what the child says. Then the child and the adult read the dictation aloud. Children who are not yet ready to do the writing required in this project could dictate their descriptions to an adult. The child would first draw the illustrations and then dictate a description. The adult would transcribe what the child said. Finally, the child and the adult would read aloud the dictated description.

Children's Literature to Support Social Studies Instruction

Accrosi, W. (1992). *My name is Pocahontas*. New York: Holiday House.

Adler, D. (2004). *George Washington: An illustrated biography*. New York: Holiday House.

Amster, M. (2000). *Sybil Ludington's midnight ride*. Minneapolis: Carolrhoda.

Ancona, G. (1985). *Freighters: Cargo ships and the people who work them*. New York: Crowell.

Atkin, S. B. (Ed.). (1993). *Voices from the fields: Children of migrant farmworkers tell their stories*. Boston: Little, Brown.

Avi. (2002). *Crispin: The cross of lead*. New York: Hyperion.

Baker, O. (1981). *Where the buffaloes begin*. New York: Frederick Warne.

Bartoletti, S. C. (2005). *Hitler Youth: Growing up in Hitler's shadow*. New York: Scholastic.

Barton, B. (1968). *Boats*. New York: Crowell.

Baylor, B. (1976). *Hawk, I am your brother*. New York: Scribner.

Bernard, C. (1974). *The book of fantastic boats*. New York: Golden Press.

Bourne, M. A. (1983). *Uncle George Washington and Harriet's guitar*. New York: Coward.

Brenner, B. (1994). *If you were there in 1776*. New York: Bradbury.

Brill, M. T. (2001). *Margaret Knight: Girl inventor*. Brookfield, CT: Millbrook.

Brown, D. P. (1985). *Sybil rides for independence*. Niles, IL: Albert Whitman.

Brown, M. (1949). *Henry-fisherman*. New York: Scribner.

Brown, M. W. (1988). *Homes in the wilderness*. New York: William Scott (Original work published 1939).

Bunting, E. (1990). *The wall*. New York: Clarion.

Bunting, E. (1994). *A day's work*. New York: Crown.

Burton, V. (1942). *The little house*. Boston: Houghton Mifflin.

Carter, K. (1963). *Ships and seaports*. Chicago: Childrens Press.

Chandra, D. & Comora, M. (2003). *George Washington's teeth*. New York: Farrar, Straus & Giroux.

Cherry, L. (1990). *The great Kapok tree*. San Diego: Harcourt Brace Jovanovich.

Cherry, L. (1992). *A river ran wild*. Sand Diego: Harcourt Brace.

Choi, S. N. (1991). *The year of impossible goodbyes*. Boston: Houghton Mifflin.

Choi, Y. (2001). *The name jar*. New York: Knopf.

Clapp, P. (1977). *I'm Deborah Sampson: A soldier in the War of Revolution*. New York: Lothrop, Lee & Shepard.

Cleaver, E. (1985). *Enchanted caribou*. New York: Atheneum.

Clifton, L. (1980). *My friend Jacob*. New York: Dutton.

Collier, J. L., & Collier, C. (1974). *My brother Sam is dead*. New York: Four Winds.

Collier, J. L., & Collier, C. (1981). *Jump ship to freedom*. New York: Delacorte.

Collier, J. L., & Collier, C. (1983). *War comes to Willy Freeman*. New York: Delacorte.

Collier, J. L., & Collier, C. (1984). *Who is Carrie?* New York: Delacorte.

Cook, N. (2001). *The world's fastest boats*. Mankato, MN: Capstone.

Corriveau, D. (2002). *The Inuit of Canada*. Minneapolis: Lerner.

Cox, C. (1999). *Come all you brave soldiers: Blacks in the Revolutionary War*. New York: Scholastic.

Creech, S. (1994). *Walk two moons*. New York: HarperCollins.

Crews, D. (1991). *Bigmama's*. New York: Greenwillow.

Cushman, K. (1995). *The midwife's apprentice*. New York: Clarion.

D'Aulaire, I., & D'Aulaire, E. P. (1946). *Pocahontas*. New York: Doubleday.

DePaola, T. (1999). *26 Fairmount Avenue*. New York: Putnam.

Dorris, M. (1992). *Morning girl*. Boston: Hyperion.

Dorros, A. (1991). *Abuela*. New York: Dutton.

Fisher, L. E. (1991). *Sailboat lost*. New York: Macmillan.

Flack, M. (1946). *Boats on the river*. New York: Viking.

Flournoy, V. (1985). *The patchwork quilt*. New York: Dial.

Forbes, E. (1943). *Johnny Tremain*. Boston: Houghton Mifflin.

Frank, A. (1967). *The diary of a young girl* (Rev. Ed., B. M. Mooyart, Trans.). New York: Doubleday.

Freeman, M. S. (1999). Fire boats. Mankato, MN: Capstone.

Freedman, R. (1987). *Lincoln: A photobiography*. New York: Clarion.

Freedman, R. (1988). *Buffalo hunt*. New York: Holiday House.

Freedman, R. (1990). *Franklin Delano Roosevelt*. Boston: Houghton Mifflin.

Freedman, R. (1993). *Eleanor Roosevelt: A life of discovery*. New York: Clarion.

Freedman, R. (2004). *The voice that challenged a nation: Marian Anderson and the struggle for equal rights*. New York: Clarion.

Friedman, I. R. (1987). *How my parents learned to eat*. Boston: Houghton Mifflin.

Fritz, J. (1967). *Early thunder*. New York: Coward McCann.

Fritz, J. (1992). *The great adventure of Christopher Columbus*. New York: Putnam & Grosset.

Garson, E. (Ed.). (1968). *The Laura Ingalls Wilder songbook*. New York: Harper & Row.

Garza, C. L. (1990). *Family pictures* (as told to Harriet Rohmer, Spanish text by R. Zubizarreta). San Francisco: Children's Book Press.

Gerstein, M. (2003). *The man who walked between the towers*. New York: Roaring Brook.

Gibbons, G. (1991). *Surrounded by sea: Life on a New England fishing island*. Boston: Little, Brown.

Goble, P. (1978). *The girl who loved wild horses*. Scarsdale, NY: Bradbury.

Goble, P. (1984). *Buffalo woman*. Scarsdale, NY: Bradbury.

Goble, P., & Goble, D. (1973). *Lone Bull's horse raid*. Scarsdale, NY: Bradbury.

Goldstein, P. (1991). *Lóng is a dragon: Chinese writing for children*. San Francisco: China Books.

Grifalconi, A. (1990). *Osa's pride*. Boston: Little, Brown.

Hackwell, W. J. (1986). *Digging to the past: Excavations in ancient lands*. New York: Scribner.

Hall, D. (1979). *Ox-cart man*. New York: Viking.

Hartford, J. (1986). *Steamboat in a cornfield*. New York: Crown.

Harvey, B. (1986). *My prairie year: Based on the diary of Elinore Plaisted*. New York: Holiday House.

Harvey, B. (1987). *Immigrant girl: Becky of Eldridge Street*. New York: Holiday House.

Harvey, B. (1988). *Cassie's journey: Going West in the 1860s*. New York: Holiday House.

Hautzig, E. (1968). *The endless steppe*. New York: Crowell.

Havill, J. (1989). *Jamaica tag-along*. Boston: Houghton Mifflin.

Hesse, K. (1997). *Out of the dust*. New York: Scholastic.

Hodges, M. (1989). *The arrow and the lamp*. Boston: Little, Brown.

Houston, J. (1965). *Tikta Liktak: An Eskimo legend*. New York: Harcourt.

Houston, J. (1967). *The white archer*. New York: Harcourt.

Hoyt-Goldsmith, D. (1992). *Arctic hunter*. New York: Holiday House.

Humble, R. (1991). *Ships, sailors, and the sea*. New York: Franklin Watts.

Huynh, Quang Nhuong. (1982). *The land I lost: Adventures of a boy in Vietnam*. New York: Harper.

Ichord, L. F. (2003). *Skillet bread, sourdough, and vinegar pie. Cooking in pioneer days*. Minneapolis: Millbrook.

Kadohata, C. (2004*). Kira kira*. New York: Atheneum.

Kalman, M. (2002). *Fireboat: The heroic adventures of the John J. Harvey*. New York: Putnam's Sons.

Kay, V. (2001). *Tattered sails*. New York: Putnam.

Keats, E. J. (1967). *Peter's chair*. New York: Harper & Row.

Kentley, E. (1992). *Boat*. New York: Knopf.

Kerley, B. (2005). *You and me together: Moms, dads, and kids around the world*. Washington DC: National Geographic Children's Books.

Krull, K. (Ed.). (1992). *Gonna sing my head off: American folk songs for children*. New York: Knopf.

Kurjian, J. (1993). *In my backyard*. Watertown, MA: Charlesbridge.

Lasky, K. (1977). *Tugboats never sleep*. Boston: Little, Brown.

Lasky, K. (1978). *Tall ships*. New York: Scribner.

Lasky, K. (2001). *Born in the breezes: The seafaring life of Joshua Slocum*. New York: Orchard.

Leeming, J. (1946). *Toy boats to make at home*. New York: Appleton-Century.

Lester, J. (1968). *To be a slave*. New York: Dial.

Levine, E. (Ed.). (1993). *Freedom's children: Young civil rights activists tell their own stories*. New York: Putnam.

Loeb, R. H. (1979). *Meet the real Pilgrims: Everyday life on Plimoth Plantation in 1627*. Garden City, NY: Doubleday.

Loeper, J. J. (1973). *Going to school in 1776*. New York: Atheneum.

Lord, B. B. (1984). *In the year of the boar and Jackie Robinson*. New York: Harper & Row.

Lowry, L. (1989). *Number the stars*. Boston: Houghton Mifflin.

Macauley, D. (1993). *Ship*. Boston: Houghton Mifflin.

MacLaughlin, P. (1985). *Sarah, plain and tall*. New York: Harper & Row.

McGovern, A. (1975). *The secret soldier: The story of Deborah Sampson*. New York: Four Winds.

McKissack, P. (2001). *Goin' someplace special*. New York: Antheneum.

Meltzer, M. (Ed.). (1984). *The Black Americans: A history in their own words*. New York: Harper & Row.

Meltzer, M. (1986). *George Washington and the birth of our nation*. New York: Franklin Watts.

Meltzer, M. (1987). *The American revolutionaries: A history in the their own words, 1750–1800*. New York: Crowell.

Millard, A. (1998). *A street through time*. New York: DK.

Miller, B. M. (2005). *Declaring independence: Life during the American Revolution*. Minneapolis: Lerner.

Miller, M. (1987). *My grandmother's cookie jar*. Los Angeles: Sloan.

Mitchell, B. (1986). *Shoes for everyone: A story about Jan Matzeliger*. Minneapolis: Carolrhoda.

Molloy, A. S. (1965). *Shaun and the boat: An Irish story*. New York: Hasting House.

Monk, I. (2001). *Family*. Minneapolis: Carolrhoda.

Moore, K. (1998). *If you lived at the time of the American Revolution*. New York: Scholastic.

Morris, A. (1990). *Loving*. New York: Lothrop, Lee & Shepard.

Morrison, V. F. (1981). *Going on a dig*. New York: Dodd, Mead.

Myers, W. D. (2001). *Bad boy: A memoir*. New York: HarperCollins.

Nabakov, P. (Ed.). (1978). *Native American testimony: An anthology of Indian and White relations*. New York: Crowell.

Norman, H. A. (1997). *The girl who dreamed only geese and other tales of the Far North*. New York: Harcourt Brace.

O'Dell, S. (1960). *Island of the blue dolphins*. Boston: Houghton Mifflin.

Ofinoski, S. (1997). *Into the wind: Sailboats then and now*. Tarryton, NY: Benchmark.

Olney, R. R. (1985). *Ocean-going giants*. New York: Atheneum.

Park, L. S. (2001). *A single shard*. New York: Clarion.

Patrick, D. (1990). *Martin Luther King, Jr*. New York: Franklin Watts.

Penner, L. R. (1991). *Eating the plates: A Pilgrim book of food and manners*. New York: Macmillan.

Polacco, P. (1992). *Chicken Sunday*. New York: Philomel.

Rachlis, E. (1960). *Indians of the Plains*. New York: American Heritage.

Rand, G. (2001). *Sailing home: A story of a childhood at sea*. New York: North/South.

Raposo, J., & Moss, J. (1971). *The Sesame Street song book*. New York: Simon & Schuster.

Rappaport, D. (2001). *Martin's big words: The life of Dr. Martin Luther King, Jr*. New York: Jump at the Sun/Hyperion.

Reiss, J. (1976). *The upstairs room*. New York: Crowell.

Rockwell, A. F. (2002). *They call her Molly Pitcher*. New York: Alfred Knopf.

Rosenblum, R. (1976). *Tugboats*. New York: Holt, Rinehart & Winston.

St. George, J. (2000). *So you want to be president?* New York: Philomel.

St. George, J. (2001). *John and Abigail Adams: An American love story*. New York: Holiday House.

San Souci, R. D. (1995). *The faithful friend*. New York: Simon & Schuster.

Santella, A. (2001). *The Inuit*. New York: Children's Press.

Say, A. (1982). *The bicycle man*. Boston: Houghton Mifflin.

Say, A. (1989). *The lost lake*. Boston: Houghton Mifflin.

Say, A. (1993). *Grandfather's journey*. Boston: Houghton Mifflin.

Scarry, H. (1982). *Life on a barge: A sketchbook*. Upper Saddle River, NJ: Prentice Hall.

Schanzer, R. (2004). *George vs. George: The Revolutionary War as seen by both sides*. Washington DC: National Geographic Children's Books.

Scott, G. (1981). *Egyptian boats*. Minneapolis: Carolrhoda.

Soto, G. (1993). *Too many tamales*. New York: G. P. Putnam.

Speare, E. G. (1958). *The witch of Blackbird Pond*. Boston: Houghton Mifflin.

Speare, E. G. (1961). *The bronze bow*. Boston: Houghton Mifflin.

Spier, P. (1970). *The Erie Canal*. New York: Doubleday.

Stanley, D. (1994). *Cleopatra*. New York: Morrow Junior.

Stanley, D. (1996). *Leonardo da Vinci*. New York: Morrow.

Stephens, B. (1984). *Deborah Sampson goes to war*. Minneapolis: Carolrhoda.

Steptoe, J. (1969). *Stevie*. New York: Harper & Row.

Stetson, E. (2002). *Knots to know: Hitches, loops, bends & bindings*. Charlotte, VT: Williamson.

Stokes, J. (1978). *Let's make a toy sailboat*. New York: David McKay.

Sullivan, G. (2001). *The Civil War at sea*. Brookfield, CT: Millbrook.

Swain, R. F. (2003). *How sweet it is (and was): A history of candy*. New York: Holiday House.

Thimmesh, C. T. (2000). *Girls think of everything: Stories of ingenious inventions by women*. Boston: Houghton Mifflin.

Tunis, E. (1952). *Oars, sails, and steam: A picture book of ships*. Cleveland: World.

Tunis, E. (1957). *Colonial living*. Cleveland: World.

Tunis, E. (1961). *Frontier living*. Cleveland: World.

Tunis, E. (1979). *Indians* (Rev. ed.). New York: Crowell.

Turkle, B. (1969). *Thy friend, Obadiah*. New York: Viking.

Uchida, Y. (1966). *Sumi's special happening*. New York: Scribner.

Uchida, Y. (1971). *Journey to Topaz*. New York: Scribner.

Uchida, Y. (1978). *Journey home*. New York: Atheneum.

Updike, J. (1999). *A child's calendar*. New York: Holiday House.

Van Allsburg, C. (1983). *The wreck of the Zephyr*. Boston: Houghton Mifflin.

Van Tol, R. (1984). *Submarines*. New York: Franklin Watts.

Vaughn, M. (2001). *The secret of freedom*. New York: Lee & Low.

Wallner, A. (2001). *Abigail Adams*. New York: Holiday House.

Walt Disney Company. (1989). *Ships* [Videocassette]. Burbank, CA: Author.

Waters, K. (1989). *Sarah Morton's day: A day in the life of a Pilgrim girl*. New York: Scholastic.

Waters, K. (2001). *Giving thanks: The 1621 harvest feast*. New York: Scholastic.

White, L. A. (2005). *I could do that! Esther Morris gets women the vote*. New York: Farrar, Strauss & Giroux.

Wibberly, L. (1959). *Johnny Treegate's musket*. New York: Farrar, Straus.

Wilder, L. I. (1935). *Little house on the prairie*. New York: Harper & Row.

Williams, S. A. (1992). *Working cotton*. San Diego: Harcourt Brace Jovanovich.

Williams, V. B. (1982). *A chair for my mother*. New York: Greenwillow.

Winnick, K. (2000). *Sybil's night ride*. Honesdale, PA: Boyd's Mills.

Winter, J. (1988). *Follow the drinking gourd*. New York: Knopf.

Wolf, D. (1975). *Chinese writing: An introduction*. New York: Holt, Rinehart & Winston.

Wong, J., & Miran, K. (2002). *Chinese calligraphy: Learn the beautiful art of Chinese writing*. New York: Troll.

Woodford, S. (1983). *The Parthenon*. Minneapolis: Lerner.

Woodson, J. (2001). *The other side*. New York: Putnam.

Wormfield, H. H. (1988). *Boatbuilder*. New York: Macmillan.

Yolen, J. (1992). *Encounter*. New York: HarperCollins.

Zeck, P., & Zeck, G. (1982). *Mississippi steamwheelers*. Minneapolis: Carolrhoda.

Ziner, F. (1961). *The Pilgrims of Plymouth Colony*. New York: American Heritage.

References

Adams, D. M., & Hamm, M. E. (1992). Portfolio assessment and social studies: Collecting, selecting, and reflecting on what is significant. *Social Education, 56*, 103–105.

Adler, S. (2001). The NCSS standards: A response to Anna Ochoa-Becker. *Social Education, 65,* 315–318.

Akenson, J. E. (1989). The expanding environments and elementary education: A critical perspective. *Theory and Research in Social Education, 27,* 33–52.

Alibrandi, M., Beal, C., Thompson, A., & Wilson, A. (2000). Reconstructing a school's past using oral histories and GIS mapping. *Social Education, 64,* 134–140.

Alleman, J., & Brophy, J. (1994a). Taking advantage of out-of-school opportunities for meaningful social studies learning. *The Social Studies, 85,* 262–267.

Alleman, J., & Brophy, J. (1994b). Trade-offs embedded in the literary approach to early elementary social students. *Social Studies and the Young Learner, 6*(3), 6–8.

Alleman, J., & Brophy, J. (1998). Assessment in a social constructivist classroom. *Social Education, 62,* 32–34.

Alleman, J., & Brophy, J. (2000). On the menu: The growth of self-efficacy. *Social Studies and the Young Learner, 12*(3), 15–19.

Alleman, J., & Brophy, J. (2001a). Assessment in the elementary grades. *Social Studies and the Young Learner, 14*(1), 13–19.

Alleman, J., & Brophy, J. (2001b). *Social studies excursions, K–3. Book one: Powerful units on food, clothing, and shelter.* Portsmouth, NH: Heinemann.

Alleman, J. & Brophy, J. (2002a). Growing up to be President: Interviews with K–3 students. *Social Studies and the Young Learner, 15*(1), 17–20.

Alleman, J., & Brophy, J. (2002b). *Social studies excursions, K–3. Book three: Powerful units on childhood, money, and government.* Portsmouth, NH: Heinemann.

Alleman, J., & Brophy, J. (2002c). *Social studies excursions, K–3. Book two: Powerful units on communication, transportation, and family living.* Portsmouth, NH: Heinemann.

Alleman, J. & Brophy, J. (2004). Building a learning community and studying childhood. *Social Studies and the Young Learner, 17*(2), 16–18.

Alleman, J. & Brophy, J. (2006). Introducing children to democratic government. *Social Studies and the Young Learner, 19*(1), 17–19.

Alleman, J. E., & Rosaen, C. L. (1991). The cognitive, social-emotional, and moral development characteristics of students: Basis for elementary and middle school social studies. In J. P. Shaver (Ed.), *Handbook of research on social studies teaching and learning* (pp. 121–133). New York: Macmillan.

Alter, G. (Ed.). (1995a). Variations on "ten themes": Applying the social studies standards to the elementary classroom [Special issue]. *Social Studies and the Young Learner, 8*(1).

Alter, G. (Ed.). (1995b). Varieties of literature and elementary social studies [Special issue]. *Social Studies and the Young Learner, 8*(2).

Alvi, K. (2001). At risk of prejudice: Teaching tolerance about Muslim Americans. *Social Education, 65,* 344–348.

Anand, B., Fine, M., Perkins, T., & Surrey, D. S. (2002). *Keeping the struggle alive: A guide to doing oral history.* New York: Teachers College Press.

Andel, M. A. (1990). Digging for the secrets of time: Artifacts, old foundations, and more. *Social Studies and the Young Learner, 3*(1), 9–11.

Anderson, C., Avery, P. G., Pederson, P. V., Smith, E. S., & Sullivan, J. L. (1997). Divergent perspectives on citizenship education: A Q-method study and survey of social studies teachers. *American Educational Research Journal, 34,* 333–364.

Angell, R. C. (1981). Reflections on the project Sociological Resources for the Social Studies. *American Sociologist, 16,* 41–43.

Archbald, D. A., & Newmann, F. M. (1988). *Beyond standardized testing: Assessing authentic academic achievement in the secondary school.* Reston, VA: National Association of Secondary School Principals.

Armento, B. J. (1991). Learning about the economic world. In V. A. Atwood (Ed.), *Elementary school social studies: Research as a guide to practice* (pp. 85–101). Washington, DC: National Council for the Social Studies.

Aronson, E., Blaney, N., Stephen, C., Sikes, J., & Knapp, M. (1978). *The Jigsaw classroom.* Beverly Hills, CA: Sage.

Atkins, C. L. (1981). Introducing basic map and globe concepts to young children. *Journal of Geography, 80,* 228–233.

Atwood, V. A. (Ed.). (1991). *Elementary social studies: Research as a guide to practice* (2nd ed.). Washington, DC: National Council for the Social Studies.

Au, K. H. (1980). Participation structures in a reading lesson with Hawaiian children: Analysis of a culturally appropriate instructional event. *Anthropology and Education Quarterly, 11,* 91–115.

Au, K. H. (1993). *Literacy instruction in multicultural settings.* Fort Worth, TX: Harcourt Brace.

Au, K. H., & Kawakami, A. J. (1994). Cultural congruence in instruction. In E. R. Hollins, J. E. King, & W. C. Hayman (Eds.), *Teaching diverse populations: Formulating a knowledge base* (pp. 5–24). Albany: State University of New York Press.

Banks, J. A. & Banks, C. A. M. (Eds.). (2003). *Multicultural education: Issues and perspectives* (5th ed.). New York: Wiley.

Banks, J. A., Cookson, P., Gay, G., Hawley, W. D., Irvine, J. J., Nieto, S., Schofield, J. W. & Stephan, W. G. (2005). Education and diversity. *Social Education, 69,* 36–40.

Barnes, B. R. (1991). Using children's literature in the early anthropology curriculum. *Social Education, 55,* 17–18.

Barr, J. B., Barth, J., & Shermis, S. (1977). *Defining the social studies.* Washington, DC: National Council of the Social Studies.

Barron, R. F. (1969). The use of vocabulary as an advance organizer. In H. L. Herber & P. L. Sanders (Eds.), *Research in the content areas: First-year report* (pp. 29–39). Syracuse, NY: Reading and Language Arts Center.

Barss, K. (1998). Re-exploring early American history: African in American [Special issue]. *Social Education, 62*(6).

Barth, J. L. (1993). Social studies: There is a history, there is a body, but is it worth saving? *Social Education, 57,* 56–57.

Barth, J. L., & Shermis, S. (1970). Defining the social studies: An exploration of three traditions. *Social Education, 34,* 743–750.

Barton, K. C. (1997). History—it can be elementary: An overview of elementary students' understanding of history. *Social Education, 61,* 13–16.

Barton, K. C. (2001). A sociocultural perspective on children's understanding of historical change. *American Educational Research Journal, 38,* 881–913.

Barton, K. C., & Levstik, L. S. (1996). "Back when God was around and everything": Elementary children's understanding of historical time. *American Educational Research Journal, 33,* 419–454.

Baum, C. G., & Cohen, I. S. (1989). Psychology and the social science curriculum. In *Charting a course: Social studies for the 21st century* (pp. 65–69). Washington, DC: National Commission on Social Studies in the Schools.

Beck, I. L., & McKeown, M. G. (1988). Toward meaningful accounts in history texts for young learners. *Educational Researcher, 17*(6), 31–39.

Beck, I. L., & McKeown, M. G. (1991a). Research directions: Social studies texts are hard to understand: Mediating some of the difficulties. *Language Arts, 68,* 482–489.

Beck, I. L., & McKeown, M. G. (1991b). Substantive and methodological considerations for productive textbook analysis. In J. P. Shaver (Ed.), *Handbook of research on social studies teaching and learning* (pp. 496–512). New York: Macmillan.

Beck, I. L., McKeown, M. G., & Worthy, J. (1995). Giving a text voice can improve students' understanding. *Reading Research Quarterly, 30,* 220–239.

Bell, K. (2002). Using moot courts in the classroom. *Social Education, 66,* 42–45.

Bennett, L. (2006). Children's voices for democracy [special issue]. *Social Studies and the Young Learner, 19*(1).

Benniga, J. S. (Ed.). (1991). *Moral education and civic education in the elementary school.* New York: Teachers College Press.

Bernard-Powers, J. (2002). Hilda Taba. In M. S. Crocco & O. L. Davis (Eds.), *Building a legacy: Women in social education, 1784–1984* (pp. 57–58). Silver Spring, MD: National Council for the Social Studies.

Berson, I. R., & Berson, M. J. (2001). Growing up in the aftermath of terrorism. *Social Studies and the Young Learner, 14*(2), 6–9.

Berson, M. J. (2004). Digital images: Capturing America's past with the technology of today. *Social Education, 68,* 214–219.

Berson, M. J. & Berson, I. R. (2004). Developing thoughtful "cybercitizens." *Social Studies and the Young Learner, 16*(4), 5–8.

Berson, M. J., Berson, I. R., & Ralston, M. E. (1999). Threshing out the myths and facts of Internet safety: A response to "Separating Wheat from Chaf." *Social Education, 63,* 160–161.

Berson, M. J., Cruz, B. C., Duplass, J. A., & Johnston, J. H. (2001). *Social studies on the Internet.* Upper Saddle River, NJ: Merrill/Prentice Hall.

Berti, A. (2005). Children's understanding of politics. In M. Barrett & E. Buchanan-Barrow (Eds.), *Children's understanding of society* (pp. 69–103). New York: Psychology Press.

Berti, A. E., & Bombi, A. S. (1988). *The child's construction of economics.* Cambridge, UK: Cambridge University Press.

Bestor, A. (1953). *Educational wastelands: The retreat from learning in our public schools.* Urbana: Illinois University Press.

Bestor, A. (1955). *Restoration of learning.* New York: Knopf.

Beyer, B. K. (1985). Critical thinking: What is it? *Social Education, 49,* 270–276.

Beyer, B. K. (1987). *Practical strategies for the teaching of thinking.* Boston: Allyn & Bacon.

Beyer, B. K., & Gilstrap, R. L. (Eds.). (1982). *Writing in elementary school social studies.* Boulder, CO: Social Science Education Consortium.

Beyer, B. K., & Penna, A. (Eds.). (1971). *Concepts in the social studies.* Washington, DC: National Council for the Social Studies.

Bickmore, K. (2002). Conflicts global and local: An elementary approach. *Social Education, 66,* 235–238.

Bigelow, W. (1992). Once upon a genocide: Christopher Columbus in children's literature. *Language Arts, 69,* 112–120.

Bisland, B. M. (2005). Walls, towers, and sphinxes: Multicultural concept construction and group inquiry. *Social Studies and the Young Learner, 17*(4), 8–12.

Bjorklun, E. C. (1995). Teaching about personal injury law: Activities for the classroom. *The Social Studies, 86,* 78–84.

Black, M. S. (1998). Using archaeology to explore cultures of North America. *Social Studies and the Young Learner, 11*(1), 11–16.

Bloom, B. S. (Ed.). (1956). *Taxonomy of educational objectives: The classification of educational goals. Handbook 1: The cognitive domain.* New York: David McKay.

Boehm, R. G., & Petersen, J. F. (1994). An elaboration of the fundamental themes in geography. *Social Education, 58,* 211–218.

Boggs, S. T., Watson-Gegeo, K., & McMillen, G. (1985). *Speaking, relating, and learning: A study of Hawaiian children at home and at school.* Norwood, NJ: Ablex.

Bolick, C. M. (2006). Teaching and learning with online historical maps. *Social Education, 70,* 133–137.

Bolick, C. M., Mcglinn, M. M., & Siko, K. L. (2005). Twenty years of technology: A retrospective view of Social Education's technology themed issues. *Social Education, 69,* 155–161.

Bower, B., & Lobdell, J. (1998). History alive! Six powerful constructivist strategies. *Social Education, 62,* 50–53.

Boykin, A. W. (1982). Task variability and the performance of Black and White schoolchildren: Vervistic explorations. *Journal of Black Studies, 12,* 469–485.

Brandt, R. (Ed.). (1992). Using performance assessment [Special issue]. *Educational Leadership, 49*(8).

Braun, J. A., & Cook, M. L. (1985). Making heritage experiences come alive for elementary school social studies students. *The Social Studies, 76,* 216–219.

Breidenstein, A., Butler, R., & Kamdar, N. (2001). Economists in the school. *Social Education, 65,* 373–378.

Brophy, J. (1985). Classroom management as instruction: Socializing self-guidance in students. *Theory Into Practice, 24,* 233–240.

Brophy, J. (1990). Teaching social studies for understanding and higher order application. *Elementary School Journal, 90,* 351–417.

Brophy, J. (1996a). *Advances in research on teaching, volume 6: Teaching and learning history.* Greenwich, CT: JAI.

Brophy, J. (1996b). Introduction. In J. Brophy (Ed.), *Advances in research on teaching, volume 6: Teaching and learning history* (pp. 1–18). Greenwich, CT: JAI.

Brophy, J. (1999). Elementary students learn about Native Americans: The development of knowledge and empathy. *Social Education, 63,* 39–45.

Brophy, J., & Alleman, J. (2002). Primary-grade students' knowledge and thinking about the economics of meeting families' shelter needs. *American Educational Research Journal, 39,* 423–468.

Brophy, J., & Van Sledright, B. (1997). *Teaching and learning history in elementary schools.* New York: Teachers College Press.

Bruner, J. (1960). *The process of education.* Cambridge, MA: Harvard University Press.

Bruner, J. (1961). The act of discovery. *Harvard Educational Review, 31,* 21–32.

Bruner, J., Goodnow, J., & Austin, G. (1956). *A study of thinking.* New York: Wiley.

Burgstahler, S., & Utterback., L. (2000). *New kids on the net: Internet activities in elementary language arts.* Boston: Allyn & Bacon.

Burroughs, S. (2002). Testy times for social studies. *Social Education, 66,* 315–318.

Burstein, J. H. & Hutton, L. (2005). Planning and teaching with multiple perspectives. *Social Studies and the Young Learner, 18*(1), 15–17.

California Department of Education. (1992). *Handbook for teaching Korean American students.* Sacramento: Author.

California Department of Education. (1998). *History-social science content standards for California public schools: Kindergarten through grade twelve.* Sacramento: Author.

Camperell, K., & Knight, R. S. (1991). Reading research and social studies. In J. P. Shaver (Ed.), *Handbook of research on social studies teaching and learning* (pp. 567–577). New York: Macmillan.

Cangemi, J., & Aucoin, L. (1996). Global thematic units are passports to learning. *Social Education, 60*(2), 80–82.

Caplan, N. S., Choy, M. H., & Whitmore, J. K. (1991). *Children of the boat people: A study of educational success.* Ann Arbor: University of Michigan Press.

Cardis, R. J., & Risinger, C. F. (1994). Contemporary trends in social studies. *Social Studies and the Young Learner, 6*(3), 4–5, 22.

Carlson, H. L., & Holm, C. (1999). Diversity and global studies: Elementary children's investigations. *Social Studies and the Young Learner, 11*(3), 6–10.

Carnegie Corporation of New York and the Center for Information and Research on Civic Learning and Engagement (2003). *The civic mission of schools.* New York: Author.

Carrol, R. F. (1987). Schoolyard archaeology. *The Social Studies, 78,* 69–75.

Case, R. (1993). Key elements of a global perspective. *Social Education, 57,* 318–325.

Cazden, C. (1983). Adult assistance to language development: Scaffolds, models, and direct instruction. In R. P. Parker & F. A. Davis (Eds.), *Developing literacy: Young children's use of language* (pp. 3–18). Newark, DE: International Reading Association.

Center for Civic Education. (1994). *National standards for civics and government.* Calabasas, CA: Author.

Charles, C. (1985). Using the natural world to teach and learn globally. *Social Education, 49,* 213–215.

Charney, R. S. (1993). *Teaching children to care: Management in the responsive classroom.* Greenfield, MA: Northeast Foundation for Children.

Chick, K. A. (2004). Making meaning for children: The events of 9–11. *Social Studies and the Young Learner, 17*(1), 25–29.

Christensen, L. M. (2006). Using art to teach history to young learners. *Social Education, 70,* 312–315.

Clarke, J. H. (1990). *Patterns of thinking: Integrating learning skills in content teaching.* Boston: Allyn & Bacon.

Clements, H. M., Fielder, W. R., & Tabachnick, B. R. (1966). *Social study: Inquiry in elementary classrooms.* Indianapolis: Bobbs-Merrill.

Cohen, R. (1996). Moving beyond name games: The conservative attack on the U.S. history standards. *Social Education, 60,* 49–54.

Collins, H. T., Czarra, F. R., & Smith, A. F. (Eds.). (1998). Global education: Challenges, cultures, and connections [Special issue]. *Social Education, 62*(5).

Cooper, B. L. (1989). Popular records as oral evidence: Creating an audio time line to examine American history, 1955–1987. *Social Education, 53,* 34–40.

Cordier, M. H., & Perez-Stable, M. A. (1996). Latino connections: Family, neighbors, and community. *Social Studies and the Young Learner, 9*(1), 20–22.

Cort, H. R., & Peskowitz, N. (1977). *A longitudinal study of man: A course of study, summary report.* Washington, DC: National Science Foundation. (ERIC Document Reproduction Service No. ED 151 275)

Cox, C. (2005). *Teaching language arts: A student- and response-centered classroom* (5th ed.). Boston: Allyn & Bacon.

Cremin, L. (1961). *The transformation of the school: Progressivism in American education.* New York: Knopf.

Crocco, M. S., & Davis, O. L. (Eds.). (2002). *Building a legacy: Women in social education, 1784–1984.* Silver Spring, MD: National Council for the Social Studies.

Cruz, B. C., Nutta, J. W., O'Brien, J., Feyton, C. M., & Govoni, J. M. (2003). *Passport to learning: Teaching social studies to ESL students.* Silver Spring MD: National Council for the Social Studies.

Cuban, L. (1984). *How teachers taught: Constancy and change in American classroom, 1890–1980.* New York: Longman.

Cullinan, B. E. (Ed.). (1993). *Fact and fiction: Literature across the curriculum.* Newark, DE: International Reading Association.

Cummins, J. (1979). Linguistic interdependence and the educational development of bilingual children. *Review of Educational Research, 49,* 222–251.

Cummins, J. (1986a). Empowering minority students: A framework for intervention. *Harvard Educational Review, 56,* 18–36.

Cummins, J. (1986b). The role of primary language development in promoting educational success for language minority students. In *Schooling and language minority students: A theoretical framework* (pp. 3–49). Los Angeles: CSULA Evaluation, Dissemination, and Assessment Center.

Cummins, J. (1989). *Empowering minority students.* Sacramento: California Association for Bilingual Education.

Cummins, J. (1992). Language proficiency, bilingualism, and academic achievement. In P. A. Richard-Amato & M. A. Snow (Eds.), *The multicultural classroom: Readings for content-area teachers* (pp. 16–26). White Plains, NY: Longman.

Cunningham, J. W., Cunningham, P. M., & Arthur, S. V. (1981). *Middle and secondary school reading.* New York: Longman.

Curtis, C. K. (1991). Social studies for students at risk and with disabilities. In J. P. Shaver (Ed.), *Handbook of research on social studies teaching and learning* (pp. 57–174). New York: Macmillan.

Curtis-Seinik, C., McCarthy, M., Nadal, K., Pfeiffer, D., Tella, A., & Wagner, N. (2006). Character education, K–12, in Uniondale. *Social Studies and the Young Learner, 18*(3), 27–29.

Czartoski, S., & Hickey, G. (1999). All about me: A personal heritage project. *Social Studies and the Young Learner, 11*(4), 11–14.

Danziger, K. (1958). Children's earliest conceptions of economic relationships. *Journal of Social Psychology, 47,* 231–240.

Darling-Hammond, L., Ancess, J., & Falk, B. (Eds.). (1995). *Authentic assessment in action: Studies of schools and students at work.* New York: Teachers College Press.

De Avila, E. A., Duncan, S. E., & Navarrete, C. J. (1987a). *Cooperative learning: Integrating language and content-area instruction.* Wheaton, MD: National Clearinghouse for Bilingual Education.

De Avila, E. A., Duncan, S. E., & Navarrete, C. J. (1987b). *Finding out/Descubrimiento: Teacher's resource guide.* Northvale, NJ: Santillana.

Delaney, M., & Oyler, C. (2001). Online expeditions: Strengths and limitations. *Social Studies and the Young Learner, 13*(3), 6–9.

Delisle, J. R. (1991). Gifted students and social studies. In J. P. Shaver (Ed.), *Handbook of research on social studies teaching and learning* (pp. 175–184). New York: Macmillan.

Dever, M. T., Sorenson, B. & Broderick, J. (2005). Using picture books as a vehicle to teach young children about social justice. *Social Studies and the Young Learner, 19*(1), 18–21.

Dewey, J. (1900). *The school and society.* Chicago: University of Chicago Press.

Dewey, J. (1902). *The child and the curriculum.* Chicago: University of Chicago Press.

Dewey, J. (1933). *How we think.* Boston: Heath. (Original work published 1910)

Dewey, J. (1976). The university elementary school: History and character. In J. A. Boydston (Ed.), *John Dewey: The middle works, 1899–1924.* Vol. 1: 1899–1901 (pp. 325–338). Carbondale: Southern Illinois University Press. (Original work published 1897)

Diaz, C. F., Massialas, B. G., & Xanthopoulos, J. A. (1999). *Global perspectives for educators.* Boston: Allyn & Bacon.

Diaz-Rico, L. T., & Weed, K. Z. (2005). *The cross-cultural, language, and academic development handbook: A complete K–12 reference guide* (3rd ed.). Boston: Allyn & Bacon.

Dimmitt, J. P., & Van Cleaf, D. W. (1992). Integrating writing and social studies: Alternatives to the formal research paper. *Social Education, 56,* 382–384.

Dockterman, D. A. (2002). *Weaving technology into your teaching.* Watertown, MA: Tom Snyder.

Donaldson, M. (1978). *Children's minds.* New York: Norton.

Dougan, A. (1988). The search of a definition of social studies: A historical overview. *International Journal of Social Education, 3*(3), 13–36.

Douglass, M. P. (1967). *Social studies from theory to practice in elementary education.* Philadelphia: JB Lippincott.

Douglass, M. P. (1998). *The history, psychology and pedagogy of geographic literacy.* Westport, CT: Praeger.

Dow, P. B. (1976). MACOS: Social studies in crisis. *Educational Leadership, 34,* 112–117.

Dow, P. B. (1991). *Schoolhouse politics: Lessons from the Sputnik era.* Cambridge, MA: Harvard University Press.

Downey, M. T. (Ed.). *History in the schools.* Washington, DC: National Council for the Social Studies.

Downey, M. T., & Levstik, L. S. (1991). Teaching and learning history. In J. P. Shaver (Ed.), *Handbook of research on social studies teaching and learning* (pp. 400–410). New York: Macmillan.

Drier, H. S., & Lee, J. K. (1999). Learning about climate: An exploration in geography and mathematics. *Social Studies and the Young Learner, 12*(1), 6–10.

Easterly, J. E. (Ed.). (1994). *Promoting global teacher education: Seven reports.* Reston, VA: Association of Teacher Education.

Echevarria, J. & Graves, A. (2006). *Sheltered content instruction: Teaching English learners with diverse abilities* (3rd ed.). Boston: Allyn & Bacon.

Echevarria, J., Vogt, M., & Short, D. (2003). *Making content comprehensible to English language learners: The SIOP model* (2nd ed.). Boston: Allyn & Bacon.

Edgington, W. D. (2001). Solving problems with twenty questions. *Social Education, 65,* 379–382.

Eggen, P. D., & Kauchak, D. (2001). *Strategies for teachers: Teaching content and thinking skills* (4th ed.). Boston: Allyn & Bacon.

Eisner, E. (1991). Art, music, and literature within social studies. In J. P. Shaver (Ed.), *Handbook of research on social studies teaching and learning* (pp. 551–558). New York: Macmillan.

Elnour, A. & Bashir-Ali, K. (2003). Teaching Muslim girls in American schools. *Social Education, 67,* 62–64.

Ember, C. R., & Ember, M. (2006). *Cultural anthropology* (12th ed.). Upper Saddle River, NJ: Prentice Hall.

Engle, S. H. (1986). Late night thoughts about the New Social Studies. *Social Education, 50,* 20–22.

Engle, S. H., & Ochoa, A. S. (1988). *Education for democratic citizenship: Decision making in the social studies.* New York: Teachers College Press.

Epstein, J. & Shiller, T. (2005). Perspective matters: Social identity and the teaching and learning of national history. *Social Education, 69,* 201–204.

Erickson, J. (2001). Learning civics by changing the community. *Social Studies and the Young Learner, 13*(3), 10–13.

Evans, M. D. (1995). Exchanging opinions through letters and editorials: A social studies activity. *Social Education, 59,* 158.

Evans, R. W. (1989b). A dream unrealized: A brief look at the history of issue-centered approaches. *The Social Studies, 80,* 178–184.

Evans, R. W. (Ed.). (1992). Defining issues-centered social studies education [Special issue]. *The Social Studies, 83*(3).

Evans, R. W. (2004). *The social studies wars: What should we teach the children?* New York: Teachers College Press.

Evans, R. W (2006). The social studies wars, now and then. *Social Education, 70,* 317–321.

Farivar, S. (1993). Continuity and change: Planning an integrated history-social science/English language arts unit. *Social Studies Review, 32*(2), 17–24.

Feinberg, J. (2002). Service learning in contemporary Japan and American. *Social Education, 66,* 368–371.

Felton, R. G., & Allen, R. F. (1990). Using visual materials as historical resources. *Social Studies, 81,* 84–87.

Fenton, E. (1967). *The new social studies.* New York: Holt, Rinehart & Winston.

Fenton, E. (1991). Reflections on the new social studies. *The Social Studies, 82,* 84–90.

Fertig, G. (2005). Connecting with our pioneer past: Letters from the homestead. *Social Education, 69,* 263–268.

Field, L. & Singer, J. Y. (2006). Talking with children about the Columbian exchange. *Social Studies and the Young Learner, 18*(4), 24–26.

Field, S. L. (1997). Teaching young citizens [Special issue]. *Social Studies and the Young Learner, 10*(1).

Field, S. L. (1998). Social studies: Gateway to literacy [Special issue]. *Social Studies and the Young Learner, 10*(4).

Field, S. L., Wilhelm, R., Nickell, P., Culligan, J., & Sparks, J. (2001). Teaching middle school social studies: Who is at risk? *Social Education, 65,* 225–230.

Finchum, M. (2006). "I" in for Indian? Dealing with stereotypes in the classroom. *Social Studies and the Young Learner, 18*(4), 4–6.

Fine, M. (1995). *Habits of mind: Struggling over values in America's classrooms.* San Francisco: Jossey-Bass.

Finn, C. E. & Ravitch, D. (1988). No trivial pursuit. *Phi Delta Kappan, 69,* 559–564.

Firek, H. (2006). Creative writing in the social studies classroom: Promoting literacy and content literacy. *Social Education, 70,* 183–186.

Fisher, A. (2001). *Critical thinking.* London: Cambridge University Press.

Fitzpatrick, C. (2000). Navigating a new information landscape. *Social Education, 64,* 33–35.

Foncault, P. (2000). Cooperative learning and conflict management in the second grade. *Social Studies and the Young Learner, 13*(1), 24–26.

Ford, J. & Neville, E. (2006). Making democracy an active force in students' lives. *Social Studies and the Young Learner, 19*(1), 8–11.

Forsythe, A. S. (1995). *Learning geography: An annotated bibliography of research paths.* Indiana, PA: National Council for Geographic Education.

Foster, S. J., & Hoge, J. D. (2000). "Dismantling the wall one brick at a time": Overcoming barriers to parochialism in social studies classrooms. *Social Education, 64,* 368–370.

Fraenkel, J. R. (1992). Hilda Taba's contributions to social studies education. *Social Education, 56,* 172–178.

Freeman, E. B., & Person, D. G. (Eds.). (1992). *Using nonfiction trade books in the elementary classroom: From ants to zeppelins.* Urbana, IL: National Council of Teachers of English.

Freese, J. R. (1997). Using the National Geographic standards to integrate children's social studies. *Social Studies and the Young Learner, 10*(2), 22–24.

Gallenstein, N. L. (2000). Group investigation: An introduction to cooperative research. *Social Studies and the Young Learner, 13*(1), 17–18.

Gandy, S. K. (2004). Teaching the electoral process in ten days. *Social Education, 68,* 332–338.

Garcia, E. (1994) *Understanding and meeting the challenge of student cultural diversity.* Boston: Houghton Mifflin.

Gardner, H. (1983). *Frames of mind: The theory of multiple intelligences.* New York: Basic Books.

Gardner, H. (1991). *The unschooled mind: How children think and how school should teach.* New York: Basic Books.

Gavrish, M. J. A. (1995). The historian as detective: An introduction to historical methodology. *Social Education, 59,* 151–153.

Gay, G. (1991). Culturally diverse students and social studies. In J. P. Shaver (Ed.), *Handbook of research on social studies teaching and learning* (pp. 144–156). New York: Macmillan.

Gay, G. (2000). *Culturally responsive teaching: Theory, research and practice.* New York: Teachers College Press.

Gay, G. (2001). Educational equity for students of color. In J. A. Banks & C. A. M. Banks (Eds.), *Multicultural education: Issues and perspectives* (4th ed., pp. 197–224). New York: Wiley.

Geographic Education National Implementation Project. (1987). *K–6 geography: Themes, key ideas, and learning opportunities.* Washington, DC: Author.

Geographic Education National Implementation Project. (1989). *7–12 geography: Themes, key ideas, and learning opportunities.* Washington, DC: Author.

Geography Education Standards Project. (1994). *Geography for life: National geography standards.* Washington, DC: Author.

Gersmehl, P. (2005). *Teaching geography.* New York: Guilford Press.

Gilligan, C. (1982). *In a different voice.* Cambridge, MA: Harvard University Press.

Gilliland, H. (Ed.). (1992). *Teaching the Native American.* Dubuque, IA: Kendall/Hunt.

Gilstrap, R. L. (1982). Writing in elementary social studies: Report of a personal search. In B. K. Beyer & R. L. Gilstrap (Eds.), *Writing in elementary school social studies* (pp. 19–29). Boulder, CO: Social Science Education Consortium.

Gilstrap, R. L. (1991). Writing for the social studies. In J. P. Shaver (Ed.), *Handbook of research on social studies teaching and learning* (pp. 578–587). New York: Macmillan.

Ginsburg, H., & Opper, S. (1979). *Piaget's theory of intellectual development* (2nd ed.). Upper Saddle River, NJ: Prentice Hall.

Goodman, J. (1992). *Elementary schooling for critical democracy.* Albany: State University of New York Press.

Grabe, M., & Grabe, C. (2000). *Integrating the Internet for meaningful learning.* Boston: Allyn & Bacon.

Grant, S. G. (1997). Appeasing the Right, missing the point? Reading the New York state social studies framework. *Social Education, 61,* 102–107.

Grant, S. G., & Van Sledright, B. A. (1996). The dubious connection: Citizenship education and the social studies. *The Social Studies, 87,* 56–59.

Gray, P. S. (1989). Sociology. In *Charting a course: Social studies for the 21st century* (pp. 71–75). Washington, DC: National Commission on Social Studies in the Schools.

Greenbaum, P. E. (1985). Nonverbal differences in communication style between American Indian and Anglo elementary classrooms. *American Educational Research Journal, 22,* 101–115.

Greenstein, F. I. (1969). *Children and politics.* New Haven, CT: Yale University Press.

Gregg, M., & Leinhardt, G. (1994). Mapping out geography: An example of epistemology and education. *Review of Educational Research, 64,* 311–361.

Griffith, B. (1991). The abandonment of social studies? *Theory and Research in Social Education, 19,* 136–151.

Groce, E. C., Groce, R. D. & Colby, S. (2005). The Big Apple's core: Exploring Manhattan. *Social Studies and the Young Learner, 18*(1), 22–27.

Gronlund, N. E. (2000). *How to write and use instructional objectives* (6th ed.). Upper Saddle River, NJ: Merrill/Prentice Hall.

Grossman, H. (1984). *Educating Hispanic students: Cultural implications for instruction, classroom management, counseling, and assessment.* Springfield, IL: Charles C. Thomas.

Gunter, M. A., Estes, T. H., & Mintz, S. L. (2006). *Instruction: A models approach* (5th ed.). Boston: Allyn & Bacon.

Haas, M. E. (2000). *A Street Through Time* used with powerful instructional strategies. *Social Studies and the Young Learner, 13*(2), 20–23.

Haas, M. E. (2004). The presidency and presidential elections in the elementary classroom. *Social Education, 68,* 340–346.

Hale-Benson, J. E. (1986). *Black children: Their roots, culture, and learning styles* (Rev. ed.). Baltimore: Johns Hopkins University Press.

Handley, L. M., & Adler, S. (1994). Standards in social studies: Curriculum concerns. *Social Studies and the Young Learner, 6*(3), 17–19.

Hanna, P. R. (1963). Revising the social studies: What is needed. *Social Education, 27,* 190–196.

Hanna, P. R. (Ed.). (1987a). *Assuring quality for the social studies in our schools.* Stanford, CA: Hoover Institution Press.

Hanna, P. R. (1987b). Society-child-curriculum. In P. R. Hanna (Ed.), *Assuring quality for the social studies in our schools* (pp. 11–19). Stanford, CA: Hoover Institution Press. (Original work published 1956).

Hansen, W. L., Bach, G. L., Calderwood, J. D., & Saunders, P. (1977). *A framework for teaching economics: Basic concepts.* New York: Joint Council for Economic Education.

Hanvey, R. G. (1976). *An attainable global perspective.* New York: Global Perspectives in Education.

Harms, J. M., & Lettow, L. J. (1994). Criteria for selecting picture books with historical settings. *Social Education, 58,* 152–155.

Hartman, K. J., & Giorgis, C. (2001). Exploring maps through children's literature. *Social Studies and the Young Learner, 13*(3), 14–16.

Hartoonian, H. M., & Van Scotter, R. (2000). Footsteps of a new millenium [Special issue]. *Social Education, 64*(1).

Harwood, A. M., & Chang, J. (1999). Inquiry-based service-learning and the Internet. *Social Studies and the Young Learner, 12*(1), 15–18.

Hatcher, B., & Olsen, M. (1984). Sidewalk social studies. *Social Education, 48,* 473–474.

Heath, J. A., & Vik, P. (1994). Elementary school student councils: A statewide study. *Principal, 74*(1), 31–32.

Heath, S. B. (1986). Sociocultural contexts of language development. In *Beyond language: Social and cultural factors in schooling language-minority students* (pp. 143–186). Los Angeles: California State University Evaluation, Dissemination, and Assessment Center.

Heimlich, J. E., & Pittelman, S. D. (1986). *Semantic mapping: Classroom applications.* Newark, DE: International Reading Association.

Hembacher, D., Okada, D., & Richardson, T. (2004). "School to career" and social studies: Making the connection. *Social Studies and the Young Learner, 16*(4), 20–23.

Herlihy, J. G. (1974). Man: A course of study, an exemplar of the New Social Studies. *Social Education, 38,* 442–443.

Hertzberg, H. W. (1981). *Social studies reform 1880–1980.* Boulder, CO: Social Science Education Consortium.

Hess, D. E. (2004). Discussion in social studies: Is it worth the trouble? *Social Education, 68,* 151–155.

Hickey, G. M. (1991). "And then what happened, Grandpa?": Oral history projects in the elementary classroom. *Social Education, 55,* 216–217.

Hickey, G. M. (1999). *Bringing history home: Local and family history projects for grades K–16.* Boston: Allyn & Bacon.

Hickey, G. M. & Kolterman, D. L. (2006). Special women in my life: Strategies for writing women into the social studies curriculum. *Social Education, 70,* 190–196.

Hicks, K., & Austin, J. (1994). Experiencing the legal system: Fairy-tale trials for fifth graders. *The Social Studies, 85,* 39–44.

Hightshoe, S. (1997). Sifting through the sands of time: A simulated archaeological dig. *Social Studies and the Young Learner, 9*(3), 28–30.

Hinde, E. R. (2005). Revisiting curriculum integration: A fresh look at an old idea. *The Social Studies, 96,* 105–111.

Hinde, E. R. & Ekiss, G. O. (2005). No child left behind . . . except in geography? GeoMath in Arizona answers a need. *Social Studies and the Young Learner, 18*(2), 27–29.

Hirshfield, C. (1991). New worlds from old: An experience in oral history at the elementary school level. *Social Studies, 82*(3), 110–114.

Hittleman, C. G., & Hittleman, D. R. (1998). Bringing grandparents into social studies: A unit of study. *Social Studies and the Young Learner, 10*(2), pp. 1–4.

Hollins, E. R., King, J. E., & Hayman, W. C. (Eds.). (1994). *Teaching diverse populations: Formulating a knowledge base.* Albany: State University of New York Press.

Hollins, E. R. & Oliver, E. I. (Eds.). (1999). *Pathways to success in school: Culturally responsive teaching.* Mahwah, NJ: Erlbaum.

Hollins, E. R., Smiler, H., & Spencer, K. (1994). Benchmarks in meeting the challenges of effective schooling for African American youngsters. In E. R. Hollins, J. E. King, & W. C. Hayman (Eds.), *Teaching diverse populations: Formulating a knowledge base* (pp. 163–174). Albany: State University of New York Press.

Hoone, C. (1989). Teaching timelines. *Social Studies and the Young Learner, 2*(2), 13–17.

Hoover, R. L., & Kindsvatter, R. (1997). *Democratic discipline: Foundation and practice.* Upper Saddle River, NJ: Merrill/Prentice Hall.

Howard, R. W. (2003). The shrinking of social studies. *Social Education, 67,* 285–288.

Huerta, G. C., & Flemmer, L. A. (2001). Latina women speak: Using oral histories in the social studies curriculum. *Social Education, 65,* 270–277.

Hunter, M. (1984). Knowing, teaching, and supervising. In P. L Hosford (Ed.), *Using what we know about teaching* (pp. 169–192). Alexandria, VA: Association for Supervision and Curriculum Development.

Imeson, J., & Skamp, K. R. (1996). A novel use of literature to integrate environmental education with social studies. *The Social Studies, 86,* 215–220.

Inkpen, T. D. (1974). A selected bibliography on man: A course of study. *Social Education, 38,* 456–457.

Irvin, J. L., Lunstrum, J. P., Lynch-Brown, C., & Shepard, M. F. (1995). *Enhancing social studies through literacy strategies.* Washington, DC: National Council for the Social Studies.

Jaffee, C. (2004). Teaching about the Middle East: Challenges and resources. *Social Education, 68,* 46–50.

Jahoda, G. (1979). The construction of economic reality by some Glaswegian children. *European Journal of Social Psychology, 19,* 115–127.

Jantz, R. K., & Klawitter, K. (1991). Anthropology and sociology. In V. A. Atwood (Ed.), *Elementary school social studies: Research as a guide to practice* (pp. 102–118). Washington, DC: National Council for the Social Studies.

Jenness, D. (1990). *Making sense of the social studies.* New York: Macmillan.

Jennings, T. E., Crowell, S. M., & Fernlund, P. F. (1994). Social justice in the elementary classroom. *Social Studies and the Young Learner, 7*(1), 4–6.

Johnson, D. D., & Pearson, P. D. (1984). *Teaching reading vocabulary.* New York: Holt, Rinehart & Winston.

Johnson, D. W., & Johnson, F. P. (2005). *Joining together: Group theory and group skills* (9th ed.). Boston: Allyn & Bacon.

Johnson, D. W., & Johnson, R. T. (1989–1990). Social skills for successful group work. *Educational Leadership, 47*(4), 29–33.

Johnson, D. W., & Johnson, R. T. (1992a). Approaches to implementing cooperative learning in the social studies classroom. In R. J. Stahl & R. L. Van Sickle (Eds.), *Cooperative learning in the social studies classroom: An introduction to social study* (pp. 44–51). Washington, DC: National Council for the Social Studies.

Johnson, D. W., & Johnson, R. T. (1992b). Encouraging thinking through constructive controversy. In N. Davidson & T. Worsham (Eds.), *Enhancing thinking through cooperative learning* (pp. 120–137). New York: Teachers College Press.

Johnson, D. W., & Johnson, R. T. (1998). *Learning together and alone: Cooperative, competitive, and individualistic learning* (5th ed.). Boston: Allyn & Bacon.

Johnson, D. W., & Johnson, R. T., & Holubec, E. J. (1994). *The new circles of learning: Cooperation in the classroom and school.* Alexandria, VA: Association for Supervision and Curriculum Development.

Johnson, D. W., Maruyama, G., Johnson, R. T., Nelson, D., & Skon, L. (1981). Effects of cooperative, competitive, and individualistic goal structures on achievement: A meta-analysis. *Psychological Bulletin, 89,* 47–62.

Joint Committee on Geographic Education. (1984). *Guidelines for geographic education: Elementary and secondary schools.* Washington, DC: Association of American Geographers and National Council for Geographic Education.

Jones, R. C. & Lapham, S. S. (2004). Teaching reading skills in the elementary social studies classroom. *Social Studies and the Young Learner, 17*(2), pullout section.

Joyce, B. R., Weil, M., & Calhoun, E. (2003). *Models of teaching* (7th ed.). Boston: Allyn & Bacon.

Kagan, S. (1989–1990). The structural approach to cooperative learning. *Educational Leadership, 47*(4), 12–15.

Kagan, S. (1997). *Cooperative learning*. San Juan Capistrano, CA: author.

Keech, A. M. (2002). Magnificent manatees: A service-learning project. *Social Studies and the Young Learner, 14*(4), 11–15.

Keefe, S. E., & Padilla, A. M. (1987). *Chicano ethnicity*. Albuquerque: University of New Mexico Press.

Keiper, T. A., & Larson, B. E. (2000). The fifty state quarters: Art and historical inquiry. *Social Studies and the Young Learner, 13*(2), pp. 5–8.

Kellough, R. D. (Ed.). (1995). *Integrating language arts and social studies for intermediate and middle school students*. Upper Saddle River, NJ: Merrill/Prentice Hall.

Kerckhoff, A. C. (1986). Effects of ability grouping in British secondary schools. *American Sociological Review, 51*, 842–858.

Kilpatrick, W. H. (1918). The project method. *Teachers College Record, 19*, 319–333.

Kilpatrick, W. H. (1925). *Foundations of method*. New York: Macmillan.

Kirp, D. L. (1990, August 12). The classroom according to Hunter. *Los Angeles Times Magazine*, pp. 16–23, 37–39.

Kirschenbaum, H. (1977). *Advanced value clarification*. La Jolla, CA: University Associates.

Kleg, M. (1993). On the NCSS curriculum guidelines for multicultural education. *Social Education, 57*, 58–59.

Kniep, W. M. (1985). *A critical review of the short history of global education: Preparing for new opportunities*. New York: Global Perspectives in Education.

Kniep, W. M. (1986). Defining a global education by its content. *Social Education, 50*, 437–446.

Kochman, T. (1981). *Black and White styles in conflict*. Chicago: University of Chicago Press.

Koeller, S. (1992). Social studies research writing: Raising voices. *Social Education, 56*, 379–382.

Kohlberg, L. (1981). *The philosophy of moral development: Moral stages and the idea of justice*. New York: Harper & Row.

Kon, J. H., & Martin-Kniep, G. O. (1992). Students' geographic knowledge and skills in different kinds of tests: Multiple-choice versus performance assessment. *Social Education, 56*, 95–98.

Koeppen, K. E. (2003). Issues-centered social studies: Promoting active citizenship in the classroom. *Social Studies and the Young Learner, 15*(4), 15–17.

Kourilsky, M. (1977). The kinder-economy: A case study of kindergarten pupils of economic concepts. *Elementary School Journal, 77*, 182–191.

Kourilsky, M. (1987). Children's learning of economics: The imperative and the hurdles. *Theory Into Practice, 26*, 198–205.

Krashen, S. (1982). *Principles and practices of second-language acquisition*. Oxford, UK: Pergamon.

Krashen, S. (1986). Bilingual education and second-language acquisition theory. In *Schooling and language minority students: A theoretical framework* (pp. 51–79). Los Angeles: California State University Evaluation, Dissemination, and Assessment Center.

Krashen, S. (2003). *Explorations in language acquisition and use*. Portsmouth, NH: Heinemann.

Krashen, S. D., & Terrell, T. D. (1995). *The natural approach: Language acquisition in the classroom*. New York: Phoenix ELT.

Krey, D. M. (1998). *Children's literature in social studies: Teaching to the standards.* Washington, DC: National Council for the Social Studies.

Kurtz-Costes, B., & Pungello, E. P. (2000). Acculturation and immigrant children: Implications for educators. *Social Education, 64,* 121–125.

Ladson-Billings, G. (1992). I don't see color, I just see children: Dealing with stereotyping and prejudice in young children. *Social Studies and the Young Learner, 5*(2), 9–12.

Ladson-Billings, G. (1995). Toward a theory of culturally relevant pedagogy. *American Educational Research Journal, 32,* 465–492.

Lamme, L. L. (1994). Stories from our past: Making history come alive for children. *Social Education, 58,* 159.

Lamy, S. L. (1987). *The definition of a discipline: The objects and methods of analysis in global education.* New York: Global Perspectives in Education.

Landorf, H. & Lowenstein, E. (2004). The Rosa Parks "myth": A third grade historical investigation. *Social Studies and the Young Learner, 16*(3), 5–9.

Laney, J. D., & Moseley, L. (1990). Who packed the suitcase? Playing the role of an archaeologist/anthropologist. *Social Studies and the Young Learner, 2*(3), 17–19.

Langer, J. A. (1981). From theory to practice: A prereading plan. *Journal of Reading, 25,* 106–110.

Lankiewicz, D. (1987). Our museum of American life. *Clearing House, 60,* 256–257.

Larkins, A. G., & Hawkins, M. L. (1990). Trivial and noninformative content in primary grade social studies texts: A second look. *Journal of Social Studies Research, 14,* 25–32.

Larson, B. E. (2005). Considering the move to electronic discussions. *Social Education, 69,* 162–166.

Laughlin, M., Black, P., & Loberg, M. (1991). *Social studies readers' theater for children: Scripts and script development.* Englewood, CO: Teacher Idea Press.

Lechner, J. V. (1997). Accuracy in biographies for children. *New Advocate, 10,* 229–242.

Ledford, C. C. & Lyon, A. (2004). Election resources and activities for grades K–5. *Social Studies and the Young Learner, 17*(1), 19–21.

Lee, J. K. (2000). The E-citizen. *Social Education, 64,* 378–379.

Lee, J. K. (2002). Ideology and the Web. *Social Education, 66,* 161–165.

Leinhardt, G., Beck, I. L., & Stanton, C. (Eds.). (1994). *Teaching and learning in history.* Hillsdale, NJ: Lawrence Erlbaum.

Leming, J., Ellington, L., & Porter-Magee, K. (Eds.). (2003). *Where did social studies go wrong?* Washington DC: Fordham Institute.

Leming, J. S., Ellington, L. & Schug, M. (2006). The state of social studies: A national random survey of elementary and middle school social studies teachers. *Social Education, 70,* 322–327.

LeRiche, L. W. (1987). The expanding environments sequence in elementary social studies: The origins. *Theory and Research in Social Education, 5,* 137–154.

Levstik, L. (1986). The relationship between historical response and narrative in a sixth-grade classroom. *Theory and Research in Social Education, 21*(1), 1–15.

Levstik, L. (1989). Historical narrative and the young reader. *Theory Into Practice, 28,* 114–119.

Levstik, L. (1990). Mediating content through literary texts. *Language Arts, 67,* 848–853.

Levstik, L. (1991). Teaching history: A definitional and developmental dilemma. In V. A. Atwood (Ed.), *Elementary school social studies: Research as a guide to practice* (pp. 68–84). Washington, DC: National Council for the Social Studies.

Levstik, L. S. & Barton, K. C. (1996). They still use some of their past: Historical salience in elementary children's chronological thinking. *Journal of Curriculum Studies, 28,* 531–576.

Levstik, L. S. & Barton, K. C. (2005). *Doing history: Investigating with children in elementary and middle schools* (3rd ed.). New York: Erlbaum.

Lewis, R. B., & Doorlag, D. H. (2006). Teaching special students in general education classrooms (7th ed.). Upper Saddle River, NJ: Pearson/Merrill/Prentice Hall.

Liben, L., & Downs, R. (1989). Educating with maps: Part I. The place of maps. *Teaching Thinking and Problem Solving, 11*(1), 6–9.

Lickona, T. (1991). *Educating for character: How our schools can teach respect and responsibility.* New York: Bantam.

Little Soldier, L. (1990). Making anthropology a part of the elementary social studies curriculum. *Social Education, 54,* 18–19.

Losey, K. M. (1995). Mexican American students and classroom interaction: An overview and critique. *Review of Educational Research, 65,* 283–318.

Lou, Y., Abrami, P. C., Spence, J. C., Poulson, C., Chambers, B., & D'Apollonia, S. (1996). Within-class grouping: A meta-analysis. *Review of Educational Research, 66,* 423–458.

Lubliner, S. (2001). *A practical guide to reciprocal teaching.* Bothel, WA: Wright.

Lybarger, M. (1991). The historiography of social studies: Retrospect, circumspect, and prospect. In J. P. Shaver (Ed.), *Handbook of research on social studies teaching and learning* (pp. 3–15). New York: Macmillan.

Lyman, F. T. (1992). Think-Pair-Share, Thinktrix, Thinklinks, and weird facts: An interactive system for cooperative thinking. In N. Davidson & T. Worsham (Eds.), *Enhancing thinking through cooperative learning* (pp. 169–181). New York: Teachers College Press.

Lyman, L., Foyle, H. C., & Azwell, T. S. (1993). *Cooperative learning in the elementary classroom.* Washington, DC: National Educational Association.

Mager, R. F. (1997). *Preparing instructional objectives: A critical tool in the develoment of effective instruction* (3rd ed.). Atlanta, GA: The Center for Effective Performance.

Mahood, W. (1980). The land of milk and honey: Simulating the immigrant experience. *Social Education, 44,* 22–27.

Maier, J. (1993). Relating here to there: Globes and world maps as advance organizers. *Social Studies and the Young Learner, 5*(3), 9–11.

Main, M., Wilhelm, R. W., & Cox, A. R. (1996). Mi communidad: Young children's bicultural explorations of the meaning of family. *Social Studies and the Young Learner, 9*(1), 7–9, 14.

Mandeville, G. K., & Rivers, J. L. (1988–1989). Effects of South Carolina's Hunter-based PET program. *Educational Leadership, 46*(4), 63–66.

Marchand-Martella, N. E., Slocum, T. A., & Martella, R. C. (2003). *Introduction to direct instruction.* Boston: Allyn & Bacon.

Martorella, P. H. (1991). Knowledge and concept development in social studies. In J. P. Shaver (Ed.), *Handbook of research on social studies teaching and learning* (pp. 370–384). New York: Macmillan.

Massialas, B. G. (1991). Education for international understanding. In J. P. Shaver (Ed.), *Handbook of research on social studies teaching and learning* (pp. 448–458). New York: Macmillan.

Massialas, B. G., & Cox, C. B. (1966). *Inquiry in social studies.* San Francisco: McGraw-Hill.

Mayhew, K. C., & Edwards, A. C. (1936). *The Dewey School: The Laboratory School of the University of Chicago 1896–1903.* New York: Appleton-Century.

McCabe, P. P. (2003). Working with the textbook: How to enhance student motivation. *Social Education, 67,* 274–277.

McCall, A. L. (1994). Including quilters' voices in the social studies curriculum. *Social Studies and the Young Learner, 7*(1), 10–14.

McCormick, T. M. (2004). Letters from Trenton, 1776: Teaching with primary sources. *Social Studies and the Young Learner, 17*(2), 5–12.

McCracken, H. (1959). *George Catlin and the old frontier.* New York: Dial.

McGowan, M. J., & Powell, J. H. (1996). An annotated bibliography of resources for literature-based instruction. *Social Education, 60,* 231–232.

McGowan, T. M. (Ed.). (1996). Telling the story of citizenship [Special issue]. *Social Education, 60*(4).

McGowan, T. M., Erickson, L., & Neufeld, J. A. (1996). With reason and rhetoric: Building the case for the literature–social studies connection. *Social Education, 60,* 203–207.

McKeown, M. G., Beck, I. L., Sinatra, G. M., & Loxterman, J. A. (1991). The contribution of prior knowledge and coherent text to comprehension. *Reading Research Quarterly, 27,* 79–93.

McLaren, P. (1994). *Life in schools: An introduction to critical pedagogy in the foundations of education.* New York: Longman.

McLaughlin, B. (1987). *Theories of second-language learning.* London: Edward Arnold.

Mehaffy, G., Sitton, G., & Davis, O. L. (1979). *Oral history in the classroom.* Washington, DC: National Council for the Social Studies.

Mehlinger, H. D. (2002). Teaching about September 11 and its aftermath. *Social Education, 66,* 303–306.

Merryfield, M. M. (2004). Elementary students in substantial culture learning. *Social Education, 68,* 270–273.

Merryfield, M. & Crocco, M. S. (2003). Women of the world [Special issue]. *Social Education, 67*(1).

Mezaros, B. (1997). Economic standards: A guide for curriculum planners. *Social Education, 61,* 324–328.

Mezaros, B., & Engstromn, L. (1998). The voluntary national content standards in economics: From standards to classroom implementation. *Social Studies and the Young Learner, 11*(2), 7–12.

Miel, A. (1952). *Cooperative procedures in learning.* New York: Teachers College Press.

Miller, E. G., & Jacobson, M. G. (1994). Teaching for global-mindedness. *Social Studies and the Young Learner, 6*(4), 4–6.

Miller, F. (2000). Biography buddy: Interviewing each other. *Social Studies and the Young Learner, 12*(3), 13–14.

Miller, J. W. (1974). Comparisons of conventional "subdued" to vivid "highly contrasting" color schemes for elementary school maps: Report of an experiment. *Journal of Geography, 73*(3), 41–45.

Miller, J. W. (1982). Improving the design of classroom maps: Experimental comparison of alternative formats. *Journal of Geography, 81*(2), 51–55.

Milson, A. J., & Downey, P. (2001). WebQuest: Using Internet resources for cooperative inquiry. *Social Education, 65,* 144–146.

Milson, A. J., & LaComb, S. (2001). World-class sounds: Music, social studies, and the Internet. *Social Studies and the Young Learner, 13*(4), 1–2.

Mohan, B. (1986). *Language and content.* Reading, MA: Addison-Wesley.

Molebash, P. (2004). Web historical inquiry projects. *Social Education, 68,* 226–229.

Molebash, P., & Dodge, B. (2003). Kickstarting inquiry with WebQuests and Web Inquiry. *Social Education, 67,* 158–162.

Moore, A. W. (1985). A question of accuracy: Errors in children's biographies. *School Library Journal, 31*(6), 34–35.

Morin, J. A. (1997). Software enhancement for a diverse family unit. *Social Studies and the Young Learner, 9*(3), 24–26.

Morris, R. V. (1998). Using artifacts as a springboard to literacy. *Social Studies and the Young Learner, 10*(4), 14–17.

Morris, R. V. (2003). Colonial America and service learning in the fifth grade. *Social Studies and the Young Learner, 15*(4), 11–14.

Morris, R. V. (2006). The land of Hope: Third-grade students use a walking tour to explore their community. *The Social Studies, 97,* 129–132.

Mosher, R., Kenney, R., & Garrod, A. (Eds.). (1994). *Preparing for citizenship.* Westport, CT: Praeger.

Muir, S. P., & Frazee, B. (1986). Teaching map-reading skills: A developmental perspective. *Social Education, 50,* 199–203.

Nash, G. B., & Dunn, R. E. (1995). History standards and culture wars. *Social Education, 59,* 5–7.

National Center for History in the Schools. (1996). *National standards for history: Basic edition.* Los Angeles: Author.

National Council for the Social Studies. (1994). *Expectations of excellence: Curriculum standards for the social studies.* Washington, DC: Author.

National Council for the Social Studies. (2006). Technology position statement and guidelines. *Social Education, 70,* 329–332.

National Council for the Social Studies Ad Hoc Committee on Ability Grouping. (1992). Ability grouping in social studies. *Social Education, 56,* 268–270.

National Council for the Social Studies Ad Hoc Committee on Global Education. (1987). Global education: In bounds or out? *Social Education, 51,* 242–249.

National Council for the Social Studies Select Subcommittee. (2001). Service-learning: An essential component of citizenship education. *Social Education, 65,* 240–241.

National Council for the Social Studies Task Force on Early Childhood/Elementary Social Studies. (1989). Social studies for early childhood and elementary school children preparing for the 21st century. *Social Education, 53,* 14–23.

National Council for the Social Studies Task Force on Ethnic Studies. (1992). Curriculum guidelines for multicultural education. *Social Education, 56,* 274–294.

National Council for the Social Studies Task Force on Revitalizing Citizenship Education. (2001). Creating effective citizens. *Social Education, 65,* 319.

National Council for the Social Studies Task Force on Scope and Sequence. (1989). In search of a scope and sequence for social studies: Report of the National Council for the Social Studies Task Force on Scope and Sequence. *Social Education, 53,* 375–387.

National Council for the Social Studies Task Force on Standards for Teaching and Learning in the Social Studies. (1993). A vision of powerful teaching and learning in the social studies: Building social understanding and civic efficacy. *Social Education, 57,* 213–223.

National Council on Economic Education. (1997). *National content standards in economics.* New York: Author.

National Council on Economic Education. (2005). The little red hen: Productive resources and incentives. *Social Studies and the Young Learner, 17*(4), pullout section.

National Institute of Child Health and Development. (2000). *Report of the National Panel. Teaching children to read: An evidence-based assessment of the scientific research literature on reading and its implication for reading instruction. Reports of the subgroups.* Washington DC: National Institute for Child Health and Human Development/U.S. Department of Education/National Institute for Literacy. www.nationalreadingpanel.org.

Neill, M. & Guisbond, L. (2005). Excluding children, lost learning: The costs of doing business with NCLB. *Social Studies and the Young Learner, 17*(4), 31–32.

Nelson, P. (2005). Preparing students for citizenship: Literature and primary documents. *Social Studies and the Young Learner, 17*(3), 21–29.

Nelson, M. R., & Stahl, R. J. (1991). Teaching anthropology, sociology, and psychology. In J. P. Shaver (Ed.), *Handbook of research on social studies teaching and learning* (pp. 420–426). New York: Macmillan.

Neufeld, P. (2006). Comprehension instruction in content area classes. *The Reading Teacher, 59,* 302–312.

Newmann, F. M. (1990a). Higher order thinking in social studies: A rationale for the assessment of classroom thoughtfulness. *Journal of Curriculum Studies, 22,* 41–56.

Newmann, F. M. (1990b). Qualities of thoughtful social studies classes: An empirical profile. *Journal of Curriculum Studies, 22,* 253–275.

Newmann, F. M. (1991). Promoting higher order thinking in social studies: Overview of a study of 16 high school departments. *Theory and Research in Social Education, 19,* 324–340.

Newmann, F. M., & Associates. (1996). *Authentic achievement: Restructuring schools for intellectual quality.* San Francisco: Jossey-Bass.

Nickell, P. (Ed.). (1999). Authentic assessment in social studies. [Special issue]. *Social Education, 63*(6).

Nitko, A. J. & Brookhart, S. M. (2006). Educational assessment of students (5th ed.). Upper Saddle River NJ: Prentice Hall.

Norton, D. E., Norton, S. E., & McClure, A. (2003). *Through the eyes of a child: An introduction to children's literature* (7th ed.). Upper Saddle River, NJ: Merrill/Prentice Hall.

Norton, J. (1992). The State v. the Big Bad Wolf: A study of the justice system in the elementary school. *Social Studies and the Young Learner, 5*(1), 5–9.

Oakes, J. (1985). *Keeping track: How schools structure inequality.* New Haven, CT: Yale University Press.

Ochoa-Becker, A. S. (2001). A critique of the NCSS curriculum standards. *Social Education, 65,* 165–171.

Ogle, D. (1986). K-W-L: A teaching model that develops active reading of expository text. *The Reading Teacher, 39,* 564–570.

Olmedo, I. M. (1996). Creating contexts for studying history with students learning English. *The Social Studies, 87,* 39–43.

Olsen, D. G. (1995). "Less" can be "more" in the promotion of thinking. *Social Education, 59,* 130–134.

Onosko, J. T. (1992). An approach to designing thoughtful units. *Social Studies, 83,* 193–196.

O'Reilly, K. (1998). What would you do? Constructing decision-making guidelines through historical problems. *Social Education, 62,* 46–49.

Ovoian, G., & Gregory, D. (1991). Can you dig it? *Social Studies Review, 30*(3), 83–88.

Owen, R. C. (1982). Anthropology and a social science/social studies: One more plea. *Social Studies, 73,* 207–211.

Paley, V. G. (1979). *White teacher.* Cambridge, MA: Harvard University Press.

Palinscar, A. S., & Brown, A. L. (1984). Reciprocal teaching of comprehension-fostering and comprehension-monitoring activities. *Cognition and Instruction, 2,* 117–175.

Pappamihiel, N.D., Lake, V. E., & Rice, D. C. (2005). Adapting a social studies lesson to include English language learners. *Social Studies and the Young Learner, 17*(3), 4–7.

Parker, F. W. (1883). *Talks on teaching.* New York: Kellogg.

Parker, F. W. (1894). *Talks on pedagogics.* New York: Kellogg.

Parker, W. C. (1991). Achieving thinking and decision-making objectives in social studies. In J. P. Shaver (Ed.), *Handbook of research on social studies teaching and learning* (pp. 345–356). New York: Macmillan.

Parker, W. C. (1995). Assessing civic discourse. *Educational Leadership, 52*(5), 84–85.

Parker, W. C. (2001). Classroom discussion: Models for leading seminars and discussions. *Social Education, 75,* 111–115.

Parker, W. C. (2006). Talk isn't cheap: Practicing deliberation n school. *Social Studies and the Young Learner, 19*(1), 12–15.

Pascopella, A. (2005). Staying alive: Social studies in elementary schools. *Social Studies and the Young Learner, 17*(3), 30–32.

Passe, J. (1988). Developing current events awareness in children. *Social Education, 52,* 531–533.

Passe, J. (1994). Media literacy in a global age. *Social Studies and Young Learner, 6*(4), 7–9.

Passe, J., & Passe, M. (1985). Archaeology: A unit to promote thinking skills. *Social studies, 76,* 238–239.

Patrick, J. J., & Hoge, J. D. (1991). Teaching government, civics, and law. In J. P. Shaver (Ed.), *Handbook of research on social studies teaching and learning* (pp. 427–436). New York: Macmillan.

Petersen, J. F., Natoli, S. J., & Boehm, R. G. (1994). The guidelines for geographic education: A 10-year retrospective. *Social Education, 58,* 206–210.

Pezone, M., & Singer, A. (1997). Empowering students through democratic dialogues. *Social Education, 61,* 75–79.

Phillips, S. U. (1972). Participant structures and communicative competence: Warm Springs children in community and classroom. In C. B. Cazden, V. P. John, & D. Hymes (Eds.), *Functions of language in the classroom* (pp. 370–394). New York: Teachers College Press.

Phipps, S. & Adler, S. (2003). Where's the history? *Social Education, 67,* 296–298.

Piaget, J., & Inhelder, B. (1969). *The psychology of the child* (H. Weaver, Trans.). New York: Basic Books.

Potter, L. A. (2003). Teaching U.S. history with primary sources [Special issue]. *Social Education, 67*(7).

Potter, L. A. (2004). Buttons to bumper stickers: Political campaign memorabilia. *Social Education, 68,* 382–387.

Potter, L. A. (Ed.). (2005). Teaching civics with primary documents [Special issue]. *Social Education, 69*(7).

Powe, F. (1998). Perspectives on the American landscape. *Social Education, 62,* 126–133.

Pratt, L., & Beaty, J. J. (1999). *Transcultural children's literature.* Upper Saddle River, NJ: Merrill/Prentice Hall.

Proctor, D. R., & Hass, M. E. (1993). Social studies and school-based community service programs: Teaching the role of cooperation and legitimate power. *Social Education, 57,* 381–384.

Qin, Z., Johnson, D. W., & Johnson, R. T. (1995). Cooperative versus competitive efforts and problem solving. *Review of Educational Research, 65,* 129–143.

Quigley, C. N., & Bahmueller, C. F. (Eds.). (1991). *Civitas: A framework for civic education.* Calabasas, CA: Center for Civic Education.

Rader, W. (1995). The Elementary School Economics Project at the University of Chicago. *The Social Studies, 86,* 85–90.

Rallis, D. N., & Rallis, H. (1995). Changing the image of geography. *The Social Studies, 86,* 167–168.

Ramirez, M., & Castaneda, A. (1974). *Cultural democracy, bicognitive development, and education*. New York: Academic Press.

Raphael, T. E. & Au, K. H. (2005). QAR: Enhancing comprehension and test taking across grades and content areas. *The Reading Teacher, 59,* 206–221.

Raths, L. E., Harmin, M., & Simon, S. B. (1978). *Values and teaching: Working with values in the classroom* (2nd ed.). Upper Saddle River, NJ: Merrill/Prentice Hall.

Reutzel, D. R., & Cooter, R. B. (2004). *Teaching children to read: Putting the pieces together* (4th ed.). Upper Saddle River, NJ: Pearson/Merrill/Prentice Hall.

Rhoades, L. (1994). Quick-start ideas for teaching current events with newspapers. *Social Education, 58,* 173–174.

Ricchiuti, L. (1998). Hanging in the Louvre: Virtual museum. *California Council for the Social Studies, 38*(1), 57–63.

Rice, M. J., & Cobb, R. L. (1978). *What can children learn in geography? A review of the research*. Boulder, CO: Social Science Education Consortium.

Richard-Amato, P., & Snow, M. A. (Eds.). (1992). *The multicultural classroom: Readings for content-area teachers*. New York: Addison-Wesley.

Risinger, C. F. (1998). Separating the wheat from the chaff: Why dirty pictures are not the real dilemma in using the Internet to teach social studies. *Social Education, 62,* 148–150.

Risinger, C. F. (2001). Teaching elementary and secondary history using the Internet. *Social Education, 65,* 297–299.

Risinger, C. F. (2005). Take your students on virtual field trips. *Social Education, 69,* 193–294.

Ritchie, D. A. (1995). *Doing oral history*. New York: Twayne.

Roberts, P. L. (1996). *Integrating language arts and social studies for kindergarten and primary children*. Upper Saddle River, NJ: Merrill/Prentice Hall.

Rodriguez, H. M., Salinas, C., & Guberman, S. (2005). Creating opportunities for historical thinking with bilingual students. *Social Studies and the Young Learner, 18*(2), 9–13.

Rong, X. L., & Hickey, M. G. (Eds.). (1998). Social studies and the new immigration [Special issue]. *Social Education, 62*(7).

Rosenshine, B., & Meister, C. (1994). Reciprocal teaching: A review of the research. *Review of Educational Research, 64,* 479–530.

Ross, D. D., & Bondy, E. (1993). Classroom management for responsible citizenship: Practical strategies for teachers. *Social Education, 57,* 326–328.

Rossi, J. A. (1996a). Creating strategies and conditions for civil discourse about controversial issues. *Social Education, 60,* 15–21.

Rossi, J. A. (Ed.). (1996b). Teaching controversial issues [Special issue]. *Social Education, 60*(1).

Rothwell, J. T. (1997). History making and the Plains Indians. *Social Education, 61,* 4–10.

Ruddell, M. R. (1997). *Teaching content reading and writing* (2nd ed.). Boston: Allyn & Bacon.

Ruggiero, V. R. (2003). *Beyond feelings: A guide to critical thinking* (7th ed.). New York: McGraw-Hill.

Rule, A. C., & Sunal, C. S. (1994). Buttoning up a hands-on history lesson: Using everyday objects to teach about historical change. *Social Studies and the Young Learner, 7*(2), 8–11.

Rulli, D. (2005). Websites for primary sources and civics education. *Social Education, 69,* 412–413.

Rushdoony, H. A. (1968). A child's ability to read maps: Summary of the research. *Journal of Geography, 67,* 213–222.

Sahr, D. E. (1997). Native American governments in today's curriculum. *Social Education, 61,* 308–315.

Sanchez, T. (2001). Heroes and heroines: Biographies to live by. *Social Studies and the Young Learner, 13*(1), 27–29.

Sandmann, A. (2004). Literature that promotes justice for all. *Social Education, 68,* 254–259.

Sandmann, A. L., & Ahern, J. F. (2002). *Linking literature with life: The NCSS standards and children's literature for the middle grades.* Silver Spring, MD: National Council for the Social Studies.

Saunders, P., Bach, G. L., Calderwood, J. D., & Hansen, W. L. (1984). *A framework for teaching economics: Basic concepts* (2nd ed.). New York: Joint Council on Economic Education.

Saxe, D. (1991). *Social studies in schools: A history of the early years.* Albany: State University of New York Press.

Saxe, D. W. (1992). Framing a theory for social studies foundations. *Review of Educational Research, 62,* 259–278.

Saxe, D. W. (1996). The national history standards: Time for common sense. *Social Education, 60,* 44–48.

Schaffarzick, J. (1979). Federal curriculum reform: A crucible for value conflict. In J. Schaffarzick & G. Sykes (Eds.), *Value conflicts and curriculum issues: Lessons from research and experience* (pp. 1–26). Berkeley, CA: McCutchan.

Shafer, F., Stearns, L., & Kallo, J. (2006). The tales of the dogs: Integrating geography and technology. *Social Education, 70,* 199–202.

Schimmel, D. (1997). Traditional rule making and the subversion of citizenship education. *Social Education, 61,* 70–74.

Schneider, E., & Gregory, L. A. (2000). Speculation and historical interpretation for fifth and sixth graders. *Social Studies and the Young Learner, 13*(2), 9–11.

Schug, M. C. (1983). The development of economic thinking in children and adolescents. *Social Education, 47,* 141–145.

Schug, M. C. (Ed.). (1985). *Economics in the school curriculum, K–12.* Washington, DC: Joint Council on Economic Education and the National Education Association.

Schug, M. C. (1994). How children learn economics. *International Journal of Social Education, 8,* 25–34.

Schug, M. C. (1996). Introducing children to economic reasoning: Some beginning lessons. *The Social Studies, 87,* 114–118.

Schug, M. C., & Walstad, W. B. (1991). Teaching and learning economics. In J. P. Shaver (Ed.), *Handbook of research on social studies teaching and learning* (pp. 411–419). New York: Macmillan.

Schug, M. C., & Western, R. D. (2003). Raising interest in economics [Special issue]. *Social Education, 67*(2).

Schwartz, S. (2000). My family's story: Discovering history at home. *Social Studies and the Young Learner, 12*(3), 6–9.

Segal, A. (2003). Maps as stories about the world. *Social Studies and the Young Learner, 16*(1), 21–25.

Seikaly, Z. A. (2001). At risk of prejudice: The Arab American community. *Social Education, 65,* 349–351.

Selwyn, D. (1995). *Arts and humanities in the social studies.* Washington, DC: National Council for the Social Studies.

Senesh, L. (1963). *Our working world: Families at work.* Chicago: Science Research Associates.

Shade, B. J. (1986). Is there an Afro-American cognitive style? An explanatory study. *Journal of Black Psychology, 13,* 13–16.

Shade, B. J. & New, C. A. (1993). Cultural influences on learning: Teaching implications. In J. A. Banks & C. A. M. Banks (Eds.), *Multicultural education: Issues and perspectives,* (pp. 317–331). Boston: Allyn & Bacon.

Shaftel, F., & Shaftel, G. (1967). *Role playing for social values: Decision making in the social studies.* Upper Saddle River, NJ: Merrill/Prentice Hall.

Sharan, S. (Ed.). (1997). *Handbook of cooperative learning methods.* New York: Praeger.

Sharan, Y., & Sharan, S. (1989–1990). Group investigation expands cooperative learning. *Educational Leadership, 47*(4), 17–21.

Sharan, Y. & Sharan, S. (1992). Expanding cooperative learning through group investigation. New York: Teachers College Press.

Shaver, J. P. (Ed.). (1991). *Handbook of research on social studies teaching and learning.* New York: Macmillan.

Sheehan, J. J. & Sibit, S. A. (2005). Adapting lessons for the special needs student. *Social Studies and the Young Learner, 18*(1), 4–6.

Shiveley, J. M. (2004). Critical thinking and visiting Websites: It must be elementary! *Social Studies and the Young Learner, 16*(4), 9 -12.

Short, D. J., Mahrer, C. A., Elfin, A. M., Liten-Tejada, R. A., & Montone, C. L. (1994). *Protest and the American Revolution: An integrated language, social studies, and culture unit for middle school American history.* Washington, DC: National Center for Research on Cultural Diversity and Second Language Learning and Center for Applied Linguistics.

Simmons, D. (1994). "Think globally, acting locally": Using the local environment to explore global issues. *Social Studies and the Young Learner, 6*(4), 10–13.

Simmons, D. (1995). Environmental education, social studies, and education reform: Why is environmental education essential education? *Social Studies and the Young Learner, 8*(1), 9–11.

Simpson, M. (Ed.). (1996). The world around us: Global education [Special issue]. *Social Education, 60*(7).

Simpson, M. (Ed.). (1997). A new view of the world: Using technology in social studies education [Special issue]. *Social Education, 61*(3).

Simpson, M. (Ed.). (2001a). Teaching about tragedy [Special issue]. *Social Education, 65*(6).

Simpson, M. (Ed.). (2002). Teaching with tech [Special issue]. *Social Education, 66*(3).

Simpson, M. (Ed.). (2003). Advancing technology in social studies [Special issue]. *Social Education, 67*(3).

Simpson, M. (Ed.). (2004). Plugging into the past: Using technology to explore history [Special issue]. *Social Education, 68*(3).

Simpson, M. (Ed.). (2005). Empowering social studies with technology [Special issue]. *Social Education, 69*(3).

Simpson, M. (Ed.). (2006). Connecting technology with social studies [Special issue]. *Social Education, 70*(3).

Sincero, P. & Woyshner, C. (2003). Writing women into the curriculum. *Social Education, 67,* 218–225.

Singleton, L. (1993). *G is for geography: Children's literature and the five themes.* Boulder, CO: Social Science Education Consortium.

Singleton, L. (1995). *H is for history: Using children's literature to develop historical understandings.* Boulder, CO: Social Science Education Consortium.

Singleton, L. (1997). *C is for citizenship: Children's literature and civic understanding.* Boulder, CO: Social Science Education Consortium.

Singleton, L. R. (2001). Following a tragic event: A necessary challenge for civic educators. *Social Education, 65,* 413–418.

Slavin, R. E. (1978). Student teams and achievement divisions. *Journal of Research and Development in Education, 12,* 39–49.

Slavin, R. E. (1980). Cooperative learning. *Review of Educational Research, 50,* 315–342.

Slavin, R. E. (1987). Ability grouping and achievement in elementary school: A best evidence synthesis. *Review of Educational Research, 60,* 471–499.

Slavin, R. E. (1989). PET and the pendulum: Fadism in education and how to stop It. *Phi Delta Kappan, 70,* 752–758.

Slavin, R. E. (1989–1990). Research on cooperative learning: Consensus and controversy. *Educational Leadership, 47*(4), 52–55.

Slavin, R. E. (1990). On making a difference. *Educational Researcher, 19*(3), 30–34.

Slavin, R. E. (1992). Cooperative learning in the social studies: Balancing the social and the studies. In R. J. Stahl & R. L. Van Sickle (Eds.), *Cooperative learning in the social studies classroom: An introduction to social study* (pp. 21–25). Washington, DC: National Council for the Social Studies.

Slavin, R. E. (1994a). *Cooperative learning: Theory, research, and practice on line* (2nd ed.). Boston: Allyn & Bacon.

Slavin, R. E. (1994b). *Using student team learning* (2nd ed.) Baltimore: Johns Hopkins University Center for Research on Elementary and Middle Schools.

Sloyer, S. (1982). *Readers' theatre: Story dramatization in the classroom.* Urbana, IL: National Council of Teachers of English.

Smagorinsky, P. (1994). Bring the courtroom to the classroom: Develop civic awareness with simulation activities. *The Social Studies, 85,* 174–180.

Smith, F. (1986a). *How education backed the wrong horse.* Victoria, BC: Abel Press.

Smith, F. (1986b). *Insult to intelligence: The bureaucratic invasion of our classrooms.* Portsmouth, NH: Heinemann.

Smith, F. (1988). *Understanding reading: A psycholinguistic analysis of reading and learning to read.* Mahwah, NJ: Lawrence Erlbaum.

Smitherman, G. (1977). *Talkin' and testifyin': The language of Black America.* Boston: Houghton Mifflin.

Soley, M. (1996). If it's controversial, why teach it? *Social Education, 60,* 9–14.

Spies, P., Bloom, J., Boucher, J., Lucking, C., Norling, L. & Theisen, R. (2004). From crisis to civic engagement: The struggle over social studies standards in Minnesota. *Social Education, 68,* 457–463.

Stahl, R. J., & Van Sickle, R. L. (1992a). Cooperative learning as effective social study within the social studies classroom: Introduction and invitation. In R. J. Stahl & R. L. Van Sickle (Eds.), *Cooperative learning in the social studies classroom: An introduction to social study* (pp. 1–7). Washington, DC: National Council for the Social Studies.

Stahl, R. J., & Van Sickle, R. L. (1992b). *Cooperative learning in the social studies classroom: An introduction to social study.* Washington, DC: National Council for the Social Studies.

Stallings, J., & Krasavage, E. M. (1986). Program implementation and student achievement in a 4-year Madeline Hunter follow-though project. *Elementary School Journal, 87,* 117–138.

Stanley, W. B. (2005). Social studies and the social order: Transmission or transformation? *Social Education, 69,* 282–286.

Steele, M. M. (2005). Teaching social studies to students with mild disabilities. *Social Studies and the Young Learner, 17*(3), 8–10.

Sternberg, R. J. (Ed.). (1994). *Thinking and problem solving* (2nd ed.). San Diego: Academic Press.

Stevens, R. (2002). A thoughtful patriotism. *Social Education, 66,* 18–24.

Stewart, L. (2006). Celebrating the life and legacy of Rosa Parks. *Social Studies and the Young Learner, 19*(1), 23–26.

Stiggins, R. J. (1994). *Student-centered classroom assessment.* Upper Saddle River, NJ: Merrill/Prentice Hall.

Stokes, S. M. (1997). Curriculum for Native American students: Using Native American values. *The Reading Teacher, 50,* 576–584.

Stoltman, J. P. (1991). Research on geography teaching. In J. P. Shaver (Ed.), *Handbook of research on social studies teaching and learning* (pp. 437–447). New York: Macmillan.

Stone, L. (1991). Intercultural and multicultural education: In V. A. Atwood (Ed.), *Elementary school social studies: Research as a guide to practice* (pp. 34–54). Washington, DC: National Council for the Social Studies.

Strang, R. (1958). *Group work in education.* New York: Harper.

Stull, A. T., & Ryder, R. J. (1999). *Education on the Internet: A student's guide.* Upper Saddle River, NJ: Merrill/Prentice Hall.

Suchman, R. (1962). *The elementary school training program in scientific inquiry: Report to the U.S. Office of Education Project Title VII, Project 216.* Urbana: University of Illinois.

Suchman, R. (1966). *Inquiry development program: Developing inquiry.* Chicago: Science Research Associates.

Swearingen, J. (1996). Promoting tolerance in preservice teachers. *Social Education, 60,* 152–154.

Switzer, T. (1986). Teaching sociology in K–12 classrooms. In S. Wronski & D. Bragaw (Eds.), *Social studies and social sciences: A 50-year perspective* (pp. 124–138). Washington, DC: National Council for the Social Studies.

Symcox, L. (2002). *Whose history? The struggle for national standards in American classrooms.* New York: Teachers College Press.

Taba, H. (1967). *Teachers' handbook for elementary social studies.* Palo Alto, CA: Addison-Wesley.

Taylor, H. E., & Larson, S. (1998). Using cooperative learning activities with students who have attention deficit learning disorder. *Social Studies and the Young Learner, 10*(4), pp. 1–4.

Taylor, H. E., & Larson, S. M. (2000). Teaching elementary social studies to students with mild disabilities. *Social Education, 64,* 232–235.

Teachers Curriculum Institute. (1995). *History alive!* Mountain View, CA: Author.

Thelan, H. (1960). *Education and the human quest.* New York: Harper & Row.

Thornton, S. J., & Vukelich, R. (1988). Effects of children's understanding of time concepts on historical understanding. *Theory and Research in Social Education, 16,* 69–82.

Tibbett, T. (2004). Listen to learn: Using American music to teach language arts and social studies. San Francisco: Jossey-Bass.

Tierney, R. J., & Readance, J. E. (2005). *Reading strategies and practices: A compendium* (6th ed.). Boston: Allyn & Bacon.

Tomlinson, C. A. (2001). *How to differentiate instruction in mixed abilities classrooms* (2nd ed.). Alexandria VA: Association for Supervision and Curriculum Development.

Tomlinson, C. A. (2003). *Fulfilling the promise of differentiated classrooms: Strategies and tools for responsive teaching.* Alexandria VA: Association for Supervision and Curriculum Development.

Trifonoff, K. M. (1997). Introducing thematic maps in the primary grades. *Social Studies and the Young Learner, 11*(1), 17–22.

Trueba, H. T. (1989). *Raising silent voices: Educating the linguistic minorities of the 21st century.* New York: Newbury House.

Tunnell, M. O. (1993). *The story of ourselves: Teaching history through children's literature.* Portsmouth, NH: Heinemann.

Tunnell, M. O., & Ammon, R. (1996). The story of ourselves: Fostering multiple historical perspectives. *Social Education, 60,* 212–215.

Turnbull, A., Turnbull, R., & Wehmeyer, M. L. (2007). *Exceptional lives: Special education in today's schools* (5th ed.). Upper Saddle River NJ: Pearson/Merrill/Prentice Hall.

Turner, T. N., & Hickey, G. M. (1991). Using radio tapes to teach about the past. *Social Studies and the Young Learner, 3*(4), 6–8.

Tye, K. E. (Ed.). (1990). *Global education.* Alexandria, VA: Association for Supervision and Curriculum Development.

Tyson, C. A. & Hinton-Johnson, K. (2003). Once upon a time: Teaching about women and social justice through literature. *Social Education, 67,* 54–57.

Ukpodoku, O. M. (2002). Multiculturalism and critical thinking. *Social Studies and the Young Learner, 14*(4), 20–23.

U.S. Department of Education. (1991). *America 2000: An education strategy.* Washington, DC: Author. (ERIC Document Reproduction No. ED 327 009).

VanFossen, P. (Ed.). (1998). Economics in elementary schools [Special issue]. *Social Studies and the Young Learner, 11*(2).

VanFossen, P. J. (2003a). Best practice economics education for young children? It's elementary. *Social Education, 67,* 90–94.

VanFossen, P. J. (2003b). Using literature circles to teach about immigration. *Social Studies and the Young Learner, 15*(4), 24–29.

VanFossen, P. J. (2004a). Past meets future: Social studies on the Internet [Special issue]. *Social Studies and the Young Learner, 16*(4).

VanFossen, P. J. (2004b). Using WebQuests to scaffold higher-order thinking. *Social Studies and the Young Learner, 16*(4), 13–16.

Van Sledright, B. A. (2002a). Confronting history's interpretive paradox while teaching fifth graders to investigate the past. *American Educational Research Journal, 39,* 1089–1115.

Van Sledright, B. A. (2002b). In search of America's past: Learning to read history in elementary school. New York: Teachers College Press.

Van Sledright, B. A. (2004). What does it mean to think historically . . . and how do you teach it? *Social Education, 68,* 230–233.

Van't Hooft, M. & Kelly, J. (2004). Macro or micro: Teaching fifth grade economics using handheld computers. *Social Education, 68,* 165–168.

Vardell, S. M. (2003). Poetry for social studies: Poems, standards, and strategies. *Social Education, 64,* 206–211.

Vermette, P. J. (1998). *Making cooperative learning work: Student teams in K–12 classrooms.* Upper Saddle River, NJ: Merrill/Prentice Hall.

Vygotsky, L. S. (1962). *Thought and language* (E. Hanfmann & G. Fakar, Trans.). Cambridge, MA: MIT Press. (Original work published 1934)

Wade, R. C. (1993). Content analysis of social studies textbooks: A review of 10 years of research. *Theory and Research in Social Education, 21,* 232–256.

Wade, R. C. (1994). Community service-learning. *Social Studies and the Young Learner, 6*(3) pp. 1–4.

Wade, R. C. (2000). Beyond charity: Service learning for social justice. *Social Studies and the Young Learner, 12*(4), 6–9.

Wade, R. C., & Everett, S. (1994). Civic participation in third-grade social studies textbooks. *Social Education, 58,* 308–311.

Walbert, K. (2004). How to do it: Oral history projects. *Social Studies and the Young Learner, 16*(4), pullout sections.

Wallace, B. (2005). Teaching thinking skills across the primary curriculum. London: David Fulton.

Walsh, H. M. (Ed.). (1992). Dealing with stereotypes and prejudices [Special issue]. *Social Studies and the Young Learner, 5*(2).

Warren, C. C. (2006). Viewing American history through Native eyes: Ideas for sharing a different perspective. *Social Studies and the Young Learner, 18*(4), 15–18.

Wasta, S., & Scott, M. (1998). Building bridges to China. *Social Studies and the Young Learner, 11*(1), 6–10.

Webeck, M. L., Black, M. S., Davis, O. L., & Field, S. (2002). Both sides of the classroom door: After 9–11, the many facets of teaching. *Social Studies and the Young Learner, 14*(3), 6–9.

Wentworth, D. R., & Schug, M. C. (1994). How to use an economic mystery in your history course. *Social Education, 58,* 10–12.

Westheimer, J. & Kahne, J. (2004). What kind of citizen? The politics of educating for democracy. *American Educational Research Journal, 41,* 237–269.

Whelan, M. (1996). Right for the wrong reasons. *Social Education, 60,* 55–57.

White, J. J. (1988). Searching for substantial knowledge in social studies texts. *Theory and Research in Social Education, 16,* 115–140.

White, J. J. (1989). Anthropology. In *Charting a course: Social studies for the 21st century* (pp. 31–36). Washington, DC: National Commission on Social Studies in the Schools.

Wieseman, K. C., & Caldwell, D. (2005). Local history and problem-based learning. *Social Studies and the Young Learner, 18*(1), 11–14.

Wiggins, G. (1989). A true test: Toward more equitable assessment. *Phi Delta Kappan, 70,* 703–713.

Wiggins, G. (1992). Creating tests worth taking. *Educational Leadership, 49*(8), 26–33.

Wiggins, G. (1993). *Assessing student performance.* San Francisco: Jossey-Bass.

Wiggins, G. (1998). *Educative assessment: Designing assessments to inform and improve student performance.* San Francisco: Jossey-Bass.

Wiggins, G. (1999). Assessing student performance: Exploring the purpose and limits of testing. San Francisco: Jossey-Bass.

Wilen, W. W. (2004). Encouraging reticent students' participation in classroom discussions. *Social Education, 68,* 51–56.

Wilen, W. W., & Phillips, J. A. (1995). Teaching critical thinking: A metacognitive approach. *Social Education, 59,* 135–138.

Wilen, W. W., & White, J. J. (1991). Interaction and discourse in social studies classrooms. In J. P. Shaver (Ed.), *Handbook of research on social studies teaching and learning* (pp. 483–495). New York: Macmillan.

Wilhelm, R. W. (Ed.). (1999). Multiculturalism in the classroom [Special issue]. *Social Studies and the Young Learner, 11*(3).

Wilkie, R. (Ed.). (1993). *Environmental education teacher resource handbook.* Milwood, NY: Kraus.

Willison, S., & Ruane, P. (1995). Promoting acceptance of diversity and service to others. *The Social Studies, 86,* 91–92.

Wilson, E. K., Rice, M. L., Bagley, W., & Rice, M. K. (2001). Virtual field trips and newsrooms: International technology into the classroom. *Social Education, 64,* 152–155.

Wilton, S. (1993). New biographies are "better than before." In M. Zarnowski & A. F. Gallagher (Eds.), *Children's literature and social studies: Selecting notable books in the classroom* (pp. 16–19). Washington, DC: National Council for the Social Studies.

Winitzky, N. E. (1991). Classroom organization for social studies. In J. P. Shaver (Ed.), *Handbook of research on social studies teaching and learning* (pp. 530–549). New York: Macmillan.

Wise, N., & Kon, J. H. (1990). Assessing geographic knowledge with sketch maps. *Journal of Geography, 89,* 123–129.

Wolfgang, C. H., & Kelsay, K. L. (1995). Discipline and the social studies classroom, Grades K–12. *The Social Studies, 86,* 175–182.

Wright, I. (1995). Making critical thinking possible: Options for teachers. *Social Education, 59,* 139–143.

Wyner, N. B., & Farquhar, E. (1991). Cognitive, emotional, and social development: Early childhood social studies. In J. P. Shaver (Ed.), *Handbook of research on social studies teaching and learning* (pp. 109–120). New York: Macmillan.

Yeich, C. (2002). Using newspapers to teach about the election: A lesson plan. *Social Education, 66,* 381–383.

Yell, M. M. (1998). The time before history: Thinking like an archaeologist. *Social Education, 62*(1), 27–31.

Yell, M. M. (2002). Inquiry with an E-book: A natural strategy for social studies. *Social Education, 66,* 184–185.

Yell, M. M., Scheurman, G., & Reynolds, K. (2004). *A link to the past: Engaging students in the study of history.* Silver Springs, MD: National Council for the Social Studies.

Yopp, H. K., & Yopp, R. H. (1996). *Literature-based reading activities.* Boston: Allyn & Bacon.

Young, K. A. (1994). *Constructing buildings, bridges, and minds: Building an integrated curriculum through social studies.* Portsmouth, NH: Heinemann.

Young, T. A., & Vardell, S. (1993). Weaving readers' theater and nonfiction into the curriculum. *The Reading Teacher, 46,* 396–406.

Zarnowski, M. (1990). *Learning about biographies: A reading and writing approach for children.* Urbana, IL: National Council of Teachers of English.

Zarnowski, M., & Gallagher, A. F. (Eds.). (1993). *Children's literature and social studies: Selecting and using notable books in the classroom.* Washington, DC: National Council for the Social Studies.

Zarrillo, J. (1989). History and library books. *Social Studies and the Young Learner, 2*(2), 17–19.

Zarrillo, J. (1994). *Multicultural literature, multicultural teaching: Units for the elementary grades.* Fort Worth, TX: Harcourt Brace.

Author Index

Accrosi, W., 238
Adams, D. M., 199
Adler, D., 72
Adler, S., 10, 11, 20
Adreasen, Dan, 121
Ahern, J. F., 236, 237, 239
Akenson, J. E., 14, 341
Alibrandi, M., 61
Alleman, Janet, 66, 100, 199, 252, 262, 266, 330
Allen, R. F., 99
Alter, G., 11, 236
Alvi, K., 13, 20, 39
American Forum for Global Education, 347
Ammon, R., 243
Amster, Marsha, 69–70
Anand, B., 61
Ancess, J., 199
Ancona, George, 112, 119
Andel, M. A., 327
Anderson, C., 260, 263
Angell, R. C., 335
Armento, B. J., 329, 330
Aronson, E., 130
Arthur, S. V., 228
Association for Supervision and Curriculum Development (ASCD), 99, 347
Atkin, S. Beth, 59, 60
Atwood, V. A., 7
Au, K. H., 37, 38, 216, 231
Aucoin, L., 348
Austin, G., 92
Austin, J., 261
Avi, 298
Azwell, T. S., 130

Bach, G. L., 331
Bagley, W., 179
Bahir-Ali, K., 39, 73
Bahmueller, C. F., 241, 243, 260, 265, 272, 274, 279
Baker, Olaf, 100, 101
Banks, C. A. M., 35, 36, 56, 66, 264
Banks, J. A., 13, 27, 35, 36, 56, 66, 264
Barnes, B. R., 325
Barnum, Jay Hyde, 121
Barr, J. B., 4, 20
Barron, R. F., 226
Barss, K., 74

Barth, J., 4, 5, 22
Bartoletti, S. C., 238
Barton, Bryon, 119
Barton, Keith, 289, 290–291, 295, 313
Baum, C. G., 335
Baylor, Byrd, 354
Beal, C., 61
Beaty, J. J., 237
Beck, I. L., 224, 225, 295, 298, 313
Bell, K., 279
Bennett, L., 260, 278
Benniga, J. S., 279
Bernard, C., 33, 114, 117, 119
Bernard-Powers, J., 16
Berson, I. R., 69, 73, 174
Berson, M. J., 69, 73, 158, 174, 178, 189
Berti, A. E., 262, 330
Bestor, A., 20
Beyer, B. K., 149, 150, 241
Bickmore, K., 277
Bigelow, W., 238
Bisland, B. M., 161
Bjorklun, E. C., 261, 279
Black, M. S., 69, 347
Black, P., 248
Blaney, N., 130
Bloom, Benjamin, 87–88, 98, 150
Boehm, R. G., 304
Boggs, S. T., 37
Bolick, C. M., 189, 314
Bombi, A. S., 330
Bondy, E., 276
Bourne, Anne, 71
Bower, B., 314
Boykin, A. W., 37
Bradford, William, 296
Brandt, R., 199, 201
Braun, J. A., 158
Breidenstein, A., 347
Brenner, Barbara, 71
Broderick, J., 73
Brookhart, S. M., 199, 201, 221
Brophy, J., 9, 66, 82, 100, 142, 149, 199, 252, 262, 266, 276, 289, 290, 313, 330
Brown, A. L., 230
Brown, Drollene, 69
Brown, Marcia, 121
Brown, Margaret W., 296–297
Bruner, Jerome, 8–9, 92, 142
Bunting, Eve, 240, 354

Burgstahler, S., 174, 186
Burroughs, S., 208
Burstein, J. H., 56
Burton, V., 334
Butler, R., 347

Cadwell, D., 161
Calderwood, J. D., 331
Calhoun, E., 85, 148, 153
California Department of Education, 16, 38, 172, 223
Camperell, K., 224, 230
Cangemi, J., 348
Caplan, N. S., 48
Cardis, R. J., 9
Carlson, H. L., 161
Carlson, Nancy L., 121
Carnegie Corporation of New York, 260
Carrol, R. F., 327
Carter, Katherine, 119
Case, R., 340, 341
Castaneda, A., 37
Cazden, C., 350
Center for Civic Education, 11, 216, 259, 260, 261, 265, 266, 268–269, 271, 272, 278, 279, 280, 282
Center for Information and Research on Civic Learning and Engagement, 260
Chandra, Deborah, 72
Chang, J., 276
Charles, C., 344
Charney, R. S., 279
Cherry, L., 162, 345
Chick, K. A., 73
Children's Book Council, 237
Choi, Sook Nyul, 59, 60
Choi, Yangsook, 354
Choy, M. H., 48
Christensen, L. M., 252
Clapp, P., 70
Clarke, J. H., 162
Cleaver, E., 240
Clements, H. M., 161
Clifton, Lucille, 354
Cobb, R. L., 302
Cohen, I. S., 335
Cohen, R., 313
Colby, S., 252
Collins, H. T., 340, 347

Comora, Madeline, 72
Cook, M. L., 158
Cook, Nick, 119
Coombs, Roy, 119
Cooney, Barbara, 121, 317
Cooper, B. L., 158
Cooter, R. B., 229, 232
Cordier, M. H., 240
Corriveau, D., 240
Cort, H. R., 20
Council for the Advancement
        of Citizenship, 265
Cox, A. R., 240, 348
Cox, C., 71, 252
Cox, C. B., 142, 143, 161
Cremin, L., 7, 66, 93
Crews, Donald, 60, 354
Crocco, M. S., 20, 73
Crowell, S. M., 264
Cruz, B., 31, 47
Cruz, B. C., 174
Cuban, L., 20
Cullinan, B. E., 236
Cummins, James, 26, 29, 31–35,
        47, 160, 322
Cunningham, J. W., 228
Cunningham, P. M., 228
Curtis, C. K., 48
Curtis-Seinek, C., 279
Cushman, K., 239, 241
Czarra, F. R., 340
Czartoski, S., 68

Danziger, K., 330
Darling-Hammond, L., 199
D'Aulaire, Edgar Parin, 238
D'Aulaire, Ingri, 238
Davies, Karin, 264
Davis, O. L., 20, 61, 69
De Avila, Edward, 136
Delaney, M., 179, 180
Delisle, J. R., 48
De Paola, Tomie, 60
Dever, M. T., 73
Dewey, John, 7, 20, 66, 142, 147
Diaz, C. F., 341
Diaz-Rico, L. T., 35
Dimmitt, J. P., 243
Dockterman, D. A., 182
Dodge, B., 179
Doorlag, D. H., 27, 40, 45
Dorris, Michael, 299
Dorros, Arthur, 26, 354
Dougan, A., 4
Douglass, M. P., 7, 301, 302, 314
Dow, P. B., 8, 20
Downey, M. T., 289, 290, 313

Downey, P., 190, 191
Downs, R., 303
Drier, H. S., 162
Duncan, Sharon, 136
Dunn, R. E., 10
Duplass, J. A., 174

Easterly, Jean, 348
Echevarria, J., 13, 35
Edgington, W. D., 148
Edwards, A. C., 20, 93, 100
Eggen, Paul, 99, 143, 148, 152,
        154–156
Eisner, E., 5, 247
Ekiss, G. O., 10
Elfin, A. M., 69
Ellington, L., 5, 10, 20, 224, 241, 263
Elnour, A., 39, 73
Ember, C. R., 35
Ember, M., 35
Engle, S. H., 6, 9, 19, 20, 99, 260,
        264, 269–271
Engstrom, L., 331
Environmental Education
        Network, 348
Epstein, J., 38, 291
Erickson, J., 279
Erickson, L., 298
Estes, T. H., 99
Evans, M. D., 243
Evans, R. W., 4, 5, 7, 9
Everett, S., 262

Falk, B., 199
Feinberg, J., 279
Felton, R. G., 99
Fenton, E., 6, 9
Fernlund, P. F., 264
Fertig, G., 73
Feyten, Carine, 31, 47
Field, L., 252
Field, S., 16, 69, 239, 260, 298
Fielder, W. R., 161
Finchum, M., 82
Firek, H., 241, 243
Fisher, A., 150
Fitzpatrick, C., 13, 174
Flack, Marjorie, 121
Flemmer, L. A., 61
Flournoy, Valerie, 339, 354
Foncault, P., 136
Forbes, E., 298
Forsythe, A. S., 302
Foster, S. J., 13
Foundation for Teaching
        Economics, 330
Foyle, H. C., 130

Fraenkel, J. R., 16
Frank, Anne, 60
Freedman, R., 81, 100, 101, 106, 238
Freeman, E. B., 236
Freeman, Marcia, 119
Freese, J. R., 304
Friedman, I. R., 298, 354
Fritz, Jean, 71, 299

Gallagher, A. F., 236, 239, 298
Gallenstein, N. L., 147
Gandy, S. K., 267
Garcia, E., 35, 66
Gardner, Howard, 22, 247, 318
Garrod, A., 279
Garson, E., 96, 297
Garza, Carmen Lomas, 60, 354
Gavrish, M. J. A., 316, 317
Gay, G., 35, 37, 48, 56
Geography Education National
        Implementation Project
        (GENIP), 304
Geography Education Standards
        Project, 11, 102, 214, 301,
        304, 311, 320
Gersmehl, P., 301, 302, 314
Gerstein, M., 239
Gibbons, Gail, 31, 113, 120
Gilligan, C., 279
Gilliland, H., 39
Gilstrap, R. L., 224, 241
Giorgis, C., 314
Global Education Network, 347
Goble, Paul, 100, 101, 240, 252, 255–256
Goldstein, P., 50
Goodman, J., 276
Goodnow, J., 92
Govoni, Jane, 31, 47
Grabe, C., 178
Grabe, M., 178
Grant, S. G., 10, 278
Graves, A., 13, 35
Gray, P. S., 335
Greenbaum, P. E., 37
Greenstein, F. I., 262
Gregg, M., 301, 302, 303, 314
Gregory, D., 327
Gregory, L. A., 162
Grifalconi, Ann, 354
Griffith, B., 4
Groce, E. C., 252
Groce, R. D., 252
Gronlund, N. E., 87, 99
Grossman, H., 37
Guberman, S., 28, 47
Guisbond, L., 10
Gunter, M. A., 99

Haas, M. E., 267, 275, 314
Hackwell, W. John, 327
Hale-Benson, J. E., 48
Hall, D., 248, 298, 317
Hallam, Roy, 290
Hamm, M. E., 199
Handley, L. M., 11
Hanna, Paul, 14
Hansen, W. L., 331
Hanvey, R. G., 340
Harmin, M., 279
Harms, J. M., 299
Hartford, John, 120
Hartman, K. G., 314
Hartoonian, H. M., 20
Harvey, Brett, 96, 297
Harwood, A. M., 276
Hautzig, Esther, 60
Havill, Juanita, 354
Hawkins, M. L., 14, 341
Hayman, W. C., 48
Heath, J. A., 273
Heath, S. B., 37
Heimlich, J. A., 228
Hembacher, D., 333, 334
Herlihy, J. G., 20
Hertzberg, H. W., 7
Hess, Diana, 245
Hesse, K., 239
Hickey, G. M., 61, 63, 68, 73, 158
Hickey, M. G., 48
Hicks, K., 261
Hightshoe, Susan, 327, 328
Hinde, E. R., 10, 224
Hinton-Johnson, K., 73, 252
Hirshfield, C., 62, 64
Hittleman, C. G., 74
Hittleman, D. R., 74
Hodges, Margaret, 21
Hoge, J. D., 13, 260, 261, 262
Hollins, E. R., 35, 39, 48
Holm, C., 161
Holubec, E. J., 133
Hoone, C., 300
Hoover, R. L., 276, 277, 279
Houston, J., 240
Howard, R. W., 10
Hoyt-Goldsmith, Diane, 240
Huerta, G. C., 61
Humble, R., 33, 114, 120
Hunter, Madeline, 89, 90, 99
Hutton, L., 56
Huynh, Quang Nhuoug, 59, 60
Hyman, Trina Schart, 354

Ichord, L. F., 96
Imeson, J., 348

Inhelder, B., 302
Inkpen, T. D., 20
Irvin, J. L., 224

Jaffee, C., 39, 73
Jahoda, G., 330
Jantz, R. K., 325, 335
Jenness, D., 7
Jennings, T. E., 264
Johnson, Caleb, 163
Johnson, D. D., 228
Johnson, D. W., 125, 126, 132–133, 136
Johnson, F. P., 126, 132, 133
Johnson, Roger T., 125, 126, 132–133, 136
Johnston, J. H., 174
Joint Committee on Geographic Education, 305
Joint Council on Economic Education, 331
Jones, R. C., 225
Joyce, B. R., 85, 92, 99, 148, 153

Kadohata, C., 298
Kagan, Spencer, 125, 131, 136, 337
Kahne, J., 260
Kallo, J., 189
Kalman, Maira, 120
Kamdar, N., 347
Kauchak, D., 99, 143, 148, 152, 154–156
Kawakami, A. J., 37
Kay, Verla, 121
Keats, Ezra Jack, 26, 354
Keech, A. M., 279
Keiper, T. A., 162
Kellough, R. D., 16
Kelly, J., 347
Kelsay, K. L., 276
Kenney, R., 279
Kentley, Eric, 120
Kerckhoff, A. C., 134
Kerley, Barbara, 354
Kilpatrick, William H., 6, 125
Kindsvatter, R., 276, 277, 279
King, J. E., 48
Kirp, D. L., 89
Kirschenbaum, H., 279
Kleg, M., 37
Knapp, M., 130
Kniep, Willard, 340
Knight, Christopher G., 120
Knight, R. S., 224, 230
Kochman, T., 48
Koeller, S., 243
Koeppen, K. E., 278

Kohlberg, L., 279
Kolterman, D. L., 61, 73
Kourilsky, Marilyn, 329, 331
Krasavage, E. M., 89
Krashen, Stephen, 26, 29, 30, 34–35, 47
Krey, D. M., 237
Krudop, Walter Lyon, 120
Krull, K., 297
Kurjian, J., 334
Kurtz-Costes, B., 13, 37

LaComb, S., 188, 252
Ladson-Billings, Gloria, 37, 39, 337
Lamme, L. L., 347
Lamy, S. L., 340
Landorf, H., 130
Laney, J. D., 325
Langer, J. A., 226
Lankiewicz, D., 158
Lapham, S. S., 225
Larkins, A. G., 14, 341
Larson, B. E., 162, 251
Larson, S. M., 48, 136
Lasky, Kathryn, 120
Laughlin, M., 248
Lechner, J. V., 238
Ledford, C. C., 267
Lee, J. K., 162, 175, 188
Leeming, J., 116
Leinhardt, G., 301, 302, 303, 313, 314
Leming, J. S., 5, 10, 20, 224, 241, 263
LeRiche, L. W., 14
Lester, Julius, 58, 60
Lettow, L. J., 299
Levine, Ellen, 59, 60
Levstik, Linda, 289, 290–291, 295, 298, 313
Lewis, R. B., 27, 40, 45
Liben, L., 303
Lickona, T., 279
Liten-Tejada, R. A., 69
Little Soldier, L., 325
Lobdell, J., 314
Loberg, M., 248
Loeb, R. H., 67
Loeper, John, 71
Lord, Bette Bao, 60, 61
Losey, K. M., 37
Lou, Y., 134
Lowenstein, E., 130
Lowry, Lois, 240, 299
Loxterman, J. A., 295
Lubliner, Shira, 230, 252
Lybarger, M., 7
Lyman, F. T., 130
Lyman, L., 130
Lyon, A., 267

Macauley, David, 117, 120
MacLaughlin, P., 298
Mager, R. F., 87, 99
Mahood, W., 248
Mahrer, C., 69, 70
Main, M., 240, 348
Mandeville, G. K., 89
Marchand-Martella, N. E., 89
Martella, R. C., 89
Martorella, P. H., 230
Maruyama, G., 126
Massialas, B. G., 142, 143, 161,
     340, 341
Mayhew, K. C., 20, 93, 100
McCabe, P. P., 252
McCall, A. L., 339
McClure, A., 237
McCormick, T. M., 69, 74
McCracken, H., 101
McGovern, A., 71
McGowan, M. J., 298
McGowan, T. M., 236, 298,
     313–314
McKeown, M. G., 224, 225, 295
McKissack, Patricia, 60
McLaughlin, B., 30
McMillen, G., 37
Mehaffy, G., 61
Mehlinger, H. D., 69, 73
Meister, C., 230
Meltzer, Milton, 59, 60, 70, 72
Merryfield, M., 73, 340, 347
Mezaros, B., 331
Miel, Alice, 136, 147
Millard, A., 314
Miller, Brandon, 71
Miller, F., 61
Miller, J. W., 303
Miller, Montazalee, 354
Milmore, Mark, 53
Milson, A. J., 188, 191, 252
Mintz, S. L., 99
Miran, K., 50
Mitchell, B., 223
Mohan, R., 47
Molebash, P., 143, 179
Molloy, Anne Stearns, 121
Monk, Isabel, 354
Montone, C. L., 69
Moore, A. W., 238
Moore, Kay, 71
Morin, J. A., 348
Morris, Ann, 354
Morris, R. V., 275, 280, 327
Morrison, Velma, 327
Moseley, L., 325
Mosher, R., 279

Moss, J., 26, 339
Myers, Walter Dean, 60

Nabakov, Peter, 59, 60
Nadel, Marc, 121
Nash, G. B., 10
National Association of Economic
     Educators, 330
National Center for Education
     Statistics, 29
National Center for History in the
     Schools, 11, 74, 192, 200,
     291, 294, 314
National Council for the Social
     Studies (NCSS), 11, 22, 23
   Ad Hoc Committee on Ability
        Grouping, 134
   Ad Hoc Committee on Global
        Education, 340
   citizenship education, 263, 279
   data collection, 202–208
   diversity, 49
   economics, 331, 348–349
   global education, 341
   history and geography, 313, 319
   instructional organization, 107
   integrated curriculum, 237
   psychology and sociology, 335, 337
   record keeping, 211
   Select Subcommittee, 274
   Task Force on Early
        Childhood/Elementary Social
        Studies, 18
   Task Force on Ethnic Studies
        Curriculum Guidelines, 36,
        261, 326, 327
   Task Force on Revitalizing
        Citizenship Education, 5
   Task Force on Scope and
        Sequence, 18, 150
   Task Force on Standards for
        Teaching and Learning in the
        Social Studies, 4, 93, 260
   technology, 173
   Website, 19
National Council on Economic
     Education, 11, 169, 330, 331,
     332, 347
National Institute of Child Health
     and Development, 230
Natoli, S. J., 304
Navarette, Cecelia, 136
Neill, M., 10
Nelson, D., 126
Nelson, M. R., 325, 335
Nelson, P., 252
Neufeld, J. A., 298

Neufeld, P., 230
New, C. A., 38
Newmann, Fred, 152–153
Nickell, P., 199, 221
Nitko, A. J., 199, 201, 221
Norman, H. A., 240
North American Association for
     Environmental Education, 348
Norton, D. E., 237
Norton, J., 261, 282, 284
Norton, S. E., 237
Nutta, Joyce, 31, 47

Oakes, J., 134
O'Brien, Jason, 31, 47
Ochoa, A. S., 6, 19, 20, 99, 260,
     264, 269–271
Ochoa-Becker, A. S., 20
O'Dell, S., 298
Ofinoski, Steven, 114, 120
Ogle, D., 95, 226
Okada, D., 333
Oliver, E. I., 35
Olmedo, I. M., 61, 62
Olney, Ross R., 120
Olsen, D. G., 150
Ovoian, G., 327
Owen, R. C., 327
Oyler, C., 179, 180

Paley, V. G., 48
Palincsar, A. S., 230
Park, L. S., 239, 298
Parker, Francis W., 7, 66
Parker, W. C., 149, 162, 272
Pascopella, A., 10
Passe, J., 327, 346
Passe, M., 327
Patrick, Diane, 237
Patrick, J. J., 260, 261, 262
Pearson, P. D., 228
Peel, E. A., 290
Penner, L. R., 67
Perez-Stable, M. A., 240
Person, D. G., 236
Peskowitz, N., 20
Petersen, J. F., 304
Pezone, M., 48
Phillips, J. A., 150
Phillips, S. U., 37
Phipps, S., 10, 20
Piaget, Jean, 290, 302
Pittelman, S. D., 228
Polacco, Patricia, 354
Porter-Magee, K., 5, 10, 20, 263
Potter, L. A., 162, 278, 296, 313
Powe, F., 57, 100

Powell, J. H., 298
Pratt, L., 237
Proctor, D. R., 275
Pungello, E. P., 13, 37

Qin, Z., 126
Quigley, C. N., 241, 243, 260, 265, 272, 274, 279

Rachlis, E., 100, 101, 106
Rader, W., 347
Rakitin, Sarah, 121
Rallis, D. N., 301
Rallis, H., 301
Ralston, M. E., 174
Ramirez, M., 37
Rand, Gloria, 120
Rand, Ted, 120
Raphael, T. E., 231
Raposo, J., 26, 339
Rappaport, D., 237
Raths, L. E., 279
Readance, J. E., 225, 229, 230, 232
Reiss, Johanna, 60
Reutzel, D. R., 229, 232
Reynolds, K., 313
Reynolds, Malvina, 26, 339
Rhoades, L., 346
Ricchiuti, L., 146
Rice, M. J., 302
Rice, M. K., 179
Rice, M. L., 179
Richard-Amato, P., 47
Richardson, T., 333
Risinger, C. F., 9, 175, 179
Ritchie, D. A., 61
Rivers, J. L., 89
Roberts, P. L., 224, 251
Rockwell, A. F., 71
Rodriguez, H. M., 28, 47
Rong, X. L., 48
Rosenblum, Richard, 120
Rosenshine, B., 230
Ross, D. D., 276
Rossi, J. A., 246
Rothwell, Jennifer Turan, 100
Ruane, P., 275
Ruddell, M. R., 229
Ruggiero, V. R., 150
Rule, A. C., 158
Rulli, D., 143
Rushdoony, H. A., 302
Ryder, R. J., 189

Sahr, D. E., 100
St. George, J., 71, 239
Salinas, C., 28, 47

Sanchez, Tony, 238
Sandmann, A., 73, 236, 237, 239, 252
San Souci, Robert, 354
Santella, A., 240
Saunders, P., 33
Saxe, D., 7, 10
Say, Allen, 26, 60, 61, 252, 253–254, 354
Scarry, Huck, 120
Schaffarzick, J., 8
Schanzer, R., 70
Scheurman, G., 313
Schimmel, D., 276, 277
Schneider, E., 162
Schug, M. C., 5, 10, 20, 224, 241, 329, 330, 332, 333
Schwartz, S., 68
Scott, Geoffrey, 121
Scott, Margaret, 48
Segal, A., 314
Seikaly, Z. A., 13, 20, 39
Selwyn, D., 224, 243, 247, 248, 249, 279
Senesh, Lawrence, 331
Shade, B. J., 37, 38
Shafer, F., 136, 189
Shaftel, F., 248
Shaftel, G., 248
Sharan, Shlomo, 143, 147
Sharan, Yael, 143, 147
Shaver, J. P., 19
Sheehan, J. J., 40
Shermis, S., 4
Shiller, T., 38, 291
Shiveley, J. M., 162, 175
Short, D., 13, 35, 66, 69, 70
Sibit, S. A., 40
Sikes, J., 130
Simmons, D., 344
Simon, S. B., 279
Simpson, M., 13, 69, 173, 189, 313, 340
Sinatra, G. M., 295
Sincero, P., 73
Singer, A., 48
Singer, J. Y., 252
Singleton, L., 69, 314
Sitton, G., 61
Skamp, K. R., 348
Skon, L., 126
Slavin, R. E., 89, 125, 126, 129, 134, 136
Slocum, T. A., 89
Sloyer, S., 248
Smagorinsky, P., 261, 279
Smiler, H., 39

Smith, A. F., 340
Smitherman, G., 48
Snow, M. A., 47
Social Science Education Consortium, 314
Soley, M., 346
Sorenson, B., 73
Soto, Gary, 240, 354
Speare, E. G., 282, 284, 298
Spencer, K., 39
Spier, Peter, 114, 121
Spies, P., 10, 289
Stahl, R. J., 134, 136, 325, 335
Stallings, J., 89
Stanley, Diane, 162, 238
Stanley, W. B., 263
Stanton, C., 313
Stearns, L., 189
Steele, M. M., 40
Stephen, C., 130
Stephens, B., 71
Steptoe, John, 354
Sternberg, R. J., 162
Stetson, Emily, 121
Stevens, R., 69
Stewart, L., 237
Stiggins, R. J., 200
Stokes, S. M., 39, 116
Stoltman, J. P., 301, 302
Stone, L., 37
Strang, Ruth, 136
Stull, A. T., 189
Suchman, R., 143, 148, 162–165
Sullivan, George, 121
Sunal, C. S., 158
Swain, R. F., 237
Swearingen, J., 348
Switzer, T., 335
Symcox, L., 10

Taba, Hilda, 16, 17, 100, 152, 153–154
Tabachnick, B. R., 161
Taylor, H. E., 48, 136
Teachers Curriculum Institute, 314
Terrell, T. D., 30
Thelan, H., 147
Thimmesh, Catherine, 223
Thompson, A., 61
Thornton, S. J., 290
Tibbett, T., 247, 252
Tierney, R. J., 225, 229, 230, 232
Tomlinson, C. A., 13, 28, 40
Trifonoff, Karen, 303, 312
Tunis, E., 33, 67, 96, 114, 121
Tunnell, M. O., 236, 243
Turkle, Brinton, 298, 299, 354
Turnbull, A., 27, 40, 45

Turnbull, R., 27, 40, 45
Turner, T. N., 158
Tye, K. E., 340
Tyson, C. A., 73, 252

Uchida, Yoshiko, 60, 61, 354
Ukpodoku, O. M., 162
U.S. Census Bureau, 29, 155
Updike, John, 354
Utterback, L., 174, 186

Van Allsburg, Chris, 121
Van Cleaf, D. W., 243
VanFossen, P. J., 13, 73, 173, 174,
        179, 189, 329, 347
Van Scotter, R., 20
VanSickle, R. L., 134, 136
Van Sledright, B., 9, 278, 289, 298, 313
Van't Hooft, M., 347
Van Tol, Roger, 121
Vardell, S., 248, 252
Vaughn, M., 339
Vennema, Peter, 238
Vermette, P. J., 135, 136
Vik, P., 273
Vogt, M., 13, 35
Vukelich, R., 290
Vygotsky, Lev, 34, 126–127

Wade, R. C., 224, 262, 275, 276, 279
Walbert, K., 61

Wallace, B., 150
Wallner, A., 71
Walsh, H. M., 335
Walstad, W. B., 329, 330
Warren, C. C., 73
Warren, Mercy Otis, 71
Wasta, Stephanie, 48
Waters, K., 67
Watson-Gegeo, K., 37
Webeck, M. L., 69, 73
Weed, K. Z., 35
Wehmeyer, M. L., 27, 40, 45
Weil, M., 85, 148, 153
Wentworth, D. R., 333
Western, R. D., 329
Westheimer, J., 260
Whelan, M., 313
White, J. J., 142, 224, 325, 326
White, L. A., 237
Whitmore, J. K., 48
Wibberly, Leonard, 71
Wieseman, K. C., 161
Wiggins, G., 199, 201
Wilder, Laura Ingalls, 96
Wilen, W. W., 142, 150, 245, 251
Wilhelm, R. W., 13, 240, 348
Wilkie, R., 344
Williams, Sherley Anne, 354
Williams, Vera B., 22, 354
Willison, S., 275
Wilson, A., 61

Wilson, E. K., 179
Wilton, S., 238
Winitzkey, Nancy, 136
Winnick, K., 69
Winslow, Edward, 296
Winter, J., 298
Wolf, D., 50
Wolfgang, C. H., 276
Wong, J., 50
Woodford, Susan, 21
Woodson, Jacqueline, 354
Wormfield, Hope Herman, 121
Worthy, J., 225, 295
Woyshner, C., 73
Wright, I., 150

Xanthopoulos, J. A., 341

Yeich, C., 99
Yell, M. M., 148, 313, 347
Yolen, Jane, 299
Yopp, H. K., 228
Yopp, R. H., 228
Young, K. A., 16
Young, T. A., 248

Zarnowski, M., 236, 238, 239, 298
Zarrillo, J., 20, 300, 317, 326, 339
Zeck, Gerry, 121
Zeck, Pam, 121
Ziner, F., 163

Subject Index

Abbreviated lesson plans, 83, 84, 85–86
Ability grouping, 134
Absolute location, 310
Abstract thinking, 330
Abuela, 26, 354
"Academic Knowledge and Skills," 14–15
Accountability, 126, 132
Activities. *See* Instructional activities
Additive cultural approach, 57, 254
Advertisements, analysis of, 334
Affective component, of environmental education, 344
Affective filter, 30
African Americans, 35, 37, 38–39. *See also* Cultural diversity; Multicultural education
African history, 293
Agenda writing, 244
Almanacs, 157
American democracy, 266–267
American Educational Research Association, 278
American Forum for Global Education, 347
American Library Association, 238
American Political Science Association, 278
American Revolutionaries: A History in Their Own Words, 70
Americas, history of, 293
Analysis
    critical thinking, 151, 159–160
    historical, 294
    inquiry learning, 146, 149
    lesson plans and instructional units, 87, 88, 89, 92
Anecdotal records, 210
Animals, 345
Answers to questions, 202
Answer verification, 231–232
Anthropology, 325–329
Anticipatory set, 89
Antonyms, 230
Anxiety, 30, 35
AppleWorks, 182
Application, 87, 88, 89
Arab Americans, 39. *See also* Cultural diversity; Multicultural education

Archaeological digs, 327–329
Archaeologists, 327
Arctic Hunter, 240
Aronson, E., 130
Arrow and the Lamp, The, 21, 22
Artifacts, 66, 158
Arts, 326. *See also* Performing arts; Visual arts
Asian Americans, 37, 38. *See also* Cultural diversity; Multicultural education
Asian history, 293
Assessments, 196–197
    authentic, 199–209
    data analysis and sharing, 212–219
    diversity and, 220
    instructional units, 115, 118–119
    purposes and goals of, 197–198
    social studies standards and, 10
    student portfolios, 209–212
    summary, 220–221
Assimilationist perspective on citizenship education, 263
Association for Supervision and Curriculum Development (ASCD), 347
Atlases, 156–157, 180, 343
Attitudes, 271–272
Audio resources, 158–160
Audiotapes, 210
Auditory activities, for students with learning disabilities, 42
Authentic assessment
    characteristics of, 199
    data gathering, 201–209
    student portfolios, 199–200
    tests and, 201
Authenticity, 299
Authentic tests, 208–209
Authority, social studies theme for, 12
Autobiographies, 336
Autonomy, 47

Background knowledge, 226–227, 233
Bad Boy: A Memoir, 60
Barton, K., 290
"Best option" approach, 229–230
Bias, 159–160, 299
Bibliographic information, 145
Bicycle Man, The, 60, 61
Bigmama's, 60, 354

Biography, 70–71, 236–239. *See also* specific books
Black Americans: A History in Their Own Words, 59, 60
Bloom, Benjamin, 87–89
Boat, 120
Boatbuilder, 121
Boats, 119
Boats on the River, 110, 121
Booklist (journal), 237
Book of Fantastic Boats, The, 31, 114, 117, 119
Born in the Breezes: The Seafaring Life of Joshua Slocum, 120
Bradford, William, 296
"Bringing Grandparents into Social Studies" (instructional unit), 74
Bronze Bow, The, 298
Brophy, J., 290
Brown, Margaret Wise, 296
Bruner, Jerome, 8–9, 92, 142
Budgeting, 334–335
Buffalo Chase, Bulls Making Battle with Men and Horses. See *Buffalo Chase, Upper Missouri*
Buffalo Chase, Upper Missouri (painting), 81, 83, 85–86, 88, 101–106
Buffalo Hunt, 100
Buffalo Woman, 240
Bulletin board displays, 111, 345
Bush, George W., 10

Caldecott Medal, 238
Candidates, 273–274
Captions, 202
Career days, 334
Career inquiries, 334
Career opportunities, 334
Careers, 348–350
Cassie's Journey: Going West in the 1860s, 297
Categories, 219
Categorizing, 154
Cause-and-effect text structures, 232, 233
CD-ROMs, 180–181, 210
Center for Civic Education, 243, 265
Chair for My Mother, A, 3, 22–24, 354
Change, social studies theme for, 12
Characters, in historical fiction, 299

Charts
  data retrieval, 241, 242, 351
  inquiry learning and critical
    thinking, 146, 160
  K-W-L, 95, 109, 110, 226
  student portfolios, 204
  students with learning disabilities, 42
Checklists, 211–214
Chicken Sunday, 354
Child-centered study, 6
Childhood experiences, 67–68
Children's books
  career-oriented, 334
  families and friends, 339, 354
  history, 298–300
  instructional units and, 119–221
  integrated curriculum, 236–241
  multicultural education, 59–61
  See also specific books
Children's Internet Protection Act
    (CIPA), 174
*Children's Literature Association
    Quarterly,* 237
Children's World Atlas, 157
Child's Calendar, A, 354
China the Beautiful (Website), 50
Chinese Calligraphy, 50
Chinese Writing: An Introduction,
    50, 51
Choral reading, 248
Chronological thinking, 294
Chronology, 96, 137–139
Citizens, roles of, 267
Citizenship, 5–6, 258–260
  content, 265–268
  environmental education and, 344
  lesson plans and instructional
    activities, 279–286
  perspectives on, 263–265
  processes, 271–277
  social studies and, 260–262
  summary, 277–279
  values, 268–271
Civic communication, 188
Civic education, writing in, 243–244
Civics, 12, 260–261. *See also*
    Citizenship
Civic values, 18, 268
Civil War at Sea, The, 121
Civitas, 265, 274, 279
Clarification, 230
Classification, 150
Classified ads, 348–350
Classroom directions, 310
Classroom management, citizenship
    and, 276–277

Classroom museums, 329
Classroom rules, 276
Classroom service projects, 275
Cleopatra, 238
Clinton, William Jefferson, 11
Cognitive demand, 31–35
Collaboration
  authentic tests, 208–209
  citizenship education and, 276–277
  See also Cooperative learning
Collages, 250
Colonial Living, 67
Combination projects, 127
*Come All You Brave Soldiers: Blacks
    in the Revolutionary War,* 71
Comments, written, 219
Community histories, 292–293
Community resources, for global
    education, 343
Community service projects, 275
Community symbols, 308
Compacting the curriculum, 46
Comparative shopping, 334
Comparison/contrast text structures,
    232, 233
Comparisons, 154–155
Compasses, 310
Completion tests, 209
Complex thinking. *See* Critical
    thinking
Comprehensible input, 30, 36, 161
Comprehension
  historical, 294
  language arts, 230–232
  lesson plans and instructional
    activities, 87, 88, 89
Comprehensive lesson plans, 83–85,
    101–105
Computer-based information, 145
Computers. *See* Internet; Technology
Computers in the Schools (journal), 189
Computer storage, 210
Computing Teacher, The (journal), 189
Concept attainment model, 90–92,
    106–107, 115
Concept formation, 153–154
Concept identification, 92
Concept mapping, 184–185
Concepts, 16–17
Conclusions, in inquiry learning, 146
Conferences, 219
Conformal map, 306
Consumer goods, oral history
    and, 69
Consumption, 12, 334–335
Contemporary realistic fiction, 240

Content, 14–17
  assessments and, 212
  children's literature, 238
  citizenship education, 265–268
  critical thinking and, 154–156
  geography, 304–305
  gifted children and, 45–46
  history, 291–294
  learning disabilities and, 40–41
  student portfolios, 209–212
  See also Curriculum; Integrated
    curriculum
Content integration, 93
Content objectives, for comprehensive
    lesson plans, 84
Context
  geography, 301
  inquiry learning and critical
    thinking, 159
  textbooks, 229, 233
Contextual redefinition, 228
Contextual support, 31–35
Continuity, social studies theme for, 12
Contributions approach, 57
Cooperative learning, 123–125
  ability grouping, 134
  group goals, 132
  history, 295
  individual accountability, 132
  inquiry learning and critical think-
    ing, 147–149, 160, 162–165
  interclass grouping, 135
  interest-oriented grouping, 134
  introduction to, 125
  lesson plans and instructional
    activities, 136–139
  planning, 133
  proximity-based grouping, 134
  research-based rationale for, 126–132
  social skills, 132–133
  social studies and, 134
  summary, 135–136
  time for, 135
*Cooperative Learning in the Social
    Studies: An Introduction to
    Social Study,* 136
*Cooperative Learning: Theory,
    Research, and Practice,* 136
*Cooperative Procedures in
    Learning,* 136
Coordinates, 310
Costs, 332–333
Council for the Advancement of
    Citizenship, 243, 265
Creative thinking activities, 46. *See
    also* Critical thinking

Crispin: The Cross of Lead, 298
Criterion-referenced tests, 208
Critical thinking, 46, 140–141
    audio and visual resources, 158–160
    citizenship education and, 263, 264
    concept formation, 153–154
    defining, 150–151
    developing, 152
    English learners, 160–161
    history, 295
    integrative model, 154–156, 165–167
    learning disabilities, 160
    lesson plans and instructional
        activities, 162–170
    Newman's research on, 152–153
    overview of, 149–150
    reference books and multimedia,
        156–157
    summary, 161–162
Cross-references, 157
Cues, 42–43
Cultural anthropology, 325
Cultural diversity, 5, 28, 35–40. *See
    also* Diversity; Multicultural
    education
Cultural groups, 35, 37
Culturally responsive pedagogy, 35
Cultural pluralism, 263, 264
Cultural universals, 66–67, 331, 340
Cultural values, 340. *See also* Values
Culture
    anthropology and, 327
    defining, 35
    history and, 293, 294
    learning and, 37–40
    segue activities and, 96
    social studies theme for, 12
    See also Cultural diversity; Diversity;
        Multicultural education
Currency, 151
Current events, 68–69, 345–346
Curricular integration, levels of,
    56–57. *See also* Integrated
    curriculum
Curriculum
    content, 14–17
    economics, 331–332
    gifted children and, 45–46
    history, 9–10, 295
    learning disabilities and, 40–41
    processes, 18
    psychology and sociology, 337
    standards, 10–12
    values, 18–19
    See also Content; Integrated
        curriculum; Transformed
        curriculum

*Curriculum Guidelines for
    Multicultural Education,* 36,
    261, 326
*Curriculum Standards for Social
    Studies. See Expectations of
    Excellence: Curriculum
    Standards for the Social Studies*
Cybersafety, 174–175, 176

Dance, 250
Dances with Wolves (movie), 81
Data
    geographic, 305–306, 311–312
    presentation of, 92
    sharing, 218–219
    social science, 243–244
Data analysis, 146, 212–219
Databases, 182, 183
Data collection. *See* Information
    gathering
Data retrieval charts, 241, 242, 351
Data verification, 149
Deborah Sampson Goes to War, 71
Decision making, 271, 332–333
*Declaring Independence: Life During
    the American Revolution,* 71
Democracy, 266–267
Democratic citizenship, 260. *See also*
    Citizenship
*Democratic Discipline: Foundation
    and Practice,* 279
Democratic values, 269–271, 293
Demonstrations, 273–274
Departmentalized elementary
    schools, 135
Description, 154–155
Description of New England, A, 165
Description text structures, 232, 233
Desktop publishing software, 182
Developmental appropriateness, 299
Dewey, John, 7, 20, 66, 142, 147
Diary of a Young Girl, The, 60
Differentiated instruction, 25–28
    cultural diversity, 35–40
    exceptionality, 40–47
    instructional activities and lesson
        plans, 48–53
    linguistic diversity, 29–35
    summary, 47–48
*Digging to the Past: Excavations in
    Ancient Lands,* 327
Digs. *See* Archaeological digs
Dimensions of language proficiency,
    31–35
Diorama, 250
Direct instruction, 89–90, 105–106
Direction, 310

Direct observation, 145
Discovery learning, 142
Discrepant event inquiry, 148–149
Discussions, 95, 149, 244–245, 273
Dispositions, 271–272
Distribution, social studies theme for, 12
Diversity, 13, 25–28
    assessments and, 220
    cultural diversity, 5, 28, 35–40
    exceptionality, 40–47
    instructional activities and lesson
        plans, 48–53
    linguistic diversity, 29–35
    summary, 47–48
    textbooks and, 235–236
    See also Multicultural education
Documents, in oral history projects, 66
Drop everything and read (DEAR), 239

Early Thunder, 71
Eating the Plates, 67
Ecological knowledge, 344
"Economic America" (curriculum
    project), 347
Economics, 329–331
    anthropology and, 326
    curriculum, 331–332
    history and, 293–294
    lesson plan for, 348–350
    teaching, 332–335
Economic thinking, 330
Economizing, 335
Editorials, 202, 203
Education for All Handicapped
    Children Act, 27
*Education on the Internet: A Student's
    Guide,* 189
Egyptian Boats, 121
*Eleanor Roosevelt: A Life of
    Discovery,* 238
Electoral process, 267–268
E-mail, 185–188, 204, 244
En Carta (CD-ROM), 180–181, 194–195
Enchanted Caribou, 240
Encounter, 299
Encyclopedias, 157, 180–181, 194–195
Endangered species, 345
Endless Steppe, The, 60
Energy consumption, 345
English learners (ELs), 13, 29
    history and, 295
    inquiry learning and critical
        thinking, 160–161
    second-language acquisition, 29–35
    textbooks and, 236
    See also Diversity; Multicultural
        education

Enrichment activities, 116–118
Enumeration, 153
Environment, 304, 305
Environmental education, 12, 344–345
Environmental Education Network, 348
Environmental policy, 345
E-pals, 188
EPALS Classroom Exchange
   (Website), 188
Equal-area maps, 306
Equity, 56
"Erie Canal, The" (song), 114
Erie Canal, The, 114, 121
Essays, 204
Essay tests, 209
Ethnic groups, 36
Ethnicity, 13. *See also* Cultural
   diversity; Diversity;
   Multicultural education
European Americans, 37, 38. *See also*
   Cultural diversity;
   Multicultural education
European history, 293
Evaluation rubrics. *See* Rubrics
Evaluation
   Bloom's taxonomy, 87, 88
   comprehensive lesson plans, 84, 85
   critical thinking, 151
   group investigation, 147
   social skills, 133
   Website information, 175–176
   See also Assessments
Evaluative comprehension, 231
Excavation, 327–329
Excel, 182
Exceptionality, 13, 40
   gifted children, 45–47
   learning disabilities, 40–45
   See also Diversity
Expanding environments scope and
   sequence, 14–16
*Expectations of Excellence: Curriculum
   Standards for the Social Studies,*
   11, 49, 107, 202, 204, 237, 279,
   319, 331, 335, 348–349, 350
Experiences, 36. *See also* Student
   experiences
Explanation, 154, 155
*Explorations in Language Acquisition
   and Use,* 47
Expository texts, 232
External links, 178
Eyewitness 3D Atlas of the World
   (CD-ROM), 180

Facts, 16–17
Faithful Friend, The, 354

Families, 338–339, 350–355
Family, 354
Family life, 291–292
Family Pictures, 60, 354
Family stories, 339
Family trees, 339
Fiction
   historical, 298–300
   instructional units, 121
   language arts, 239–241
   See also specific books
Fifth Amendment, 282–285
Filmstrips, 158
Financial contributions, to political
   parties, 273–274
Finding Out/Descubrimiento, 136
Fire Boats, 119
*Fireboat: The Heroic Adventures of
   the John J. Harvey,* 120
First Amendment, 267
"Five People in My Family" (song),
   26, 339
Focused examination, 159
Folk dance, 250
Folklore, 293
Folktales, 239–240
Follow the Drinking Gourd, 298
Food gathering/production, 325
Formative assessment, 197
Foundation for Teaching
   Economics, 330
*Framework for Teaching Economics:
   Basic Concepts,* 331
Franklin Delano Roosevelt, 168
*Freedom's Children: Young Civil
   Rights Activists Tell Their Own
   Stories,* 59, 60
*Freighters: Cargo Ships and the People
   Who Work Them,* 112, 119
Friendship, 338–339
Frontier Living, 96

Gardner, Howard, 22, 247, 318
Gazeteers, 157
Generalizations, 16–17, 154, 155
Geographic information, 305–306,
   311–312
Geographic questions, 305, 306
Geography, 5, 287–289
   content, 304–305
   history and, 293
   lesson plans and instructional
      activities, 314–322
   overview and research, 301–303
   processes, 305–306
   segue activities and, 96
   summary, 312–314

teaching, 306–312
   transformation process and, 59
Geography Education National
   Implementation Project
   (GENIP), 304
Geography for Life, 11, 102
George Catlin and the Old Frontier, 101
*George vs. George: The Revolutionary
   War as Seen by Both Sides,* 70
*George Washington and the Birth of
   Our Nation,* 72
*George Washington: An Illustrated
   Biography,* 72
George Washington's Teeth, 72
Gifted children, 13, 40, 45–47. *See
   also* Diversity; Exceptionality
*Girls Think of Everything: Stories of
   Ingenious Inventions by
   Women,* 223
*Girl Who Dreamed of Only Geese and
   Other Tales of the Far North,
   The,* 240
Girl Who Loved Wild Horses, The, 240
*Giving Thanks: The 1621 Harvest
   Feast,* 67
Global Connections (newsletter), 347
Global connections, social studies
   theme for, 12
GlobaLearn Website, 180
Global education, 267, 340–344
Global Education Network, 347
Globes, 306
Goals
   assessments, 197–198
   cooperative learning and, 133
   group, 126, 132
   See also Objectives
Goals 2000: Educate America Act,
   11, 331
Going on a Dig, 327
Going to School in 1776, 71
Goin' Someplace Special, 60
*Gonna Sing My Head Off: American
   Folk Songs for Children,* 297
Governance, social studies theme
   for, 12
Governing agencies, 273–274
Government, 12, 261, 266–267. *See
   also* Citizenship
Grades, 219
Grandfather's Journey, 252, 253–254
Graphic organizers, 226–227, 232, 234
Graph Master, 182
Graphs
   inquiry learning and critical
      thinking, 146, 160
   students with learning disabilities, 42

Great Adventure of Christopher Columbus, The, 299
Great Kapok Tree, The, 345
Grids, 310, 320–322
Group activities, 97–98. *See also* Cooperative learning
Group formation, 128, 147
Group goals, 126, 132
Grouping, 154
Grouping patterns, 36
Group investigation, 147–149, 162–165
Group membership, 336
Group Project Evaluation Form, 197, 198
Group Projects, 124, 127–129
Groups, social studies theme for, 12
Group symbols, 308
Group Work in Education, 136
Guidelines for Geographic Education: Elementary and Secondary Schools, 305
Guided practice, 90

Hallam, Roy, 290
Handbook of Research on Social Studies Teaching and Learning, 136, 162
Hawk, I Am Your Brother, 354
Henry-Fisherman, 121
Heritage, 293
Higher-order thinking. *See* Critical thinking
Hispanic Americans, 35, 37. *See also* Cultural diversity; Multicultural education
Historical analysis and interpretation, 294
Historical comprehension, 294
Historical fiction, 298–300
Historical issues, 294
Historical novels, 239
Historical pageant, 249
Historical research capabilities, 294
History, 5, 287–289
    anthropology and, 326–327
    content, 291–294
    controversy over, 9–10
    lesson plans and instructional activities, 314–322
    multicultural education and, 69–72
    overview and research, 289–291
    processes, 294
    summary, 312–314
    teaching, 295–300
History–Social Science Content Standards, 172, 223

History/Social Science for K–12 Teachers (Website), 179
Hitler Youth: Growing Up in Hitler's Shadow, 238
Homes in the Wilderness, 297
Hornbook (journal), 237
House on Maple Street, The, 334
How My Parents Learned to Eat, 298, 354
Humanities, 5. *See also* Social studies
Human statues, 249–250
Human systems, 304
Hunter, Madeline, 89–90
Hyperlinks, 178
Hypermedia, 184
HyperStudio, 184
HyperText Transfer Protocol, 177
Hypotheses, 142, 144–145, 149. *See also* Inquiry learning
Hypothesizing, 154, 155

I Could Do That! Esther Morris Gets Women the Vote, 237
Identity, social studies theme for, 12
If You Lived in the Time of the American Revolution, 71
If You Were There in 1776, 71
Illustrations, 146, 299
I'm Deborah Sampson: A Soldier in the War of Revolution, 70
Immigrant Girl: Becky of Eldridge Street, 297
Immigrant students. *See* Cultural diversity; Multicultural education
Immigration, 293
Incentives, 333
Independent practice, 90
Independent reading, 239
Indians of the Plains, 100
Individual accountability, 126, 132
Individual activities, 97, 98
Individual development, social studies theme for, 12
Individuals, social studies theme for, 12
Individual service projects, 275
Individuals with Disabilities Education Act (IDEA), 27
Inferences, 159
Inferential comprehension, 231
Informal conferences, 219
Information. *See* Data
Information age, 13. *See also* Technology
Information books, 119–121, 236–239. *See also specific books*

Information gathering
    authentic assessments, 201–209
    e-mail and, 187–188
    inquiry learning and critical thinking, 145–146
    technology and, 174–181
    writing and, 243–244
In My Own Backyard, 334
Input, 90
Inquiry learning, 140–141
    audio and visual resources, 158–160
    English learners, 160–161
    group investigation, 147–149, 162–165
    learning disabilities, 160
    lesson plans and instructional activities, 162–170
    overview of, 142–143
    reference books and multimedia, 156–157
    summary, 161–162
    teaching sequence for, 143–146
Inquiry processes, 18
Inquiry projects, 127
Institutions, social studies theme for, 12
Instructional activities
    citizenship education, 279–286
    cooperative learning, 136–139
    differentiated instruction, 48–53
    geography and history, 314–322
    inquiry learning and critical thinking, 162–170
    integrated curriculum, 252–256
    lesson plans and instructional units, 97–98, 101–122
    multicultural education, 74–78
    oral activities, 206
    social sciences, 348–355
    social studies, 21–24
    technology, 190–195
    textbooks, 235
Instructional materials and resources, 36
    anthropology, 327
    collaborative learning, 133
    comprehensive lesson plans, 84
    Group Projects, 128
    history, 295
    inquiry learning and critical thinking, 145, 156–160
    instructional units, 96–97
    learning disabilities and, 41–42
    psychology and sociology, 337
    See also Technology
Instructional objectives. *See* Lesson objectives

Instructional processes, 28
  gifted children and, 46
  learning disabilities and, 40, 41–43
Instructional prompts and cues, 42–43
Instructional strategy, 153, 225–236
Instructional unit grid, 118
Instructional units, 80–82
  instructional activities, 97–98,
    108–118
  instructional resources, 96–97
  integrated, 93
  oral history and, 69–72
  organizing framework, 107–118
  planning principles, 93–98
  scope, 93–94
  sequence, 94–96, 97
  summary, 98–101
  support plans, 118–122
  teaching sequence, 89–92
  See also Lesson plans
Integrated curriculum, 222–224
  children's literature, 236–241
  lesson plans and instructional
    activities, 252–256
  multicultural education, 56–57
  performing arts, 247–250
  social studies textbooks, 224–236
  speaking and listening, 244–247
  summary, 251–252
  visual arts, 247–248, 250–251
  writing, 241–244
Integration, 337
Integrative model, for critical
    thinking, 154–156, 165–167
Interclass grouping, 135
Interest groups, 273
Interest-oriented grouping, 134
Internal links, 178
International affairs. *See* Global
    education
International organizations, 343
Internet, 13
  geography and, 306
  information gathering through,
    174–180
  See also E-mail; Technology
Interpretation
  critical thinking, 151, 159–160
  historical, 294
*Interracial Books for Children
    Bulletin,* 237
Interviews, 62–66, 336. *See also*
    Three-Step Interview
*In the Year of the Boar and Jackie
    Robinson,* 60, 61
*Into the Wind: Sailboats Then and
    Now,* 114, 120

Inventors, 293–294
Investigation. *See* Group
    investigation
Involvement. *See* Student involvement
Island of the Blue Dolphins, 298
Issues-centered study, 5

Jamaica Tag-Along, 354
Jigsaw, 111, 124, 130
Job shadowing, 334
Johnny Treegate's Musket, 71
Johnny Tremain, 298
Joint Council on Economic
    Education, 331
Journal prompts, 95
Journals, 202–203
Journey Home, 60
Journey to Topaz, 60, 61
Jump Ship to Freedom, 71
Juvenile novels, 71

Kagan, Spencer, 125, 131, 136, 337
"Kid-friendly" definitions, 230
Kilpatrick, William H., 6, 125
Kinesthetic activities, for students
    with learning disabilities, 42
Kira Kira, 298
*Knots to Know: Hitches, Loops, Bends,
    and Bindings,* 121
Knowledge, 87–88, 89
Knowledge acquisition, 5–6
K-W-L chart, 95, 109, 110, 226

Labeling, 154
Laboratory School of the University of
    Chicago, 93
*Land I Lost: Adventures of a Boy in
    Vietnam,* 59, 60
Language Arts (journal), 237
Language arts, 224
  children's literature, 236–241
  social studies textbooks, 224–236
  speaking and listening, 244–247
  writing, 241–244
Language arts processes, 18
Language experience approach
    (LEA), 355
Language proficiency. *See* Dimensions
    of language proficiency
Language usage, for inquiry learning
    and critical thinking, 160–161
Latitude, 310
Laura Ingalls Wilder Songbook, The,
    96, 297
Law-related education (LRE), 261
Laws, writing, 244
Learning

culture and, 37–40
  service, 274–276
"Learning about Climate," 162
*Learning and Leading with
    Technology* (journal), 189
Learning disabilities, 13, 40–45, 160,
    295. *See also* Diversity;
    Exceptionality
Learning processes, 5–6
Learning structures, 125
*Learning Together and Alone:
    Cooperative, Competitive, and
    Individualistic Learning,* 136
Legalist perspective on citizenship
    education, 263
Legal rights, 282–286
Legend, 307
Leonardo da Vinci, 162
Lesson objectives, 87–89
Lesson plans, 80–82
  abbreviated, 85–86
  citizenship education, 279–286
  comprehensive, 84–85, 101–105
  concept attainment model, 90–92,
    106–107, 115
  cooperative learning, 136–139
  differentiated instruction, 48–53
  direct instruction, 89–90, 105–106
  formats, 83–86
  geography and history, 314–322
  guidelines, 82–83
  history, 295
  inquiry learning and critical
    thinking, 162–170
  integrated curriculum, 252–256
  lesson objectives and, 87–89
  multicultural education, 74–78
  social sciences, 348–355
  social studies, 21–24
  summary, 98–101
  teaching sequence, 89–92
  technology, 190–195
  See also Instructional units
Let's Make a Toy Sailboat, 116
Letter grades, 219
Letters, 204
Levstik, L., 290
Life history, 68
Life on a Barge: A Sketchbook, 120
Lincoln: A Photobiography, 168
Lincoln School, 93
Linear presentation software, 182, 184
Linguistic diversity, 13, 28, 29–35. *See
    also* Diversity; Multicultural
    education
Links, 178
Listening, 153, 244–247

Literacy, Website, 177–179
Little House books, 96
Location, absolute and relative, 310
Lone Bull's Horse Raid, 240, 252, 255–256
Lóng Is a Dragon, 50, 51
Longitude, 310
Lost Lake, The, 26, 354
Loving, 354

Macroeconomics, 331
Making Cooperative Learning Work: Student Teams in K–12 Classrooms, 136
"Man: A Course of Study," 8
Man Who Walked Between the Towers, The, 238–239
Mapquest (Website), 306
Map-reading activity, 112
Maps, 205
   directions, 310
   grids, 310, 320–322
   Internet, 306–307
   processes, 305
   relief, 312
   research, 301, 302–303
   scale, 308, 310, 318–319
   student-made, 311–312
   symbols, 307–308, 309
   thematic, 312
Martin Luther King, Jr., 237
Martin's Big Words: The Life of Dr. Martin Luther King, Jr., 237
Matching tests, 209
Materials. *See* Instructional materials and resources
Media literacy, 346
Meet the Real Pilgrims, 67
Mental map, 311
Mercator projection, 306
Metacognitive strategies, 230
Mexican Americans. *See* Hispanic Americans
Microeconomics, 331
Microsoft Excel, 182
Midwife's Apprentice, The, 239, 241
Migrations, 293
Mini-murals, 336
Mini-units. *See* Instructional activities
Minority groups, 37. *See also* Cultural diversity; Multicultural education
Minutes, writing, 244
Mississippi Steamwheelers, 121
Mock trials, 282–286
Modalities, multiple, 42
Modeling, 90

Morning Girl, 299
Mourt's Relation, 296–297
Multicultural Classroom: Readings for Content-Area Teachers, 47
Multicultural education, 54–56
   children's books, 59–61
   dimensions of, 56–59
   lesson plans and instructional activities, 74–78
   oral history, 61–72
   summary, 72–73
   See also Cultural diversity; Diversity
Multimedia, 146, 156–157, 210, 337
Multimedia School (journal), 189
Multiple-choice tests, 209
Multiple-form products, in student portfolios, 207–208
Multiple grouping patterns, 36
Multiple intelligences, 318
Multiple modalities, 42
Murals, 250, 336
Museums, classroom, 329
Muslim Americans, 39. *See also* Cultural diversity; Multicultural education
My Brother Sam Is Dead, 71
My Friend Jacob, 354
My Grandmother's Cookie Jar, 354
My Name Is Pocahontas, 238
My Prairie Year: Based on the Diary of Elinor Plaisted, 96, 297

Name Jar, The, 354
Narrative texts, 232
National Academy of Sciences, 8
National Assessment of Educational Progress, 301
National Association of Economic Educators, 330
National Content Standards in Economics, 11, 330, 331, 347
National Council for the Social Studies (NCSS)
   Ad Hoc Committee on Ability Grouping, 134
   Ad Hoc Committee on Global Education, 340
   citizenship education, 263, 279
   data collection, 202–208
   diversity, 49
   economics, 331, 348–349
   global education, 341
   history and geography, 313, 319
   instructional organization, 107
   integrated curriculum, 237
   psychology and sociology, 335, 337
   record keeping, 211

   Select Subcommittee, 274
   social studies standards, 11, 22, 23
   Task Force on Early Childhood/Elementary Social Studies, 18
   Task Force on Ethnic Studies Curriculum Guidelines, 36, 261, 326, 327
   Task Force on Revitalizing Citizenship Education, 5
   Task Force on Scope and Sequence, 18, 150
   Task Force on Standards for Teaching and Learning in the Social Studies, 4, 93, 260
   technology, 173
   Website, 19
National Council on Economic Education, 330, 331, 347
National Digital Map Library, 306–307
National Geographic Our World: A Child's First Picture Atlas, 157
National Geography Standards, 166
National heritage, 293
National projects, on citizenship education, 265
National Standards for Civics and Government, 11, 259, 260, 261, 265, 266, 268, 271, 279, 280, 282
National Standards for History, 11, 74, 200, 216, 291, 294, 317
Nations, 267, 343, 344
Native Americans
   cultural diversity, 35, 37, 39
   lesson plans, 99–100, 101–107
   See also *Buffalo Chase, Upper Missouri;* Cultural diversity; Multicultural education
Native American Testimony: An Anthology of Indian and White Relations, 59, 60
Native Hawaiians, 37, 38. *See also* Cultural diversity; Multicultural education
Newberry Medal, 238, 298
Newmann, Fred, 152–153
News. *See* Current events
NewsCurrents, 346
News media, 346
New social studies, 8–9, 142
Newspapers, 346
New York Times Almanac, 156
No Child Left Behind (NCLB), 10
Nonwritten products, in student portfolios, 204–207
Norm-referenced tests, 208

North American Association for
  Environmental Education, 348
Notes, 203
Novels, juvenile, 71
Number the Stars, 240, 299

*Oars, Sails, and Steam: A Picture
  Book of Ships,* 31, 114, 121
Objectives
  comprehensive lesson plans, 84, 85
  direct instruction, 90
  English learners, 36
  lesson, 87–89
Objectivity, 151
Observation, direct, 145
Ocean-Going Giants, 120
Online expeditions, 179–180
Open-ended journal prompts, 95
Operators, 178
Oral activities, 206
Oral history, 61
  benefits of, 61–62
  instructional units and, 69–72
  project guidelines, 62–66
  student experiences and, 66–69
Oral reports, 146
Organizations
  international, 343
  participation in, 273
  psychology and sociology, 337
Osa's Pride, 354
Other Side, The, 354
Our Working World, 331
Outline maps, 311
Out of the Dust, 239
Overview
  comprehensive lesson plans, 84
  Group Projects, 128
Ox-Cart Man, 248, 298, 317–318

Pantomime, 113
Parent conferences, 219
Parker, Francis W., 7, 66
Parthenon, The, 21
Participation processes, 18. *See also*
  Student involvement
Participatory writing, 274
Patchwork Quilt, The, 339, 354
*Patterns of Thinking: Integrating
  Learning Skills in Content
  Teaching,* 162
Peel, E. A., 290
Peer pressure, 336
People
  global education and, 343
  multicultural education and, 71–72
  social studies theme for, 12

study of, 4–5
transformation process and, 59
Perceptual global education, 340
Performance assessment. *See*
  Authentic assessment
Performing arts
  assessments, 207
  integrated curriculum, 247–250
  processes, 18
  projects, 127
Peter's Chair, 26, 354
Petitions, circulating, 273–274
Photographs, 210
Physical anthropology, 325
Physical systems, 304
Piaget, Jean, 290, 302
Pictures, for inquiry learning and
  critical thinking, 160
Pilgrims of Plymouth Colony, The, 163
Places, 12, 304. *See also* Geography
Plan book grid, 85–86
Planning
  cooperative learning, 133
  group investigation, 147
Plants, 344–345
Playground rules, 276
Plays, 249
Pocahontas, 238
Political campaigns, 244, 273–274
Political candidates, 273–274
Political causes, 273–274
Political organization, anthropological
  study of, 326
Political parties, 273–274
Politics. *See* Citizenship; Civics;
  Government
Portfolios, student, 199–200, 209–212
Positive interdependence, 132
Poverty. *See* Cultural diversity
Power, social studies theme for, 12
PowerPoint, 182
Practice
  guided and independent, 90
  learning disabilities, 42
  social skills, 133
Predicting, 230
Prejudice, 337–338
Preparing for Citizenship, 279
Preparing Instructional Objectives, 87
"Preparing Tomorrow's Teachers to
  Use Technology," 172
PreReading Plan (PreP), 226
Presentations
  group investigation, 147
  instructional units and lesson
    plans, 92
  learning disabilities, 42

Presentation software, 182, 184
Primary sources, 145, 296–298
Principles, 266–267. *See also* Values
Prints, 158
Problem-and-solution text structures,
  232, 233
Problem identification, 142, 143–144
Problem solving, 6, 142. *See also*
  Inquiry learning
Processes, 18
  citizenship education, 271–277
  geography, 305–306
  history, 294
Process integration, 93
Process objectives, for comprehensive
  lesson plans, 84, 85
Process of Education, The, 8
Production, social studies theme
  for, 12
Progressive Education, 7–8, 142
Progressivism, 7, 142
Projects, for oral history, 62–66. *See
  also* Instructional activities;
  Instructional units; Lesson
  plans
*Promoting Global Teacher Education:
  Seven Reports,* 348
Prompts, 42–43, 95
Proximity-based grouping, 134
Psychology, 335–339
Public issues, 273, 274
Public Law 94–102, 27
Public officials, 244, 273, 274
Public symbols, 274
Purchases, comparative, 334
Purposes
  American democracy, 266–267
  assessments, 197–198
  direct instruction, 90
  textbooks, 234–235

Quality, of historical fiction, 299
Question–answer relationships
  (QARs), 231–232
Question classification, 231–232
Questioning, 230
Questions
  geographic, 305, 306
  oral history interviews, 63–64
  yes/no, 149

Race, 13. *See also* Cultural diversity;
  Diversity; Multicultural
  education
Rating scales, 211, 212–214, 215
Read-aloud, 112–113
Readers' theater, 248

Reading
environmental education and, 345
independent, 239
public issues, 273
testing alternatives to, 209
See also Children's books;
Textbooks
Reading strategies, 230–231
Reading Teacher, The (journal), 237
Realia, 158
Reasoning
economics and, 330
teaching, 154–156, 165–167
See also Critical thinking
Reciprocal teaching, 230–231
Recording, 181–185
Records, teacher, 210–212
Recycling, 344
Reference books, 156–157
Reflective thinking, 142
Regional histories, 293
Regions, 304, 344. *See also* Geography
Relationships, 159
Relative location, 310
Relief maps, 311–312
Religion, 326
Report cards, 219
Reports
group investigation, 147
oral, 146
research, 243
summary, 203
Research
citizenship education, 262
cooperative learning and, 126–132
critical thinking, 152–153
geography, 301–303
history, 289–291, 294
Research reports, 243
Residence patterns, 326
Resources. *See* Instructional materials
and resources
Responsibility, environmental, 344
Rights, 282–286
River Ran Wild, A, 162
Role play, 243, 248
Roles, in cooperative learning, 133
Rubrics, 202, 203, 211
Rules
classroom and playground, 276
economics and, 333
writing, 244

Safety. *See* Cybersafety
Sailboat Lost, 121
*Sailing Home: A Story of a Childhood
at Sea,* 120

Sarah Morton's Day, 67
Sarah, Plain and Tall, 298
Scaffolding, 350
Scale, 303, 308, 310, 318–319
Scales, 219
Scholastic Children's Encyclopedia, 156
Scholastic Newstime, 346
School Library Journal, 237
*School Library Media Activities
Monthly,* 157
School service projects, 275
Schools of California Online
Resources in Education
(SCORE), 48, 179
School-to-career education, 333–334
Science, 12, 293–294
Scientists, 293–294
Scope, 14–16
instructional units, 93–94
transformation process, 57–58
Scoring rubrics. *See* Rubrics
Scripts, 203
Search engines, 177–178
Second-language acquisition, 29–35
Secret of Freedom, The, 339
*Secret Soldier: The Story of Deborah
Sampson,* 70–71
Segue activities, 96, 116
Semantic maps, 228–229, 339
Sequence, 14–16, 94–96, 97. *See also*
Teaching sequence
Sequence text structures, 232, 233
Service learning, 274–276
Service projects, 275
Sesame Street Song Book, 26, 339
Sharing
data, 218–219
technology, 181–185
Shaun and the Boat: An Irish Story, 121
Sheltered instruction, 35
Ship, 117, 120
Ships (video), 113
Ships and Seaports, 119
Ships, Sailors, and the Sea, 31,
114, 120
*Shoes for Everyone: A Story About Jan
Matzeliger,* 223
Shopping, comparative, 334
Simulation
anthropology, 328
economics, 334
Single group studies, 326–327
Single Shard, A, 239, 298
SIOP (Sheltered Instruction
Observation Protocol), 35
Sixth Amendment, 282–285
Sketch maps, 311

*Skillet Bread, Sourdough, and
Vinegar Pie: Cooking in
Pioneer Days,* 96
Slavin, R. E., 89, 125, 126, 129, 134, 136
Small-group activities, 97, 98
Social action approach, 57
Social Education (journal), 13, 48,
73–74, 100, 189, 221, 237,
278, 279, 296
Social sciences, 5, 6, 323–325
anthropology, 325–329
current events, 345–346
economics, 329–335
environmental education, 344–345
global education, 340–344
information gathering, 243–244
lesson plans and instructional
activities, 348–355
psychology and sociology, 335–339
summary, 347–348
See also Citizenship; Geography;
History; Social studies
Social skills, 132–133
Social stratification, 326
Social studies, 2–3
citizenship education and, 260–262
cooperative learning and, 134
critical thinking and, 152–153
curriculum, 14–19
definitions of, 4–6
lesson plans and instructional
activities, 21–24
summary, 19–20
teaching, history of, 6–13
See also Anthropology;
Assessments; Citizenship;
Cooperative learning; Critical
thinking; Current events;
Curriculum; Diversity;
Economics; Environmental
education; Geography; Global
education; History; Inquiry
learning; Instructional
activities; Instructional units;
Integrated Curriculum; Lesson
plans; Multicultural education;
Psychology; Social sciences;
Sociology; Technology;
Textbooks
Social Studies, The (journal), 189
Social Studies and the Young Learner
(journal), 13, 99, 189, 237,
278, 279
Social Studies on the Internet, 189
Society, 12, 305
Society for American Archaeology, 347
Sociology, 335–339

Sociopolitical knowledge, 344
Songs, about families and friends, 339
So You Want to Be President?, 239
Spatial relationships, 302–303, 304
Speaking, 244–247
"Specially Designed Academic
    Instruction in English," 35
Speculation, 144–145
Spreadsheets, 182, 183
Standardized tests, 208
Standards
    assessments and, 216–218, 219
    comprehensive lesson plans, 84
    instructional units, 107–108
    social studies, 10–12
    student portfolios and, 199–200
State histories, 293
State v. The Big Bad Wolf (mock
    trial), 282
Steamboat in a Cornfield, 120
Stereotyping, 327, 337–338
Stevie, 354
Stories, 202
Student achievement. *See* Assessments
Student conferences, 219
Student experiences
    English learners, 36
    oral history and, 66–69
Student involvement, for students
    with learning disabilities, 42
Student-made maps, 311–312
Student portfolios, 199–200,
    209–212
Students with special needs. *See*
    Exceptionality; Learning
    disabilities
Student Teams–Achievement
    Divisions (STAD), 124, 129
Student work product
    gifted children, 46–47
    students with learning disabilities,
    40, 41, 43–45
Study guides, structure-based,
    232, 234
Study print, 158
Subgroups, 128
Submarines, 121
Substantive global education, 340
Suchman, R., 143, 148, 162–165
Sumi's Special Happening, 354
Summarization, 151, 230
Summary, 347–348
Summary reports, 203
Summative assessment, 197
*Surrounded by Sea: Life on a New
    England Fishing Island,*
    31, 113, 120

Surveys, 145
Sustained silent reading (SSR), 239
Sybil Ludington's Midnight Ride,
    69–70
Sybil Rides for Independence, 69
Sybil's Night Ride, 69
Symbols, 274, 302–303, 307–308, 309
Synonyms, 230
Synthesis, 87, 88, 89, 151

Taba, Hilda, 16, 17, 100, 152, 153–154
Tactile activities, for students with
    learning disabilities, 42
Tall Ships, 120
Task characteristics/requirements, for
    students with learning
    disabilities, 43
Task criteria, for students with
    learning disabilities, 44
Task modality, for students with
    learning disabilities, 42
Tattered Sails, 121
Taxonomy of Educational Objectives,
    87–89
Teacher records, 210–212
Teaching
    economics, 332–335
    geography, 306–312
    global education, 341–344
    history, 295–300
    psychology and sociology, 337
*Teaching Children to Care:
    Management in the
    Responsive Classroom,* 279
Teaching Diverse Populations, 48
Teaching sequence
    history, 295, 297–298
    inquiry learning, 143–146
    lesson plans and instructional
    units, 84, 85, 89–92
    textbooks, 232–235
Technical correctness, 151
Technology, 171–173
    current events and, 346
    e-mail, 185–188
    history of, 293–294
    information age, 13
    information gathering, 174–181
    inquiry learning, 145
    lesson plans and instructional
    activities, 190–195
    recording and sharing, 181–185
    social studies theme for, 12
    summary, 188–189
Technology processes, 18
Television advertisements, analysis
    of, 334

Tests
    assessments and, 201
    authentic, 208–209
    instructional units, 115–116
Text, in historical fiction, 299
Textbooks, 36, 224–226
    background knowledge, 226–227
    comprehension, 230–232
    diversity and, 235–236
    teaching sequence, 232–235
    vocabulary, 227–230
Text structures, 232, 233, 234
Thematic maps, 312
Themes, 96
Thinking and Problem Solving, 162
Thinking processes, 18
Thinking strategy, analysis of, 92
Think-Pair-Share, 124, 130–131
Three-column, single-sheet lesson
    plan, 86
Three-Step Interview, 124, 131–132
*Through the Eyes of a Child: An
    Introduction to Children's
    Literature,* 237
Thy Friend, Obadiah, 298, 299, 354
Tiering assignments, 46, 116
Tikta Liktak: An Eskimo Legend, 240
Time
    authentic tests, 208
    cooperative learning, 128, 133, 135
    social studies theme for, 12
Time Almanac, 156
TimeLiner, 182
Time lines, 300
Time management, 277
To Be a Slave, 3, 59, 60, 74–76
Too Many Tamales, 240, 354
Top of the News (journal), 237
Topography, 311–312
Toy Boats to Make at Home, 116
Trade, 333
Transcultural Children's Literature, 237
Transformation approach, 57
Transformation model, 263, 264
Transformation process, 57–59
Transformed curriculum, 54–56
    children's books, 59–61
    dimensions of, 56–59
    lesson plans and instructional
    activities, 74–78
    oral history, 61–72
    summary, 72–73
Transmission model, 263
Travel brochure project, 344
True/false tests, 209
*Try How Sweet It Is (And Was):
    A History of Candy,* 237

Tugboats, 120
Tugboats Never Sleep, 120
26 Fairmount Avenue, 60

*Uncle George Washington and
    Harriet's Guitar,* 72
Understanding
    assessment of, 212–214
    direct instruction, 90
    social skills, 133
Uniform Resource Locator (URL),
    177, 178
U.S. Constitution, 266–267, 282–285
U.S. Department of Education, 11, 172
Unit grid, 118
Unit of study. *See* Instructional
    activities
Unit plans. *See* Instructional units
Upstairs Room, The, 60
*Using What We Know About
    Teaching,* 99

Value assumptions, 269–270
Values, 18–19
    assessment of, 214, 216
    citizenship education, 266–267,
        268–271
    comprehensive lesson plans,
        84, 85
    cultural, 340
    history and, 293
    universal, 340
Videotapes, 210

Vignettes. *See* Instructional activities
Virtual field trips, 179–180, 191–194
Virtual tours, 344
Visual activities, for students with
        learning disabilities, 42
Visual arts
    assessments, 205–206, 210
    integrated curriculum, 247–248,
        250–251
    processes, 18
    projects, 127
Visual resources, 158–160
Vocabulary
    English learners and, 36
    textbooks, 227–230, 234
*Voices from the Fields: Children of
    Migrant Farmworkers Tell
    Their Stories,* 59, 60
*Voice That Challenged the Nation:
    Marian Andrews and the
    Struggle for Equal Rights,* 238
Voting, 273
Vygotsky, Lev, 34, 126–127

Wall, The, 354
War Comes to Willy Freeman, 71
Web Inquiry Project, 179
WebQuest, 179, 190–191
Website accuracy, 175–176
Website literacy, 177–179
Weekly Reader (magazine), 273, 346
Where the Buffaloes Begin, 100
White Archer, The, 240

Who Is Carrie?, 71
Whole-group activities, 97–98
Wilson Library Bulletin, 237
Winslow, Edward, 296
Witch of Blackbird Pond, The, 280,
        282–285, 298
Word processing, 182
Word structure, 230
Workforce education, 333–334
Working Cotton, 354
Work product. *See* Student work
        product
World affairs. *See* Global education
World Book, 156
World's Fastest Boats, The, 119
World Wide Web (WWW),
        information gathering
        through, 174–180. *See also*
        E-mail; Internet; Technology
Wreck of the Zephyr, The, 121
Writing, 241–244
    participatory, 274
    testing alternatives to, 209
Written comments, 219
Written products, in student
        portfolios, 202–204
Written projects, 127

Year of Impossible Goodbyes, The,
        59, 60
*You and Me Together: Moms, Dads,
    and Kids Around the
    World,* 354